D0564061

Ideas and Foreign Policy

A volume in the series

Cornell Studies in Political Economy

EDITED BY PETER J. KATZENSTEIN

A full list of titles in the series appears at the end of the book.

The papers in this volume grew out of a panel sponsored by the Committee on Foreign Policy Studies of the Social Science Research Council.

Ideas and Foreign Policy

BELIEFS, INSTITUTIONS, AND POLITICAL CHANGE

Edited by

JUDITH GOLDSTEIN *and*

ROBERT O. KEOHANE

CORNELL UNIVERSITY PRESS

Ithaca and London

WITHDRAWN

CALVIN T. RYAN LIBRARY
U. OF NEBRASKA AT KEARNEY

Copyright © 1993 by Cornell University

All rights reserved. Except for brief quotations in a review, this book, or parts
thereof, must not be reproduced in any form without permission in writing
from the publisher. For information, address Cornell University Press, Sage House,
512 East State Street, Ithaca, New York 14850.

First published 1993 by Cornell University Press
First printing, Cornell Paperbacks, 1993

Library of Congress Cataloging-in-Publication Data
Ideas and foreign policy : beliefs, institutions, and political change
  / edited by Judith Goldstein, and Robert O. Keohane.
     p.   cm.—(Cornell studies in political economy)
   Includes bibliographical references and index.
   ISBN 0-8014-2931-5 (cloth : alk. paper).—ISBN 0-8014-8152-X (pbk.)
   1. International relations—Philosophy. 2. International economic
relations—Philosophy. I. Goldstein, Judith. II. Keohane, Robert O. (Robert
Owen), 1941– . III. Series
JX1391.I33   1993
327—dc20   93-8556

Printed in the United States of America

Cornell University Press strives to use environmentally responsible suppliers
and materials to the fullest extent possible in the publishing of its books. Such
materials include vegetable-based, low-VOC inks and acid-free papers that are
recycled, totally chlorine-free, or partly composed of nonwood fibers. Books that
bear the logo of the FSC (Forest Stewardship Council) use paper taken from
forests that have been inspected and certified as meeting the highest standards
for environmental and social responsibility. For further information, visit our
website at www.cornellpress.cornell.edu.

Cloth printing   10 9 8 7 6 5 4 3 2 1

Paperback printing 10 9 8 7 6 5 4

Contents

CONTENTS

vi

Acknowledgments

This book would not exist except for the financial support of the Foreign Policy Program of the Social Science Research Council (SSRC). The project was conceived in 1988—while we both were Foreign Policy Fellows—as a result of the Program's offer to sponsor research workshops for Fellows interested in similar topics. This enterprise dates to such a workshop in January 1989. After that discussion, we asked the SSRC to support two additional conferences in order to bring together a broad range of scholars to consider the role of ideas in politics, and especially in foreign policy. Both of these conferences, in January 1990 and April 1991, were held at the Center for Advanced Study in the Behavioral Sciences, Stanford, California. Participants at both conferences were critical in the shaping of this project through either their memos, their papers, or their participation: Anne-Marie Burley, Barry Eichengreen, James Fearon, Jeffry Frieden, Ernst B. Haas, Peter Haas, Peter Hall, David Lumsdaine, Richard Madsen, Bruce Bueno de Mesquita, James Morrow, Richard Moss, John Odell, Kenneth Oye, Robert Putnam, Jack Rakove, Douglas Rivers, John Ruggie, and Janice Thomson.

We thank Miles Kahler for encouraging the project in his capacity as chair of the Foreign Policy Committee of the SSRC. There would be no book were it not for his intellectual and material support.

We express our gratitude to all ten of the scholars whose papers make up this volume. Not only was their intellectual guidance critical to the success of the project, but they must be thanked as well for their patience with our not always welcomed comments and repeated demands for revisions.

JUDITH GOLDSTEIN

Stanford, California

ROBERT O. KEOHANE

Cambridge, Massachusetts

Contributors

JOHN FEREJOHN is Professor of Political Science and Senior Fellow, Hoover Institution, Stanford University.

GEOFFREY GARRETT is Assistant Professor of Political Science, Stanford University.

JUDITH GOLDSTEIN is Associate Professor of Political Science, Stanford University.

JOHN A. HALL is Professor of Sociology, McGill University.

NINA P. HALPERN is Assistant Professor of Political Science, Stanford University.

G. JOHN IKENBERRY is Associate Professor of Political Science, University of Pennsylvania.

ROBERT H. JACKSON is Professor of Political Science, University of British Columbia.

PETER J. KATZENSTEIN is Walter S. Carpenter, Jr., Professor of International Studies, Cornell University.

ROBERT O. KEOHANE is Stanfield Professor of International Peace, Harvard University.

CONTRIBUTORS

STEPHEN D. KRASNER is Graham Stuart Professor of Political Science, Stanford University.

KATHRYN SIKKINK is Assistant Professor of Political Science, University of Minnesota, Minneapolis.

BARRY R. WEINGAST is Professor of Political Science and Senior Fellow, Hoover Institution, Stanford University.

PART I

INTRODUCTION AND INTELLECTUAL HISTORY

CHAPTER ONE

Ideas and Foreign Policy: An Analytical Framework

JUDITH GOLDSTEIN AND
ROBERT O. KEOHANE

This book is about how ideas, which we define as beliefs held by individuals, help to explain political outcomes, particularly those related to foreign policy. As social scientists we are interested in using empirical evidence to evaluate the hypothesis that ideas are often important determinants of government policy. Our argument is that ideas influence policy when the principled or causal beliefs they embody provide road maps that increase actors' clarity about goals or ends-means relationships, when they affect outcomes of strategic situations in which there is no unique equilibrium, and when they become embedded in political institutions.

For milennia philosophers and historians have wrestled with the issue of the role of ideas in social and political life, and for as long as social science has existed its practitioners have debated these questions. In many ways this volume is an extension of the approach first enunciated by Max Weber. Like Weber, we do not argue that ideas *rather than*

We thank participants at two conferences on the role of ideas in foreign policy, sponsored by the Social Science Research Council, which we organized and chaired at the Center for Advanced Study in the Behavioral Sciences, Stanford, California, January 18–20, 1990, and April 19–20, 1991. We are particularly grateful to James Fearon, Geoffrey Garrett, Ernst B. Haas, Peter Hall, Nannerl O. Keohane, Stephen D. Krasner, Henry Nau, Daniel Philpott, and Jack Snyder for critiques of earlier drafts of this chapter.

interests (as interpreted by human beings) move the world. Instead, we suggest that ideas *as well as* interests have causal weight in explanations of human action.

If the study of the impact of ideas on policy is so old, why revive it now? Simply because in modern political economy and in international relations, the impressive elaboration of rationalist explanations of behavior has called into question old assumptions about whether the substantive content of people's ideas really matters for policy. To many economists, and to political scientists captivated by their modes of thinking, ideas are unimportant or epiphenomenal either because agents correctly anticipate the results of their actions or because some selective process ensures that only agents who behave as if they were rational succeed. In such functional arguments, effects explain causes through rational anticipation or natural selection.[1] The extreme version of this argument is that ideas are just hooks: competing elites seize on popular ideas to propagate and to legitimize their interests, but the ideas themselves do not play a causal role.[2] These interests may be strictly material—in many economic models, individuals are wealth-maximizers—but they also may encompass broader utility functions, in which such values as status and power are included. Whatever the details, in this rationalist view interests are given and logically prior to any beliefs held by the actors.

The most widely accepted systemic approaches to the study of international relations, realism and liberal institutionalism, take rationalist models as their starting points. Both realism and institutionalism assume that self-interested actors maximize their utility, subject to constraints. In such models, actors' preferences and causal beliefs are given, and attention focuses on the variation in the constraints faced by actors.[3] Most analysts who rely on such approaches have relegated ideas to a minor role.[4]

---

[1] See Kenneth Shepsle, "Institutional Arrangement and Equilibrium in Multidimensional Voting Models," *American Journal of Political Science* 23 (1979): 27–60. For a sophisticated discussion, see Paul Milgrom, Douglass North, and Barry Weingast, "The Role of Institutions in the Revival of Trade: The Law Merchant, Private Judges, and the Champagne Fairs," *Economics and Politics* 2 (1990): 1–23.

[2] Kenneth A. Shepsle, "Comment," in *Regulatory Policy and the Social Sciences*, ed. Roger Noll, pp. 231–37 (Berkeley: University of California Press, 1985).

[3] A striking contrast can be found in the work of Henry R. Nau, who emphasizes purposes and ideas in *The Myth of America's Decline: Leading the World Economy into the 1990s* (New York: Oxford University Press, 1990), esp. chap. 1. Classical liberal arguments have also emphasized the role of domestic politics and society in shaping preferences. See Andrew Moravcsik, "Liberalism and International Relations Theory," Working Paper no. 92-6, Center for International Affairs, Harvard University (October 1992).

[4] Ideas, like political culture, have traditionally been granted the status of "unexplained variance." For such a treatment of ideas in realist analysis, see Stephen Krasner, *Defending*

In this volume we seek to show that ideas matter for policy, even when human beings behave rationally to achieve their ends. Indeed, rationalist analysts of international politics have often recognized that the assumption of rationality, like that of egoism, "is a theoretically useful simplification of reality rather than a true reflection of it."[5] But even if we accept the rationality premise, actions taken by human beings depend on the substantive quality of available ideas, since such ideas help to clarify principles and conceptions of causal relationships, and to coordinate individual behavior. Once institutionalized, furthermore, ideas continue to guide action in the absence of costly innovation.[6] Hence this volume criticizes approaches that deny the significance of ideas, but does not challenge the premise that people behave in self-interested and broadly rational ways.

More far-reaching criticisms of rationalistic models have become common in the literature on international relations. According to this "reflectivist" view, beliefs are a central element of all research because, in the words of Alexander Wendt, analysis turns on how "knowledge-able practices constitute subjects." Reflectivists "share a cognitive, inter-subjective conception of process in which identities and interests are endogenous to interaction, rather than a rationalist-behavioral one in which they are exogenous."[7] This reflectivist critique is irrefutable in

---

the National Interest (Princeton: Princeton University Press, 1978). Among rationalistic works that seek to explain cooperation in a nonrealist way but do not focus on ideas are Robert O. Keohane, *After Hegemony: Cooperation and Discord in the World Political Economy* (Princeton: Princeton University Press, 1984), and Kenneth A. Oye, ed., *Cooperation under Anarchy* (Princeton: Princeton University Press, 1986).

[5] Keohane, *After Hegemony,* p. 108.

[6] A notable study of the role of ideas on policy is Peter A. Hall, ed., *The Political Power of Economic Ideas: Keynesianism across Nations* (Princeton: Princeton University Press, 1989). The research design of that study, however, differs from ours. Hall controls for knowledge of Keynesian ideas of macroeconomic management in a variety of countries, and accounts for the variety of outcomes on the basis of other variables, such as the orientation of the governing party, the structure of the state and state-society relations, the structure of political discourse, and the impact of World War II. We explore a variety of issue areas, with each author seeking to show how variations in the ideas available affected policy outcomes.

[7] Alexander Wendt, "Anarchy Is What States Make of It: The Social Construction of Power Politics," *International Organization* 46 (Spring 1992): 392. For a discussion of reflective vs. rationalistic views, see Robert O. Keohane, "International Institutions: Two Approaches," *International Studies Quarterly* 32 (December 1988): 379–96, reprinted in Keohane, *International Institutions and State Power: Essays in International Relations Theory* (Boulder, Colo.: Westview, 1989), pp. 158–79. For examples of the reflectivist critique not otherwise cited, see Richard Ashley and R. B. J. Walker, "Speaking the Language of Exile: Dissident Thought in International Studies," *International Studies Quarterly* 34 (September 1990): 259–68; Thomas J. Biersteker, "Critical Reflections on Post-positivism in International Relations," *International Studies Quarterly* 33 (September 1989): 263–67; Robert Cox, *Production, Power, and World Order* (New York: Columbia University Press, 1987); Yosef Lapid, "The Third Debate: On the Prospects of International Theory in a

the abstract and reminds researchers to investigate not just what strategies are devised to attain interests but how preferences are formed and how identities are shaped. The key issue, however, is not whether identities matter but *how* they matter, and how their effects can be systematically studied by social scientists. Unfortunately, reflectivist scholars have been slow to articulate or test hypotheses. Without either a well-defined set of propositions about behavior or a rich empirical analysis, the reflectivist critique remains more an expression of understandable frustration than a working research program.

This volume was written as a challenge to both rationalist and reflectivist approaches. Although we concede that the rationalist approach is often a valuable starting point for analysis, we challenge its explanatory power by suggesting the existence of empirical anomalies that can be resolved only when ideas are taken into account. We demonstrate this need to go beyond pure rationalist analysis by using its own premise to generate our null hypothesis: that variation in policy across countries, or over time, is entirely accounted for by changes in factors *other than* ideas. Like reflectivists, we explore the impact of ideas, or beliefs, on policy. But this volume also poses an explicit challenge to the antiempiricist bias of much work in the reflectivist tradition, for we believe that the role played by ideas can and should be examined empirically with the tools of social science.

Our line of argument should also be distinguished from that suggested by psychological approaches. Cognitive psychology has shown convincingly that people frame information in ways that depart significantly from ideal-typical rationality.[8] Political scientists have used psychological insights and social-psychological work on group decision making to build a substantial literature stressing how cognitive processing affects foreign policy choices.[9] Work on foreign policy has emphasized how collective myths that affect conceptions of self-interest can be created and then perpetuated through propaganda and social-

---

Post-positivist Era," *International Studies Quarterly* 33 (September 1989): 235–54; Alexander Wendt, "The Agent-Structure Problem in International Relations Theory," *International Organization* 41 (Summer 1987): 335–70.

[8] Daniel Kahneman and Amos Tversky, "Choices, Values, and Frames," *American Psychologist* 39 (1984): 341–50; Amos Tversky and Daniel Kahneman, "The Framing of Decisions and the Psychology of Choice," *Science* 211 (1981): 453–58.

[9] See, inter alia, Robert Jervis, *Perception and Misperception in International Politics* (Princeton: Princeton University Press, 1976); Deborah Welch Larson, *Origins of Containment: A Psychological Explanation* (Princeton: Princeton University Press, 1985); Richard Ned Lebow, *Between Peace and War: The Nature of International Crisis* (Baltimore: Johns Hopkins University Press, 1981); Robert Jervis, Richard Ned Lebow, and Janice Gross Stein, *Psychology and Deterrence* (Baltimore: Johns Hopkins University Press, 1985).

ization of children in schools.[10] On issues such as deterrence, a vigorous debate has ensued about the relative adequacy of rationalist theories versus interpretations based on cognitive psychology.[11]

Cognitive psychology certainly concerns ideas, since it investigates beliefs of individuals about social reality that identify possibilities for action, reflect moral principles, and specify causal relationships. This volume, however, is concerned not with the implications of cognitive psychology for interpretation of reality but with another facet of the role of ideas. We focus on the impact of particular beliefs—shared by large numbers of people—about the nature of their worlds that have implications for human action. Such beliefs range from general moral principles to agreement on a specific application of scientific knowledge. When we refer to ideas in this volume, we refer to such beliefs. Since all of these beliefs were processed through human brains, it seems safe to assume that cognitive psychology played a role in their emergence; but we are interested in the impact of particular beliefs, not on the relationship between beliefs and objective reality (however defined and determined). We do not seek to explain the sources of these ideas; we focus on their effects.

In our critique of both rationalist and reflective approaches to the study of foreign policy, we conceive of beliefs in a manner consistent with the logic of these two schools of thought and not that suggested by cognitive analyses. A sophisticated rationalist view could agree that interests are always interpreted through psychological processes, yet hold that knowledge of these interests, thus interpreted, enables the observer to understand behavior. Similarly, a reflectivist approach would not dispute that psychological forces are at work on the human brain. But like their rationalistic colleagues, reflectivists are far more interested in shared behavioral regularities attributable to linguistic constraints, for example, than in error attributable to deficiencies in human processing.[12] Reflectivist research focuses not on misinterpretations of human environments but on the constraints imposed by language, culture, and history on all aspects of individuals' abilities to define and act on "objective" interests.

In this introduction, we present the analytical structure for this volume. We begin by distinguishing three types of beliefs: world views,

---

[10] Stephen Van Evera, "The Cult of the Offensive and the Origins of the First World War," *International Security* 9 (Summer 1984): 58–107; Jack Snyder, *Myths of Empire: Domestic Politics and International Ambition* (Ithaca: Cornell University Press, 1991).

[11] See "The Rational Deterrence Debate: A Symposium," *World Politics* 41 (January 1989).

[12] See, e.g., Friedrich Kratochwil, "The Force of Prescriptions," *International Organization* 38 (Autumn 1984): 685–708.

principled beliefs, and causal beliefs. We then outline three causal pathways by which ideas can affect policy: by providing principled or causal road maps, affecting strategies where there is no unique equilibrium, and becoming embedded in institutions. In the next section we present a chart that links our types of beliefs with these causal pathways, showing how each chapter in the volume focuses on a given type or types of beliefs, and a specific causal pathway. Finally, we make a case for an empiricist methodology to study the impact of beliefs on policy.

THREE TYPES OF BELIEFS

At the most fundamental level, ideas define the universe of possibilities for action. As John Ruggie has pointed out, "fundamental modernist concepts such as market rationality, sovereignty, and personal privacy would not have been comprehensible before the development of appropriate terms of social discourse."[13] These conceptions of possibility, or *world views*, are embedded in the symbolism of a culture and deeply affect modes of thought and discourse. They are not purely normative, since they include views about cosmology and ontology as well as about ethics. Nevertheless, world views are entwined with people's conceptions of their identities, evoking deep emotions and loyalties. The world's great religions provide world views; but so does the scientific rationality that is emblematic of modernity.

Ideas have their broadest impact on human action when they take the form of world views. The world's major religions, for instance, have deeply affected human social life in a variety of ways and across millennia.[14] Similarly, it has often been argued that new conceptions of sovereignty led, at the Peace of Westphalia in 1648, to a new international order, dominated by independent states.[15] Still, the connections between world views and shifts in material power and interests are complex and need investigation. They do not all run in one direction.

Of the major ideas discussed in this volume, none—neither human rights nor sovereignty nor Stalinism—would have made any sense in those premodern soieieties in which people's lives were governed by

[13] Memo prepared for the SSRC-sponsored conference on ideas and foreign policy, Stanford, California, January 18–20, 1990.

[14] Max Weber, *The Protestant Ethic and the Spirit of Capitalism* (1904–5; rpt. New York: Scribner's, 1958), and "The Social Psychology of the World Religions" (1913), in *From Max Weber: Essays in Sociology*, ed. H. H. Gerth and C. Wright Mills (New York: Oxford University Press, 1958).

[15] Leo Gross, "The Peace of Westphalia, 1648–1948," *American Journal of International Law* 42 (1948): 20–41; John Gerard Ruggie, "Continuity and Transformation in the World Polity: Toward a Neorealist Synthesis," *World Politics* 35, no. 2 (1983): 261–85.

notions of magic or fate. Indeed, all of the chapters in this book take for granted a world view according to which human beings are assumed to be active agents in the construction of their own destinies. For traditionalist or religious fundamentalist societies even today, the individualistic and secular scientific premises of this world view remain intellectually and morally alien. Since all of the subjects discussed in this volume have been profoundly affected by modern Western world views, and our authors all share this modernist outlook, we can say relatively little about the impact of broad world views on politics. Only John Ferejohn and Stephen Krasner, writing about events in the seventeenth century, explicitly focus on changes that appear to have been affected by the intellectual movement toward individualistic, human-centered thinking. Understanding the impact of world views on general politics or foeign policy would require a broader comparative study of cultures, such as that on which Hedley Bull was engaged at the end of his too-brief career.[16]

Our second category of ideas, *principled beliefs*, consists of normative ideas that specify criteria for distinguishing right from wrong and just from unjust. The views that "slavery is wrong," that "abortion is murder," and that human beings have the "right of free speech" are principled beliefs. Principled beliefs are often justified in terms of larger world views, but those world views are frequently expansive enough to encompass opposing principled beliefs as well. For instance, although many opponents of slavery justified their arguments with references to Christianity, Christianity had tolerated slavery for almost two millennia. Principled beliefs mediate between world views and particular policy conclusions; they translate fundamental doctrines into guidance for contemporary human action. Millions of people have died on behalf of their principled beliefs; many people now alive are willing to do so. The revolutions of 1989 in Eastern Europe attest to the continuing vibrancy of principled beliefs in politics: people risked their lives in mass demonstrations, although material self-interest alone would have led them to be "free riders."

Changes in principled beliefs, as well as changes in world views, have a profound impact on political action. In Chapter 6, for example, Kathryn Sikkink argues that the killing, torture, and maltreatment of millions of innocent people during World War II led both Europeans and Americans to believe that human rights should properly be a matter for international agreement and regulation, not shielded from international surveillance by the doctrine of sovereignty. The effects on policy

---

[16] Hedley Bull and Adam Watson, eds., *The Expansion of International Society* (Oxford: Clarendon, 1984).

were profound, since new ideas on human rights conditioned the definition of nations' interests. "The adoption of human rights policies," she suggests, "represented not the neglect of national interests but a fundamental shift in the perception of long-term national interests."

The ideas in a third category, *causal beliefs,* are beliefs about cause-effect relationships which derive authority from the shared consensus of recognized elites, whether they be village elders or scientists at elite institutions. Such causal beliefs provide guides for individuals on how to achieve their objectives. Scientific knowledge may reveal how to eliminate smallpox, for instance, or how to slow down the greenhouse effect in the earth's atmosphere. Similarly, the Hungarian and Polish revolutions in the fall of 1989 showed people in East Germany and Czechoslovakia that unarmed mass protests could bring down long-standing repressive governments. Under such conditions, the efficacy of individual action depends on support from many other people, and therefore on the existence of a set of shared beliefs. Causal beliefs imply strategies for the attainment of goals, themselves valued because of shared principled beliefs, and understandable only within the context of broader world views.

Changes in the conceptualization of cause-effect relationships take place more frequently and more quickly than do changes in either world views or principled beliefs. Thus specific policy shifts can often be traced to such changes, particularly when technical knowledge is expanding. The foreign policies of the United States and many other countries with respect to regulation of the production of chlorofluorocarbons (CFCs), for example, changed dramatically between 1985 and 1990, largely in response to new scientific evidence about the hole in the atmospheric ozone layer over Antarctica. Policy shifted because scientific models linked ozone loss to cancer and climate change, and attributed much of it to increased levels of CFCs in the atmosphere.[17] John Ikenberry's discussion of the importance of monetary theory in the postwar economic settlement (Chapter 3) provides another example of how causal ideas—here ideas about the functioning of the economy—influence policy outcomes. Similarly, Nina Halpern argues in Chapter 4 that Stalinist economic ideas, which postulated a radically different set of relationships between market participants, became a guide for economic development in Eastern Europe.

Our categorization of beliefs is clearest in the abstract; in social life

---

[17] Richard Elliot Benedick, *Ozone Diplomacy: New Directions in Safeguarding the Planet* (Cambridge: Harvard University Press, 1991); Edward A. Parson, "Protecting the Ozone Layer," in *Institutions for The Earth: Sources of Effective International Environmental Protection,* ed. Peter M. Haas, Robert O. Keohane, and Marc A. Levy (Cambridge: MIT Press, 1993), pp. 27–74.

all three aspects of ideas may be linked. Doctrines and movements often weave conceptions of possibilities and principled and causal ideas together into what may seem to be a seamless web. The "epistemic communities" studied by Peter Haas and other scholars, for example, are constituted by knowledge-based experts who share both cause-effect conceptions and sets of normative and principled beliefs.[18] Nevertheless, it is worthwhile for purposes of causal analysis to distinguish ideas that develop or justify value commitments from those that simply provide guidance as to how to achieve preferred objectives.[19]

THE IMPACT OF IDEAS ON POLICY

The central issue of this volume concerns causality: Do ideas have an impact on political outcomes, and if so, under what conditions? The most egregious error that proponents of the role of ideas have made is to assume a causal connection between the ideas held by policy makers and policy choices. Ideas are always present in policy discussions, since they are a condition for reasoned discourse. But if many ideas are available for use, analysts should not assume that some intrinsic property of an idea explains its choice by policy makers. Choices of specific ideas may simply reflect the interests of actors. It is crucial for anyone working on ideas and policy to recognize that the delineation of the existence of particular beliefs is no substitute for the establishment of their effects on policy. Advocates of an ideational approach to political analysis must begin by identifying the ideas being described and the policy outcomes or institutional changes to be explained. We must also provide evidence about the conditions under which causal connections exist between ideas and policy outcomes.

In general, we see ideas in politics playing a role akin to that enunciated by Max Weber early in this century: "Not ideas, but material and ideal interests, directly govern men's conduct. Yet very frequently the

[18] Peter M. Haas, "Introduction: Epistemic Communities and International Policy Coordination," *International Organization* 46 (Winter 1992): 1–35. Our interest in ideas extends beyond epistemic communities, but the recent work on epistemic communities provides substantial support, within particular institutional contexts, for the thesis that ideas matter. Peter Haas contributed significantly to our thinking on these issues through his participation in our meetings.

[19] This distinction parallels Weber's between "substantive rationality," which applies "criteria of ultimate ends," and "formal rationality," which denotes that "action is based on 'goal-oriented' rational calculation with the technically most adequate available methods." See Max Weber, *Economy and Society*, ed. Guenther Roth and Claus Wittich (Berkeley: University of California Press, 1968), p. 85. It is also similar to the distinction in rational choice analysis between preferences and strategies.

'world images' that have been created by ideas have, like switchmen, determined the tracks along which action has been pushed by the dynamic of interest."[20] Ideas help to order the world. By ordering the world, ideas may shape agendas, which can profoundly shape outcomes. Insofar as ideas put blinders on people, reducing the number of conceivable alternatives, they serve as invisible switchmen, not only by turning action onto certain tracks rather than others, as in Weber's metaphor, but also by obscuring the other tracks from the agent's view.[21]

We do not suggest a theory for the creation of these switches, or even a fully worked-out model to explain the process by which ideas are selected. Rather, we suggest three causal pathways through which ideas hold the potential of influencing policy outcomes.[22] The first pathway derives from the need of individuals to determine their own preferences or to understand the causal relationship between their goals and alternative political strategies by which to reach those goals. On this pathway, ideas become important when actors believe in the causal links they identify or the normative principles that they reflect. Thus *ideas serve as road maps*. Analysis of this pathway does not account for which ideas are available and persuasive, but once an idea is selected, this pathway limits choice because it logically excludes other interpretations of reality or at least suggests that such interpretations are not worthy of sustained exploration.

On our second pathway, ideas affect strategic interactions, helping or hindering joint efforts to attain "more efficient" outcomes—outcomes that are at least as good as the status quo for all participants. Here *ideas contribute to outcomes in the absence of a unique equilibrium*. They may serve as focal points that define cooperative solutions or act as coalitional glue to facilitate the cohesion of particular groups—which may even prevent agreement on a wider basis. In any case, policy varies because of the choice of some ideas rather than others.

Whatever the reason for the enactment of a policy idea, the choice itself has long-lasting implications. Once ideas become embedded in rules and norms—that is, once they become institutionalized—they constrain public policy. Policies are influenced by earlier road maps,

[20] Max Weber, "Social Psychology of the World's Religions," p. 280.

[21] For instance, the hegemony of utilitarian, market-oriented language and modes of thinking in contemporary capitalist democracies rules out certain community-based and value-laden policies as irrational, excluding them from serious consideration as public policy.

[22] We borrow the idea of causal pathways from a working paper by David Dessler, "The Architecture of Causal Analysis," Center for International Affairs, Harvard University, April 1992.

by past agreement to some policy focal point, or by the existence of some coalitional pattern rather than another. In short, *ideas embedded in institutions specify policy in the absence of innovation.* Analysis of this institutional path says nothing about why ideas were originally adopted; in fact, ideas may become important solely because of the interests and power of their progenitors. But once a policy choice leads to the creation of reinforcing organizational and normative structures, that policy idea can affect the incentives of political entrepreneurs long after the interests of its initial proponents have changed.

The way ideas influence policy outcomes varies with the paths. Still, on all three paths, ideas matter: policy would have been different in the absence of the idea in question. To illustrate this key point, each chapter illuminates how public policy was constrained because of the available set of ideas, choices from that set, or the bias that prevailing ideas exert on the range of acceptable future policies. Although we hold neither that a theory of ideas can stand alone nor that we can understand politics without understanding interests and power, we suggest that policy outcomes can be explained only when interests and power are combined with a rich understanding of human beliefs.

Ideas as Road Maps

Rationalistic analysis typically stipulates, but does not explain, individuals' preferences for some outcome. Yet people's preferences for particular policy outcomes are not given but acquired. World views and principled beliefs structure people's views about the fundamental nature of human life and the morality of practices and choices. They reflect beliefs about the nature of the universe, and about right and wrong. To understand the formation of preferences, we need to understand what ideas are available and how people choose among them.

Furthermore, even the most rationalistic analysts agree that people have incomplete information when they select strategies by which to pursue their preferred outcomes. The ideas individuals hold therefore become important elements in the explanation of policy choice, even if preferences are clear and actors are motivated purely by self-interest. If actors do not know with certainty the consequences of their actions, it is the *expected* effects of actions that explain them. And under conditions of uncertainty, expectations depend on causal beliefs as well as on institutional arrangements for authoritative decision making. Causal ideas help determine which of many means will be used to reach desired goals and therefore help to provide actors with strategies with which to further their objectives; embodied in institutions, they shape the solutions to problems.[23]

Four of our chapters suggest that ideas are critical to the understanding of public policy because they serve as road maps in uncertain environments. John Ikenberry suggests in Chapter 3 that there was considerable uncertainty over the course of action that would further the interests of the country that was effectively in a position to determine the new order after World War II: The United States. "A variety of designs for postwar order were advocated by officials within the American government and elsewhere, all claiming to advance American interests." In this case, the transmission mechanism that propelled a particular set of ideas forward was the epistemic community. Ikenberry suggests that ideas inspired by Keynes determined policy outcomes because they were embraced by a group of well-placed government specialists and economists in the United States, who then promoted these views as the most efficient means to wealth and prosperity. This community of experts fostered agreement by reshaping governmental conceptions of interests, building new political coalitions, and legitimating hegemonic U.S. power.

Nina Halpern sees a similar role for ideas in her explanation for the adoption of Stalinist economic policies in countries not under the control of the Soviet Union. The most common explanations for the spread of command economies after World War II are power-based. Countries faced military invasion if they failed to follow the Soviet developmental road. Halpern admits in Chapter 4 that fear of Soviet punishment may be the best explanation for many of the East European cases. Yet in other cases, notably that of China, the power-based explanation is simply untenable. In fact, in some instances a Stalinist political economy was adopted *against* the wishes of the Soviet Union. In these cases, Soviet ideas, not Soviet power, explain the choice of economic policy.

The ideas here were essentially causal: they prescribed not only how to industralize the economy but how to do so in an ideologically correct way. Halpern suggests that Stalinist ideas were used because of "their ability to resolve two of the major problems facing the postrevolutionary governments." These problems—uncertainty over just what was the socialist road and the need for agreement on a common policy—led to the adoption of economic programs that were neither functionally

---

[23] Ideas, embodied in institutions, may shape the stream of solutions, to be matched conjuncturally with a separate stream of problems. See M. D. Cohen and J. G. March, "A Garbage Can Model of Organizational Choice," *Administrative Science Quarterly* 17 (1972): 1–25.

determined by economic or political factors nor imposed by the Soviet Union. Moreover, once these initial policy choices were made, the ideas they embodied were institutionalized and came to constrain even future leaders who did not believe in the merits of the Stalinist model.[24]

Discussing a very different case, Robert Jackson argues in Chapter 5 that principled as well as causal ideas serve as guides for national behavior. Jackson suggests that after World War II, European empires became inconsistent with "the normative framework of anticolonialism," embodied in juridical statehood and legitimated by principles of democracy and equality. Further, it was this change in the thinking of the colonizers that led to the wave of decolonization that began in the mid-1950s, and not changes in the international power structure, in the demands of the colonies themselves, or in the economic benefits of colonialism. Jackson maintains that the "previous norms governing independent statehood—which required acquisition of (Western-style) 'civilization' and demonstrated capacity for self-government on the part of colonial subjects—were abandoned and replaced by new ones that had few empirical conditions attached to them. As a consequence, many colonies that hitherto had little real prospect of soon gaining self-government now had a categorical entitlement to become independent states as soon as possible."

Once the colonial powers voluntarily loosened the strings of their control, all colonies were able to demand their autonomy. Only this change in the colonists' stance on self-determination, and not the inability of states to control their colonies, can explain the rapid transformation in international politics that occurred in the decade starting in the mid-1950s. Ideational change was imperative, according to Jackson, because colonialism represented a deeply held set of normative relations, not only an asymmetric constellation of international power: "To view it exclusively from a narrow utilitarian perspective of costs and benefits is to overlook everything else about it, which amounts to a good deal."

Thus the timing and extent of decolonization can be explained only by the ascendence of new principled ideas about self-determination. This is not to imply that the interests of the European states were unchanged, or that power did not matter, but that changes in interests and power, or their implications for the cost-benefit ratio of holding colonies, were not sufficient to explain the extent and pace of decolonization.

---

[24] In *Myth of America's Decline* Nau makes a strikingly similar argument about U.S. foreign economic policy, which he interprets in light of competing conceptions of national purpose, which have both analytical and prescriptive dimensions. See his chap. 1, esp. pp. 27–32.

Kathryn Sikkink suggests in Chapter 6 that the atrocities of World War II gave birth to the idea that a guarantee of human rights was a responsibility shared by the community of nations. Yet European and American reactions to violations of human rights after the war differed greatly. The revelation of German atrocities during World War II led Europeans to concentrate on the use of international law, especially the European Court of Human Rights, to protect citizens against violations of their rights by their own governments. The United States, by contrast, emphasized human rights violations under Third World and communist regimes, rather than portraying them as important issues within American society.

Sikkink suggests that her European case exemplifies how an idea at one point in time may cast a very long shadow over political debate and policy outcomes. Even though the idea of giving human rights considerations an important place in foreign policy is quite old, its impact on American public policy was felt only after other cards had fallen into place. Thus attention came to focus on human rights only with "the convergence of détente, public disillusionment with Vietnam, and the initial successes of the civil rights movement." For Sikkink, ideas explain elements of American foreign policy even though there was a considerable time lag between the common acceptance of the notion of human rights and its incorporation into a strategy of maximizing American interests abroad. Sikkink suggests (as Peter Katzenstein also argues persuasively in Chapter 10) that nations react quite differently to similar material circumstances because of fundamental differences in normative beliefs about politics.

In sum, when we view politics as an arena in which actors face continual uncertainties about their interests and how to maximize them, the need for ideas to act as road maps becomes apparent. Ideas serve the purpose of guiding behavior under conditions of uncertainty by stipulating causal patterns or by providing compelling ethical or moral motivations for action. Ideas can be broad or narrow; they can stipulate what is right and wrong, provide new social visions, or merely suggest what economic policy will steer a nation toward increased wealth. New ideas may even lead—even if not immediately—to a significant change in the very constitution of interests. This change may come about when an existing set of ideas is discredited by events or when a new idea is simply so compelling that it captures the attention of a wide array of actors. There is a difference, of course, between the ways in which causal and principled ideas relate to uncertainty. Causal ideas respond directly to uncertainty by reducing it, whereas principled ideas enable people to behave decisively despite causal uncertainty. Principled ideas can shift the focus of attention to moral issues and away from purely instrumental ones focused on material interests and power.[25]

Depressions, wars, the decline of a political party, and the overthrow of a government may all cause ideas to become important because all constitute exogenous shocks that undermine the existing order. At such moments radical shifts in the political agenda may occur because of the common acceptance of some new normative or causal set of beliefs. The logic here is the opposite of that suggested by a functional model. Ideas are important even though actions based on their premises may lead to no gain in efficiency. Whereas a functional approach leads analysts to look to the purposes to which ideas are put, this first path suggests that the uncertainties that confront political actors can lead to reliance on beliefs as guides to action *even if* those ideas do not lead to benefits for society at large.

Coordination: Ideas as Focal Points and Glue

The folk theorem of repeated games emphasizes that players' rational strategies often fail to result in a unique equilibrium outcome: "In a very wide class of situations of strategic interaction—indeed, in virtually any game that takes place over time or in which there is a nontrivial informational structure—almost any outcome can occur in some game theoretic equilibrium."[26] Thus, from a game-theoretic perspective, ideas may be important precisely because unique predictions cannot be generated solely through an examination of interests and strategic interactions (utility functions and payoff matrices). Because almost all games with repeated play have multiple equilibria, the ideas held by players are often the key to a game's outcome.[27] It is not only the set of objective constraints and opportunities that guides action; individuals rely on beliefs and expectations when they select from a range of viable outcomes.

On this pathway, the key role played by ideas is to alleviate coordination problems arising from the absence of unique equilibrium solutions.[28] Ideas can serve as focal points, as solutions to problems

[25] For an excellent discussion of morality and foreign policy, see Robert McElroy, *Morality and American Foreign Policy* (Princeton: Princeton University Press, 1992).

[26] Memo by John Ferejohn, written for our January 18–20, 1990, conference, pp. 8–9.

[27] This is the insight of the folk theorem. See Drew Fudenberg and Eric Maskin, "The Folk Theorem in Repeated Games with Discounting or with Incomplete Information," *Econometrica* 54 (1986): 533–54. This is true even in the more restrictive situation in which players have both complete and perfect information; that is, they know the strategies selected by players in the past and they are completely aware of the payoff structure.

[28] For an interesting related discussion, see Lisa Martin, "The Rational State Choice of Multilateralism," in *Multilateralism Matters*, ed. John Gerard Ruggie, pp. 91–121 (New York: Columbia University Press, 1993).

associated with incomplete contracting, or as the means to counteract problems of collective action. When political actors must choose between sets of outcomes that would represent Pareto improvements for all, and when there are no "objective" criteria on which to base choice, ideas focus expectations and strategies.[29] Political elites may settle upon courses of action on the basis of shared cultural, normative, religious, ethnic, or causal beliefs. Other policies may be ignored. As Geoffrey Garrett and Barry Weingast state the issue, "to assert that institutions help assure adherence to the rules of the game is to overlook a prior and critical issue. If the members of a community cannot agree to one set of rules, the fact that institutions might facilitate adherence to them would be irrelevant."[30]

Chapter 7, in which Garrett and Weingast investigate the move toward an internal market within the European Community (EC), provides a functional analysis of the role of ideas. Their explanation proceeds in three steps. They begin with the observation that the European countries faced a classic collective action problem in the early 1980s. They wanted to reduce barriers to trade to stimulate European economic performance, but there were strong temptations for individual countries and firms to defect. Hypothetically, these temptations could be reduced through the codification and monitoring of an agreed set of rules. Many sets of rules were consistent with these desiderata, however, and EC members disagreed over which should be chosen.

A further barrier to the successful completion of the international market lay in what they call an incomplete contracting issue. It was impossible for the members to know whether the rules they chose would cover every type of dispute that might arise within the internal market. As a result, the countries had to consider delegating considerable political authority to some agent to interpret and to apply some general "rules of the game" to all future trade disputes in Europe. Members would agree to give up such authority, however, only if they were confident that the delegated authority would in fact act in accordance with their general wishes.

Garrett and Weingast claim that ideas were crucial elements that helped to determine which of many rules were selected. "Given that most agreements are likely to be incomplete, . . . shared beliefs about

[29] For the generalized argument, see David Kreps, "Corporate Culture and Economic Theory," in *Perspectives on Positive Political Economy*, ed. James Alt and Kenneth Shepsle (Cambridge: Cambridge University Press, 1990).

[30] Geoffrey Garrett and Barry Weingast, "National Autonomy, European Law, and the Internal Market: Norms, Institutions, and European Integration," paper prepared for our April 1991 conference, p. 18.

the spirit of agreements are essential to the maintenance of cooperation." These ideas do not necessarily arise spontaneously, but must be engineered. In this case, parties were able to coalesce around principled ideas embedded in court decisions asserting the supremacy of EC law over domestic laws and the principle of mutual recognition as the central rule for organizing market exchanges in the EC. Garrett and Weingast point out, however, that these ideas were able to serve as a focal point only because they did not contradict the interests of the most powerful actor, Germany.[31] EC law has allowed German goods and services freer access to other European markets, but it has not sought to undermine the elaborate domestic regulatory framework that the German government and capitalists feel is central to their international competitiveness.

In sum, Garrett and Weingast argue that "a cooperative agreement in Europe based solely on decentralized, self-interested behavior could neither have emerged in the mid-1980s nor would be likely to sustain itself after 1992. Because the participants had—and continue to have— divergent preferences over the potential paths to cooperation, the lack of a natural unique path has been a great barrier to the realization of collective gains."

That the idea of mutual recognition—enunciated as a rule by the European Court of Justice in the *Cassis de Dijon* case—became the central feature of the move toward a single European market was not inevitable. Which idea is chosen as the focal point cannot be fully explained by rational choice theory. What this approach suggests, however, is that some focal point was necessary to ensure coordination, to signal commitments, and to promote cooperation in a game in which the cooperative equilibrium was difficult to sustain.

In Chapter 8 John Ferejohn suggests a quite different analysis of the way ideas help political actors deal with strategic interaction. Ferejohn observes that in mid-seventeenth-century England, fiscal pressures led to an increase in legislative independence in contrast to the pattern in continental Europe. Ferejohn explains that English and continental policies diverged because beliefs about the role of the monarchy diverged. Up until the 1620s, the theory of kingship embraced in England comprised two strands—one that granted the king the right to impose taxes and a second that required him to secure the legislature's consent to any taxes he wished to impose. Ferejohn writes of the divergence in the 1620s between the theories accepted by the king and by Parliament.

---

[31] In *The Strategy of Conflict* (Cambridge: Harvard University Press, 1960), Thomas Schelling discussed focal points as clues for coordinating behavior. Schelling was less

How ideas contributed to conflict is at the heart of Ferejohn's chapter. In England, he argues, the incompleteness of the Reformation "produced profound religious division and distrust within the governing elite. . . . This chronic distrust delimited the set of acceptable and stable institutional arrangements that could evolve." Bifurcated ideologies emerged: both absolutist and constitutional doctrines were elaborated and sharpened. Ferejohn describes the resulting situation in game-theoretic language: "In a sense, the transition in this period was between two different strategic equilibria: one based on extensive trust between crown and subject and the other based on more explicitly formulated rules and procedures for resolving conflict." As in the case of the Single European Act, ideas served the function of creating focal points for coalitions. In the seventeenth century, however, the incompatibility of the ideas relied on by king and Parliament eventually worsened problems of strategic interaction between them by weakening trust, and led to civil strife.

Institutionalization

Ideas can matter in a third sense. Regardless of how a particular set of beliefs comes to influence politics, use of those ideas over time implies changes in existing rules and norms. Ideas have a lasting influence on politics through their incorporation into the terms of political debate; but the impact of some set of ideas may be mediated by the operation of institutions in which the ideas are embedded. Once ideas have influenced organizational design, their influence will be reflected in the incentives of those in the organization and those whose interests are served by it. In general, when institutions intervene, the impact of ideas may be prolonged for decades or even generations. In this sense, ideas can have an impact even when no one genuinely believes in them as principled or causal statements. One of the best examples of this process is seen in the case of legal doctrines—socially constructed sets of ideas that constrain contemporary policy making.[32]

Our third causal path focuses on how political institutions—administrative agencies, laws, norms, and operating procedures—mediate between ideas and policy outcomes.[33] In this model, ideas become

---

concerned with the functioning of ideas as focal points than with preexisting features of situations that actors could use to concert their expectations.

[32] We are indebted to John Ferejohn for this example.

[33] We define norms as implicit prescriptions accepted as valid by a particular society to govern relationships within it or by more than one society to govern their relations with one another. The concept of norms, however, is contested, and we have not imposed this definition on all of the authors in this volume.

institutionalized at some point in time. Although this institutionalization may reflect the power of some idea, its existence may also reflect
the interests of the powerful.[34] But even in this case, the interests that
promoted some statute may fade over time while the ideas encased in
that statute nevertheless continue to influence politics. Thus at a later
time, these institutionalized ideas continue to exert an effect: it is no
longer possible to understand policy outcomes on the basis of contemporary configurations of interest and power alone.[35]

When ideas are powerfully institutionalized, we must both analyze
the contemporary importance of old rules and socially embedded
norms and undertake an archaeology of ideas in order to understand
how one set of ideas rather than another came to be institutionalized.
Consider, for instance, Judith Goldstein's work on United States trade
policy. Contemporary variations in the treatment of industries in U.S.
trade policy are not fully explained by variations in their economic
positions or political resources. Different laws apply to antidumping
and escape-clause issues, and we can understand these laws only by
exploring the circumstances under which they were first enacted, including the ideas about trade policy then held by the powerful.[36]

This process—whereby an idea that becomes institutionalized essentially for reasons of power and interest ultimately has an independent
impact—is illustrated in Stephen Krasner's study of the origins of the
nation-state system in Chapter 9. The common wisdom is that the
contemporary system of sovereign states can be traced back to a single
epoch-making event that embodied a set of new ideas about political
order—the Treaty of Westphalia in 1648. But Krasner points out that
historical periods cannot be so easily and cleanly delineated. Sovereignty existed in fairly modern forms long before the mid–seventeenth
century. Violations of its norms have since been widespread. Krasner
argues, moreover, that the origins of sovereignty as an organizing political idea did not predate the existence of nations themselves. Rather,

[34] In this model, therefore, whether ideas shaped institutions at their creation is less
important than the effects of the institution that embodies the ideas.

[35] The importance of the institutionalization of ideas was particularly brought home
to us by James E. Alt, "Crude Politics: Oil and the Political Economy of Unemployment
in Britain and Norway, 1970–85," *British Journal of Political Science* 17 (April 1987):
149–99. Alt shows how Norway's institutionalization of sectoral ideas about the economy,
in the form of a disaggregated model used by the Norwegian Ministry of Finance,
enabled it to react effectively to increases in the price of crude oil. Britain's treasury
relied on models that had institutionalized aggregate conceptions of the economy, using
a single equation for all exported manufactures. For this as well as for larger political
reasons, Britain was less able than Norway to limit the unemployment-creating effects
of oil price increases. See ibid., pp. 161–63.

[36] Judith Goldstein, *Ideas, Interests, and American Trade Policy* (Ithaca: Cornell University
Press, 1993).

"ideas have been used to codify existing practices rather than to initiate new forms of order. Ideas have not made possible alternatives that did not previously exist; they legitimated political practices that were already facts on the ground."

Krasner suggests that the notion of sovereignty did not precipitate the creation of nations. Rather, the Treaty of Westphalia was conservative, looking backward to the political order that preceded the Thirty Years' War. The treaty itself, Krasner suggests, could be read more as a legitimation of the Holy Roman Empire than the beginning of the modern international order. When Jean Bodin actually articulated the theory of sovereignty at the end of the sixteenth century, the practice was already established. Indeed, Lutheranism had already promoted sovereignty by legitimating the claims of national rulers for independence from Rome.

Still, Krasner admits that whatever the explanation for the emergence of sovereignty around the time of Westphalia, the idea subsequently influenced politics. Although a far more fluid concept than that envisioned by international law, the idea of sovereignty has had a considerable impact on the behavior of states by virtue of its embodiment in international institutions and of its functional utility. Even if the interaction between practice and ideas neither was frozen nor determined a unique outcome, the existence of sovereignty did preclude a broad range of alternative political practices.

Krasner rightly points out that politically relevent ideas are not formulated independently of interests and power. As he notes, "before and after Westphalia the notion of sovereignty has been, in one way or another, up for grabs. . . . New problems have generated new institutional solutions." However, the significance of an idea such as sovereignty should not be dismissed because it had its origins in the material interests of the powerful: indeed, the intensity of controversies about sovereignty suggests how important its institutionalization is to political actors, even if institutional arrangements can change under pressure.

In Chapter 10 Peter Katzenstein similarly suggests that politics is influenced by a complex array of ideas that are embedded in institutions and rooted in the past. His analysis of state responses to terrorism in Germany and Japan emphasizes the role of highly institutionalized social norms. These norms are reflections of principled beliefs (for instance, about civil liberties) as well as largely implicit views of how society should be organized and how state power relates to social order. Japan and Germany, often regarded as similar in international position and domestic politics, have radically different systems of internal security, even given similarities in "objective" levels of threat. Katzenstein argues that variation in the behavior of these countries can be accounted for only by the differences in the "normative context that frames political choices" in the two countries. Research, he argues, must begin with the social and normative bases of the interests of actors, since the "assumption that actors know their interests, though convenient for analytical purposes, sidesteps some of the most important political and intriguing analytical questions in contemporary politics."

Katzenstein argues that in Germany and Japan norms and beliefs not only are important explanations of internal security policies but, more strikingly, are also critical to the very constitution of problems policy makers seek to address. Thus Germany's response to international problems is conditioned by a belief in an international Grotian community. Policy makers in Japan, in contrast, see no such community. Rather, armed with a Hobbesian view of the international system, Japan sees no problem with the export of a domestic issue such as terrorism. This norm-driven variation is also manifest in general security policy. German policy is informed by the concept of a security partnership in which German security is inextricably intertwined with that of other European countries. Japan's Hobbesian view of international politics, in contrast, translates into a view of competition whereby cooperation derives from being "flexible in the redefinition of short-term into long-term interests." Whereas German leaders are willing to become enmeshed in international political structures, Japanese norms lead policy makers to go it alone, even if by doing so they must accept international vulnerability in economic and security affairs.

To varying degrees, all of the chapters in this volume exemplify the importance of institutionalized ideas. Garrett and Weingast see institutionalized legal ideas as constraining the possibilities for action, limiting choice. If institutions occupying authoritative positions (such as the European Court) are imbued with particular sets of ideas, those ideas may become influential. Similarly, Stalinist conceptions of political economy, international human rights policies in Europe after the 1940s and in the United States after the 1970s, the idea of statehood for former colonies, and ideas about sovereignty and political representation, all ultimately exerted distinctive effects because they became institutionalized.

In sum, ideas that become institutionalized play a role in generalizing rules and linking issue areas. When collective action requires persuasion rather than mere coercion, and when consistency of policy is demanded on the basis of principles institutionalized in the form of rules, reasons must be given for proposed courses of action; when reasons are required, ideas become important. The significance of law in the European Community, and therefore of beliefs incorporated in legal doctrines, demonstrates how the demand for reasons can enhance the impact of ideas on policy, spreading it beyond areas originally contemplated by policy makers.[37] Indeed, one consequence of international institutions is that they provide settings in which governments must provide reasons (whether genuine or not) for their positions. The existence of international institutions gives states greater incentives to make their policies more consistent with one another and with prevailing norms, so that they can be more successfully defended in international forums.

IDEA PATHS AND IDEA TYPES

We can organize our chapters by our three theoretical pathways and the types of ideas in question as in Table 1.

Table 1. Types of ideas analyzed by contributors to this volume, by causal pathway

Pathway	World views	Principled beliefs	Causal beliefs
Need for road maps		Jackson Sikkink	Ikenberry Halpern
Absence of unique equilibria	Ferejohn	Garrett-Weingast	
Institutional persistence	Krasner	Katzenstein	

Each of the categories in this table indicates one way in which changes in ideas, or in conditions that affect the impact of ideas, can affect policy. As Ferejohn suggests world views changed fundamentally in the seventeenth century. Changes in principled ideas helped to bring about the collapse of colonialism in the 1950s, according to Robert Jackson, and fostered pressure for protection of human rights in the United States during the 1970s, as Kathryn Sikkink argues. Changes in causal beliefs affected Anglo-American economic policy in the early 1940s and Stalinist economic policies after World War II. Two examples not examined here illustrate the impact of changes in casual ideas. In the nineteenth century, national health policies shifted and interna-

---

[37] For this point we are particularly indebted to arguments made separately by Anne-Marie Burley and Peter Hall.

tional coordination became feasible when the causes of such diseases as cholera and yellow fever were scientifically identified.[38] During the last decade, shifts in foreign policies toward production of CFCs have resulted from scientific work showing the link between CFCs and the ozone layer.[39]

The table also indicates that the categorization of ideas as principled or causal does not always neatly reflect reality. Katzenstein and Garrett and Weingast discuss mixtures of principled and causal beliefs that shaped policy. Some distinctions, furthermore, are not captured by this typology. The impetus for change in ideas, for example, may come from outside the issue area ultimately affected as well as within it. World War II, which significantly altered views toward international protection of human rights, was certainly fought neither to free colonies nor to protect the rights of people within established national states; yet it had both effects. Furthermore, changes in prevailing ideas—world views, principled beliefs, or causal beliefs—typically become institutionalized at some point, as Jackson points out in regard to colonialism. In this sense, all of the chapters are relevant to the third row of the table, the institutionalization of ideas.

Each of our three pathways suggests ways in which changes in the underlying conditions, rather than changes in ideas themselves, can alter the impact of ideas on policy. Indeed, ideas often become politically efficacious only in conjunction with other changes, either in material interests or in power relationships. Uncertainty in an issue area can increase, perhaps because of the failure of an older set of causal inferences, making room for new ideas. John Ikenberry's discussion of Keynesianism and the Anglo-American negotiations illustrates such a process. In the second pathway, change can occur when perceptions of new benefits to be realized from cooperation give coordination problems new salience and lead actors to search for ideas that will enable them to cooperate. The development of policies of mutual recognition in the European Community during the 1970s and especially the 1980s, as Garrett and Weingast discuss, illustrates such a process. Finally, institutions that embody a set of ideas can be strengthened, perhaps for reasons unrelated to those ideas themselves, as Katzenstein demonstrates in his discussion of German and Japanese practices with respect to international security.

Both our causal pathways and our case studies suggest that changes

---

[38] Richard N. Cooper, "International Cooperation in Public Health as a Prologue to Macroeconomic Cooperation," in Richard N. Cooper, Barry Eichengreen, Gerald Holtham, Robert D. Putnam, and C. Randall Henning, *Can Nations Agree? Issues in International Economic Cooperation* (Washington, D.C.: Brookings, 1989), pp. 178–254.

[39] Benedick, *Ozone Diplomacy*, p. 10.

in ideas need not immediatly lead to an alteration in policy. Changes in ideas are frequently felt only after the preexisting policy consensus in an issue area has been destabilized. Periods in which power relations are fluid and interests and strategies are unclear or lack consensus generate demands for new ideas. In such times, articulations of principled and causal beliefs that were ignored earlier may exert an impact on policy. Kathryn Sikkink argues, for example, that new beliefs about the need to protect human rights did not lead the United States immediately to support international protection. Such policy changes were inhibited by racial segregation in the United States and by the Cold War. Détente, the achievement of formal legal protection for civil rights, and revulsion against the Vietnam War created the conditions under which these beliefs could exert an impact on policy formation.

THE METHODOLOGY OF THIS VOLUME

Reflectivist students of the impact of ideas on policy often argue that interests cannot be conceptualized apart from the ideas that constitute them, and that it is therefore futile to try to distinguish interests and ideas analytically, as we seek to do. Adoption of such a view, however, would foreclose the possibility of evaluating the hypothesis that ideas are hooks against our argument that they often exert a major impact on policy. Reflectivists who assert that interests cannot be evaluated apart from the ideas that constitute them set aside materialist and rationalistic arguments without subjecting them to serious empirical evaluation. Thus a potentially rich debate is consigned to the purgatory of incompatible epistemologies.

We recognize that ideas and interests are not phenomenologically separate and that all interests involve beliefs, and therefore ideas as we conceive them. Yet, for us the important question is the extent to which *variation* in beliefs, or the manner in which ideas are institutionalized in societies, affect political action under circumstances that are otherwise similar. Does it matter that policy makers in China believed in Stalinist political economy, or that elites in the West after World War II were deeply imbued with conceptions of human rights? That is, do people behave differently than they would if they were just pursuing individual self-interest in a narrowly utilitarian sense?

This point of comparison—the materialistically egocentric maximizer of modern economic theory—allows us to formulate the null hypothesis that is central to the research design of this volume. For each chapter, the null hypothesis is that the actions described can be understood on the basis of egoistic interests in the context of power realities: that variations of interests are not accounted for by variations in the character of the ideas that people have. Evidence must then be brought to bear so that we can assess, insofar as possible, the validity of the null hypothesis in relation to the assertion that ideas mattered. In our view, only when the null hypothesis is carefully addressed and comparative evidence brought forth will the issue be joined and substantial progress be made toward understanding the conditions under which ideas affect foreign policy.

At the same time, we recognize that an exploratory investigation such as this one will at best provide preliminary evidence in support of our hypothsis. Considerable uncertainty surrounds all work in this field. A key problem is that students of the role of ideas must interpret what is in people's heads: their conceptions of what is true, reflecting their own attempts to create meaning in their lives. Such a study presents a host of methodological difficulties. The student of ideas must engage in attempts at *Verstehen*, the interpretation of meaning through empathetic understanding and pattern recognition, made possible by a shared language and shared tradition. Yet in our view, an observer's judgments generated by *Verstehen* should be treated as hypotheses rather than conclusions. Unless the interpreter's judgments are evaluated according to systematic standards for assessing the quality of inferences, they remain only the personal view of the observer. After all, we do not observe beliefs directly; we observe only claims about beliefs and actions presumably based on beliefs. Thus our descriptions of beliefs require inferences, which need insofar as possible to be tested.[40]

How can we reconcile our demand for systematic social science with our recognition of the role of interpretation? Clearly, this is a circle that cannot be easily squared. Our approach is to ask for a method of inquiry that involves careful attempts at both description and causal inference. The first step is what we refer to as *evidentiary inference*. Any set of evidence about beliefs and policies is potentially biased. Only some documents will have survived; others will have been destroyed, and some of the extant documents may have been forged. Different reports of the same event often contradict one another. Thus whether the events observed are far in the past or occurred yesterday, the analyst must employ what Marc Bloch called the critical method: "True progress [in history] began on the day when, as Volney put it, doubt became

---

[40] For a clear discussion of *Verstehen* and hermeneutics, which argues that the position taken here is too closely linked to "ideal language" or neopositivist views of the philosophy of science, see Paul Diesing, *How Does Social Science Work?: Reflections on Practice* (Pittsburgh: University of Pittsburgh Press, 1991), chap. 5, esp. pp. 141–42.

an 'examiner.'" The historian makes inferences about what actually happened, and attaches probabilities to those inferences.[41]

After undertaking this task of evidentiary inference, the investigator engages in *descriptive inference*. With respect to the study of ideas, descriptive inference has two components: first, the distinction between random and systematic aspects of behavior; and second, assessment of the extent to which self-reported and observed behavior reflect beliefs. Even if all information is accurate, it is not necessarily representative. Interviews will have been conducted with only some participants and on certain days, when those informants' recollections were affected by their current preoccupations. The policies themselves may be the result of random or conjunctural phenomena, not understood or realized by political actors. Thus, in undertaking an inquiry of this nature, the analyst needs to consider how inferences about what happened would have been affected had the available documents been somewhat different, had interviews been conducted in a different context, or had policies been adopted under other circumstances. Under those conditions, how different would the reported beliefs and policies have been? Descriptive inference requires us to think in terms of counterfactuals. Only then can an analyst describe a pattern of behavior that represents the typical beliefs and policies that would have occurred had it been possible both to repeat the process of investigation and to repeat the actual events a number of times. Such a pattern represents the systematic component of what we have actually observed.[42]

Having described as well as possible the observed pattern of statements about beliefs and apparently related behavior, the investigator also has to make inferences about the extent to which this pattern is indicative of actual beliefs. Political actors may systematically dissimulate. They also may hold contradictory beliefs, and be more aware of some of them than of others. At this stage it is important to evaluate hypotheses by examining the degree to which alleged beliefs are consistent with one another and with observed behavior.

In view of the exploratory nature of this enterprise, descriptive inference is probably the most important task carried out by the authors of the case-study chapters below. Relying largely on primary and secondary accounts of events and statements, the authors seek valid descriptive generalizations, without which no causal analysis will be of much value. Yet ultimately we wish to shed light on the *impact* of ideas on

[41] Marc Bloch wrote that "the majority of problems of historical criticism are really [complex] problems of probability": *The Historian's Craft* (New York: Knopf, 1953), p. 129. The quotation in the text is on p. 81.

[42] This paragraph draws on Gary King, Robert O. Keohane, and Sydney Verba, *Scientific Inference in Qualitative Research: Designing Social Inquiry* (Princeton: Princeton University Press, forthcoming).

policy, a task that requires some effort, however tentative, at causal inference. The first step in a causal account is to establish covariation between ideas and outcomes. That established, we also need to ask whether we can identify a path leading from ideas to policy. In which of the ways sketched above, if any, were ideas linked to policy? If at least one process connecting beliefs and policies can be identified, we need to check for spurious correlation by asking about the external constraints that affected both beliefs and outcomes. It is possible that some set of forces, typically involving power and interests, constrained both beliefs and outcomes. It could be argued, for example, that the political and economic dominance of the United States after World War II led both to the prevalence of capitalist ideology in the West and to the creation of liberal political and economic institutions. If, as this argument claims, hegemony alone explained all the variation in the form of postwar institutions, any alleged causal connection between capitalist ideology and liberal institutions would be spurious.

We recognize from the outset that the causal arguments offered here are incomplete. In terms of research design, they are indeterminate because the cases on which they are based are fewer than the explanatory variables considered. Our theories are not sufficiently well developed to limit the number of explanatory variables, and our empirical work is not sufficiently extensive to provide a large number of similar cases against which to evaluate complex theories. All we can expect at this stage is arguments that evaluate the plausibility of the view that ideas matter for policy. We do suggest, however, that the causal hypotheses offered in this book are sufficiently plausible to merit further research.

We do not demand methodological perfection. If we did, we would be studying voting behavior or congressional roll calls instead of a subject so murky as the role of ideas in foreign policy. But we do hope that a distinctive feature of this particular attempt to examine the role of ideas will be its methodological self-consciousness and the care with which both descriptive and causal inferences are made.

CONCLUSION

Ideas can be categorized as world views, principled beliefs, and causal beliefs. They can have impacts on policy by acting as road maps, helping to cope with the absence of unique equilibrium solutions, and becoming embedded in durable institutions. Policy changes can be influenced by ideas both because new ideas emerge and as a result of changes in underlying conditions affecting the impact of existing ideas. Ideas matter, as a result of a system of interacting multiple causes of which they are a part.

Ultimately, we study the role of ideas partly to understand our own role—as "scribblers," in Keynes's phrase. As scholars, we devote our lives to the creation, refinement, and application of ideas. If we really thought ideas were irrelevant, our lives as social scientists would be meaningless. Our exploration of the impact of ideas on foreign policy is also a search for personal meaning and relevance in our own lives.

CHAPTER TWO

Ideas and the Social Sciences

JOHN A. HALL

One striking, perhaps less than endearing feature of social science is the way in which questions that vex or approaches that dominate one particular discipline come to haunt another. Thus archaeology endorsed functionalism at the precise moment sociologists abandoned it; and functionalism was then revived by geography—but necessarily not for long, given that that discipline had several paradigm changes within a decade! Involvement in conceptual revolutions of this sort can have enormous sex appeal. Accordingly, it is wise to remember Poincaré's aphorism: Whereas natural scientists discuss results, social scientists argue about their concepts. The presumption that it points to— that once conceptual and technical tools are really sharp, understanding social life will be easy—is surely so questionable as to induce a healthy skepticism toward the very enterprise of paradigm generation.[1] "Theoretical praxis," to use the awful term invented by Western Marxists, does not necessarily make for powerful social science.

The author of this analytic review of the ways in which the social sciences have conceptualized the impact of ideas is a sociologist. Given the general intimation that Max Weber's travails in this area—which will be analyzed carefully in this chapter—are of especial importance, this is scarcely surprising. This is not to say that the task at hand is

This chapter is heavily indebted to the comments of many friends: Stephen Rytina, Michael Smith, Patricia Crone, Axel van den Berg, Judith Goldstein, Peter Hall, Nicos Mouzelis, and Robert Keohane.
[1] See Thomas Kuhn's contrast between the Hobbesian world of the social scientists and the consensual and accumulative practices of natural scientists in *The Structure of Scientific Revolutions* (Chicago: University of Chicago Press, 1962), p. x.

altogether welcome. It is certainly not possible to claim that sociology has quietly been accumulating and codifying truths that can now confidently be passed on to a wider audience. Very much to the contrary, sociology has been the most prone of all the social sciences to engage in theoretical extravaganzas, and it has exhibited this penchant to the worst possible effect when it has dealt with the impact of ideas. Hence one purpose of this essay must be negative: to explain error, and thereby to prevent its repetition. If the pomposity of posing as a social science health inspector can be excused for a moment, it is worth stressing immediately that the contributors to this volume seem to me to have freed themselves from the crucial error that will be identified. Differently put, they occupy a middle ground in which both belief and circumstance are given their proper due. But this chapter has a second purpose, and it is one that is happily and decidedly positive. One consequence of the marked improvement in sociology's cognitive track record over the last decade has been the specification of those rare moments when ideological power has constructed social reality.[2] This exciting intellectual development has depended upon the realization that Emile Durkheim has quite as much to tell us about the impact of ideas as does his great German contemporary.

AN ANTITHESIS

Perhaps mercifully, there is insufficient space here to describe the history of the generation and abandonment of the myriad of paradigms that have plagued sociology for most of the postwar period. What is possible, however, is to demonstrate that beneath the sound and fury lay a fundamental debate between "idealists" and "materialists"—the same division, in analytic terms, as that drawn by Robert Keohane between "rationalists" and "reflectivists" in contemporary American political science.[3] It should be noted that theorists are considered here insofar as they illustrate these two categories. As sophisticated thinkers are often aware of the limitations of their own thought and accordingly try to insulate themselves from criticisms whose provenance they can often predict, the clarity of the analysis is gained at the

[2] I argue the case for genuine cognitive advance in "Theory," in *Developments in Sociology*, ed. M. Haralambos, vol. 2 (Ormskirk: Causeway Press, 1986), and in "'They Do Things Differently There,' or, The Contribution of British Historical Sociology," *British Journal of Sociology* 40 (1989).

[3] Robert O. Keohane, "International Institutions: Two Approaches," *International Studies Quarterly* 32 (1988).

cost of losing sight of some complex and entertaining intellectual gymnastics.[4]

Meaning Makes the World Go Round

It is almost impossible now to credit the extent of the intellectual hegemony exerted by Talcott Parsons not just over sociology but over social science more generally, and for a full two decades at that. There were many reasons for this dominance, from the way in which abstruse language helped professionalization to the fit between Parsonianism and resurgent American liberalism, and they merit a study in themselves.[5] Attention here, however, must focus on the Parsonian conceptualization of the way ideas affect social life.

In a sense everything was present in his first and best book, *The Structure of Social Action*. Immense influence was exerted by Parsons's definition of a society as a bounded territory ruled over by a state monopolizing violence within whose borders norms are shared. If this definition seemed fairly neutral, it proved to be the case that Parsons was far more affected by the legacy of Durkheim than by that of Weber, with Marx famously not receiving any systematic attention whatever: Parson's central concern was cohesion or order. It was this concern that led Parsons to emphasize that he was writing against classical utilitarianism, on the grounds that mere self-interest could not establish a stable society. This is not to say that Parsons was as anticapitalist as most sociological theorists have been; rather he was giving maximum emphasis to Durkheim's argument against Herbert Spencer, that consensus must lie behind contracts if a Hobbesian state of nature is to be avoided. This concern with consensus was the seed from which grew all of Parsons's later thought. Whereas *The Structure of Social Action* formally proposed a multidimensional and multicausal sociology that paid proper attention to social actors, the later Parsonian oeuvre became completely obsessed with one dimension of social reality. Behind all of structural functionalism's specification of functional prerequisites and the varied analyses of polity, economy, and cultural order stood the insistence that normative integration was the sole bedrock of social order. And if the action frame of reference was supposedly maintained, it was emptied of content by a concept of socialization that turned human beings into mere receptacles of societal programming. This was

[4] Striking use is made of this insight by Jeffrey Alexander in *Twenty Lectures: Sociological Theory since World War II* (New York: Columbia University Press, 1987), a useful history on which I have drawn extensively for this chapter.
[5] Alexander offers striking insights into the fit between Parsonianism and a particular moment of American history. See ibid., chaps. 1 and 2 and passim.

a classically idealist view in which shared meanings made the world go round.

The central change that came to be directed at Parsons was that his theory could not explain social change.[6] Strictly speaking, this was not correct: indeed, more troubling was the fact that Parsons had two mutually incompatible theories of social change.[7] On the one hand, Parsons paid obeisance to Durkheim's insistence on structural differentiation; but on the other, and with increasing emphasis, he argued, in his view in the spirit of Max Weber, that social change resulted from the spelling out in history of the doctrines inherent in the world religions.[8] This view of Weber proved to be extremely influential, not least because it led to a general interpretation of classical sociological theory in which the idealism of Weber was (favorably) contrasted with the materialism of Marx. What was not in question for Parsons was the nature of modernity itself, toward whose definition his analysis of pattern variables was supposed to contribute. This certainty lay at the back of such substantive investigations as he made: most important, he saw Nazism as an atavism resulting from strains in the transition to modernity.[9]

It was precisely this confident universalism that was criticized by a second analytic position that gave great—indeed, much greater—prominence to the role of ideas in social life. The most rigorous articulation of the position in question has been that offered by Peter Winch in various attempts to spell out the implications of the philosophy of the later Wittgenstein for social science.[10] Winch draws many of his

[6] This charge was made by European thinkers, some of whom will be noted in a moment, indebted to Marx. But it is important to remember that the structuralist Marxism of Althusser curiously ended up replicating Parson's view of society to a quite amazing extent, as has been definitively shown by Axel van den Berg, *The Immanent Utopia* (Princeton: Princeton University Press, 1990). Modern Western Marxism as a whole, seeking to explain the nonoccurrence of revolution, tends toward idealism; that is, it tends to say that the workers are, in one way or another, brainwashed into accepting the system: see José Merquior, *Western Marxism* (London: Paladin, 1986).

[7] Randall Collins, *Theoretical Sociology* (New York, 1988), pp. 66–67.

[8] In this vein, Parsons insisted—in *Societies: Evolutionary and Comparative Perspectives* (Englewood Cliffs, N.J.: Prentice-Hall, 1966), p. 113—that "I am a cultural determinist. . . . I believe that . . . the normative elements are more important for social change than . . . material interests." Interestingly, the hugely influential German philosopher/social scientist Jürgen Habermas arrived at exactly the same conclusion in his *Communication and the Evolution of Society* (Boston: Beacon, 1979).

[9] Talcott Parsons, "Democracy and Social Structure in Pre-Nazi Germany" and "Certain Primary Sources and Patterns of Aggression," both reprinted in his *Essays in Sociological Theory* (New York: Free Press, 1954).

[10] Peter Winch, *The Idea of a Social Science* (London: Routledge, 1958) and "Understanding a Primitive Society," *American Philosophical Quarterly* 1 (1964). Ernest Gellner has usefully pointed out—in "Concepts and Society," in his *Cause and Meaning in the Social Sciences* (London: Routledge, 1973), p. 44—that the ideas of the later Wittgenstein are

examples from anthropological fieldwork, particularly that of E. E. Evans-Pritchard, and his position has close parallels to the work of Clifford Geertz, a student of Parsons whose influence extends well beyond the borders of anthropology.[11] In what ways does this position parallel Parsonianism and in what ways does it advance beyond it?

The simplest and most important claim made is that "they do things differently there"—or, in Pascal's apposite formulation, "truth is different on the other side of the Pyrenees." A particular view is being alluded to here, derived from the later Wittgenstein's view that "the limits of my language are the limits of my world." What this view suggests is that the belief system of a society has "commanding heights," which, once captured, dictate the way in which social life is conducted. A very striking literary expression of this view is George Orwell's *1984*. A part of the plot of that novel concerns the perfection of the social dictionary, the presumption being that once a concept—say that of revolution—has been removed, practical activity will thereafter be impossible. This notion is of course utterly idealist, although it is probably more rigorously so than the sociological theory of Parsons: it is less a question of positive socialization into the leading norms of society via an education system than the fact that our form of life so penetrates us that alternatives cannot even be envisaged.

But this position goes far beyond Parsonianism because of the way in which its relativist starting point affects its view of the nature of social science. Winch notes the Azande's acceptance of witchcraft and its rejection by Europeans, and suggests that "it is clear that [Evans-Pritchard] would have wished to add . . . the European is right and the Zande wrong. This addition I regard as illegitimate."[12] Witches exist for the Azande, as scientific concepts do for us; equally, Winch tells us that it is only for us that contradictions, say in light of a refutation of an oracle, matter—for the Azande they do not exist. What matters is that there is no way whatsoever in which one can judge between these viewpoints: there is no neutral point free of context, and universalism

---

very similar to the brilliant opening pages on the social construction of categories of Emile Durkheim's introduction to *The Elementary Forms of the Religious Life* (London, 1915).

[11] Clifford Geertz's position is particularly clearly seen in relatively early essays such as "Religion as a Cultural System," in *The Religious System*, ed. Donald Cutler (Boston, 1966), and "Ideology as a Cultural System," in *Ideology and Discontent*, ed. David Apter (New York, 1964). Geertz has been especially influential on such historians as Robert Darnton (*The Great Cat Massacre and Other Episodes in French Cultural History* [New York: Basic Books, 1984]) and Lynn Hunt (*Politics, Culture and Class in the French Revolution* [Berkeley: University of California Press, 1984]).

[12] Winch, "Understanding a Primitive Society," cited in Ernest Gellner, "The New Idealism—Cause and Meaning in the Social Sciences," in his *Cause and Meaning*, p. 59.

must accordingly be abandoned. One whole set of questions that this observation raises concerns the extent to which relativism is as attractive as it seems: it may discourage missionaries and intervention, but it equally blocks social reform and probably encourages intolerance to societal dissidents. But what matters here is the prescription for social science. All that is possible is the exploration of different conceptual systems: meaning becomes all and cause absolutely nothing.

Both for the sake of completeness and because of its growing importance in much modern social theory, it is worth noting a third analytic position, spiritually different even if logically largely similar. Poststructuralist theorists such as Michel Foucault and Jacques Derrida have offered arguments analogous to those of Winch and Geertz in insisting that we are trapped within the terms of particular discourses. But whereas anthropological relativists seem almost nervous in their wish to preserve traditional practices, poststructuralists gaily point to what they conceive as positive consequences of relativism. Western science is seen as but one discourse among others, and a particularly disciplinary and "logocentric" one at that. Perhaps oddly, given the supposed power of discourse over us, they suggest that we should not restrict ourselves to the terms of any single discourse. Why should we not consider all the intellectual products on offer at the theoretical emporia, and help ourselves to whatever we please, to suit the occasion at hand? Not surprisingly, what poststructuralists claim to be mere playfulness others see as anarchy.

Conflict and Calculators

Most developments in sociological theory between roughly 1960 and 1980 had at their heart a revolt againt the work of Talcott Parsons. The thinkers considered here form an intellectual group because all completely rejected the passive, plastic view of human behavior that lay at the heart of Parsonianism. Men and women were not just concept fodder but purposive and calculating agents. If this view seems absolutely opposed to the Parsonian ethic, it is as well to remember immediately that fighting an enemy always influences one's mind: in the case of sociological theory, as we shall see later, many traces of Parsons can in fact be found in those who sought to reject him absolutely.

The best-known set of thinkers who attacked Parsons were self-proclaimed "conflict" theorists such as David Lockwood, Ralf Dahrendorf, and John Rex.[13] These European thinkers were leftist, and had, so to

[13] David Lockwood, "Some Notes on *The Social System*," *British Journal of Sociology* 7 (1956); Ralf Dahrendorf, *Class and Class Conflict in Industrial Society* (London: Routledge,

speak, absorbed both Marxist theory and practical labor movement politics with their mothers' milk. For such theorists the view of society as operating consensually represented a utopia at best and a highly biased and conservative defense of American capitalism at worst. Against Parsons, they insisted on the normality of conflict within society, usually seen as the working out of social inequalities: power, in its visceral and zero-sum sense, was placed by such thinkers at the center of sociological analysis, with order being seen as something imposed by the powerful. These thinkers were prone to pay rather little attention to matters of belief, not least because they felt that ideologies prevalent in society merely reflected the interests of the powerful. All of this added up to an ethic opposed in general to the influence of Parsons. But analytically specific claims were being made, perhaps especially clearly and representatively by Rex.[14]

Rex sought to go beyond the rather neutral assertion that men and women are purposive calculators, seeking the best means by which to realize their ends. His rejection of the idea of normative integration was so intense that it led him to suggest that rationality had content: "instrumental rationality" had something like universal validity because actors could see their material interests and acted upon them; that is, they were not taken in by cloudy ideological statements, preferring instead something more real. Rex believed that this argument was indebted to Marx, but it was in fact much closer to that of Pareto: for Marx, despite his polemical attacks on hypocrites and opportunists, did recognize the reality of belief, whereas Pareto cynically regarded matters of belief as always and inevitably affairs of illusion and manipulation. Rex's substance as a theorist was demonstrated by his recognition that his view of human nature was pulling him toward a view of society as being made up of the material interests of rationally calculating individuals. Interestingly, his basic Marxist sympathies led him to reject individualism and to hold to a group view of social life, which led him into a terrible conundrum: the social change he desired was dependent upon solidarity among the dispossessed, and he half recognized that solidarity could be achieved only through shared moral norms.

But the route that Rex rejected was taken by George Homans, whose loathing for Parsons, dutifully reciprocated, long divided and enlivened the Department of Social Relations at Harvard, where they were

---

1957); John Rex, *Key Problems in Sociological Theory* (London, 1961). The most complete statement of conflict theory was, however, made a generation later: Randall Collins, *Conflict Sociology* (New York: Academic Press, 1979).

[14] A brilliant discussion of Rex is offered in Alexander, *Twenty Lectures*, pp. 127–55.

colleagues. Homans famously insisted on "bringing men back in" and sought to construct sociological theory from the bottom up in terms of the reciprocal exchanges made by self-interested actors.[15] Two points must be made about Homans's position. First, it was extraordinarily— that is, naively—self-confident about its basic image of the human being. In his principal treatise, Homans calmly justifies his restriction to American material in this way: "Though I believe that the general features of elementary social behavior are shared by all mankind, I believe it as a matter of faith only, and the evidence that I shall in fact adduce is almost wholly American."[16] Second, Homans is scarcely troubled by the Durkheimian/Parsonian anxiety about social cohesion. This attitude can be seen particularly clearly at the end of a passage in which he describes how helpful he found Pareto in justifying his position as a rich and Republican Bostonian who felt himself to be under personal attack from Marxists in the 1930s:

> I was ready to believe Pareto because he provided me with a defense. His was an answer to Marx because an amplification of him. Marx had taught that the economic and political theories of the bourgeoisie—and I was clearly a bourgeois—were rationalizations of their interests. Pareto amplified Marx by showing that this was true of most theories of human behavior. ... At least the proletariat had no more intellectual justification in demanding my money or my life—and it looked as if they were demanding both, and my liberties to boot—than I had for defending myself. Emotional justification was something else again. ... If we could only meet as honest men—or honest rationalizers—we might divide up the take without fighting. It was the intellectual guff talked about by the alleged leaders of the proletariat that put one's back up and got in the way of a settlement.[17]

If interests ruled, social order could be assured because a natural harmony would be struck up between them. All in all, social exchange theory did not envisage conflict in anything like the way European leftist sociologists saw it.

The fullest drawing together of the various strands in this whole position is probably that contained in the modern rational choice Marxism of John Roemer and Jon Elster.[18] While it is clearly the case

[15] George Homans, "Bringing Men Back In," *American Sociological Review* 29 (1964).

[16] George Homans, *Social Behavior: Its Elementary Forms* (New York: Harcourt Brace & World, 1961), p. 7.

[17] Ibid., p. 79, cited in Alexander, *Twenty Lectures*, p. 161.

[18] An interesting but hostile (because) orthodox Marxist account of this new development is Ellen Meikins Wood, "Rational Choice Marxism," *New Left Review*, no. 160 (1986). This article led to an interesting exchange between Wood, Alex Callinicos, and Alan Carling in *New Left Review*, no. 184 (1990).

that rational choice theory can take a variety of forms, in Elster's case we can be quite clear that it comprises the belief not just that humans calculate but that they do so on the basis of their "real" interests, the corollary being, Elster insists, that inquiry into social life must be based on the presumptions of methodological individualism.[19] Clarity on this point is easy to come by because of the publication of a new work by Elster, a work that is certainly an "autocritique" and perhaps a repudiation of his earlier position. The very title of this volume—*The Cement of Society*—reveals its content: social order results from norms, and norms have a life of their own such that it becomes impossible at times to discover "pure material interests."[20] As this is a point at which Parsonianism seems to be having some sort of revenge, it is clearly time to turn away from describing the debate between idealism and materialism so as to establish why it is so utterly misconceived.

ITS FALSITY

"Pure materialists" who regard belief at best as an unimportant mask for interest hold to a highly implausible position insofar as they suggest that human history would have run the same course even had paganism, world religions, and Marxism never been invented. Furthermore, as Patricia Crone points out, this view "begs the question as to why anyone *bothers* to invent religion. The Marxist answer is that religion justifies the position of those who control the means of production, but why should that be necessary? Either the productive forces are irresistible, in which case there is no need to justify them: or else they need to be justified, in which case they are not irresistible."[21] Still more important is the actual softness that hides behind the seeming toughness of rational choice theories, which see individuals as calculating interest. The absurdity becomes utterly apparent when we think of trying to "calculate" whether to marry someone. We need a *coup de foudre* for this sort of passage in life for the simple reason that our

---

[19] The fullest and most sophisticated statement of the importance of rational choice theory for sociology is now James Coleman, *Foundations of Social Theory* (Cambridge: Harvard University Press, 1990). Jon Elster's principal statement on rational choice Marxism is *Making Sense of Marx* (Cambridge: Cambridge University Press, 1985).

[20] Jon Elster, *The Cement of Society* (Cambridge: Cambridge University Press, 1989). A similar story of a rapprochement with Parsonian concerns can be told about Dahrendorf, whose approbation of conflict turned out, on closer inspection, to depend upon shared background assumptions about not letting things get out of hand! For a discussion of Dahrendorf's social philosophy as a whole, see John A. Hall, *Diagnoses of Our Time* (London: Heinemann, 1981), chap. 5.

[21] Patricia Crone, *Pre-industrial Societies* (Oxford: Basil Blackwell, 1989), p. 138.

identities are involved: calculation presumes a solidary and singular self, a bundle of sensations, and it is accordingly all but useless when a decision involves what we are or may become. Rational calculation is not much of a guide when we confront massive life events; safe passage through those events depends heavily upon the performance of various rituals.[22] This is attested to by those who have experienced trauma, as most of us do when someone close to us dies. Equally, it is a solid literary theme in Dostoevsky, Goncharov, and Sartre, all of whose characters, like Hamlet, are "unmanned" by too much thought—the point being that habitually most people manage to function because they possess the sure framework of a system of values.[23] For another thing, toughness can mask tautology. Macaulay's attack on James Mill retains its canonical status in this matter. Noting that "interest" could not predict behavior, Macaulay rightly insisted that to invoke it after the event tells us nothing.[24] Exactly this point was made by Raymond Aron against what he considered to be false realists who posited a single conception of national interest:

> . . . whatever the diplomacy of a state may be, nothing prevents one saying after the fact that it was dictated by considerations of 'national interest', as long as 'national interest' has not been strictly defined.
>
> Indeed, the so-called theory of 'national interest' either suggests something as undeniable as it is vague—that each actor thinks first of itself— or else tries to oppose itself to other pseudo-theories, for example that the foreign policy of states is dictated by political ideology or moral principles. Each of these pseudo-theories means something only in connection with the other. To say that the Soviet Union conducts its foreign affairs on the basis of its 'national interest' means that it is not guided exclusively by its ambition to spread Communism. Such a proposition is undeniable, but to conclude from it that the rulers of a non-Communist Russia would

[22] Ernest Gellner, "The Gaffe-Avoiding Animal, or, A Bundle of Hypotheses," in his *Relativism and the Social Sciences* (Cambridge: Cambridge University Press, 1985).

[23] This comment sets me apart from Weber's second thesis, namely, that the modern world would inevitably become "disenchanted." According to this theory, modernity suffers from opportunity costs such that an increase in affluence is achieved only at the price of a diminution of moral certainty. Under the legal rational authority of modernity, it seemed that human motivation would move from being *wertrational* to becoming *zweckrational;* that is, modernity would so undermine human values that we would be left stranded, mere calculators without purpose—such *Fachmenschen* being, in his eyes, decidedly inferior to the early Puritans, whose obsessive inner motivations had created a new world. Differently put, Weber believed that the problems faced by Hamlet and by Dostoevsky's characters would become generalized in a world in which "God is dead." Weber's theory does help us to understand the behavior of intellectuals, far more prone both to suffer and to seek to escape feelings of disenchantment than their fellow citizens, but its great intellectualism is probably of less use in understanding the inconsistencies and continuities in the lives of other social actors.

[24] The debate can now best be followed in Jack Lively and John Rees, eds., *Utilitarian Logic and Politics* (Oxford: Clarendon, 1978).

have had the same diplomatic policy . . . is simply absurd. The purpose of the empirical study of international relations consists precisely in determining the historical perceptions that control the behaviour of collective actors and the decisions of the rulers of these actors.[25]

This sophisticated viewpoint lay behind Aron's very striking attack in the late 1960s on the mechanical nature of American theory as it was applied to Vietnam—a theory that failed to realize that the "stake" involved was not the same on both sides.[26]

It is extremely important to stress that weaknesses in one position do not mean that victory goes to the other side by default. For there is quite as much to object to in the equally one-sided view that culture is everything and circumstance nothing. In particular, the slide between saying that humans have values (absolutely true) and the insistence that societies are held together/constrained by a set of values (very largely false) is illegitimate. A rather large amount of empirical evidence is now available to show that lower classes rarely share the values of official culture.[27] Needless to say, such evidence should not be taken to mean that "real" and "material" interests are the sole concern of such social actors. What is at issue instead is the nature of ideology.

For no-holds-barred idealism to make sense, for us to agree that we are, as Winch suggests, conceptually constrained, ideologies are required to be clear, coherent, and capable of directing social life, as in Orwell's dystopia. Later I will admit that *some* ideologies do have this character. But *most* ideologies simply are not like that: they are rag bags, replete with many options usable by different groups at will. Thus the villagers of thirteenth-century Montaillou felt themselves to be opposed to the church hierarchy—but in the name of the "true" Christianity symbolized by the poverty of Christ.[28] More generally, Christianity was sufficiently flexible to accommodate itself to empire, to its absence, and to a system of states, and it equally managed to endorse slavery and then to oppose it. It remains vital, in other words, to examine not just belief but the circumstances that make it seem plausible to particular actors at particular historical junctures. In other words, the social sciences cannot do without a firm sense of social struc-

[25] Raymond Aron, "What Is a Theory of International Relations," *Journal of International Affairs* 21 (1967): 192.

[26] Raymond Aron, "Remarques sur l'évolution de la pensée stratégique (1945–1968)," *European Journal of Sociology* 9 (1969). Aron commented further on this point in *Penser la guerre: Clausewitz*, vol. 2, *L'Age planetaire* (Paris: Gallimard, 1976), pp. 199–210.

[27] Michael Mann, "The Social Cohesion of Liberal Democracy," *American Sociological Review* 35 (1970); Nicholas Abercrombie, Stephen Hill, and Bryan Turner, *The Dominant Ideology Thesis* (London: George Allen & Unwin, 1980); Ernest Gellner, *Nations and Nationalism* (Oxford: Basil Blackwell, 1983), chap. 2.

[28] Emmanuel Le Roy Ladurie, *Montaillou* (London: Scolar, 1980).

ture—something largely absent from most of the approaches examined earlier.

As the debate over the nature of rationality has gone on for some time, it is possible to point to some high-level epistemological conclusions that have been reached. Poststructuralists are of course perfectly correct to insist that Western cognitive practices are but one way of approaching the world—that is, such practices are ethics of cognition not firmly grounded in the nature of things.[29] For practical purposes, however, the endless stream of material benefits brought by this style of thought makes it extremely unlikely that its lack of ultimate grounding will lead it to be widely questioned. Moreover, the fact that the adoption of modern cognitive norms has so spectacularly increased human power allows us to hope that there may be a relation between increasing technological power and the attainment of permanent truth.[30]

A further consideration of great import for social science is related to this observation. Social scientists do and can have a decided measure of trust in the cognitive achievements of Western science. If Winch is entirely correct to urge that all human beings try to make sense of their world, it is the merest conceit to suggest that in cognitive matters magic is equivalent to science; if all humans are equal in trying to make sense of their world, the historical emergence of science clearly made the members of one society, thanks to their possession of powerful cognitive rules, privileged and thereby more equal than others. Social science ought to take the beliefs of the people it studies seriously, but it cannot accept everything that those beliefs assert. At the least, it is necessary to bracket the view of Muslim believers, say, that Islam spread because it was true in order to examine the social conditions that created it and to which it responded. At most, social scientists cannot do their job without actually disbelieving what they are told, albeit this is *not* to doubt that the beliefs are real to the people involved: we understand how magical belief systems work in a self-maintaining, nondisprovable, and circular way, for example, *because* we hold constant to universal/Western views of consistency.

Occupying the Middle Ground

What has been said to this point—that human beings have values, but that equally they are purposive calculators—suggests that we must

[29] Ernest Gellner, "An Ethic of Cognition," in *Spectacles and Predicaments* (Cambridge: Cambridge University Press, 1979).

[30] John A. Hall, *Liberalism* (London: Paladin, 1987), pt. 3.

stand somewhere between the false extremes identified. It is well worth while exploring further why we must occupy the middle ground. We can do no better than to begin with genetics.

The most striking single fact about human history is the extraordinary diversity of social forms produced by beings possessed of either the same or very nearly the same genetic inheritance. Differently put, whereas most species have a form of social organization encoded in their genes, the human animal seems to be programmed instead to pay attention to culture. Diversity is possible because humans learn through cultural means. "Living in accordance with nature is an attractive idea," Crone observes, "but in the human case it actually means living with culture."[31]

Sociology has pointed to two central roles that culture fulfills for social life. First, culture provides meaning, for most of human history, by means of organized religion. If Marx can loosely be seen as insisting that food production is basic to human life, Max Weber insisted quite as strongly that the central problem faced by human societies was that of theodicy; that is, the necessity of offering an explanation for birth, suffering, and death. This formulation is unhappy insofar as it suggests that there is a natural fit between human need and social meaning. Rather organized social life—in which individuals have to participate if they wish to achieve their ends—depends upon repressing or prohibiting many of our genetically encoded drives, notably, as Freud correctly noted, those concerned with sexuality. Human society is thoroughly unnatural, and it is its unnaturalness that makes ritual so important a means for the management of key passages in personal and social life.

Second, culture provides rules of social action without which it would be impossible, despite Homans's cheery optimism, for human beings within a society to understand each other at all. It is extremely important to note that the world religions, very much in contrast to their supposed otherworldliness, are, naturally and inevitably, in large part compendia of rules for managing daily life. Even a quick glance at Max Weber's studies of world religions shows that he worked in this spirit, trying quite as much to explain the creation, content, spread, and maintenance of belief systems as to analyze the ways in which they then influence the social order of which they are a part. Weber interestingly explains the insignificance of the impact of Buddhism in terms of its pure otherworldliness; that is, its failure to provide, for example, a marriage service until the twentieth century. What matters

---

[31] Crone, *Pre-industrial Societies*, p. 81.

for him—as it does for Ann Swidler more recently—is the ability of a belief system to handle practical problems.[32]

This is a good moment to emphasize that Weber's approach is scarcely that of a simple-minded idealist. We can highlight this point by spelling out what the Protestant ethic thesis really implies about the role of ideas in social life. Weber's account of the rise of "bourgeois rational capitalism in the West" is distinctively *not* idealist; it did *not*, as Parsons suggested, assert that all the world civilizations were capable of capitalist development, and that it was the presence of a distinctive ideology that made all the difference. In fact, Weber argued that the world civilizations differed from one another in many, many ways: the West was as unique in its form of politics, its legal system, its kinship system, and its cosmopolitan historical inheritance as it was in its beliefs. These uniquenesses are a nice blending of more "ideal" and more "material" or institutional matters, and that blend certainly justifies the claim, made in the last paragraph of *The Protestant Ethic and the Spirit of Capitalism*, that a naive materialism was not being replaced by an equally simple idealism. Equally, Weber's account follows his own methodological injunction to comply with both "causal adequacy" (the differential growth rates of Catholic and Protestant countries) and "adequacy at the level of meaning" (the establishment of a motivational connection without which genuine causation could not be assumed). There is nothing here that a sophisticated Marxist could not accept. Indeed, Anthony Giddens has helpfully pointed out that Weber was reacting to the crude materialism of German Marxists of the late nineteenth century rather than to Marx himself—whose position, for all the gleeful polemics unmasking hypocrisy, is by no means naively materialist. Giddens rightly insists that the accounts of the rise of capitalism offered by Marx and Weber are not analytically opposed at all, albeit each has strengths that the other lacks.[33]

A full appreciation of Weber's work at this point needs to go a little further. Ideas are not held to be determinant in some free-floating way. On the contrary, Weber insists that an "elective affinity" is at work between idea and circumstance. This technical term of eighteenth-century chemistry became more widely known when Goethe used it as the title of a novel in 1809. In the fourth chapter of that novel a discussion, nuanced and disputed, is held as to the precise nature of affinity. One argument made there is worth noting:

[32] Max Weber, *The Religion of India* (New York: Free Press, 1958), pt. 3; Ann Swidler, "Culture in Action: Symbols and Strategies," *American Sociological Review* 51 (1986).

[33] Anthony Giddens, "Marx, Weber, and the Development of Capitalism," *Sociology* 4 (1970).

Those natures which, when they meet, quickly lay hold on and mutually affect one another we call affined. This affinity is sufficiently striking in the case of alkalis and acids which, although they are mutually antithetical, and perhaps precisely because they are so, must decidely seek and embrace one another, modify one another, and together form a new substance.[34]

I suspect that it is precisely this notion of modification that was at the back of Weber's mind. Thus the disciplined ideas and practices of the Puritans, at once ascetic and this-worldly, made sense of and accordingly modified the lives of the inhabitants of uniquely autonomous European cities. More generally, the famous essay "The Social Psychology of the World Religions," written to serve as the coda for the collected works on the sociology of religion, argued that distinctive social groups would be attracted to different religious styles—peasants to magic, city dwellers to religions of the book, and warriors to fatalism.[35] Ideas and circumstances are held to interrelate and interpenetrate in ways both deep and subtle.

A conclusion is forced upon us by this discussion. Any attempt to suggest that history results from a single factor, always possessed—at least "in the last instance"!—of "ultimate primacy," is bound to be simplistic, Crone points out:

> . . . human societies have acquired a complexity that makes them far more difficult to explain than those of other animals (which are difficult enough as it is). But it nonetheless remains obvious that they represent a compromise between a variety of fundamental needs, both natural *and* cultural ones, in interaction with a natural *and* cultural environment. The addition of culture has not resulted in a *simplification* of evolutionary patterns whereby one factor has acquired overriding importance and the rest been reduced to frills; on the contrary, it has greatly complicated matters, making the achievement and maintenance of the compromise a highly intricate affair. . . .[36]

In this spirit, sophisticated rational choice theory can say that it simply wishes to consider the way actors maximize their preferences—given, that is, that their preferences are value-laden; equally, Giddens can talk about the need for a "double hermeneutic," designed precisely to theorize human action within cultural frames.[37] More immediately,

[34] Johann Wolfgang von Goethe, *Elective Affinities*, trans. R. J. Hollingdale (London, 1971), pp. 52–53.

[35] Max Weber, "The Social Psychology of the World Religions," in *From Max Weber*, ed. H. H. Gerth and C. Wright Mills (Oxford: Oxford University Press, 1946).

[36] Crone, *Pre-industrial Societies*, pp. 140–41.

[37] Anthony Giddens, *The Constitution of Society* (Oxford: Polity, 1986).

Chapter 1 of this volume clearly grants that "interest" is culturally constructed, that no action takes place without benefit of meaning.

If the recognition of the reality of culture is a marked and necessary achievement, transcending a pernicious and misleading antithesis, this is not to deny that occupying the middle ground can be uncomfortable. The inevitable interpenetration of belief and circumstance—the fact that they often do not have, to use David Hume's expression, "distinct existences"—raises the specter of the impossibility of cognitively powerful social science. Must we abandon the attempt, so integral to the most striking social science theory, to specify the interactions of polity, ideology, and economy? If everything is mixed up with everything else in some sort of dreadful mishmash, how then can causal analysis be undertaken? Do not despair. These difficulties can be surmounted.

It is possible to locate the sway of ideas even when one occupies the middle ground. The most immediate way is to recognize the lags that occur between institutional and ideational change. As long as the fit between idea and circumstance remains tight, as seems to be the case with the examples provided by Peter Katzenstein in Chapter 10, it is impossible to specify an independent ideational impact. But those occasions when circumstance changes and response remains culturally bound do allow us to study ideas as an independent variable. Judith Goldstein has strikingly demonstrated the importance of, in effect, those temporary lags when institutionalized ideas are so sticky that they fail to keep up with changes in structural matters.[38]

Great care needs to be taken with this sort of research. Insofar as it is based on the acknowledgment that social actors have both ideal and material interests, it has much to recommend it. But insofar as it suggests that this lag is a distortion of something more basic, it strays unhelpfully close to the false antithesis between idealism and materialism. Let us accordingly insist not just that social actors have ideal and material interests, but that there is no one-way direction between them such that people really concentrate on earthy economic activities most of the time: to the contrary, at times people offer lip service to seeming practicality while in fact pursuing more exalted aims. Jules Ferry spoke the language of his age, Raymond Aron once noted, when he suggested that colonies would pay; but that was a front behind which lay both the desire for glory and the perception of pressures of state competi-

[38] Particularly striking is Judith Goldstein, "The Impact of Ideas on Trade Policy: The Origins of U.S. Agricultural and Manufacturing Policy," *International Organisation* 43 (1989).

tion.[39] In other words, neither ideal nor material interest is "basic" or "true": the identity of workers in Northern Ireland is stratified by religion, and it is time that the economistically inclined ceased to be surprised by this fact. Not everyone is, below the surface, just like us: and insofar as a distinction can be drawn between ideal and material interests, it is *their* definition of *their* material interests that is analytically important.

There is another point at which an independent ideational impact can sometimes be detected. If a Marxist would be able to accept Weber's account of the rise of capitalism, it remains the case that Marxism imagines, effectively, in the spirit of B. F. Skinner, that there is a virtual correspondence between circumstance and idea such that the stimulus of circumstance will *automatically* bring forth an ideological response. There is no reason why we should accept this idea. In this context we should remember that Weber, for all his awareness of "elective affinities," nonetheless felt that Protestantism had genuine cultural significance. Bluntly, Protestants invented a new world of rationality for irrational reasons. These people were driven for religious reasons, by a concept of calling, and not in any way by an appreciation of the material benefit that their conduct would bring; they did not know what the new world would be, nor did they intend to create it. It is perhaps worth noting in this context that the purpose of writing the two articles that make up *The Protestant Ethic and the Spirit of Capitalism* was to encourage—by recalling prior historical achievements—the middle class of Wilhelmine Germany, against whose supine ways Weber had polemicized powerfully and at length, to become a genuine historical actor, to seize control of Germany and influence the destiny of the modern world.[40]

The character of this type of ideational impact deserves emphasis. A class or group must believe in its moral destiny if it is to be capable of great collective acts. Powerful ideological codification can—as was the case, in Weber's view, with the Protestant ethic—affect the historical record by enhancing morale. Equally, a failure of ideological imagination can lead to political ineffectiveness. By and large, the working class has lacked precisely this sort of force.[41] If there is some general

[39] Raymond Aron, *Imperialism and Colonialism* (Leeds: Leeds University Press, 1959). Cf. Aron, *Peace and War*, trans. Richard Howard and Annette Baker Fox (Garden City, N.Y.: Doubleday, 1966).

[40] Wolfgang Mommsen, *Max Weber and German Politics, 1890–1920* (Chicago: University of Chicago Press, 1984).

[41] Michael Mann, *Consciousness and Action in the Western Working Class* (London: Macmillan, 1973). In this paragraph I am also drawing on Michael Mann's Foreword to Gianfranco Poggi's excellent *Calvinism and the Capitalist Spirit* (London: Macmillan, 1983), esp. p. 8.

acceptance of that point, it is less well known that a similar lack of force has sometimes affected members of the elite. The lack of confidence felt by the French *noblesse de robe* in the late seventeenth and early eighteenth centuries was much exacerbated, the Marxist writer Lucien Goldmann famously demonstrated, by the tortuous and tragic mental world created by Pascal and Racine, their ideological representatives.[42] In both cases, the absence of a heroic conception of group identity had social consequences.

THE SOCIAL CONSTRUCTION OF REALITIES

If ideas lag in lending force to reality or fail to do so at all, they have also, at their strongest, actually constructed the pattern of social relations. Differently put, we can now turn away from ideas embedded in reality to the analysis of ideas of an altogether more autonomous character. We can gain understanding of such ideas best if throughout we keep in mind the famous metaphor, drawn from the era of railway expansion of his time, by means of which Weber sought to capture the most fundamental way in which ideas can affect social reality: "Not ideas, but material and ideal interests, directly govern men's conduct. Yet very frequently the 'world images' that have been created by ideas have, like switchmen [at railway junctions], determined the tracks along which action has been pushed by the dynamic of interest."[43]

Any complete and uncritical acceptance of this metaphor is likely to restrict vision, making it difficult to recognize the most fundamental way in which ideas affect the historical record. The essential problem is that the metaphor takes for granted that the railway lines or tracks have already been laid; that is, that a social order is already in place. But the moments of most autonomous ideological power have been those in which intellectuals have served—to make use of Michael Mann's fundamental amendment of Weber—as "tracklayers"; that is, as the creators of society.[44] This point can best be fully elucidated by consideration of Durkheim's work within the context of a particular example.

If we accept Durkheim's view that the presence of norms defines a society, then the society of northwestern Europe between, say, 800 and 1100 was Latin Christendom. Now to say this is in fact to improve and

---

[42] Lucien Goldmann, *The Hidden God* (London: Routledge, 1956).

[43] Weber, "Social Psychology of the World Religions," p. 280.

[44] Michael Mann, *Sources of Social Power*, vol. 1, *A History of Power from the Beginning to 1760 A.D.* (Cambridge: Cambridge University Press, 1986), p. 28 and chaps. 10 and 11.

to revise Durkheim. Quite as much as crude Marxism, Durkheim viewed belief as a reflection of other social processes. But in the early Middle Ages, Christianity was not the reflection of society. It *was* society. For it was the church that issued rules about external warfare and, to a lesser extent, about matters of internal peace. Christian intellectuals were primary tracklayers, whereas their Chinese colleagues were filling in details of the space previously mapped out by military conquest. And if we inquire into the genesis of this ideological power, we are forced into the proper appreciation of the central contribution that Durkheim makes to the understanding of ideology. Christian society was initially created in the Roman Empire by the sending of messages, the epistles, between communities of city dwellers—artisans, women, freed slaves—who could have no part in official culture but yet stood above the minimal world of the peasantry. We can best understand the birth of this world religion if we bear in mind Durkheim's view that "religion is society worshipping itself": Christianity made people otherwise marginalized into a community. This insight needs to be taken very seriously. Religion, or ideology more generally, tends to be seen in highly intellectualist terms. To concentrate exclusively on ideas in this sense is, however, a mistake. *Community matters quite as much as doctrine to most believers.*

The claim being made is unfamiliar, and accordingly needs amplification. Most obviously, attention is being devoted to intellectuals as specialized actors within society. One way in which the behavior of intellectuals has been conceptualized is in terms of their own self-interest—though it can scarcely be offensive by this point to insist that "self-interest" be read as including both material and ideational components. There is much to be said for this approach to intellectuals. It is worth noting, for example, that the emergence of the European state system is itself best explained by the self-interested actions of the papacy. If one motive of the church in promoting states was to protect its property, a more fundamental one was to retain its independence: the crowning of Charlemagne had been a terrible mistake, likely to subordinate the church in the West as it had been so reduced in the East, which popes thereafter counteracted by conferring the numinous aspects of rule widely—on kings rather than just on the emperor. Balance-of-power politics was more or less invented, in other words, by the papacy.

Nonetheless, this is, in the end, too narrow and restrictive a view of the activities of intellectuals for a full understanding of the historical record. We can understand why by spelling out the essentially political presupposition behind Weber's view of society. His sociology of religion as a whole depends largely upon the interests of intellectuals—whether as bureaucrats or as spiritual experts—in the agrarian era; thus it is very much of a piece with his general view of society as comprising different groups, whether military, ideological, political, or economic in character, each of which is a bearer of a particular vision.[45] This group view of society improves upon the Marxist notion of base and superstructure: whereas Marx places intellectuals in the superstructure, Weber stresses that intellectuals have material interests just as workers and the propertied have their own cultures. Furthermore, the Weberian group view gives us a firm sense of social structure as a struggle for dominance among these various groups. If social science amounts to a power accounting among such groups, then the impact of ideas will be seen on those occasions when intellectuals dominate other social actors. To think in these terms came naturally to Weber. He was intellectually a child of Nietzsche, and accordingly took for granted, as Foucault did much later, that social life was an arena of struggle. Power in this view is essentially a zero-sum affair.

Though I do not deny the earthy realism of the Weberian view of society, I do insist that it would be ridiculous to endorse it in its entirety. Sometimes a cohesive group can indeed subjugate others to its will. But power is not always distributive and zero-sum in character: it can be based on cooperation. The skills of a particular group can allow it to lead society, to render services in such a way that society lends it its power. This is the situation especially of intellectuals, whose characteristic style of life, after all, places limited tools of command at their disposal. Differently put, intellectuals may have their own interests, but they become important social actors on occasion to the extent to which large numbers of people, quite often because they find themselves in conditions of crisis, come to believe their messages to be true. People are not idiots, and it is accordingly unlikely that such credence is lent for long without some sort of basis in fact; that is, unless intellectuals perform genuine social services, above and beyond the feathering of their own nests.

There is no mystery to this type of ideological power: to the contrary, it positively invites causal analysis. Its *form* depends upon growth in organizational infrastructures. Christianity was able to spread because a measure of literacy made it possible to send epistles from one congregation to another; equally the spread of mass literacy from the eighteenth century underlies the spread of nationalism. Its *content* is nothing less than identity. Benedict Anderson has very helpfully characterized nationalism as a process of "imagining communities"—that

---

[45] The best appreciation of Weber in this regard—that is, as a theorist of collective actors—remains Carlo Antoni, *From History to Sociology* (Detroit: Wayne State University Press, 1959).

is, he realizes that the novelty of nationalism is its ability to make us feel that we share a destiny with people whom we have never met.[46] The image of imagining is exactly right—and it applies quite as much to class and civilization as to nation. In Chapter 3 John Ikenberry clearly shows the importance that this sort of imagining can have. The intellectual community he examines did not merely provide ideas that switched British and American interests onto a common track: rather they made previously isolated actors realize that they were in some sense a community, and accordingly that they shared an interest. The social construction of identities, in other words, is necessarily prior to more obvious conceptions of interest: a "we" needs to be established before its interests can be articulated.

The creation of new social identities by intellectuals—that is, their capacity to link people across space so as to form a new community— is necessarily a rare historical phenomenon.[47] But moments of such creation need to be taken very seriously by scholars of international relations. Latin Christendom provided a common culture within which states then competed. If states gained ever greater autonomy, the commonness of European culture remained long after Christianity's extensive powers had been lost. Its survival can be seen particularly clearly on those occasions when transnational ideological currents shake the system of states. The most famous such instance is the creation of nationalism by the French Revolution, a result of which was the Holy Alliance's belief in the preservation of social order as the bedrock of international order. Nationalism was not, of course, so easily contained: while it strengthened some states and occasionally made them more aggressive by turning them into nation-states, it helped to destroy others. Bluntly, no international relations theory that fails to recognize the ability of intellectuals to imagine national communities within Austria-Hungary at the end of the nineteenth century has any chance of understanding the origins of World War I.

To say that Weber's metaphor has the power to restrict vision is not to argue that it is without any truth whatsoever. The Weberian emphasis on the consequences of doctrine needs to be complemented rather than refuted or abandoned. For an element of sense does reside in the notion that ideas can serve as switchmen. As I noted earlier, there are occasions when idealist analysis, in the strongest sense, has something to be said for it. The repertory of options available within an ideology

---

[46] Benedict Anderson, *Imagined Communities* (London: Verso, 1983).

[47] An astute analysis of ideological power in general, stressing that only rarely does it have the capacity to restructure history, is offered by Jack Goldstone, *Revolution and Rebellion in the Early Modern World* (Berkeley: University of California Press, 1991), chap. 5.

once it is encoded may—in my opinion rarely—be so limited that it becomes necessary to speak not of temporary but of permanent lags. This is a question not of transient temporary stickiness before ideas become realigned with interest but rather of a genuine inability to conceive certain possibilities.

Specifying such conceptual constraints is by no means easy. Given the sloppiness to which facile idealist analysis is prone, this sort of explanation should, in my opinion, be entertained only after more structural accounts have been exhausted. But remarkable work has been done in this vein, most notably by the intellectual historian Quentin Skinner.[48] And this viewpoint very probably helps us understand the rise of the West, albeit not in exactly the way Max Weber intended. Without for a moment abandoning the notion of morale outlined above, we can and must doubt some of the details of Weber's historical claims for Protestantism. It is doubtful, despite the force of Weber's work on the morale of Protestants, that other cultures ruled out a rational work ethic. This inference may have some validity with respect to Indian civilization, but it seems not to have applied to the Chinese.[49] Yet Jack Goldstone has felt it useful and necessary to make an argument about the ideological legacy of the Judeo-Christian tradition, stressing its insistently eschatological tone, when he seeks to explain the progressive nature of Occidental revolutions.[50] The development of science may equally depend upon the particular terms of discourse encoded in the Western legacy.[51] The "law of nature" concept rests upon the combination of Greek investigation into nature and a Judaic conception of a hidden, austere, and orderly deity, which reveals neither its designs nor the order of things, but forces humanity to interpret the surface appearance of things as clues to its grand design.[52] The poverty of Muslim science may well be explicable in part by the very different terms in which the deity is conceived: as all-powerful as the deity of the West but differing from it in being prone to interfere

[48] James Tully, ed., *Meaning and Context: Quentin Skinner and His Critics* (Princeton: Princeton University Press, 1988).

[49] Robert M. Hartwell, "Financial Expertise, Examination, and the Formulation of Economic Policy in Northern Sung China," *Journal of Asian Studies* 30 (1970–1971).

[50] Goldstone, *Revolution and Rebellion*, chap. 5.

[51] Ernest Gellner, *Plough, Sword, and Book* (London: Collins, 1988), chaps. 2–5. It is well worth highlighting that Gellner, the hammer of woolly idealism, feels it necessary to allow an element of ideological power in his own analytic history of the world.

[52] The great seventeenth-century scientists, not least Newton, were driven to understand God's purpose—as is apparent in the fact that they produced nearly as much theology as science. On this whole matter, see John Milton, "The Origin and Development of the Concept of 'Law of Nature,'" *European Journal of Sociology* 23 (1981). The argument here is very much in the spirit of what is probably Max Weber's best book, and certainly one of his central works: *Ancient Judaism* (New York: Free Press, 1952).

occasionally in the workings of the world. More generally, what is noticeable about Islam is its intransigence, its difficulty in adapting to new circumstances, given that "the gates of interpretation" are held to have finally closed very soon after the death of Muhammad.[53]

CONCLUSION

In this chapter I have taken my stand between Weber and Durkheim. It has been necessary to do so for the simplest of reasons: a proper understanding of the ways in which ideas affect society depends upon the insights of both thinkers. But the stance is not easy to maintain in view of the very different ethics of the two thinkers. It may be helpful to make a final comment upon the stance I have taken before we turn to a final complexity.

If Weber helps us see intellectuals as one power grouping among others, an appreciation and modification of Durkheim shows that intellectuals can affect society by constructing allegiances and identities. The discovery that intellectuals can construct social identities should not be exaggerated: above all, it should not be so licentiously used that we return to anything like a Parsonian world view. To begin with, it is important to remember that the exercise of this type of ideological power is rare. If all societies possess norms, it is very important to remember that such shared rules are often secondary to or created by other sources of social power. Thus Chinese culture followed behind military power, just as new norms were imposed on Germany and Japan after geopolitical defeat.[54] More important, normative cohesion is, given social complexity, almost certain always to be incomplete. One reason is that many social orders, especially in preindustrial circumstances, do not even attempt to integrate the people into official culture—which is to say that the cohesiveness of culture among the elite is not of paramount importance for the maintenance of, say, preindustrial empires.[55] If it is true, in more modern circumstances, that class struggle takes place within national societies, the fact that it is indeed *struggle* that is involved should encourage skepticism about the strength of shared norms within cohesive communities. The strongest claim that

---

[53] Michael Cook and Patricia Crone, *Hagarism* (Cambridge: Cambridge University Press, 1977), esp. chaps. 11, 12, and 14.

[54] On the nature of integration in China and in preindustrial circumstances generally, see Michael Mann, "States, Ancient and Modern," *European Journal of Sociology* 18 (1977).

[55] For an argument that degree of cohesion between elements of the preindustrial elite is the key variable in understanding comparative social development, see John A. Hall, *Powers and Liberties* (Berkeley: University of California Press, 1986), pt. 1.

can be made for intellectuals is that they can sometimes define the boundaries within which other types of social interaction then take place.

Here we come to a final complexity. Social identities are complex. Groups can have identities that transcend the bounds of a particular territory. This is often the case with respect to intellectuals, but the generalization applies equally to the nobility of the European early Middle Ages and to capitalist actors in the modern world, both capable of functioning across the boundaries of nation-states.[56] Though we are forced to use the term "society," it is best to remember that our identities are both multiple and overlapping. I, for instance, as a British subject, am ruled in part by the European Community; as a member of international academic and capitalist society, I am also dependent upon NATO—and thereby upon the United States, whose sway in that organization (and, I believe, in capitalist society) remains paramount.[57] Social reality is complex, and so must be our social science.

International relations theory, especially at points where it has problematized realism, has done a great deal to advance general social science theory at this point.[58] But the insights of recent "interdependency" theorists—above all, that as interactions flow through and beyond nation-states, so do norms—need now to be generalized. What they think of as a modern development has been true for most of history: upper-class solidarity has often been spread across the state system, as realism probably requires anyway, just as capitalism has. As important, *nationalist* foreign policy, when it has been in evidence, should encourage investigation: such policy cannot be taken for granted because it is not natural. All in all, foreign policy analysis needs to take the process of identity formation very seriously indeed. Sometimes identities have been formed by those dreamings of intellectuals which international relations, in the world as much as in the academy, ignores at its peril.

[56] Cf. Albert Hirschman, *Exit, Voice, and Loyalty* (Cambridge: Harvard University Press, 1970). Our knowledge of the extent to which the identity of, say, the top management of IBM is determined by participation in capitalist society rather than in the society of the United States is woefully inadequate.

[57] Mann, *Sources of Social Power*, 1: chap. 1.

[58] Robert Keohane and Joseph Nye, *Power and Interdependence* (Boston: Little, Brown, 1977), pp. 23–27.

PART II

REDUCING UNCERTAINTY: IDEAS AS ROAD MAPS

CHAPTER THREE

Creating Yesterday's New World Order: Keynesian "New Thinking" and the Anglo-American Postwar Settlement

G. JOHN IKENBERRY

The construction of an open world economic order in the aftermath of World War II remains one of the remarkable accomplishments of the twentieth century. Agreements reached by the United States and Britain during the war and ratified at Bretton Woods in 1944 marked a decisive move toward openness—a bit astonishing given the ravages and dislocations of war and competing postwar interests. But an open system was built, and one different from anything the capitalist world had seen before. The Anglo-American agreements established rules for a relatively open and multilateral system of trade and payments, but did so in a way that would reconcile openness with the commitments of national governments to full employment and economic stabilization. Despite rapidly shifting global power capabilities, rising national economic vulnerabilities, and divergent and competing agendas within and between Britain and the United States, an innovative postwar agreement was engineered. Not surprisingly, the leading scholar of

This chapter draws on material published in two articles: "A World Economy Restored: Expert Consensus and the Anglo-American Post-War Settlement," *International Organization* 46 (Winter 1991/92); and "The Political Origins of Bretton Woods," in *The Rise and Decline of the Bretton Woods System*, ed. Michael Bordo and Barry Eichengreen (Chicago: University of Chicago Press, 1992). Research support was provided by the Peter B. Lewis Fund at the Center of International Studies, Princeton University. Geoffrey Herrera provided valuable research assistance.

57

Anglo-American economic diplomacy characterized the postwar settlement as a "political miracle."[1]

Miracles aside, how does one explain the Anglo-American postwar settlement? Can a simple interest-based argument explain the settlement, or do we need to probe more deeply into the manner in which interests were defined, coalitions were forged, and power was legitimated in the aftermath of world war? I argue that we must probe more deeply. An adequate explanation must grapple with the problem of how interests came to be defined by governments on both sides of the Atlantic at a critical historical juncture, which in turn requires an understanding of the way in which evolving policy ideas influenced governments' conceptions of their interests.

The underlying economic interests and power position of the United States and Britain set the broad limits on the shape of postwar economic order. But these factors cannot explain why the settlement took the shape it did, nor can they fully explain how a transatlantic agreement was ultimately cobbled together. A set of policy ideas inspired by Keynesianism and embraced by a group of well-placed government specialists and economists was crucial in defining government conceptions of postwar interests, building coalitions in support of the postwar settlement, and legitimating the exercise of American power, particularly as these British and American experts engineered a shift from the contentious trade issues to monetary issues, an area where an emerging "middle ground" had been created by Keynesian ideas. These experts and their "new thinking" were important in overcoming political stalemate both within and between the two governments. In effect, this group of British and American experts intervened at a particularly fluid moment in history to help the British and American political establishments identify their interests, thereby creating the bases of postwar economic cooperation.

This argument involves several claims. First, as deliberations on postwar order began during the war, divergent views within and between the British and American political establishments posed obstacles to agreement. The most important differences in perspective were between American officials at the State Department, who wanted to reconstruct an open trading system, and British officials in the wartime cabinet, who wanted to ensure full employment and economic stability, and who, as a consequence, contemplated the continuation of the imperial preference system and bilateral trading. One vision was of a non-

---

[1] Richard N. Gardner, "Sterling-Dollar Diplomacy in Current Perspective," *International Affairs* 62 (Winter 1985/86): 21.

discriminatory, multilateral trading system; the other, although not fully articulated, was of preferential economic groupings.

Second, a community of policy specialists and economists assembled within and outside the British and American governments during the war articulated a set of ideas about monetary order and the organization of the postwar world economy that cut through these differences and moved their governments toward agreement. These experts identified and gave content to a set of interests that were later embraced by wartime British and American leaders. In effect, the "new thinking" of these experts transformed the way people thought of or framed the issue of postwar economic order and, as a consequence, changed the outcome.

Third, the ideas articulated by these experts were important as they defined a middle ground between old political divisions, opening up new possibilities for coalition building. What ultimately mattered in the ratification of the Bretton Woods agreement was not that it was based on policy ideas advanced by an expert community but that the policy ideas resonated with the larger political environment. The ideas on monetary order advanced by British and American experts had political virtues: they defined a middle ground between the old and contentious alternatives between laissez-faire and interventionism. These ideas ultimately carried the day because they created the conditions for larger political coalitions within and between governments—coalitions that themselves reflected a more general postwar reworking of sociopolitical order in Western capitalist democracies.

In sum, I argue that a transatlantic group of economists and policy specialists, united by a common set of policy ideas and a shared view that past economic failures could be avoided by innovative postwar economic arrangements, led their respective governments toward agreement by identifying a set of common Anglo-American interests that were not clearly seen by others. The episode reveals that particular historical moments can provide expert groups wielding new policy approaches and philosophies with opportunities to decisively shape a government's conception of the national interest.

At critical turning points, such as the end of a major war, structures of power and interests matter—just as they always do. But at these turning points, uncertainties about power structures and unhappiness with past or current definitions of interests provide openings for rethinking. The uncertainty of war and its aftermath provided opportunities for policy specialists to shape the resolution of debates, particularly those that involved complex issues of monetary policy. At such moments, moreover, elites are interested in building institutions that have a measure of legitimacy, and that concern reinforces the value of authoritative policy ideas. For all these reasons, it is necessary to search for the connections between policy ideas, their carriers, and underlying forces of power and interests.

EXPLAINING THE ANGLO-AMERICAN SETTLEMENT

The Anglo-American agreement on a postwar economic order did not simply reestablish economic openness, it created a new type of open system. The agreement embodied a unique blend of laissez-faire and interventionism, allowing for the operation of a relatively open system of trade and payments while also providing arrangements to support domestic full employment and social welfare. This evolving synthesis of liberal economic and social welfare goals, captured in John Ruggie's notion of "embedded liberalism," was built on a historic political compromise: "unlike the economic nationalism of the thirties, the international economic order would be multilateral in character; but unlike the liberalism of the gold standard and free trade, its multilateralism would be predicated upon domestic interventionism."[2] After years of economic turmoil and war, an open and novel international economic order was established.

The most straightforward explanation for the success of the Anglo-American agreement appeals to the underlying distribution of power capabilities.[3] According to this view, the postwar economic order reflected the efforts of the United States, as an ascending hegemonic power, to build a system congenial with its interests. The most fundamental dynamic at work in the economic diplomacy of the 1940s, therefore, really involved attempts by the United States to break down the barriers to global economic openness, making compromises where necessary.

To be sure, the hegemonic position of the United States did set the basic terms of negotiations. European governments, including Great

---

[2] John G. Ruggie, "Embedded Liberalism Revisited: Institutions and Progress in International Economic Relations," in *Progress in Postwar International Relations*, ed. Emanuel Adler and Beverly Crawford (New York: Columbia University Press, 1991), p. 203. See also John G. Ruggie, "International Regimes, Transactions, and Change: Embedded Liberalism in the Postwar Economic Order," in *International Regimes*, ed. Stephen D. Krasner (Ithaca: Cornell University Press, 1983).

[3] Robert Gilpin provides perhaps the most powerful and simple theory for explaining the organization and reworking of international order. A prevailing international order is a reflection of the underlying distribution of material capabilities of states within the system. Over time that distribution of power shifts, leading to ruptures in the system, hegemonic war, and the eventual reorganization of international order that reflects the new underlying power capabilities: Gilpin, *War and Change in World Politics* (New York: Cambridge University Press, 1981).

Britain, as we shall see, had very mixed views about postwar order. American efforts to overcome European obstacles and induce acceptance of a liberal order required a series of compromises and delays in the implementation of agreements, largely because of the economic and political vulnerabilities of a war-ravaged Britain and continental Europe.[4] Nonetheless, the United States used its resources to influence the direction of policy change. Hegemonic power, however, has limitations as an explanation for the emergence of liberal multilateralism after the war.[5] Coercive efforts, such as the British loan, were less successful than they were often thought to be. Moreover, as we shall see, the substantive content of the system was shaped by Great Britain as well as by the United States and in ways that would be unanticipated by simple considerations of power.

Explanations might also trace Anglo-American agreement to convergent shifts in underlying national economic interests. Interests of this sort in both the United States and Britain pointed in the direction of a relatively open system, particularly if protections and safeguards could be provided. What is missing in this explanation, however, is an account of how these structural conditions manifested themselves. To argue that a particular outcome is economically functional or in the interest of a group or nation is not to explain that outcome. This is particularly important because in both Britain and the United States there were, as economic planning and negotiations got under way during the war, major obstacles to agreement on even the most general outlines for postwar economic order.

These interest-based explanations of postwar economic order are not so much wrong as incomplete. They are inadequate in two respects. First, a range of postwar "orders" was compatible with America's broad interest in an open world economy.[6] A variety of designs for postwar

---

[4] On the bargain struck between the United States and Europe after World War II over multilateralism and regional integration, see Benjamin J. Cohen, "The Revolution in Atlantic Economic Relations: The Bargain Comes Unstuck," in *The United States and Western Europe: Political, Economic, and Strategic Perspectives,* ed. Wolfram Hanreider (Cambridge, Mass.: Winthrop, 1974).

[5] For a critique of power-based explanations of bargaining outcomes, including the Bretton Woods settlement, see John S. Odell, "From London to Bretton Woods: Sources of Change in Bargaining Strategies and Outcomes," *Journal of Public Policy* 8 (1989): 294–95. Others have made more general critiques of the limits of American hegemonic power after World War II. Much of this work is summarized in Joseph S. Nye, Jr., *Bound to Lead: The Changing Nature of American Power* (New York: Basic Books, 1990), esp. pp. 87–95. See also G. John Ikenberry, "Rethinking the Origins of American Hegemony," *Political Science Quarterly* 104 (Fall 1989): 375–400.

[6] This point is made forcefully by John Ruggie. See "Multilateralism: The Anatomy of an Institution," in *Multilateralism: Theory and Practice of an Institutional Form,* ed. Ruggie (New York: Columbia University Press, 1993).

order were advanced by officials within the American government and elsewhere, all claiming to advance American interests. Why did the system take on the features it did, rather than some other features? To ask this question is really to ask why interests were defined the way they were by officials at the highest levels of government. More specifically, why did an American government with a State Department that championed laissez-faire and free trade end up backing a system more concerned with safeguarding the emerging welfare state?

Second, how did a transatlantic coalition in support of the Anglo-American settlement get cobbled together? The alternative to the post-war settlement might not have been just another set of trade and mone-tary arrangements; it might have been stalemate and disorder—this, after all, was the experience of the last attempt at a postwar settlement after World War I. Agreement at Bretton Woods might have failed or gone the way of the Treaty of Versailles, a well-intentioned interna-tional agreement that fell prey to diverging national interests. How was agreement achieved amid the divergent and conflicting national and bureaucratic positions?

These questions lead us to probe the manner in which interests were defined and coalitions were forged during the Anglo-American negoti-ations.[7] It is in this regard that the policy ideas about monetary order were crucial in moving negotiations from stalemate to agreement.[8] A group of British and American monetary specialists, embracing dis-tinctive policy ideas, proved important in altering the debate about postwar economic order: they crystallized areas of common interest

[7] Empirical debates of this sort require close attention to the sequence of events (i.e., "process tracing"), the use of counterfactuals, and, when possible, comparisons with similar historical episodes (in this case, the settlement after World War I).

[8] This argument builds on a body of literature that links international cooperation to the activities of policy experts and evolving economic ideas. One strand of this literature argues that the convergence of conceptual frameworks among economics experts is a necessary precondition for successful cooperation. See Richard Cooper, "International Cooperation in Public Health as a Prologue to Macroeconomic Cooperation," in *Can Nations Agree? Issues in International Economic Cooperation*, ed. Richard Cooper et al. (Wash-ington, D.C.: Brookings, 1989); and Barry Eichengreen and Marc Uzan, "The 1933 World Economic Conference as an Instance of Failed International Cooperation," Work-ing Paper no. 90-149, University of California, Berkeley, Department of Economics. Another strand of the literature makes similar arguments, but focuses on the role of transnational policy communities (or "epistemic communities") in fostering cooperation. The argument here is that under conditions of uncertainty, when government leaders do not know what positions to take on economic, scientific, and other technical policy areas, transnational communities of experts can intervene to shape policy decisively and lead governments toward interstate agreement. See Peter Haas, "Knowledge, Power, and International Policy Coordination," special issue of *International Organization* 46 (Winter 1992). A final strand of this literature explores the more general relationship between evolving bodies of knowledge and beliefs and political outcomes. This volume is part of this larger enterprise.

between the two governments, and they elaborated a set of politically resonant ideas that served to build larger coalitions within and between governments.

UNDERLYING STRUCTURES OF INTERESTS

Before we examine the competing British and American views on postwar economic order and the initial deadlock in negotiations that they produced, it is important to establish a point made earlier: the underlying structures of interests set the broad parameters around which an agreement could be built, but they were not imperatives that inevitably produced the agreement. At a very deep level incentives for agreement existed, but serious blockages stood in the way.

The United States did have a basic and increasingly robust interest in an open system, and American political elites recognized this fact. In the 1930s, with the apparent collapse of the international economy and the emergence of German and Japanese regional economic blocs, American statesmen and intellectuals debated the plausibility of regional alternatives to an open world economy. This issue grew in importance in the early 1940s, as political elites debated whether the United States should get involved in the war. The academic culmination of this debate came with the work of Nicholas Spykman, who articulated what became the conventional wisdom, that a hemispheric bloc would not be sufficient to protect American economic and geopolitical interests.[9] Military planners in the War and Navy departments during the war also began to conceive of postwar American strategic interests in global terms.[10] In 1941 similar views emerged in discussions among economic and political experts at the Council on Foreign Relations on the nature of the Grand Area—that is, the core regions of the world that the United States depended upon for its economic viability.[11] The attack on Pearl Harbor only strengthened this evolving view: that the United States would need to work with Great Britain to reintegrate as much of the world economy as possible. Moreover, in the two decades between the world wars, the internationally oriented sectors of the American economy had expanded considerably, increasing the nation's stake in a

[9] Nicholas John Spykman, *America's Strategy in the World: The United States and the Balance of Power* (New York: Harcourt, Brace, 1942).

[10] See Melvyn P. Leffler, *A Preponderance of Power: National Security, the Truman Administration, and the Cold War* (Stanford: Stanford University Press, 1991).

[11] See "Methods of Economic Collaboration: The Role of the Grand Area in American Economic Policy," in council on Foreign Relations, *Studies of American Interests in the War and Peace*, E-B34 (July 24, 1941).

wider capitalist world order.[12] These economic and national security debates and underlying economic shifts all pointed in the same direction and reinforced liberal international thinking among political elites.

The underlying set of British interests is more difficult to specify. Fred Block argues that British participation in an American-sponsored system was not inevitable. He describes the central alternative to liberal multilateralism as "national capitalism." Block argues that "there is good reason to believe that after the war, there might have been substantial experiments with national capitalism among the developed capitalist countries." He goes on to argue that "the reason these controls were not elaborated into full-scale experiments with national capitalism was that it became a central aim of United States foreign policy to prevent the emergence of national capitalist experiments and to gain widespread cooperation in the restoration of an open world economy."[13]

This view is invoked by those who argue that Britain (and other European nations) had political values and economic interests that might have led to alternative (perhaps regional or bilateral) postwar arrangements if not for the hegemonic power of the United States. This matter is still disputed but the strong version of the argument, that Britain could have remained within its Commonwealth and imperial system, is probably incorrect.[14] It is true that the United States did confront considerable resistance to liberal multilateralism in Europe.[15] European reservations about a liberal economic order were part of broader differences between the United States and Europe over such matters as empire, spheres of influence, and regionalism.[16]

The United States did meet considerable resistance to its liberal postwar agenda, but it is less clear that Britain (and continental Europe) had viable alternatives to participation in an American-sponsored sys-

---

[12] See Jeff Frieden, "Sectoral Conflict and U.S. Foreign Economic Policy, 1914–1940," *International Organization* 42 (Winter 1988).

[13] Fred Block, *The Origins of International Economic Disorder* (Berkeley: University of California Press, 1977), p. 9.

[14] See the contrasting views of Robert Skidelsky and Benjamin Rowland in Rowland's *Balance of Power or Hegemony: The Interwar Monetary System* (New York: New York University Press, 1976).

[15] See David Watt, "Perceptions of the United States in Europe, 1945–1983," in *The Troubled Alliance: Atlantic Relations in the 1980s*, ed. Lawrence Freedman (New York: St. Martin's Press, 1983).

[16] This is a theme of Charles Maier in "The Two Postwar Eras and the Conditions for Stability in Twentieth-Century Western Europe," in Maier, *In Search of Stability: Explorations in Historical Political Economy* (New York: Cambridge University Press, 1987). On the British case, see William Roger Louis, *Imperialism at Bay: The United States and the Decolonialization of the British Empire, 1941–1945* (New York: Oxford University Press, 1978).

tem. It would have been very difficult and costly for the British to construct an alternative system organized around bilateral trade and the imperial preference system. Although British political elites were of divided opinion, not cooperating with the United States would ultimately have been difficult to sustain. For those British officials who held this view, their task was to use what intellectual and political capacities Britain had to shape the agreement in ways that served their socioeconomic goals, and to find ways to secure that agreement within a conflictual and fragmented political landscape.

Underlying structures of interests provide enough information to explain the fact that the postwar system was more or less open. But this information is not enough to explain the character of that open system. Nor is it enough to explain, even if we agree that Britain and the United States have common "objective" interests in a liberal multilateral system, how the many conflicting political positions were reconciled.

CONFLICTING ANGLO-AMERICAN PLANS FOR POSTWAR ORDER

It is important to appreciate the wide-ranging and often conflicting views on postwar order that emerged from the British and American governments—conflicting views that created obstacles to agreement. In the United States, views ranged from the free-trade proposals of the State Department to the views of New Deal planners who favored expanded government managment of the economy over institutions to promote the free flow of trade and capital. Lurking behind American wartime debates was a domestically minded and tightfisted Congress. In Britain the splits were even more profound, not least because the virtues of a liberal multilateral system were less apparent. Conservatives were reluctant to abandon the imperial preference system and many on the left saw an open economy to be a dangerous threat to economic planning and social welfare policies. Situated between these groups were economic advisers to the wartime government who were not eager to return to bilateral trade and the preference system but who thought that such an option might be necessary to protect Britain's postwar balance of payments and, in any event, might be used to extract concessions from the United States (that is, agreement to a more forgiving and expansionary system—precisely the "new thinking" that Keynes and his American counterparts were seeking to develop).

Within the Roosevelt administration the most vocal advocates of a system of free trade and multilateralism were in the State Department, led by Secretary Cordell Hull.[17] Throughout the Roosevelt period, Hull and other State Department officials never wavered in their conviction that an open international trading system was central to American economic and security interests, and that such a system was fundamental to the maintenance of peace. These ideas were given expression in the Atlantic Charter, signed by Roosevelt and Churchill during the war.

The consistency of the State Department position could be found in its ongoing opposition to the British imperial preference system. The 1932 Ottawa Agreements, according to Cordell Hull, represented "the greatest injury, in a commercial way, that has been inflicted on this country since I have been in public life."[18] Hull believed that the bilateralism and economic blocs of the 1930s, maintained by Britain but also by Germany and Japan, were a root cause of the instability of the period and the onset of war.[19] Charged with responsibility for commercial policy, the State Department championed tariff reduction agreements, most prominently in the 1934 Reciprocal Trade Agreement Act and the 1938 U.S.-British trade agreement.

Another camp within the Roosevelt administration was composed of economic planners and New Dealers, and their central concern was the domestic economy. This group, which included Harry Hopkins, Vice-President Henry Wallace, and Keynesian economists within the National Resources Planning Board, were interested in an expanded role for government in the management of the economy in the service of full employment and social welfare. This collection of officials, as Fred Block argues, had little sympathy with the State Department's multilateral vision. "They favored a world system made up of national capitalisms because of the priority they gave to the pursuit of full employment. They believed that the maintenance of high levels of employment and the development of national planning throughout the world should take precedence over the opening of economies to the free flow of investment and trade."[20] Yet these officials were not isolationists.[21] They favored international arrangements to foster expansionary domestic economic policies and institutions to channel capital to underde-

[17] E. F. Penrose, *Economic Planning for the Peace* (Princeton: Princeton University Press, 1953), p. 15.

[18] Quoted in Armand Van Dormel, *Bretton Woods: Birth of a Monetary System* (London: Macmillan, 1978), p. 25.

[19] See Robert A. Pollard, *Economic Security and the Origins of the Cold War, 1945–1950* (New York: Columbia University Press, 1985), pp. 11–12.

[20] Block, *Origins of International Economic Disorder*, pp. 36–37.

[21] See Richard Gardner, *Sterling-Dollar Diplomacy in Current Perspective* (New York: Columbia University Press, 1980), p. 15; and Alfred E. Eckes, Jr., *A Search for Solvency: Bretton Woods and the International Monetary System, 1941–1971* (Austin: University of Texas Press, 1975), p. 4.

veloped areas. Thus competing schools of thought on postwar order divided the Roosevelt administration.

The British political establishment was similarly divided. Before World War II, British attitudes toward the imperial preference system split largely along party lines.[22] The core of the Conservative party favored the maintenance of empire, and the Ottawa preference system was part of these special relations. "A section of the Conservative Party," E. F. Penrose points out, "valued the system of preferential duties on Empire goods as a force making for solidarity within the British Commonwealth of Nations."[23] These individuals stressed the importance of Commonwealth ties: it was a symbol of Great Britain's great-power status. "In Britain," Roy Harrod writes, "some resented the idea [of dismantling imperial preferences] mainly on sentimental grounds that we should be asked to abrogate this valuable symbol of Commonwealth and Empire unity."[24] Moreover, such Commonwealth nations as Canada, Australia, and New Zealand had risen in support of a beleaguered Britain during the war. These conservatives identified British interests with those of the Commonwealth.[25]

Others in the Conservative party were less enthusiastic about imperial preferences. Churchill was sympathetic with the free-trade position. Although "he acquiesced in a certain degree of protectionism as a *fait accompli*," Penrose writes, "he still thought there was a general presumption on the side of free trade and felt no enthusiasm for the system of Empire preferences adopted at Ottawa."[26] His major consideration was to protect the unity of his ruling coalition and to push on with the war.

The forces of support and opposition to the imperial preference system began to change during the war. The deterioration of the country's economic position made preferences more attractive to some British officials who otherwise would not have supported discriminatory trade practices.[27] To some of these officials the preference system might be a way to protect Britain's payments balance after the war, at least in the short term, particularly if the international economy fell into recession. They realized that turning away from multilateral trade

---

[22] On the general schools of thought among British foreign policy elites, see D. Cameron Watt, *Succeeding John Bull: America in Britain's Place, 1900–1975* (Cambridge: Cambridge University Press, 1984), pp. 16–17.

[23] Penrose, *Economic Planning*, p. 19.

[24] R. F. Harrod, *The Life of John Maynard Keynes* (London: Macmillan, 1951), p. 515.

[25] "Perhaps their most active and uncompromising member was Leopold Amery, who had great energy, high integrity, and keen political insight but little facility in economic reasoning": Penrose, *Economic Planning*, p. 20.

[26] Ibid., p. 20.

[27] Ibid., p. 14.

and payments would mean relying on trade restrictions and currency controls. That course would split the world into blocs, but a bloc system would insulate Britain from low-cost foreign competition and the deflationary effects of an American recession.[28]

Other officials were more skeptical of bilateral trade and the preference system, even as a fallback option, but they saw the threatened recourse to this option as a way to gain bargaining leverage with the United States.[29] To these officials, the only real option was to cooperate with the United States, but they wanted to do so in a manner that would allow Britain to achieve its economic objectives.[30]

As discussions began during the war, as we can see, there were striking divisions between and within the British and American governments. In Washington, the State Department articulated a remarkably unadorned vision of nineteenth-century free trade. In London, the wartime government, worried about the stability of its political coalition and the fragility of its impending postwar economic position, entertained notions of regional and managed economic arrangements. At the time, the construction of an open postwar economic order was not an obvious or inevitable outcome.

Anglo-American Monetary Experts and Their Policy Ideas

Amidst these divisions within and between the British and American governments, the Anglo-American monetary experts articulated their ideas. The Bretton Woods agreement is often seen as the result of the ideas and diplomacy of John Maynard Keynes and Harry Dexter White.[31] Indeed, these economists, particularly Keynes, were pivotal

[28] For a discussion of the relationship between British domestic economic problems, particularly the need for full employment, and an open international economic order that surveys various positions on multilateralism and its alternatives, see Allan G. B. Fisher, *International Implications of Full Employment in Great Britain* (London: Royal Institute of International Affairs, 1946). See also Eckes, *Search for Solvency*, pp. 64–65.

[29] These officials believed that Britain "could not afford to abandon any device that might assist her to retain or enlarge her export trade. Such motives were honourable and not fundamentally inconsistent with what the State Department had in mind. Most of those who held such opinions would not have deemed it a wise long-run policy to push the system of Imperial Preference further and build a self-supporting British Empire *bloc*": Harrod, *Life of Keynes*, p. 515.

[30] This was the position of most officials at the British Foreign Office and the Treasury. See the Foreign Office report "Note on Post-War Anglo-American Economic Relations," 15 October 1941, FO371/28907.

[31] The definitive history of this episode remains Gardner, *Sterling-Dollar Diplomacy*. Gardner's interpretation of the events places much more emphasis than I do on the differences between the American and British plans as they were advanced by White and Keynes, respectively. Whereas Gardner sees the Anglo-American negotiations more

figures in the devising of monetary plans, and they led their delegations in the celebrated Anglo-American negotiations during the war. But they were also part of a larger collection of economists and policy specialists who were located in the British and American Treasury departments, in other government offices, and in universities and policy institutions. While many of the beliefs held by this loose community of specialists reflected the evolving views of professional economists, the community itself was given form by the demands of the British and American governments to deliberate on postwar economic matters.

In both Britain and the United States, most of the ideas that made their way into the Bretton Woods agreement were widely shared among what could be called liberal-minded international economists, many of whom were Keynesians, and whose views reflected, more than anything else, lessons learned from recent historical experience as well as the ongoing evolution in professional economic thought. This consensus among economists and monetary specialists was a reflection less of the common acceptance of a specific economic doctrine or theory than of a more or less common professional reaction to the recent upheavals and malaise in the world economy. Out of these lessons grew agreement on the broad outlines of a desirable postwar economy and the general policies and institutions that would sustain it.

This policy consensus included rough agreement on three essentials. First, there was a common belief in the desirability of currency stability and the convertibility of currencies. Convertibility would be ensured by the abolition of exchange controls and restrictions. Disagreement could be found on the role of gold and other mechanisms for establishing stability in exchange relations, but currency exchange adjustments, when necessary to correct payments imbalances, were to be subject to international agreement. Behind the thinking of these specialists was the view that monetary arrangements must seek to avoid the political and economic instability of the interwar period. "In the interval between the wars," Keynes argued in an early draft of his monetary proposals, "the world explored in rapid succession almost, as it were, in an intensive laboratory experiment all the alternative false approaches to the solution."[32] The painful adjustments of the gold standard ruled

---

as a clash between officials representing different national interests, I see the expert negotiators as finding common cause in devising a plan that would reflect their economic thinking while also being capable of ratification by the American Congress. Eckes, *Search for Solvency,* is a sophisticated political history of the events that also stresses the role of experts in promoting agreement. Van Dormael, *Bretton Woods,* is a fairly straightforward and detailed history of the negotiations, relying primarily on British documents.

[32] "Post-War Currency Policy," in *The Collected Papers of John Maynard Keynes* (London: Cambridge University Press, 1980), 25: 22.

out policy ideas of this sort. The currency fluctuations, exchange controls, and discriminatory policies of the 1930s also discredited ideas associated with floating exchange rates.[33]

Second, the American and British experts agreed that some form of international reserves would need to be available as short-term assistance so as to allow expansionary solutions to balance-of-payments deficits. American and British experts, as we shall see, disagreed over how generous this fund would be and over the obligations of creditor and deficit nations (disagreements that emerged more from divergent domestic circumstances than from professional judgments). But they agreed that international stabilization funds should be available so as to allow governments to pursue multilateral and expansionary solutions to capital and trade imbalances.[34]

Third, and most generally, the Anglo-American specialists, some of whom were inspired by Keynes's pioneering work, agreed that new techniques of international economic management should be devised that could reconcile the movement of capital and trade with policies that promoted stable and full-employment economies. There was need for new levels of international management and supervision of national monetary and trade policies.[35] Thus, although these experts generally favored an open world economy, it was also to be a managed world economy, and in this sense their ideas differed from the policy views found in the State Department, which favored free trade. This difference was articulated by Harry Dexter White in 1942:

> The theoretical basis for the belief still so widely held, that interference with trade and with capital and gold movements, etc., are harmful, are hangovers from a nineteenth century creed, which held that international economic adjustments, if left alone, would work themselves out toward an "equilibrium" with a minimum of harm to world trade and prosperity. It is doubtful whether that belief was ever sound.[36]

In contrast to the thinking of Cordell Hull and the State Department, these specialists agreed with Harry Dexter White that international investment, capital movements, exchange rate parities, and commodity

---

[33] Odell, "From London to Bretton Woods," p. 299.

[34] Eckes, *Search for Solvency*.

[35] Anne-Marie Burley argues in "Regulating the World" (unpublished paper) that the techniques and operating philosophy of American postwar planners involved the transfer of a regulatory approach to domestic problems to foreign policy. This argument complements the argument here, that a managerial approach to monetary policy was inspired by Keynesian thinking.

[36] Harry Dexter White, March 1942 draft, White Papers, Box 8, Mudd Library, Princeton University.

prices were all potentially legitimate means for solving economic problems. An important purpose of the international stabilization fund and the other proposed postwar institutions was to separate legitimate from illegitimate economic practices.[37]

These views shared by British and American specialists reflected changes in economic thinking stimulated largely by the turmoil of the 1930s.[38] But they also reflected a broader confluence of intellectual and political thought. The Keynesian policy revolution was still spreading in British and American policy circles, but its political consequences had already taken hold: politicians and government officials, equipped with modern tools of economic policy, were increasingly capable of managing national economies. As a consequence, they would need to attend, more than ever before, to policies that promoted full employment and social welfare—a responsibility formally accepted by the British government in May 1944 with the publication of the White Paper on Employment Policy.[39] Innovations in economic and social policy allowed politicians to promise more to the electorate, but they also would need to deliver the socioeconomic goods.[40] Such new socioeconomic goals of government were at odds with the deflationary discipline of the gold standard: contraction and unemployment were not a satisfactory solution for deficit nations. "Even if this policy had its advantages," Keynes wrote in 1944, "it is surely obviously out of the question and might easily mean the downfall of our present system of democratic government."[41]

The ideas of British and American monetary planners also resonated with the revival of American internationalism in the late 1930s. One benchmark of the earlier thinking came in the first year of the Roosevelt administration. When, at the London Economic Conference of 1933, Franklin Roosevelt declared that the "sound internal economic system of a nation is a greater factor in its well-being than the price of its currency," the message was that the United States would take little responsibility for developments within the world economy.[42] By the

[37] Ibid.

[38] See Edward M. Bernstein, "Reflections on Bretton Woods," in *The International Monetary System: Forty Years after Bretton Woods,* proceedings of a conference sponsored by the Federal Reserve Bank of Boston, May 1984, pp. 17–18.

[39] See William H. Beveridge, *Full Employment in a Free Society* (London: Allen & Unwin, 1944).

[40] See Robert Skidelsky, "The Political Meaning of the Keynesian Revolution," in *The End of the Keynesian Era: Essays on the Disintegration of the Keynesian Political Economy,* ed. Skidelsky, pp. 33–40 (London: Macmillan, 1977).

[41] Memo from Keynes to Sir Wilfred Eady and Richard Hopkins, March 28, 1944, in *Collected Writings of Keynes,* 27:373–74.

[42] Quoted in Charles Kindleberger, *The World in Depression, 1929–1939,* rev. ed. (Berkeley: University of California Press, 1986), p. 216.

time the United States entered the war, official thinking had changed, and Roosevelt advanced the claim at the Bretton Woods conference in 1944 that "the economic health of every country is a proper matter of concern to all its neighbors, near and distant."[43] The change in Roosevelt's views reflected the renewal of internationalist thinking in American foreign economic policy.

The rise of Keynesianism and American internationalism, still under way as Anglo-American postwar planning began, provided a stimulus to that planning as well as a ready audience. These new attitudes contrasted sharply with those that attended planning after World War I, changes that were noted by Jacob Viner, a leading American economist and postwar planner, in 1942. "There is wide agreement today that major depressions, mass unemployment, are social evils, and that it is the obligation of governments . . . to prevent them." Moreover, there is "wide agreement also that it is extraordinarily difficult, if not outright impossible, for any country to cope alone with the problems of cyclical booms and depressions . . . while there is good prospect that with international cooperation . . . the problem of the business cycle and of mass unemployment can be largely solved."[44] A remarkable sense of economic possibility and social purpose infused the thinking of Viner and the other American and British planners.

The American group of experts was based, during the Roosevelt administration, in the Treasury Department. Under the leadership of Henry Morgenthau, a group of international economists was assembled within the department in the mid-1930s to work on exchange rate stabilization. Jacob Viner and Harry Dexter White were leading members of this group.[45] The group's early efforts culminated in the Tripartite Agreement of 1936, which established at least the principle of international monetary cooperation.[46] By 1941 White had risen at Treasury to take overall responsibility for foreign economic policy. Soon thereafter, in December 1941, Morgenthau directed White to prepare a memorandum on the establishment of an inter-Allied stabili-

[43] Roosevelt's opening message to the Bretton Woods Conference, July 1, 1944, in U.S. Department of State, *Proceedings and Documents of United Nations Monetary and Financial Conference*, vol. 1 (Washington, D.C.: U.S. Government Printing Office, 1948), p. 71.

[44] Jacob Viner, "Objectives of Post-War International Economic Reconstruction," in *American Economic Objectives*, ed. William McKee and Louis J. Wiesen (New Wilmington, Pa.: Economic and Business Foundation, 1942), p. 168.

[45] David Rees, *Harry Dexter White: A Study in Paradox* (New York: Coward, McCann & Geoghegan, 1973), p. 62.

[46] John Morton Blum, *From the Morgenthau Diaries: Years of Crisis, 1928–1938* (Boston: Houghton Mifflin, 1959), pp. 131–34.

zation fund—a fund that would "provide the basis for postwar international monetary arrangements."[47]

Although the specific origins of the proposals contained in White's original plan are unclear, the ideas were generally shared by many of White's professional and departmental colleagues. In the late 1930s, newly trained economists, mostly from Harvard and embracing Keynesian ideas, had begun to find places in the United States government.[48] By the start of the war, Keynesians had come to occupy positions in the Bureau of the Budget, the Department of Commerce, and the Treasury. During the war they also assumed positions at the Office of Price Administration and the National Resources Planning Board, which was also involved in postwar planning.[49] At Treasury, although Henry Morgenthau was not a Keynesian, key posts came to be occupied by those who were.[50] Taken together, when work began at Treasury on postwar monetary proposals, the experts surrounding White shared his basic views concerning the need for far-reaching and innovative economic proposals.

This community of experts extended outside of government as well. Most of the important ideas that found their way into White's proposal were also discussed during the war by a series of expert planning and discussion groups sponsored by the Council on Foreign Relations. The Economic and Financial Group, which was part of the council's War and Peace Studies Project, was led by Alvin Hansen and Jacob Viner, and it provided an extraordinary vehicle for the concentration of expertise and planning.[51] The Economic and Financial Group also pro-

---

[47] John Morton Blum, *From the Morgenthau Diaries: Years of War, 1941–1945* (Boston: Houghton Mifflin, 1967), pp. 228–29.

[48] John Kenneth Galbraith, "How Keynes Came to America," in *Economics, Peace and Laughter* (Boston: Houghton Mifflin, 1971). See also Walter S. Salant, "The Spread of Keynesian Doctrines and Practice in the United States," in *The Political Power of Economic Ideas: Keynesianism across Nations*, ed. Peter A. Hall (Princeton: Princeton University Press, 1989); Herbert Stein, *The Fiscal Revolution in America* (Chicago: University of Chicago Press, 1969); and Alan Sweezy, "The Keynesians and Government Policy, 1933–1939," *American Economic Review* 62 (May 1972): 116–24.

[49] Margaret Weir, "Ideas and Politics: The Acceptance of Keynesianism in Britain and the United States," in Hall, *Political Power of Economic Ideas*, p. 56. See also Marion Clawson, *New Deal Planning: The National Resources Planning Board* (Baltimore: Johns Hopkins University Press, 1981).

[50] Block, *Origins of International Monetary Disorder*, p. 39.

[51] G. William Domhoff argues that the origins of the Bretton Woods proposals are traced to the deliberations of the council's War and Peace Studies Project and the Economic and Financial Group. See *The Power Elite and the State* (New York: Aldine De Gruyter, 1990), chap. 6. For an earlier argument along these lines, see Laurence H. Shoup, "Shaping the Postwar World: The Council on Foreign Relations and United States War Aims during World War II," *Insurgent Sociologist* 5 (Spring 1975).

vided an important forum for discussions with British economists after monetary planning got under way in 1941.[52]

The British community of economic experts concerned with postwar monetary planning was overshadowed by John Maynard Keynes.[53] After World War I Keynes had written a well-known polemic, *The Economic Consequences of the Peace*, which harshly criticized the terms of the postwar settlement and forecast destructive trade and monetary policies and the eventual collapse of the European economy.[54] Two decades later, the prophetic nature of Keynes's views, along with the success of his pioneering economic theory, left Keynes in a commanding position to influence British postwar policy. During the war Keynes was given an office at Treasury to work on wartime economic administration and financial negotiations.[55] As postwar planning began at the Treasury, other international economists, such as Lionel Robbins and James Meade, were actively involved in the deliberations.[56]

British officials involved in planning shared the views of the American economists at Treasury that currency stability must be anchored in international agreement. "Exchange depreciation," Keynes wrote to Jacob Viner in 1943, "is nothing like as fashionable as it used to be, and experience has taught many countries what a futile expedient it is except in quite special circumstances."[57] Yet the single most striking belief that the British economists working on postwar monetary arrangements shared was that the currency exchange commitments must not undermine expansionary domestic policies. British economists (and many politicians as well) had by the mid-1930s come to believe that the return to gold in 1925 was a decision that brought economic misery to the domestic economy, and that the departure from gold in 1931 was associated with recovery.[58] The overriding view of British economists in government during the war was that social welfare and

[52] Interview, William Diebold, Jr., New York, August 14, 1990. Diebold was research secretary for the Economic and Financial Group in 1941 and 1942.

[53] See Hans Singer, "The Vision of Keynes: The Bretton Woods Institutions," in *The United Kingdom and the United Nations*, ed. Erik Jensen and Thomas Fisher, pp. 235–45 (London: Macmillan, 1990).

[54] John Maynard Keynes, *The Economic Consequences of the Peace* (New York: Harcourt, Brace & Howe, 1920).

[55] As we shall see, however, Keynes's first negotiations with the American government during the war dealt with lend-lease and postwar trade relations.

[56] Weir, "Ideas and Politics," p. 55. Also see Richard Gardner, "The Political Setting," in *Bretton Woods Revisited*, ed. A. L. K. Acheson, J. F. Chant, and M. F. J. Prachowny (Toronto: University of Toronto Press, 1972), p. 24.

[57] Keynes to Jacob Viner, June 9, 1943, in *Collected Writings of Keynes*, 25:323.

[58] Stephen Clarke, "The Influence of Economists on the Tripartite Agreement of September 1936," *European Economic Review* 10 (1977): 375–89. See also Peter Hall, *Governing the Economy: The Politics of State Intervention in Britain and France* (New York: Oxford University Press, 1986), pp. 49–50.

economic management must dictate postwar international economic plans, rather than the other way around.

In sum, monetary "new thinking" emerged within a community of British and American economic planners during the war. The colonizing of parts of the British and American bureaucracies by Keynesian economists strengthened the sense of community among these experts. Many of the views these Anglo-American experts held, particularly those concerning past monetary experience, were also shared by a larger international community of economists and policy makers.[59] As we shall see, although views differed among the British and American monetary planners, their shared ideas served to transform the negotiations on postwar economic order.

From Trade Stalemate to Monetary Agreement

Before the rise of this "new thinking," Anglo-American discussions of postwar economic order focused primarily on trade, and the result was stalemate. These first discussions were triggered in 1941 during negotiations over lend-lease, and disagreements surfaced immediately. State Department officials wanted to use this occasion to secure a promise that the British would open up the imperial preference system. British officials resisted and sought to tie the dismantling of discriminatory practices to a larger program of postwar reconstruction that ensured economic expansion and employment stability. The principles and mechanisms of that larger settlement, however, remained obscure.

Discussions began in the summer of 1941 when John Maynard Keynes, who had been appointed as adviser to the chancellor of the exchequer, arrived in Washington to negotiate the terms of the lend-lease agreement. Disagreement emerged over the proposed terms of Article VII, which set forth the framework for postwar settlement of mutual aid obligations. The article provided that in meeting these lend-lease obligations, neither country would lay down any condition that would obstruct commerce, and that both countries would take measures to reduce trade barriers and eliminate preferential duties. In a meeting at the State Department, Keynes asked if this provision "raised the question of imperial preferences and exchange and other trade controls in the post-war period." Assistant Secretary Dean Acheson acknowledged that it did, although it was not meant to impose unilateral obligations on the British Empire. Keynes strongly objected to this provision. "He said that he did not see how the British could make

[59] See League of Nations, *International Currency Experience* (Geneva, 1944).

such a commitment in good faith," Acheson reported; "that it would require an imperial conference and that it saddled upon the future an ironclad formula from the Nineteenth Century. He said that it contemplated the impossible and hopeless task of returning to a gold standard where international trade was controlled by mechanical monetary devices and which had proved completely futile."[60] Keynes argued that to maintain economies in balance without great excesses of imports or exports, countries in the postwar period would need exchange controls, precisely the types of measures that seemed to be prohibited by Article VII.

Behind the clash between Keynes and the State Department were differing views about the virtues of an open world trading system. State Department officials considered the construction of such a system to be an absolute necessity—a matter of principle. Keynes and his colleagues in contrast, were hostile to American efforts to rebuild what they considered to be an out-of-date laissez-faire trade system—or what Keynes called "the lunatic proposals of Mr. Hull."[61] As long as the focus of Anglo-American discussions was on trade, agreement on an overall economic settlement was beyond reach.

The difficulty of Anglo-American negotiations over Article VII led some British officials to reconsider the virtues of bilateral bargaining and imperial preferences. Leading economists in the British government voiced reservations over bilateralism in late 1941. About this time, Keynes was also rethinking his views. An American official who knew Keynes during this period notes the change: "In his own mind, Keynes had dropped, or was on the verge of dropping, the argument that hard bilateral bargaining would have to be resorted to; and he was replacing it by a plan for an international institution to deal with balance-of-payments questions."[62] Keynes came to the view that perhaps an agreement could be reached with the United States for a monetary order that would be expansionary; an order that could keep the trading system open but safeguard against depression.[63]

On the American side, as we have seen, there were conflicts between the departments of State and Treasury over postwar planning. The stalemate on postwar economic order, arrived at in the discussions of trade arrangements, did not prevent officials at Treasury from proceeding with monetary planning, and in the process, monetary negoti-

---

[60] "Memorandum of Conversation, by the Assistant Secretary of State [Acheson]," July 28, 1941, in *Foreign Relations of the United States, 1941*, vol. 3 (Washington, D.C.: U.S. Government Printing Office, 1959), pp. 11, 12.

[61] Harrod, *Life of Keynes*, p. 512.

[62] Penrose, *Economic Planning*, p. 18.

[63] Eckes, *Search for Solvency*, p. 65.

ations became the cutting edge of postwar planning. The centrality of monetary planning was traceable to the initial contentiousness of Anglo-American discussions of trade and to the relative smoothness with which British and American monetary experts were able to find common ground.

What followed was a ferment of monetary planning on both sides of the Atlantic. In Britain, Keynes listened to arguments from various quarters and retreated to the country to produce his famous plan for an International Clearing Union. What emerged was an ambitious plan for far-reaching cooperation in monetary relations, involving mechanisms for both orderly adjustment of exchange rates and the mobilization of credit that would prevent resort to deflation as a means to correct maladjustments.[64] The Clearing Union would have the authority to create and manage an international currency that would be used to manage intercountry balances. This overdraft facility would have the authority to create and manage $25 billion to $30 billion of a new international currency to settle payments balances. As Alfred Eckes notes, this "distribution of new financial assets would allow members—particularly heavily indebted countries like Britain—to remove restrictions on all capital movements, maintain stable exchange rates, and pursue stimulative domestic policies without fear of an external payments crisis."[65] A key provision of Keynes's Clearing Union was the pressure it sought to put on both deficit and surplus countries to correct payments imbalances. Among the measures he proposed was a tax on the excess reserves of creditor nations and specific policy guidance from the Clearing Union's governing board to restore payments equilibrium.

American planning got under way in early 1942 under the direction of Harry Dexter White. The plan was similar to Keynes's in its attempt to eliminate exchange controls and restrictive financial practices, and it provided rules for alterations in rates of exchange. Although it provided relief for monetary authorities in international difficulties, it differed from Keynes's plan in proposing relatively modest resources for this purpose and severely limiting the obligations of creditor nations to contribute to that relief. The Clearing Union scheme obligated creditor nations to accept clearing units (Bancors) up to the amount of these units available. The White plan restricted the obligation of creditors to the amount they subscribed to the fund.[66]

---

[64] The initial draft (and subsequent versions) of the Keynes plan are published in Keynes's Collected Writings, 25:21–40.

[65] Eckes, *Search for Solvency*, p. 66.

[66] The White plan is published in "Memorandum by the Secretary of the Treasury [Morgenthau] to President Roosevelt," May 15, 1942, in *Foreign Relations of the United*

These two plans formed the basic framework of negotiations that followed throughout 1943 and up to the Bretton Woods conference. Many of the compromises were made in favor of White's less ambitious plan, but many of the British demands were also met. The capital was to be subscribed under the compromise plan; there would not be a new international currency. Moreover, the primary responsibility for restoring international equilibrium would fall on the deficit countries and not, as Keynes had proposed, shared with surplus countries. The power of member nations to change their exchange rates was increased in the emerging agreement, which addressed the British interest in flexibility. Finally, Keynes's attempt to address short-term postwar financial problems was left out of the plan. Wartime debts as well as reconstruction loans would be dealt with by other bilateral agreements and a development bank.[67]

The crucial breakthrough in Anglo-American negotiations came in September 1943, when the British side agreed to abandon the Clearing Union idea of unlimited liability of creditor countries. Lionel Robbins noted later that "once we had recognized the political unacceptability of the unlimited liability of the creditor, the rest was a compromise between essentially friendly negotiators."[68] After this concession, much of what followed involved practical adjustments to specific national interests and domestic politics.

The agreement between British and American monetary planners was particularly important because it served to transcend the stalemate over the postwar trade system. The "embedded liberal" ideas of the Anglo-American monetary experts paved the way for agreement between the two governments. Once agreement was reached in this area, the State Department found its old-style trade proposals of secondary significance in the emerging postwar settlement. The debate on postwar economic order had been redefined.

THE KEYNESIAN COMPROMISE AND POLITICAL COALITION BUILDING

The new Anglo-American monetary ideas also had a political resonance within the wider circles of British and American politics. The Bretton Woods ideas allowed political leaders and social groups across the political spectrum to envisage a postwar economic order in which

---

States, 1942, vol. 1 (Washington, D.C.: U.S. Government Printing Office, 1943), pp. 171–90.

[67] Penrose, Economic Planning, pp. 55–60.

[68] Lionel Robbins, Autobiography of an Economist (London: Macmillan, 1971), p. 200.

multiple and otherwise competing political objectives could be combined. The alternatives of the past—of the nineteenth century and of the interwar period—suggested options that were much too politically stark. Outside the narrow transatlantic community of government economists, politicians were looking for options that could steer a middle course. In the end, the ability of "new thinkers" to articulate ideas that spoke to the practical needs of British and American politicians was a particularly profound aspect of their work.

Throughout their discussions with American officials, the British were looking for a middle ground between bilateralism (and the imperial preference system) and laissez-faire. Ambassador Halifax cabled the British Foreign Office in October 1942, after a visit from John Foster Dulles (at the time a corporation lawyer in New York):

> The most interesting point on the economic side of the discussion was Mr. Dulles' exposition of the Cordell Hull School of free trade, and the place which it had in the plans of the Administration. I said to him that I thought that we did not clearly understand what the significance of the Hull policies was. There was a feeling in some quarters here that we were faced with two alternatives, either we must revert to a completely 19th century system of laissez-faire, or else we must safeguard our balance of payments position by developing a bilateral system of trade with those countries whose natural markets we were. It seemed to me that neither of these courses would work, the first was clearly impossible, the second might be disastrous. I asked Mr. Dulles whether there might not be some middle course which would take account of our special difficulties and which at the same time would satisfy Mr. Cordell Hull on the question of discrimination, preferences, etc.[69]

The comments of the British ambassador reveal a historical moment when political elites were open to new policy ideas. Later in the year, when Keynes and the British shifted negotiating partners—from the State Department (and trade policy) to the Treasury (and monetary policy)—opportunities for finding that middle ground emerged.

In both Britain and the United States, the onset of war stimulated and widened political debate on the future of world economic order. Even before the war, politicians and editorialists on the left and right staked out a wide range of positions on the proper direction of world trade and monetary order. In American liberal and progressive circles, wartime views affirmed the goals of full employment and economic planning, and included calls for postwar world economic federation

---

[69] Dispatch from Ambassador Halifax to the Foreign Office, October 21(?), 1942, FO371/31513.

and multilateral cooperation. Liberal and progressive spokesmen stressed different goals: some advanced vague commitments to liberal internationalism, others favored the primacy of economic planning, and still others reaffirmed a commitment to free trade. Most commentators agreed that a new economic order must be built; there was little agreement on what that meant.

Once the Bretton Woods proposals were on the table, however, the various liberal and progressive commentators largely fell in line behind the ageement. Keynesian planners saw the agreement as an attempt to bring Keynesian management to the world economy; free traders saw a commitment to trade expansion. As both a practical and an intellectual matter, few economic planners or internationalists saw any real alternative to Bretton Woods. In Britain the Bretton Woods proposals also played a politically integrating role.

In Britain and the United States the Bretton Woods proposals represented a middle way that generated support from both the conservative free-traders and the new prophets of economic planning. Wartime economic "new thinking" helped refine the political mainstream, making possible new coalitions. Like a piece of crystal, the Bretton Woods agreement had many surfaces—it projected different things to different groups. No other internationalist proposal could command such a broad coalition.

Conclusion

As World War II raged, politicians and intellectuals contemplated the shape of the postwar order. Even before victory was assured, British and American officials planned for peace. To understand the postwar settlement that eventually emerged, it is necessary to refer to underlying power realities and national economic interests. But these factors alone are insufficient to explain the type of postwar economic agreement that emerged or, for that matter, why a settlement was even successfully cobbled together. Anglo-American agreement was fostered by a community of experts composed of liberal-minded British and American economists and policy specialists who shared a set of technical and normative views about the desirable features of international monetary order. The ideas articulated by this group of experts fostered agreement by altering the political debate about postwar policy.

The initial negotiations on postwar economic order, led by the State Department, dealt with trade arrangements and deadlocked without agreement. British and American officials differed over the desirable level of trade openness and national autonomy. The United States wanted to move immediately to lower tariff barriers and reestablish a multilateral trading system. Britain, concerned with its fragile economy and trade imbalances and not wanting to lose national control over economic management, resisted such moves. No bargain was possible between them.[70] (See Figure 1.)

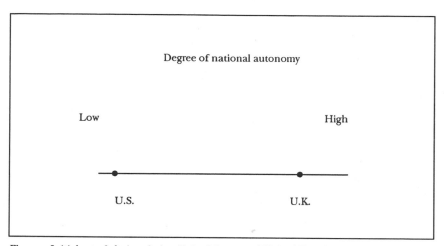

Figure 1. Initial set of choices facing United States and United Kingdom

The "new thinking" of British and American treasury officials served to break this stalemate by transforming the choices for postwar economic order, and consequently the debate over it. The new ideas provided a way to cut through the old divisions by pointing to a new set of rules and institutions that could provide an open and multilateral trade and monetary system while also safeguarding national economic autonomy. These ideas allowed national control over trade and monetary issues to vary independently. The new ideas transformed the choice space so that now it represented not a single dimension of national autonomy but autonomy in two separate domains (Figure 2).

The status quo, Q, represents a high level of autonomy on both the trade and monetary dimensions. The United States is concerned primarily with opening world trade and hence is located almost straight above Q, while Britain is concerned primarily with monetary issues and is located horizontally to the right of Q. The key implication of the transformed debate is that there are now gains from exchange between the United States and Britain. The lens-shaped region formed by the two nations' preference arcs indicate the region in which both states are better off than they are under Q. The contract curve indicates

---

[70] I am indebted to Barry R. Weingast for assistance in this section.

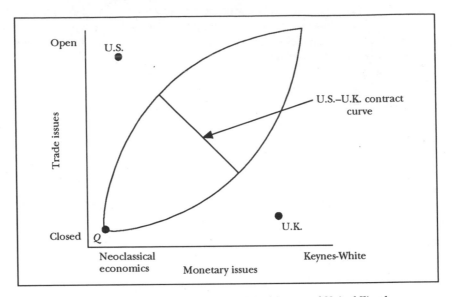

Figure 2. Idea-transformed set of choices facing United States and United Kingdom

those points that are Pareto-optimal for the two states; that is, the point at which it is not possible to make one state better off without making another worse off. By transforming the way policy makers framed the issue, the ideas had the principal effect of allowing the parties to conceive and choose policies that made them better off than they were under Q.

Seen in this way, agreement on postwar monetary order was fostered by the efforts of a group of monetary experts who, despite the many differences between them, shared a set of evolving ideas about the desirable organization of monetary relations and world economic order. These ideas eventually took hold, undercutting the State Department's more conventional but contested free-trade position and revealing a realm of common Anglo-American interests.

Shaping Government Conceptions of Interests

Not all increments of historical time are equal. There are junctures or "break points" at which possibilities for major change are particularly great and the scope of possible outcomes is unusually wide. These are moments of historical possibility—what H. R. Trevor-Roper calls "lost moments of history."[71] In this century, the several years sur-

[71] H. R. Trevor-Roper, "The Lost Moments of History," *New York Review of Books,* October 27, 1988.

rounding 1945 would surely be one such moment. Nobody knew how the world order would be reorganized, but everybody believed that reorganization was inevitable. The ending of a major war or the aftermath of large-scale economic crisis alters the parameters of policy making: dissatisfaction with past policy creates a new willingness by political leaders to reevaluate their interests, goals, and doctrines; disruptions and breakdown of rules and institutions create a need for nonincremental decision making; and the collapse of old political coalitions requires a search for new coalitions. At these moments, the removal of obstacles to change occurs simultaneously with the presence of impulses to change. When this happens on a global scale, fundamental change is possible.

At these critical turning points, the interests and capacities of the dominant groups, states, and classes matter, as they always do, but uncertainties about power structures and dissatisfactions with prevailing definitions of interests create opportunities for the recasting of interests. At the core of the postwar settlement were British and American political leaders who were open to the redefinition of national economic policy interests. Keynes, White, and the other "new thinkers" were particularly well situated to shape the resolution of these uncertainties: the transgovernmental "alliance" that they formed allowed them to shape the agenda, taking the initiative away from the free-trade-oriented State Department; the complexity of the issues gave them a privileged position to advance proposals; their ideas were particularly well suited to building winning political coalitions.

Building New Political Coalitions

The consensus among British and American monetary experts provided a basis for breaking through various layers of conflicts and deadlocks within and between the British and American governments. Most immediately, the consensus among Anglo-American experts cut through conflicts by shifting the ground of debate from trade to monetary issues. In a more general way, the monetary agreement served the purpose of political compromise by articulating ideas that created possibilities for new political coalitions. The policy ideas embraced by Anglo-American "new thinkers," not fully available in an earlier era, provided a solid intellectual foundation for a political middle ground between an unregulated open system and bilateral or regional groupings. This is the point made by Albert Hirschman about Keynesianism: that economic ideas "can supply an entirely new common ground for positions between which there existed no middle ground whatsoever."[72] It was the British (Keynes in particular) who were most intent on finding a middle ground—something that in the early Anglo-American discussions over postwar trade arrangements seemed so elusive. The Bretton Woods agreement articulated a middle position between a nineteenth-century-style free-trade system and regional or national capitalist arrangements. The policy views of the monetary experts were intellectually synthetic and politically robust: they provided a respectable position between extremes and set the stage for political compromise between British and American governments, and they foreshadowed (and perhaps enabled) a broader sociopolitical reordering of coalitions within postwar Western capitalist democracies.[73]

Policy ideas do more than simply "enlighten" political elites. They have a political as well as a cognitive impact. They provide opportunities for new coalitions of interests, or at least they can give intellectual force or inspiration to those groupings. Ideas do change minds, but it is their practical value in solving political dilemmas that gives them a force in history. The welfare state did not come into being because of emerging ideas about social welfare, such as T. H. Green's lectures on the social responsibility of the state at Oxford in the 1870s or the later writings of Charles Booth and Sir William Beveridge, although the ideas of these individuals did influence elites of their day. Many good ideas never find an audience and many bad ideas are around for generations. As the Anglo-American settlement suggests, policy ideas matter because they provide opportunities for elites to pursue their interests in more effective ways. This may be the most profound way in which ideas matter.

Legitimating Hegemonic Power

American leaders certainly wanted to promote American interests, and they were willing to use the nation's power capabilities to do so. But one can also detect a desire on the part of many officials to promulgate a postwar system that would have a normative appeal to elites in other nations. American officials realized that building international economic order on a coercive basis would be costly and ultimately counterproductive. This is not to say that the United States did not

[72] Albert O. Hirschman, "How the Keynesian Revolution Was Exported from the United States, and Other Comments," in Hall, *Political Power of Economic Ideas*.

[73] The rise of postwar political coalitions around Keynesian social democracy has been widely discussed. A nice analysis of the rise (and fall) of Keynesian social democracy in Britain is found in David Marquand, *The Unprincipled Society: New Demands and Old Politics* (London: Jonathan Cape, 1988).

exercise hegemonic power; it is to say that there were real limits to the coercive pursuit of the American postwar agenda. Historical records do show that American officials wanted to avoid looking as if they were imposing policies on the Europeans. This general observation helps explain why American officials paid more than insignificant attention to the normative bases of the postwar settlement, and why they were willing to make adjustments along the way to give the system a certain legitimacy.

Timing and Circumstance

Finally, the role of ideas in politics appears to be both powerful and fragile: powerful in shaping the definition of interests at particular historical junctures—Max Weber's "switchman" role—and fragile in that the conditions that allow for the play of these ideas are so highly dependent on an array of enabling circumstances.

The Anglo-American settlement is illustrative. The ideas of the monetary planners did play a switchman role in altering the debate about postwar order. But the conditions that allowed these ideas to influence the settlement were circumstantial and complex. The monetary ideas that proved so influential were not, strictly speaking, new. Why didn't these ideas play a role earlier—after World War I or between the wars—in fostering international economic agreement? Circumstances mattered. The range of legitimate policy ideas on monetary relations was much wider before World War II. The experience of the 1930s was crucial in discrediting monetary ideas associated with floating exchange rates. The lessons learned by British economists and politicians from the disastrous return to the gold standard in 1925 were also crucial in narrowing the range of expert views. Moreover, the war itself gave economic planners an opportunity to devise international rules and institutions in a way not fully available in the 1930s. The war also served to attract economists into the British and American governments, most of whom were trained in the "new thinking." In short, the fate of competing ideas and the political standing of the ideas' advocates mattered.

Beyond these immediate factors were more diffuse shifts in thinking among British and American elites about the socioeconomic role of government. Economic crisis in the 1930s and the progressive rise of the modern welfare state had a profound impact on the way many political elites thought about postwar order—and what they sought to achieve in a postwar settlement. Full employment, economic stabilization, and social welfare—these were words that repeatedly found their way into discussions of postwar economic order during the 1940s.

Nothing similar was evident after World War 1, when the rapid return to laissez-faire and the autonomic forces of economic life were the order of the day. As a result, British and American elites in 1945 had a different set of perceptions and objectives as they confronted postwar order than did their predecessors in 1919. In this sense, diffuse background shifts in British and American political and intellectual life had a powerful if subtle impact on the demand for new ideas.

CHAPTER FOUR

Creating Socialist Economies: Stalinist Political Economy and the Impact of Ideas

NINA P. HALPERN

As elites and economists throughout much of the world struggle to determine how to reform or transform socialist economies, an inquiry into the origins of such systems may not seem very compelling. Yet as one examines the problems facing such disparate countries as Hungary, the Czech Republic, Slovakia, Bulgaria, Mongolia, and China, one is struck by their similarity. What should be done with the unprofitable and inefficient state-owned enterprises that dominate the economy? How can entrepreneurship be developed in a setting where the state has long been almost the sole source of and distributor of capital? While China attempts to distinguish between the ownership and management of state assets without altering the major institutions of the state economy, the East European countries wonder how to create the necessary but absent infrastructure of a free-market economy. Varied as the choices for the future may be, the current problems are very much a legacy of similar past choices. If we can understand why these very different nations developed such similar politico-economic institutions, we may be able to discern the likely nature of future change.

On a more academic level, the similarity of the economic paths followed by countries with quite different economic endowments and cultural backgrounds provides fruitful grounds for exploration into the role of ideas in determining policy choices. The source of the politico-economic strategies adopted by these countries is not hard to identify: they are close imitations of the development strategy and institutions of the Soviet Union, introduced during Stalin's reign. After World War

II, all the countries whose leaders identified themselves as communist adopted the basic policies, institutions, and concepts of the Stalinist political economy. Despite partial modifications in subsequent decades, with the exception of Yugoslavia, socialist countries are still wrestling primarily with the problems generated by that model and set of institutions. It is beyond doubt that Stalin's particular policy choices had a dramatic influence on all the countries that later became socialist; the sources of this influence, however, are more controversial.

For those who deny the influence of ideas on policy, the adoption of such similar institutions in different national settings is easily explained as a product of power relationships and political interests. The USSR, having installed communist regimes in most of Eastern Europe, could certainly dictate to them their policies and institutions. Thus East European elites' professions of loyalty to Stalin and his ideas demonstrate nothing more than an interest in protecting their political positions and, given Stalinist terror, their lives. Even in China and Yugoslavia, where communist regimes achieved power essentially on their own and therefore did not owe their political existence or control over society to the Soviet army, Stalin could offer strong inducements in the form of economic and military aid. If such aid was not essential to maintain political power, it was at least necessary for economic development, which might determine political survival in the long run. According to this viewpoint, the adoption of Stalinist institutions throughout the communist world had nothing to do with the force of ideas; communist elites did not follow Stalin's example, they followed his orders. Had Stalin not chosen to dictate a complete imitation of the Soviet path, these leaders would have chosen quite different policies and institutions.

I do not deny the importance of Stalin's personal power or the influence of Soviet aid on the choices of other communist elites. The mechanisms of control that Stalin established within the East European "satellites" have been well described.[1] Moreover, Stalin's ability to dictate to East European elites the timing and substance of their policy choices is strongly suggested by the uniformity of the various governments' movements. Stalin's personal power, however, does not explain the persistence of his ideas and policies after his death. Nor does it account adequately for policy choices in the two countries where communist elites triumphed through their own strength and did not depend on the Soviet army to stay in power: Yugoslavia and China.

---

[1] Zbigniew Brzezinski, *The Soviet Bloc* (Cambridge: Harvard University Press, 1960); Charles Gati, *The Bloc That Failed: Soviet–East European Relations in Transition* (Bloomington: Indiana University Press, 1990).

China, despite its claim that the Stalinist model was its eventual goal, initially adopted a set of policies quite different in some respects from Stalinism; its move to full-blown Stalinism was fully implemented only after Stalin's death. In Yugoslavia, Tito asserted his personal independence of the Soviet Union in several ways, including adoption of Stalinist policies more rapidly than Stalin wanted and at a time when other East European countries were being held to a slower and somewhat different path. Tito insisted on following Stalinist ideas rather than Stalin's wishes. Accordingly, the personal-power argument leaves us with certain anomalies: how to account for the strength of those ideas in places where Stalin lacked that personal power, against his wishes, and after his death?

These anomalies suggest the need for an explanation that confers more power on the ideas themselves. Stalinist ideas derived their power primarily from their ability to resolve two of the major problems facing the postrevolutionary governments. The first was the high degree of uncertainty about the right way, both morally and practically, to develop a socialist economy. The second was the need for coordination—that is to ensure that whether or not the optimal answer to the first set of questions had been discovered, sufficient unity of action could be achieved to develop and implement *some* set of effective policies. The Soviet Union had faced exactly these problems after its revolution, and, after a lengthy period of debate and policy reversals, had resolved them in practice through Stalin's personal power to make decisions. But once Soviet experience had been codified into a set of ideas about the political economy of socialist development, those ideas could help resolve the uncertainty and coordination problems of socialist governments established afterward. Any preexisting set of ideas about what socialism meant and how to achieve socialist economic development, particularly one that had demonstrated its validity by taking an economically backward nation to the status of world power, would possess tremendous power.

Thus my argument for the power of Stalinist ideas rests on two premises. First, in the absence of alternatives and with the appearance of success, their answer to the question how to develop socialism largely persuaded communist elites. Second, the regime that rejected this alternative would face great uncertainty as to what path to take and what actions might be taken by others (including other domestic actors and other communist nations). Even if the regime was not convinced that the Stalinist notion of socialism was ideal, strong incentives nevertheless existed to adopt it and to punish any deviations from it. Overwhelming incentives might well force deviations from this ideology, but pressure would be felt to limit such deviations.

These pressures, if not belief in the ideas themselves, would exert their influence on actual policy. In the postrevolutionary period, however, these countries were not simply setting policy but also building institutions. Stalinist ideas therefore became incorporated into the institutions of these socialist countries. And once incorporated there, they have proved remarkably impervious to reform. The East European revolutions of 1989 were directed against this enduring legacy of Stalinist institutions, and, as I have suggested, that legacy continues to pose enormous policy problems for the new governments.

In the case of the East European countries that depended on the Soviet army for their very existence, clear evidence for these propositions cannot be derived from an examination of their early experiences; the alternative explanation that their choices were purely a response to Stalin's commands is impossible to disprove. Thus the case for the role of ideas must rest upon a close examination of the early experiences of the other two countries, China and Yugoslavia. These two cases provide strong, if not conclusive, evidence for my arguments, and permit extrapolation to the remaining East European countries.

STALINIST POLITICAL ECONOMY

An argument that ideas influenced policy outcomes requires a clear specification of those ideas. Ideas, however, operate at several levels. As Chapter 1 of this volume points out, ideas can be conceptions of possibility, principled, or causal. The notion of communism as a desirable end state clearly falls in the first category. Marx is largely responsible for the underlying shift in ideas that made a communist revolution conceivable, and Lenin introduced the notion that such a revolution might occur in an underdeveloped country. My concern here, however, is not the broad shift in world view that made communism appear possible or applicable to underdeveloped countries but rather ideas about socialism, defined as the path to communism. Although Marx spoke in some of his writings about lower and higher stages of communism, it was left to Lenin and especially to Stalin to struggle with the question what that path toward communism should look like. In particular, they faced the question how, as they strove for the classless society that Marx had identified as communist, they could simultaneously produce the material abundance that he had predicted. The answer to this question necessarily entailed both principled and causal ideas. That is, because socialism is defined as the path to the ideal state of communism, to define something as socialist was to label it "correct." At the same time, action to achieve the goal of economic development, and especially industrialization, could hardly be undertaken without some notion of causal relationships. The Soviet leaders had to choose their economic policies in a setting where, for principled reasons, the capitalist path was excluded, but no socialist alternative had yet been defined. The answers they eventually developed under the leadership of Stalin constituted the first "political economy of socialism." This set of ideas is what I will call "Stalinist political economy" (or, for variation, "the Soviet model").

Soviet economic policy went through several stages, but by the late 1920s it was launched upon a distinctive path. The Soviet textbook on political economy written in the early 1950s, along with Stalin's own 1952 *Economic Problems of Socialism in the U.S.S.R.*,[2] essentially codified, both in the distinctive socialist jargon, the policy choices that Stalin had already made. Described in Western rather than socialist terms, Stalinist political economy identified the most appropriate set of property relations, sources of growth, proper allocation of national income between investment and consumption, conception of how macro- and microeconomic decisions could best be made, and concepts for measuring value.[3] It consisted of a causal argument that these were the best ways to promote economic growth, and a principled one that only these choices were correctly "socialist"—that is, leading toward the classless society of communism.

The property relations specified by Stalinism consisted nominally of two types: state ownership for industry and collective ownership for agriculture. Industry was nationalized, and factories' entire residual was subject to state disposal. Managers were also appointed by the state (in the communist setting, "state" refers to the Communist Party or the bureaucracy that it controlled). Agriculture was collectivized and the peasants were dispossessed of their land and property (as is well known, in an extremely rapid and bloody fashion). Although nominally the collectives had the right to control their residual after paying taxes to the state, in fact mandatory procurement policies and the so-called

[2] J. V. Stalin, *Economic Problems of Socialism in the U.S.S.R.* (Peking: Foreign Languages Press, 1972).

[3] This discussion of Stalinist political economy draws on but does not duplicate the following works: Wlodzimierz Brus, "Stalinism and the 'People's Democracies,'" in *Stalinism: Essays in Historical Interpretation*, ed. Robert C. Tucker (New York: Norton, 1977); Alexander Erlich, "'Eastern' Approaches to a Comparative Evaluation of Economic Systems," in *Comparison of Economic Systems*, ed. Alexander Eckstein (Berkeley: University of California Press, 1971); Alexander Erlich, "Stalinism and Marxian Growth Models," in Tucker, *Stalinism*; Isaac Deutscher, "Dogma and Reality in Stalin's 'Economic Problems,'" *Soviet Studies* 4 (April 1953): 349–63; J. Miller, "A Political Economy in the Making," *Soviet Studies* 4 (April 1953): 403–33; Alec Nove, *Political Economy and Soviet Socialism* (London: Allen & Unwin, 1979) and *The Economics of Feasible Socialism* (London: Allen & Unwin, 1983); Stalin, *Economic Problems of Socialism in the U.S.S.R.*

price scissors (prices set by the state so that peasants were squeezed between very low agricultural procurement prices and very high prices for the goods they purchased) also served to place the agricultural residual at the disposal of the state. In agriculture, Stalinism thus demanded collectivism in form (he cautioned against nationalizing agriculture and used the coexistence of the two forms of ownership as justification for the continued operation of the "law of value" under socialism) but virtual state ownership in practice.

Stalinism was quite specific on the sources of growth: growth would occur only if producer goods developed faster than consumer goods (the so-called law of priority development of the means of production). In practice, then, investment should be directed overwhelmingly into heavy industry. By specifying the desirability of a very high rate of growth (achieved through a system of five-year plans that set very high growth targets), Stalinism also demanded that a very high percentage of national income be directed toward investment rather than consumption.

Stalinism mandated that both macro- and microeconomic decisions would be made by state bureaucrats. Through overall balancing, planners would determine what should be produced and how (that is, with what resources) factories would produce it. The direction of production and investment would be determined by planners through bureaucratic directives, not by consumers through market behavior. Institutionally, this system entailed the construction of a large government bureaucracy, with numerous specialized bureaus responsible for managing production of diverse products.

Finally, Stalinism had a distinctive set of concepts for measuring value and growth. Planning and accounting were based on quantities of products, not on prices. Prices were set according to the "labor theory of value"; that is, basically on a cost-plus basis without allowance either for the cost of capital or for the impact of scarcity. No criteria existed for allocating investment funds between equally desirable end products. National income was measured in gross, not net, terms.

This is the model of political economy that Stalin developed. Why it developed in this way is not our concern here. I am not arguing that Stalin made his policy choices on the basis of this set of ideas about how a socialist economy should operate. In fact, although there is some room for arguing that Marxism influenced these choices at least by ruling out certain alternatives, such as an unfettered free market, there is also little doubt that much of Stalinism consisted of ad hoc responses based on personal interests or perhaps whim. A different leader might well have made very different choices. But once those choices were made and a doctrine was developed to justify them, that doctrine later exerted an independent influence on the policy choices of countries that later identified themselves as socialist.

CHINA

In many ways China constitutes the best case for examining the proposition that Stalinist ideas had an independent impact on initial policy choices, and, through institutionalization, an enduring impact on later ones. Explanations based on coercion or interests seem most inadequate in this case. Stalin was not in a position to dictate policy to the Chinese communists, who, unlike Eastern Europeans, had achieved power on their own and thus did not depend on him for political support. And if desire for Soviet economic and military aid had produced compliance with Stalin's commands, one would expect to see early Chinese policy essentially duplicating that of Eastern Europe, which it did not. Other facts are at odds with the argument that the Chinese were trying primarily to please Stalin rather than following their preferred policies. The Chinese did not fully adopt Stalinist policies until after Stalin's death—at a time when those policies were being somewhat modified in the USSR itself. Finally, the basic Stalinist model has persisted in China to the present time, despite the fact that China broke relations with the USSR in the early 1960s. Thus neither coercion nor economic incentive seems to explain adequately why China has so fully adopted Stalinist policies.

On other grounds of interests one might have expected China to choose policies quite different from the USSR's. On efficiency grounds, the Stalinist model fitted quite badly with China's resource endowments. China differed greatly from the USSR in having a very large population and a much lower ratio of surplus grain to population. When the communists took power, China was also much less industrialized than the Soviet Union had been at the time of its revolution. For these reasons, the Chinese economy was far less able to support the Stalinist policy of very rapid industrialization financed by a squeeze on the peasantry.

Second, when they took power the Chinese leaders had already governed large pieces of territory for many years from their capital, Yenan, during the Sino-Japanese War; during this period they had accumulated many experiences that might have been developed into an alternative model of socialism. The Yenan policies of decentralized governance and local self-sufficiency were adopted to address the problems of governing scattered rural areas with minimal communications in the face of an economic blockade enforced by both the Japanese and the Kuomintang; they were quite different from Stalinist policies. This alternative set of policies could easily have been legitimated by their success in producing a communist victory over both the Japanese and the Kuomintang. Nevertheless, Mao opted to follow the Soviet model.

What gave Stalinist ideas their power to shape policy in China? In other words, why did Mao and other leaders seize on those ideas and use them as their guide for China's own policies and institutions? First, because the Yenan experience seemed inadequate as a guide to building a highly industrialized socialist country, China needed some alternative vision of what a socialist economy should look like. Looking back, Mao argued that because China lacked experience and knowledge about industrialization, it had to learn from other countries: "We couldn't manage the planning, construction and assembly of heavy industrial plants. We had no experience, China had no experts, the minister himself was an outsider [that is, he lacked expertise in economics], so we had to copy from foreign countries."[4] As the only one that had industrialized under socialism, the Soviet Union was the sole foreign country that could provide a principled as well as practical guide to industrialization; that is, a set of methods that not only worked but was agreed to be socialist.

The second reason, the need for coordination, helps explain the timing and completeness with which China eventually embraced Stalinism. Although Stalinism provided the only available model of socialist industrialization, Chinese leaders recognized that in Chinese conditions these policies might not be optimal, at least initially. Thus, immediately after the revolution, China officially adopted not Stalinism but a policy known as "New Democracy," which diverged in important respects from Stalinism. New Democracy, defined as a presocialist stage of economic recovery and preparation for socialism, was much vaguer than Stalinism: it was explicitly intended as a temporary response to postwar conditions, not as a model for the future. As such, it provided no clear guide to what policies were acceptable on grounds of either principle or efficiency. In these conditions, coordination of the making and implementation of policy became a serious problem. Stalinism provided a set of ideas that, even if not optimal at the time, was preferred to conflict and lack of coordination.

New Democracy, 1949–1953

From 1949 to 1953 the leaders identified China as in a presocialist phase, New Democracy. New Democracy differed from Stalinism

---

[4] Stuart Schram, ed., *Chairman Mao Talks to the People* (New York: Pantheon, 1974), p. 98.

mostly in calling for cooperation with elements of the bourgeoisie who had not collaborated with the Japanese rather than for a dictatorship of the proletariat. Thus, rather than confiscating all bourgeois property, the leadership maintained the capitalist economy so that it could help create the necessary economic conditions for the adoption of socialism. Similarly, in the countryside, rather than attacking the rich peasants and establishing collectivized agriculture, the leadership maintained private landownership and the rich peasant economy. At the behest of Stalin, the East European countries had earlier gone through a similar stage, called people's democracy, but by 1949 Stalin had forced them to leave this stage and adopt his system in its entirety. Some evidence exists that China's policies, particularly in agriculture, were adopted despite the opposition of Stalin.[5] Thus the decision to pursue these policies appears to have been quite autonomous.

New Democracy's deviations from Stalinism do not indicate that the Chinese leaders planned to develop an independent route to socialist development, or ever questioned the equation of Stalinism and socialist economic development. At the time, New Democracy was always described as a presocialist stage during which China could develop the necessary conditions for socialism; that is, approaching the level of industrialization the USSR had achieved at the time of its revolution.[6] In other words, the Stalinist model was said to be inappropriate then because China lacked the necessary conditions to implement it, not because any alternative way of building socialism was believed to exist. New Democracy itself was defined largely in relation to future policies—that is, by what it did not yet do: it did *not* expropriate capitalist private property or attack the rich peasant economy. The need for explicit declaration of such a presocialist phase stemmed precisely from the shared assumption that as a socialist country, China *would* adopt Stalinist policies. Recognizing the precarious state of the economy, China's leaders wanted to prevent premature nationalization of industry and collectivization of agriculture, which they knew would interfere with their immediate goal of restoring the economy and perhaps alienate the population excessively before they had consolidated their political control (in the fall of 1950 China also found itself at war with the United States in Korea, so that popular support was extremely important). Current accounts of policy discussions during this early period[7] make it clear that the reiteration of the need for a New Democratic stage was designed to prevent "leftism" on the part of cadres for

[5] Bo Yibo, *Ruogan zhongda juece yu shijiande huigu* [Reminiscences of some important policies and events] (Beijing: Zhonggong Zhongyang Dangxiao Chubanshe, 1991), p. 118.

[6] *Gongheguo zouguode lu, 1953–1956* [The path followed by the Republic, 1953–1956] (Beijing: Zhongyang Wenxian Chubanshe, 1991), p. 29.

[7] E.g., Bo, *Ruogan zhongda juece.*

whom the Soviet model appeared the "natural" course to take after the revolution.

By describing New Democracy as a presocialist phase, the leaders could deviate from Stalinism without countenancing development of any non-Stalinist alternatives for future policy. Other leadership actions also foreclosed the development of such alternatives. In particular, Chinese leaders took steps to ensure that in the future, Chinese economists would be unable or unwilling to offer any advice that deviated from the logic of Stalinist political economy.

Both before and after 1949, Mao often argued that because the Chinese communists lacked experience and knowledge in running an industrialized economy, they must learn from the Soviet Union. Of course, in this new situation they might instead have turned to their own economists for advice. China had economists trained in Western economics, some of whom had earned Ph.D.'s in the United States or England. Far from seeking advice from these economists, the leaders prevented them from teaching, sent them off to participate in land reform, shut down their professional economics associations and some of their economic research institutes, and subjected them to "thought reform."[8] Rather than being enlisted to provide advice on how to deal with China's economic problems and achieve industrialization, China's economists became themselves targets for transformation.

But China badly needed such advice, and so in addition to seeking Soviet assistance, its leaders attempted to create a contingent of economists who could offer it. Many students were sent to study economics in the USSR, and measures were taken to reindoctrinate all of China's economists. Stalinist political economy became the only acceptable set of ideas, both causal and principled, on how the economy functioned. The Soviet textbook on socialist political economy became China's textbook, and Stalin's contribution to political economy was greeted with as much acclaim in China as in the USSR. The topics, concepts, and categories of Stalinist political economy—definitions of ownership, the "role of the law of value," and so on—were all adopted by Chinese economists.[9] Although Mao at one point suggested that adoption of Stalinist economic theory was needed primarily to displace the hegemony of neoclassical economics ("We had to make use of Soviet experience and Soviet experts to break down the bourgeois ideology of

[8] Nina Halpern, "Policy Communities in a Leninist State: The Case of the Chinese Economic Policy Community," *Governance* 2 (January 1989): 23–41.

[9] Cyril Chiren Lin, "The Reinstatement of Economics in China Today," *China Quarterly*, no. 85, pp. 1–48; Zhang Xunhua, *Shehui kexue zhengming daxi, shehuizhuyi jingji lilunjuan* [Social science contentions, socialist economic theory volume] (Shanghai: Renmin Chubanshe, 1991).

China's old experts"),[10] in fact Stalinist orthodoxy was enforced even for economists who were long-time Party members who professed adherence to Marxism. Thus, even as they adopted policies quite different from Stalin's, Chinese leaders took steps to make sure that *economic theory* would duplicate Stalinist logic. In doing so, they preempted the development of any possible alternative set of ideas on how to develop a socialist economy. If the Chinese leaders were making obeisance to the Stalinist model only in order to maintain Stalin's support and actually were contemplating adoption of an alternative long-term strategy for development, this behavior would be hard to understand.

In other ways Chinese leaders gave evidence of preparing to embark upon a Stalinist path as soon as conditions warranted. They adopted as their goal the rapid industrialization of the country, with emphasis on heavy industry. In preparation, they began to develop the organizational infrastructure for the adoption of Stalinist-style planning and management of the economy. As early as 1952 the bureaucracy was being remodeled along Stalinist lines, and the techniques of central planning were being learned from Soviet advisers.

The Movement to Stalinism

In all these ways, Chinese leaders made it clear that New Democracy was intended only to prepare the conditions for the adoption of Stalinist approaches to economic development. In 1949, Chinese leaders anticipated that this presocialist stage would last ten to fifteen years or more.[11] Why, then, did they switch course in the latter part of 1953 (several months after Stalin's death) and initiate the "general line for the transition to socialism"—that is, the adoption of Stalinist property relations in both industry and agriculture?

Three possible explanations present themselves. The first is that given a model of what a socialist economy should be, emotional pressure existed to introduce that model as soon as possible. Whatever the rhetoric about needing to act according to China's particular conditions, the Chinese may have found it difficult to remain in a declared state of inferiority (in terms of progress toward communism) to both the USSR and Eastern Europe. The second explanation, recently offered by the Chinese leader Bo Yibo, is that conditions changed in the intervening years so that Mao now believed it possible to implement Stalinism sooner than he had expected. Specifically, economic recovery

---

[10] Schram, *Chairman Mao Talks to the People,* pp. 98–99.
[11] Bo, *Ruogan zhongda juece,* p. 213.

had been faster than anticipated,[12] and campaigns undertaken largely for ad hoc political reasons (the three- and five-anti campaigns, directed against corruption) had brought government bureaucrats and businessmen sufficiently under control so that accommodationist policies no longer seemed necessary. Also, the end of the Korean war provided an opportunity to concentrate on industrialization before the conflict between international socialism and imperialism inevitably heated up again.[13] The third explanation is that unlike Stalinism, New Democracy provided neither a principled statement of how to reach communism nor a detailed practical guide to policy, and therefore failed to produce the necessary coordination of action at either the central or the lower level. All three of these explanations may help account for the shift, but the last is probably the most important.

Because New Democracy was adopted to signal cadres what *not* to do, and because it was justified as a response to practical conditions that precluded the initiation of socialism, it was never elaborated as a positive model of how to develop the economy. As a result, a good deal of uncertainty prevailed over what New Democracy meant and what specific policies it allowed. This uncertainty manifested itself in cadre demands for clear signals on what was acceptable, divergent local responses to policy problems, and, eventually, policy conflict at the top. Such conflict and diversity of practice produced pressures to move toward a more concrete model that could establish agreement on proper policy. Since Stalinism both provided a clear guide to action and was the avowed model for future policy, it was the most obvious and easiest means of resolving this uncertainty and coordinating policies. Even if it was not the optimal response to China's conditions at the time, it was far preferable to continued uncertainty about proper policy and some of the inappropriate (in Mao's view) decisions being taken under New Democracy.

This proposition is perhaps best illustrated by a brief description of policy conflicts over agriculture. Agriculture is often pointed to as the area where Chinese leaders were least interested in adopting the Stalinist model, both because Stalin's violent collectivization had proved very costly and because the Chinese communists' experience in governing was largely in the countryside, so they regarded themselves as knowledgeable in this sphere. In fact, agriculture was collectivized even more rapidly in China than in the East European countries, though with less violence. But like the policy of rapid industrialization, collectivization did not begin immediately after the revolution. New Democracy called

---

[12] This point is also emphasized by *Gongheguo zouguode lu,* p. 31.
[13] Bo, *Ruogan zhongda juece,* pp. 216–17.

instead for "maintaining" the rich peasant economy (ruling out Stalin's attacks on the kulaks) and promoting mutual-aid teams (which involved no formal organization or pooling of land or tools) rather than collective farming of common land.

Today Chinese leaders and economists often assert that mutual-aid teams were simply a temporary device until industrialization and agricultural mechanization supplied the necessary conditions for introducing Soviet-style collective farms.[14] Support for this assertion is provided by an examination of the nature of the conflicts that arose within the leadership over agricultural policy during 1951–1952 (that is, after land reform). Disagreements existed over a wide range of issues— whether supply and marketing cooperatives would precede production cooperatives; whether class polarization was a serious problem at the time; whether rich peasants should be allowed to hire other peasants and lend money at interest; and so on—but no hint of any noncollective future for agriculture entered this debate.

Agreement that Soviet-style collectives constituted the eventual future for Chinese agriculture, however, did not preclude the development of serious conflict over how to respond to developments after land reform. The official policy of "neutrality" toward the rich peasant (adopted despite the lack of understanding, if not outright opposition, of Stalin)[15] did not provide answers to a large number of questions about what types of peasant behavior should be allowed. Leaders differed over whether rich peasants should be allowed to collect rents[16] and over how long the rich peasant economy should be maintained. In areas where land reform had been adopted in 1948 (the so-called early liberated areas), by the end of 1949 some rich peasants, and even some cadres, were taking advantage of New Democratic policies to hire long-term laborers and to lend money and grain at interest (activities associated with the landlords who had just been dispossessed of their land). A report written at the time described a great deal of confusion as to whether or not these activities should be allowed. The Party organization department's response to a request for clarification was a nonresponse, quite compatible with New Democratic vagueness: The Party took no official position on these questions.

But this ambiguity in turn produced conflict among top Party leaders who held very different views on the major dangers of the time. Leaders in Shanxi province, one of the "early liberated areas," called attention to dangers of peasant "spontaneity" and called for raising the level

[14] E.g., ibid., p. 194.
[15] Ibid., p. 118.
[16] Ibid., pp. 124–28.

of mutual-aid teams in the direction of collective farming. Liu Shaoqi, the second highest party leader, after Mao, harshly accused the Shanxi leaders of going against New Democratic policies, even as Gao Gang, the top Party leader in the Northeast, supported them. Eventually Mao stepped in and upheld Gao Gang, clearly displeased with Liu's reading of the meaning of New Democracy. But it was precisely the ambiguity of New Democracy that had permitted Liu to arrive at a policy position that Mao found so unacceptable.[17]

As time passed, therefore, the official position that China was in a presocialist stage requiring flexibility and cooperation with "bourgeois classes" produced confusion among cadres, conflict among top leaders, and interpretations of policy that Mao found unacceptable. Clearly, some way had to be found to provide clearer signals on appropriate policy and implementation. Stalinism, as the only accepted model for the future, was the most obvious, indeed at that point the only, set of ideas that could produce immediate consensus on the proper path to the economy's development. Although it would hardly eliminate all uncertainty and disagreement, it was far less ambiguous than New Democracy. Thus the need, much earlier than any of the leaders had anticipated, to declare that China had entered the socialist stage.

To summarize the argument thus far, the Chinese leaders' behavior after 1949 suggests that they never contemplated developing any alternative to the Stalinist model of socialism. Indeed, even as they insisted that China was not ready for that set of policies and, in the face of some opposition from Stalin, adopted alternative policies, they both insisted that these alternatives were *not* socialist and systematically ensured that in the future their own economists would be able to provide only Stalinist solutions to policy problems. The evidence strongly suggests that they did so because they neither imagined nor wished to imagine that socialism could be defined otherwise, or that socialist industrialization could be achieved in any other way. The timing of their movement to adopt Stalinist policies, on the other hand, seems to have been motivated largely by the need to reduce uncertainty and to coordinate the making and implementation of policy, which made the issue of whether China had fully achieved the necessary conditions for implementation of socialism seem far less significant. Reinforcing the lessening of concern about the conditions necessary for socialism was the unexpectedly rapid success in achieving economic recovery and social control. Stalin's ideas about socialist political economy, held by the Chinese leaders from the beginning, were fully implemented in 1953 be-

[17] Ibid., chap. 9.

cause changing conditions had made them seem both more relevant and more necessary.

Institutionalization of Stalinism

Thus, beginning in 1953, the Chinese for all intents and purposes adopted the Soviet model of economic development. Between 1953 and 1955 they adopted a five-year economic plan (preparation began as early as 1952, but the plan was actually adopted in 1955) incorporating the basic attributes of Stalinist planning: a heavy-industry bias and a very high level of investment. They continued to model their economic institutions on the Soviet Union's, acquiring the organizational capacity not only for centralized planning but also for product-by-product management of the industrial economy. And during 1955 mutual-aid teams, a very low stage of collective economy, were rapidly transformed into collectives along the lines of the Soviet model (agriculture had already been subjected to "unified purchasing and sales," which allowed for the implementation of a price scissors policy). In sum, after three years of indoctrinating Chinese economists and others with the ideals and theories of Stalinist political economy, China moved to adopt Soviet institutions in toto.

The process by which Stalinist notions of political economy were adopted and institutionalized in China provides evidence that a need for principled and practical guides to policy, as well as for coordination of the making and implementation of policy, can endow a set of ideas with force quite independent of the power of their creator. Subsequent stages of Chinese development suggest that those ideas, once institutionalized, can continue to exert their influence even if they are seen to produce serious problems.

Beginning in the mid-1950s, the Chinese began to recognize that the extensive application of the Stalinist model in the Chinese setting was producing some problems, particularly overcentralization of decision making and inadequate agricultural growth. The Great Leap Forward, although the product of many factors, was designed in part to address the inadequacies of the Stalinist model. Although Great Leap policies were far more mobilizational than Soviet ones, however, in important ways they remained basically Stalinist.[18] They retained Stalinist property relations, the role of planning as a tool for economic development and for direction of investment into heavy industry, and the gen-

---

[18] Mark Selden, "Mao Zedong and the Political Economy of Chinese Development," in *Marxism and the Chinese Experience,* ed. Arif Dirlik and Maurice Meisner (Armonk, N.Y.: M. E. Sharpe, 1989), pp. 43–58.

eral categories of Stalinist economic thinking, such as an emphasis on gross output rather than productivity. Even after the Soviets pulled out their advisers in the early 1960s and Mao began to identify the Soviet Union as "revisionist," Stalinist economic thinking continued to be the major influence on Chinese economic policy and discourse. After the Cultural Revolution and Mao's death, as the Chinese embarked on a major analysis of their existing economy and a serious reform effort, neither they nor most Western observers doubted that the Chinese economy remained, in its essentials, a "Soviet-style" economy. The enormous shake-up of the Cultural Revolution and fifteen years of polemics with the Soviet Union about the proper model of socialism had not fundamentally transformed Chinese political-economic institutions or methods (although they had produced serious economic and political problems). The Chinese continued to have a centrally planned economy, in which industry was state-owned and managed by a large group of ministries specializing along product lines. Agriculture was still collectivized. Why, more than twenty years after Mao first suggested (in his 1956 speech "On the Ten Major Relationships") the need to learn the negative as well as positive lessons of the Soviet experience, and after all of the attacks on the overcentralization and bureaucratism inherent in China's Stalinist system, did China still cling to a basically Stalinist economy?

The failure of Chinese economic policy to break significantly with the Soviet model, despite Mao's criticisms and large-scale political movements such as the Great Leap Forward and later the Cultural Revolution, reflects both the continued influence of Stalinist thought upon Chinese leaders, particularly Mao, and the institutionalization of Stalinist practices and thinking within both China's administrative structure and its economics profession. Despite Mao's dissatisfaction with the results of implementing the Soviet model, he never fundamentally rejected Stalin's ideas or authorized a search for an alternative model of a socialist economy. During the course of the Great Leap Forward, Mao encouraged the study of political economy. He himself returned to Stalin's writings, reading *The Economic Problems of Socialism in the USSR* and the Soviet textbook on political economy published under Stalin's direction; in 1959 he called upon all Party members to study Stalin's work critically in order to learn some "political economy."[19] And he did not do so as a negative lesson; that is, Stalin's writings were not held up as an object of attack. On the contrary, Mao hoped that Stalin's writings on objective economic laws and the law of

[19] Mao Tsetung, *A Critique of Soviet Economics*, trans. Moss Roberts (New York: Monthly Review Press, 1977).

value (written as a critique of the Soviet Union's own voluntarism during the 1930s) would encourage cadres to desist from some of the most radical tendencies of the Leap.

One must not exaggerate Mao's approval of the Stalinist model or downplay some of the differences between later Chinese and Soviet practices. Mao did have some very specific criticisms of Stalin's writings and practices, to which he traced Khrushchev's revisionism. His critique reflected the lessons he drew from China's own experience, during the Yenan period as well as during the Great Leap Forward. He criticized Stalin particularly for his neglect of the superstructure (political institutions and ideas) and mass mobilization, for neglecting agriculture and overemphasizing heavy industry, and for overemphasizing technological change as a route to communism.[20] But he never suggested that the Stalinist strategy gave rise to a nonsocialist system until Khrushchev made use of these errors to take the USSR along the revisionist path, or put forward any clear alternative vision—in an economic sense—of what socialism means.

By the mid-1950s, Stalinist concepts and categories of thought had become well institutionalized within the Chinese economics discipline and the economic bureaucracy. Chinese economic discussions in the 1950s and 1960s did produce a few innovative figures whose work might eventually have led in new policy directions.[21] But even the most innovative economists were limited by working within the set of concepts and assumptions of Stalinist economics. Western economic concepts were ruled out entirely. The handful of economists who began to strike out in new directions, even if not purged, made little progress in persuading the bulk of economists, whose unwillingness to question traditional assumptions stemmed from both training and fear. And bureaucrats who had learned to work with a given set of concepts, statistics, and methods were virtually impervious to the merits of other approaches and ideas. After the Great Leap Forward, as leaders sought an explanation of what had gone wrong, one economist who traced the problems to fundamental categories of thinking adopted from the Soviet Union was quickly dismissed by planning bureaucrats, who had little interest in rethinking their basic procedures for running the economy.[22]

After Mao died, the more independent lines of thought initiated

[20] Ibid.

[21] Lin, "Reinstatement of Economics"; Barry J. Naughton, "Sun Yefang: Toward a Reconstruction of Socialist Economics," in *China's Establishment Intellectuals*, ed. Carol Lee Hamrin and Timothy Cheek (New York: M. E. Sharpe, 1986), pp. 124–54.

[22] Sun Yefang, *Shehuizhuyi jingjide ruogan lilun wenti* [Some theoretical problems in socialist economics] (Beijing: Renmin Chubanshe, 1979), pp. iv–vi.

after the Great Leap Forward were resurrected and taken much further. Only then did it become acceptable to critique some of the basic Stalinist formulations, such as the notion that commodity production applied only in exchange between the state and the collective sector. It also became officially acceptable to look to capitalist economies for methods of running the economy. These doctrinal changes, even without any clear alternative model, have given rise to a dialogue and reform process that have substantially altered the Chinese political economy. Most striking is the decollectivization of agriculture, the growth in the urban private and "collective" sectors, and the reduction in the degree of economic activity subject to mandatory state planning. These important changes were made possible in part by the leadership's willingness to acknowledge that some of the current problems derived from the adoption of the Stalinist model. But there are also distinct limits to the ideological reformulations that have been permitted; for example, the debate must still revolve around the proper combination of plan and market, the proper role of the law of value, and new forms of management rather than ownership. This approach has placed definite limits on the evolution of the Chinese reform movement, both by permitting periodic cutoffs of particular lines of argument or policy suggestions (after the purge of the reformist Party head, Zhao Ziyang, in 1989, for example) privatization of the state sector was ruled out as a policy or topic of theoretical exploration[23] and by affecting social expectations. Thomas Bernstein has argued, for example, that the failure to articulate a new ideological understanding of the eventual goal of agricultural organization—the adoption of the reforms in a "contingent manner"—has made the peasants wary of change.[24] Even though agriculture is the sector where institutional change has gone furthest and endured longest, peasants are still more concerned about minimizing their political vulnerability than about maximizing their long-term profits. Thus, although Stalinist ideas and institutions are now subject to substantial questioning, they continue to influence economic policy choices and outcomes in China.

YUGOSLAVIA

The Yugoslav case will receive far less attention here, because Yugoslavia did eventually break with the Stalinist approach and follow an

---

[23] Nina Halpern, "The Impact of Tiananmen on the Political Climate of Economic Reform," *Issues and Studies* 27 (March): 78–97.

[24] Thomas Bernstein, "Ideology and Rural Reform: The Paradox of Contingent Stability," Conference on State and Society in China: The Consequences of Reform, 1978–

independent path that I am less interested in tracing. More important for my purposes here is the involuntariness of that break, and the autonomous power that Stalinist ideas demonstrated during the early years of Yugoslavia's economic policy. We can see that autonomy when we examine the conditions under which Yugoslavia adopted Stalinist economic policies. It adopted those policies more rapidly than any other East European country and more rapidly than Stalin wished.

Before the Break

From the beginning Tito and the other Yugoslav leaders emphasized Yugoslavia's differences from the other East European countries: specifically, they claimed that their revolution had been both autonomous and socialist. Thus their notion of "people's democracy" (the stage that Stalin insisted the East European countries had then reached) differed from Soviet formulations.[25] But the Yugoslavs' insistence that their revolution and form of people's democracy differed from those of other East European countries was not meant to suggest that Yugoslavia's path would differ from the USSR's; according to Milovan Djilas's later statement, ideas akin to the "Polish road to socialism" articulated by Wladyslaw Gomulka in the fall of 1947 were at that time unthinkable for the Yugoslav leaders.[26] Rather, it was meant to suggest that Yugoslavia could move more rapidly than the others to adopt Stalinist policies.

This emphasis on Yugoslavia's advanced status within Eastern Europe did not cause obvious problems for the USSR, even if it perhaps should have served as a warning of Tito's independent nature. The Soviets' insistence on the presocialist stage of people's democracy and gradualist policies within Eastern Europe may have reflected beliefs about what was politically possible within those countries; more likely it reflected a foreign policy aimed at reassuring the West.[27] Thus what did cause conflict with Stalin was Yugoslavia's foreign policy, which was far more radical than the Soviet Union's.[28] This radicalism was reflected in Yugoslavia's drive to incorporate Albania and Bulgaria and its support for a Greek communist uprising, actions that Stalin feared would undermine his strategy of reassuring the West and thus increasing his influence in the world.

1990, Claremont, Calif. Forthcoming in *China's Rural Reforms: Ideological and Political Constraints* (Armonk, N.Y.: M. E. Sharpe).

[25] A. Ross Johnson, *The Transformation of Communist Ideology, 1945–1953* (Cambridge: MIT Press, 1972), p. 26.

[26] Cited in Ivo Banac, *With Stalin against Tito: Cominform Splits in Yugoslav Communism* (Ithaca: Cornell University Press, 1988), p. 26.

[27] Ibid., p. 23; Johnson, *Transformation of Communist Ideology*, p. 9.

[28] Banac, *With Stalin against Tito*, pp. 28–29.

Tito's independence in foreign policy, which threatened to disrupt Soviet attempts to avoid conflict with the West, was matched by his insistence on organizational independence from the USSR and Stalin. Tito, to the great dissatisfaction of Stalin, resisted Stalin's efforts to infiltrate the Yugoslav Communist Party and refused to accept Stalin's decisions on who should be purged from the Party. He denied Stalin the control he exercised over every other East European communist party. This, too, was a major source of the conflict that led to Yugoslavia's eviction from the Cominform and the cessation of Soviet aid.[29]

Tito's demonstrated willingness to contradict Stalin's expressed demands makes it highly unlikely that he adopted Stalinist economic policies simply to fulfill Stalin's wishes—particularly since Soviet policy at the time called for a greater degree of gradualism. The Yugoslavs accepted such gradualism only in the sphere of agricultural collectivization, although even in this sphere they were somewhat ahead of the other East European countries. In other areas, though, they moved rapidly ahead with the adoption of Stalinist approaches to economic development. In particular, Yugoslavia was the first East European country to adopt a five-year economic plan oriented toward rapid industrialization. Tito made the decision to adopt such a plan in early 1946; the new head of the Economic Council (appointed after the earlier one was removed because of his opposition to this decision) was sent to the USSR to study Soviet planning, and the plan was adopted upon his return, in April 1947.[30] In Dennison Rusinow's words, it was "fantastically ambitious," calling for a fivefold increase in gross industrial output over 1939 levels, envisaging a rise in investment to 27 percent of social product, and focusing on heavy industry.[31] Despite limited emphasis on agricultural collectivization, Yugoslav policy followed Stalinism in directing investment overwhelmingly into industry; the 8 percent of investment directed toward agriculture was lower than that of any East European country except the relatively industrialized Czechoslovakia.[32] According to Ivo Banac, the Soviets were unhappy with the overambition of Yugoslav planning, but "once again, they were faced with accomplished facts."[33] Tito also reorganized the various levels of government to cope with the demands of the plan, bringing Yugoslavia institutionally closer to the Soviet model.[34] Despite the more

---

[29] Adam B. Ulam, *Expansion and Coexistence: The History of Soviet Foreign Policy, 1917–1967* (New York: Praeger, 1968), pp. 462–63.

[30] Johnson, *Transformation of Communist Ideology*, pp. 35–36.

[31] Dennison Rusinow, *The Yugoslav Experiment: 1948–1974* (Berkeley: University of California Press, 1978), p. 20.

[32] Banac, *With Stalin against Tito*, p. 20.

[33] Ibid.

[34] Rusinow, *Yugoslav Experiment*, p. 22.

cautious approach to agricultural collectivization, therefore, the Yugoslavs gave every indication of believing that Stalinist approaches to industrialization were the proper and efficacious route to economic development.

After the Break

Thus the Yugoslavs' initial decisions to embark upon a Stalinist path to socialism are not easily traced to political or economic interests derived from Soviet preferences. Instead, like the Chinese, the Yugoslav leaders readily grasped at Stalinism as an efficacious and legitimate guide for economic development. Immediately after Stalin evicted Yugoslavia from the Cominform, they moved even further in the direction of full-fledged Stalinism, particularly by dramatically speeding up the collectivization of agriculture. The timing of this move was seemingly motivated by instrumental considerations, because Stalin's attacks on Yugoslavia had pointed to its slowness in agricultural collectivization as evidence of a nonsocialist nature. But other evidence suggests that the desire to prove Stalin wrong was the primary motivating factor only in the timing of agricultural collectivization, not in the policy itself. A. Ross Johnson has traced in great detail the evolution of Yugoslav doctrine and practice after the 1948 break with the USSR, and has found that ironically (since this was the policy realm in which Yugoslavia had earlier diverged most notably from Soviet practices), Yugoslav policy responses to serious agricultural problems continued to be restricted by a belief in the general correctness of Soviet-style collective agriculture until the late 1950s.[35] In agriculture, then, Yugoslav policy after the break demonstrated the continued hold of Stalinist ideas long after they had lost any possible value in cementing Yugoslavia's relationship with the USSR.

In industry, however, this was not the case. After their excommunication, Yugoslav theoreticians gradually developed a critique of Stalinism that initially pointed to Soviet international behavior, but soon came to focus on domestic policies and institutions. According to Deborah Milenkovich, the discussions in early 1950 contained three threads: (1) a critique of Soviet organization, focusing on bureaucratic centralism; (2) an emphasis on participatory forms of government as Marx's true meaning of socialism and the path to the withering away of the state; and (3) a new analysis of the roles of plan and market in socialism.[36]

[35] Johnson, *Transformation of Communist Ideology,* chap. 8.
[36] Deborah Milenkovich, *Plan and Market in Yugoslav Economic Thought* (New Haven: Yale University Press, 1971), p. 66.

Djilas has described how these threads came together, were sold to Tito, and became the basis of the development of what is widely agreed to be the only truly distinct non-Stalinist economic model in the communist world.

> Soon after the Yugoslav Party was expelled from the Cominform, [Djilas] says, he started "to re-read Marx's *Capital*," but this time "with much greater care, to see if I could find the answer to the riddle of why, to put it in simplistic terms, Stalinism was bad and Yugoslavia good." In the process he rediscovered the Marxian principle of social self-management, with its antibureaucratic and anti-elitist implications. . . . "One day—it must have been in the spring of 1950—it occurred to me that we Yugoslav communists were now in a position to start creating Marx's free association of producers."[37]

With the development of a conception of socialism based on this insight and with Tito's acceptance, the Yugoslavs began moving in the direction of a new model of socialist economic development centered on workers' councils. A gradual transformation also took place in other aspects of Stalinist economic institutions and practices, including an immediate reorganization of economic ministries and abolition of general directorates (which functioned between the ministries and the factories) and of supply allocation plans.[38] Over the next two decades, the dynamics of reform in this new ideological context eventually produced a far more market-oriented system with the introduction of decentralized decision making, first for production and sales and later for investment. Alone in the socialist world the Yugoslavs could be said to have pioneered a new political economy of socialism—one that often appears in comparative economic textbooks under the heading of the "worker-managed economy." If we seek to understand the origins of this model, it is probably impossible to improve on Johnson's detailed analysis, which concluded:

> If political liberalization in some form was necessary for Tito's continued defiance of Stalin, given the international situation of 1948–1953, the doctrines of the withering away of the state, worker self-management, and the new role of the Party suggested, within a Marxist framework, *how* such political decompression could be carried out (and how it could be limited). Without this ideological factor, it would be difficult to explain the establishment of workers' councils, councils of producers, and other organs of mass participation.[39]

[37] Quoted in Rusinow, *Yugoslav Experiment*, p. 51.
[38] Milenkovitch, *Plan and Market*, p. 82.
[39] Johnson, *Transformation of Communist Ideology*, p. 232.

The Yugoslavs' willingness to move away from Stalinist ideas about industrial development does not indicate that earlier these ideas had functioned only as "hooks." It does, however, indicate that ideas will not be maintained at any cost, and that when ideas cease to perform certain necessary functions, they are likely to be replaced by others. For Yugoslavia, after the break with the USSR, Stalinism could no longer serve the functions of either legitimation or economic development. Legitimation was rendered impossible by Stalin's continued denunciation of the Yugoslavs as nonsocialist; a claim to be the true follower of a living leader who continually denounces you is simply not viable in the long run. Moreover, the economic embargo against Yugoslavia enforced by all socialist countries, as well as the increased military spending necessitated by fear of a Soviet attack, rendered the earlier plans for Stalinist-style industrialization inoperable.[40] Thus Stalinist notions of political economy lacked the minimal functional properties to permit the Yugoslavs to continue to embrace them. Unwillingly, they were forced to invent a new doctrine of socialism that could meet the needs for a guide to action, legitimation, and coordination earlier filled by Stalinism. Despite this development, their early history makes quite clear that had Stalin not eliminated all ties between Yugoslavia and other socialist countries, the Yugoslavs would have chosen instead to follow his ideas.

CONCLUSION

As the cases of China and Yugoslavia clearly indicate, Stalin's ideas exercised an independent power to influence the policy choices and institutions of other countries by offering persuasive answers to the most compelling questions they faced: What did socialism mean? How should a socialist economy be developed? How could the making and implementation of policy be coordinated? These questions could be answered in a variety of ways, but Stalinism represented a unique set of ideas that had already been formulated and moreover was associated with success. It is hardly surprising that neither Mao nor Tito seems to have contemplated any alternative notion of socialism, at least until Tito found himself forced to do so. The implication of these two cases is that because the other East European countries faced the same needs and pressures as China and Yugoslavia, they would have been likely to adopt Stalinist ideas even if Stalin had granted them a much greater degree of independence than he did.

[40] Banac, *With Stalin against Tito*, p. 132.

The Chinese case suggests that ideas that are accepted as correct need not necessarily exert their influence immediately: they must first seem relevant to the situation in which one finds oneself. The Chinese initially did not believe that the conditions necessary for socialism existed in their country, so their attention centered at first on creating those conditions. But because they had accepted a particular idea of socialism, pressures soon built to put it into practice. Primary among those pressures was the need for coordination: they needed an acceptable, agreed-upon guide to policy and its implementation. This need, as well as enhanced control over society and economy, produced a more rapid adoption of Stalinist political economy than China's leaders had anticipated. And once the Stalinist model was fully institutionalized within both the economics discipline and the political infrastructure, it proved remarkably resilient. It continues to shape Chinese policy to this day.

The Yugoslav case demonstrates that although ideas can sometimes be hooks, or justifications for policies adopted for reasons of interest, they can also be pursued even when they go against the national interest. Yugoslavia's relations with the USSR would certainly have been smoother if Tito had been willing, like other East European leaders, to tailor his policies to Stalin's wishes instead of his theories. The idea of moving toward socialism and acceptance of Stalin's definition of socialism motivated him far more than Stalin's policy pronouncements. The Yugoslav case also demonstrates that ideas do not necessarily prevail against all counterincentives; faced with a fairly desperate situation, Yugoslavia eventually relaxed its hold on Stalinism. Facing the same needs for legitimation, information, and coordination as the other socialist states, Yugoslavia was forced to embark upon the difficult and costly path of defining its own version of socialism.

The overall conclusion to be drawn from these cases is that, particularly after a revolution, countries seize on preexisting ideas to guide them through times of high uncertainty and to allow them to legitimate and coordinate their actions. This solution can often produce a more slavish imitation of another country's experience than might seem merited on grounds of pure efficiency. And once the practices and doctrines taken from abroad have been institutionalized, they may have very long-lasting effects. Decades from now the countries of Eastern Europe may marvel at their willingness in this current period of revolution to adopt so wholeheartedly the ideas and institutions of Western capitalism. But at this time their need for ideas is no less urgent than it was after their socialist revolutions. And the ideas they adopt are likely to have equally long-lasting effects. One can only hope that fifty years from now their current choices will appear more fortunate than those they made nearly fifty years ago.

CHAPTER FIVE

The Weight of Ideas in Decolonization: Normative Change in International Relations

ROBERT H. JACKSON

NORMATIVE IDEAS IN INTERNATIONAL RELATIONS

Social and political ideas can become institutionalized as normative frameworks of human relations—like the rules of a competitive game—within which utilitarian interests and purposive activities are played out. Rules define the game, but coaches and players determine the plays. Within the rules any stratagem that seeks to maximize self-interest can be employed—such as attempting in baseball to steal second base by taking out the second baseman or shortstop covering the bag. There is no necessary conflict between interests and rules. Conflict occurs only when rules governing the activity are infringed. Furthermore, rules are artificial: rule-governed activities have a structure or architecture. Rules can therefore be changed at least in principle if not always in practice. Systems of law usually provide a procedure or institution for changing rules.[1] But if the rules are changed, the game will also change. If four strikes were permitted in baseball, we should expect not only different stratagems and plays on the part of coaches and players but also longer games and very likely more hits and runs. Even the skills and players could be affected by this rule change: the

I am grateful to Robert Keohane and three anonymous readers for helpful comments on an earlier version of this chapter. I also acknowledge the financial support of the Social Sciences and Humanities Research Council of Canada.
[1] See H. L. A. Hart, *The Concept of Law* (Oxford: Clarendon, 1961), chap. 5.

balance between pitching and hitting might be tilted in favor of the latter.

Similar jurisprudential reasoning can be applied to political institutions. Within the rules of free democratic elections, various electoral stratagems that are known to expert advisers and consultants can be used by candidates in their attempts to be elected. But such campaign stratagems could not include the act of breaking into the electoral offices of a rival candidate and stealing his secret campaign strategy. At that point the pursuit of interests comes into conflict with norms: in this case a law that forbids breaking and entering. Furthermore, when the rules or institutions of a political game are changed, the way the game is played is also likely to change. If the U.S. Constitution authorized the president to make foreign policy without congressional involvement, we might expect a more directed and disciplined system of American foreign relations. If a parliamentary system were instituted in the United States, it would be a dramatically different political game: among other things, the frequent stalemates between the executive and legislative branches might be ended. One could speculate about other conceivable consequences—intended and unintended—of such changes.

Fundamental institutional change happens rarely in political life, but it does happen occasionally. And when it happens it usually reflects new ideas, whether conceived within a society or imported from abroad. As we shall see, normative ideas—what Robert Keohane and Judith Goldstein label "principled beliefs"—that originated in the West were a crucial factor in the abolition of colonialism and the institution of self-determination in the greater part of the non-Western world in the middle of the present century.

A few comments on the jurisprudential approach adopted here may be helpful at the outset.[2] "Ideas" and "interests" are in my view both concepts and therefore ideas. If I claim that something is or is not in my interest, for example, I am expressing my understanding of the situation in which I find (or expect to find) myself and the advantages or disadvantages it has (or might have) for me. This is an instrumental idea. Likewise if I claim something is of concern to me, such as the inequality of men and women or the discriminatory practices of the police, I am again expressing an idea. This is a noninstrumental or

---

[2] The model on which my argument rests is analyzed in Michael Oakeshott, "The Rule of Law," in *On History and Other Essays*, pp. 119–64 (Oxford: Basil Blackwell, 1983). For its application to international relations see Terry Nardin, *Law, Morality, and the Relations of States* (Princeton: Princeton University Press, 1983), chap. 1; and Robert H. Jackson, *QuasiStates: Sovereignty, International Relations, and the Third World* (Cambridge: Cambridge University Press, 1990), chap. 2.

normative idea. Hence both my interests and my concerns are shaped by my understanding, which is to say my thoughts and ideas about myself in relation to the social world around me—which consists of other people with their thoughts and ideas regarding their situations.[3]

Ideas are conceived in the first chapter as constraints on human interaction: railway "switchmen," in Max Weber's terminology. Ideas can affect our perceptions and—as Weber puts it—"obscure the other tracks from view."[4] But ideas can also shape our conceptions and the institutions that embody them. As indicated, social reality is constructed from ideas: the interactions and transactions of human agents are determined in significant part by their understanding of what is appropriate conduct in the circumstances. When normative ideas become embedded in institutions, they in effect alter the tracks—and the trains that run along them. One institutionalized idea may preempt another—freedom precludes slavery, citizenship bars subject status, independence repudiates colonial status. If any one side of these contrasting pairs is instituted, the other side is not only (perceptually) obscured but (conceptually) eliminated as a normative option.

This preemptive process of normative change is particularly characteristic of social and political institutions: a liberal society based on individual equality and freedom cannot accommodate slaves or serfs; a democratic voting system based on the universal franchise cannot deny votes to women or minorities; an economic system based on free markets cannot accommodate state ownership of the means of production; an international system based on self-determination cannot deny independence to Asians and Africans. One cannot have effectively established among the same set of people at the same time monogamous and polygamous marriage, Catholicism and Protestantism, a parliamentary system and a presidential system, a single-member-constituency electoral system and proportional representation, and so forth. If norms of self-determination are institutionalized, norms of colonialism are ruled out.

It is important to be clear about this point: I am not claiming that societies cannot embody many conflicting normative ideas and institutions at the same time. I am calling attention to an institutional logic of human societies: that if an institution is operative among one set of people, then an alternative institution that contradicts it cannot also be operative among them at the same time. One may of course have

---

[3] This is the outlook of philosophical idealism, which underlies the jurisprudential approach taken in this chapter. For further discussion of these points see R. G. Collingwood, *The Idea of History* (New York: Oxford University Press, 1956), pt. 5.

[4] H. H. Gerth and C. Wright Mills, eds., *From Max Weber: Essays in Sociology* (New York: Oxford University Press, 1958), pp. 63–64.

conflicting normative ideas and institutions among different sets of people at the same time: almost any contemporary Western pluralistic society is very likely to contain both religious believers and atheists, Catholics and Protestants, liberals and conservatives, beef eaters and vegetarians, lovers of Bach and fans of Elvis—the actual possibilities are almost endless. One may also have conflicting normative ideas and institutions among the same set of people at different times: England was once a Catholic country but became in the sixteenth century officially and predominantly Protestant; the Soviet Union was a communist one-party state but contemporary Russia is a (fragile) multiparty democracy.

Historical change often is marked by a change of principled beliefs and the institutions that embody them. During normal times institutions—if they are successfully institutionalized—can be taken for granted as social givens and everybody can get on with the business of looking after his or her interests. Change at such times is likely to be incremental. Institutions become an issue only when they are called into serious question by a sufficient number of people who object to them and are committed to alternative principled beliefs to replace them with. Colonialism is a case in point: an international institution that had been taken for granted became controversial, received widespread criticism against which it was not effectively defended, lost its moral force, and was displaced by an alternative international institution that embodied the normative idea of self-determination. Demands for self-determination and self-government by non-Western leaders and their Western supporters interrupted the normal business of colonialism in the middle of the twentieth century and in fairly short order fundamentally changed the way the international community henceforth was prepared to conduct itself with respect to the Third World.

THE NORMATIVE FRAMEWORK OF COLONIALISM

When old normative ideas and the institutions that embody and express them are displaced by new or contrary ones, a different regime is inaugurated. Something like this process of change was evident in the decolonization process in parts of Asia and most of Africa, the Caribbean, and Oceania. Previous norms governing independent statehood—which required acquisition of (Western-style) "civilization" and demonstrated capacity for self-government on the part of colonial subjects—were abandoned and replaced by new ones that had few conditions attached to them. As a consequence, many colonies that hitherto had little real prospect of soon gaining self-government now had a categorical entitlement to become independent states as soon as possible. They exercised it almost without exception. The change was unambiguous, rapid, and conclusive: within a decade, from about the mid-1950s to the mid-1960s, the international system was transformed from one that included a large number of legal overseas dependencies of European colonial powers—formal empires—to one in which most colonies had become independent states and the universal end of Western colonialism was clearly in sight. The normative ideas of self-determination and self-government not only preempted colonialism but also precluded its reform—into international trusteeship, say, or associate statehood. The change thus acquired revolutionary and categorical characteristics.

Nineteenth-century colonialism was not only a system of power for the pursuit of Western national or commercial interests; it was also a regime of justification expressed by domestic and international law. It is obvious that Western powers had certain military and economic interests in partitioning the non-Western world into various dependencies. They staked their claims on a wide scale in the latter half of the century; but they rarely if ever did so outside of a legal and moral framework that, while accommodating the interests of the great powers, also recognized and respected the legitimate concerns and rights of all sovereign states, large and small. It even recognized—if only in an embryonic way—the human rights of conquered and colonized non-European populations. Utilitarian interests and normative practices usually went hand in hand.

When the British government acquired and exercised colonial jurisdiction, for example, it did so in accordance with a Foreign Jurisdiction Act that set down precise rules for the occupation and administration of overseas territory. The act did not define Britain's national interest in foreign territory—that was a question of military and economic expediency determined by the government—but it did define the rules of the game in the acquisition and governance of such territory, and those rules were enforced by British courts of law.[5] The act was required reading for colonial lawyers and administrators. And when representatives of Britain, France, Germany, Austria-Hungary, Italy, Spain, and various other European states as well as the United States met in Berlin in 1884–1885 to partition the continent of Africa and distribute the parts among themselves, they did so by discussion and negotiation, which resulted in a treaty—the General Act—that spelled out the mu-

---

[5] See F. W. Maitland, *The Constitutional History of England* (Cambridge: Cambridge University Press, 1908), pp. 339–41.

tual rights and obligations of the high contracting parties.[6] The great powers certainly looked after their military and commercial interests—and we would surely be surprised if they had not. But these interests were fitted into an international normative framework that acknowledged the mutual rights and responsibilities of all signatories, large and small.

Like the British Foreign Jurisdiction Act, the General Act provided a normative framework not only for the acquisition of territory in the African continent but also for its colonial governance afterward. All signatories were duty bound to follow certain procedures concerning the physical occupation of territory and to avoid any resort to war among themselves. And the partition was achieved without the warfare that had been so characteristic of the earlier efforts of European states to colonize the North and South American continents. The signatories were also bound afterward to treat one another's African territories as "under the rule of neutrality" in the event of future war, which meant they could not use them "as a base for warlike operations" (art. XI). Even though this rule was not observed during the two world wars, colonial boundaries changed very little throughout the colonial era and indeed right down to the present.

Although war among themselves was prohibited by the General Act, the occupying powers could use force against recalcitrant African political authorities. This provision was entirely consistent with the international law of the day, which justified conquest and did not yet recognize the sovereign rights of most non-European governments.[7] The treaty did, however, acknowledge limited nonsovereign or (as we would say) human rights of Africans and the responsibilities of the signatories to protect them. The act carried forward the antislavery movement, which was injected into international relations and international law at various congresses in the nineteenth century largely by the efforts of Britain: occupying powers were duty bound to "suppress slavery and especially the slave trade." Of course they were also duty bound to "protect and favour" Christian missionaries, explorers, scientists, and other agents of "civilization." The treaty in this regard reflected ideas, beliefs, convictions, and prejudices that were prominent among Europeans in the latter half of the nineteenth century and first decades of the twentieth.

These norms were embodied in treaties of that time which involved

---

[6] See Sir Edward Hertslet, *The Map of Africa by Treaty* (London: John Murray, 1967), 2: 468–85.

[7] See M. F. Lindley, *The Acquisition and Government of Backward Territory* (London: John Murray, 1926).

non-Western jurisdictions. When Western powers began to encroach on China in the 1840s, for example, all encroachments were marked by treaties between those powers and the Chinese government, which—as one observer wrote—"formed the foundation on which has been erected the superstructure of the diplomatic and commercial relations between China and upwards of a score of foreign nations."[8] Likewise, when Japan was obliged to enter the international system in the latter half of the nineteenth century, it was required to abandon its traditional foreign practices and submit to the formal methods and institutions of the Western powers, "the most fundamental of which were the diplomatic/consular system and international law."[9]

These international relations rarely expressed raw power and were almost always corseted within a framework of noninstrumental rules of one sort or another. The external projection and exercise of armed force, or for that matter national wealth, usually had to be justified by something in addition to utilitarian considerations. Of course it was the law of the powerful (and the successful and the adventurous), but it was still law no doubt because there was always more than one great power. International rules of this sort provided a foundation of confidence, certainty, and reciprocity in the relations of not only the great powers but all the sovereign states that collectively formed an international society.[10] The rules of international law and diplomacy constituted the normative framework of that society, which was almost entirely Eurocentric.

All partitions, encroachments, unequal treaties, treaty ports, and other impositions on the non-Western world disclosed general principles of empirical statehood and positive sovereignty which were characteristic of the nineteenth-century society of states. These were the rules that Western states had no difficulty in living with. The colonial framework rested on the central postulate of classical international law: that independence was a question of empirical conditions—that is, whether statehood was a reality or not. If a political system consisted in an effective national government capable of enforcing its authority according to Western standards of "civilized" conduct in the populated territory it claimed to govern, then it was independent and ought to be recognized by other sovereign political systems. By this standard the

---

[8] H. B. Morse quoted in Gerrit W. Gong, "China's Entry into International Society," in *The Expansion of International Society*, ed. Hedley Bull and Adam Watson (Oxford: Clarendon, 1984), p. 176.

[9] Hidemi Suganami, "Japan's Entry into International Society," in Bull and Watson, *Expansion of International Society*, p. 193.

[10] See Martin Wight, "De systematibus civitatum," in *Systems of States*, pp. 21–45 (Leicester: Leicester University Press, 1977).

Ottoman Empire and Japan gained admission as sovereign states to Western-dominated international society in the nineteenth century. Recognition was required to be reciprocal: both the Turks and the Japanese were obliged to adopt, as a condition of membership, what then were still European norms and practices concerning international law, diplomacy, commerce, and so forth. Thus they were required to give up their traditional rules and practices for dealing with foreign "infidels" and "barbarians."

But if a political system was not a demonstrable reality or was not "civilized," it had no claim to recognition and membership in international society. On the contrary, sovereign states (mostly Western powers) had a right to intervene in such countries to establish a tutelary regime. For some commentators—such as John Stuart Mill—intervention was not only a right but also a duty if the aim was to install constitutional government, the rule of law, free trade, and other "civilized" norms in what were deemed to be "barbarous" societies.[11] Consequently, populated territory outside Europe could be acquired by conquest, purchase, exchange, or other means without the consent of the indigenous population, who—as barbarians—were conceived as not yet capable of giving or withholding such consent. Half the populated territory of the globe in continents and oceans beyond the West was brought under Western governance and the actions were justified more or less according to such normative ideas. These colonial norms of the old European state system persisted in some places until the middle of the twentieth century—although in the final decades of the colonial era they were expressed in terms of "development" instead of "civilization" and "barbarism."[12]

If non-Western peoples were to become independent, they would have either to drive out the occupying power by force and hope to be recognized as such or to wait until they qualified for sovereignty by graduating from the school of colonial development. Otherwise the rules of the positive sovereignty game would have to be changed. Since anticolonial nationalists and their supporters were not likely to wait for graduation—which might still be generations or even centuries away— and usually lacked the power to escape outright from the old norms, they were obliged to discredit them. They did so primarily by making reference to political and moral ideas that legitimated their claims and discredited those of the colonial powers. The core ideas were equality

[11] J. S. Mill, "A Few Words on Non-intervention," in *Essays in Politics and Culture by J. S. Mill*, ed. Gertrude Himmelfarb, pp. 368–84 (New York: Doubleday/Anchor, 1963).
[12] See Gerrit W. Gong, *The Standard of "Civilization" in International Society* (Oxford: Clarendon, 1984).

and self-determination, which—like most other features of anticolonial nationalism—ironically originated in the West. Anticolonialism was at base an ideological struggle in which the ideas of colonialism could be defeated even if the agents of colonialism could not. And colonial powers were deprived of crucial legitimacy even where their power remained unimpaired. This was the case throughout large parts of Asia, most of subsaharan Africa, and virtually all of the Caribbean and Oceania. This international change, which turned the morality and legality of colonialism upside down, was one of the most significant normative transformations of the twentieth century.

The entire colonial enterprise was deeply normative: to view it exclusively from a utilitarian perspective of costs and benefits is to overlook everything else about it, which amounts to a good deal. Great political acts, such as those that resulted in Western colonialism or those that rebelled against it, are rarely if ever contemplated or undertaken without elaborate justification that can warrant the sacrifices involved. Pure interest and power are no less exceptions in human relations than pure morality and legality. The real world is usually some combination of the two. Even though international relations can occasionally be governed by power and expediency alone—during wars, for instance, when mutual recognition, diplomacy, consular relations, legitimate commerce, and other normative interactions between states are often interrupted—colonialism for the most part is not a case in point. Indeed, the colonial system was vulnerable to moral criticism because it was in very significant part a normative order based on a now discredited doctrine of civilization which often had the appearance in practice of racial supremacy: its legitimacy could therefore be questioned, disputed, denied, undermined, and even destroyed.

THE NORMATIVE FRAMEWORK OF ANTICOLONIALISM

Self-determination

Ideas can—as Chapter 1 of this volume makes clear—destabilize old institutions based on discredited ideas and serve as the basis of new institutions. Demands for independence based on equality and self-determination eventually deprived colonialism of its moral defenses and put in its place alternative norms for justifying independent statehood. Normative ideas themselves can also change: the idea of self-determination assumed different shapes with different content as it was transported over time and space and employed in different circumstances. By the time it reached subsaharan Africa it was far different from what it had been when it left Europe.

Self-determination is an idea usually attributed to the French Revolution of 1789 and subsequent movements for national unification or separation in nineteenth- and early twentieth-century Europe.[13] It originally postulated peoples rather than princes (or dynasties) as the only valid grounds of international legitimacy: *national* self-determination. Hence the German-speaking and the Italian-speaking nationalities rather than the numerous and institutionally heterogeneous states into which they were previously divided became (apart from Austria and small pockets of German speakers scattered across Eastern Europe) two new independent states in the 1860s. These nation-states rested, at base, on a normative idea concerning political identity and legitimacy which did not begin to circulate widely among Europeans (and their overseas cousins in North and South America) before the late eighteenth century.[14]

In Central and Eastern Europe, movements for national self-determination had the contrary effect of dividing up multinational jurisdictions that formerly were united under imperial states. Before, during, and after World War I numerous subject nationalities—Bohemians, Lithuanians, Poles, Hungarians, Serbians, Romanians, Bulgarians, among others—proclaimed their right to independence from the German, Russian, Austro-Hungarian, and Turkish empires, which were destroyed in that war. Here the "self" was a distinctive and usually smaller nationality that elected to go it alone or—as in the cases of Czechoslovakia and Yugoslavia—unite with other such nationalities to form a new country of their own. "Determination" signified the desire and willingness of such peoples to govern themselves as independent states. It was accepted by the victorious Allied powers and, indeed, by all other independent states. National self-determination received quasi-official status at the 1919 Paris Peace Conference, which founded the League of Nations, and, as a consequence, numerous previously subjugated nationalities in Central and Eastern Europe were recognized as sovereign states.

The line was drawn with Europeans, however. Non-European nationalities of the old Ottoman Empire in the Middle East were—apart from the Turks—not recognized as sovereign states. They became "mandated territories" under League supervision. National self-determination in

[13] See Alfred Cobban, *The Nation State and National Self-determination*, rev. ed. (New York: Crowell, 1969), chap. 3.

[14] Self-determination (like nationalism) is of course prefigured in earlier European developments, such as the English civil war of the 1640s. In this respect it resembles the origins of the idea of sovereignty analyzed by Stephen Krasner in chap. 9.

1919 did not extend to what we today know as the Third World. This was still a colonial domain governed according to the norms described above. Most non-European peoples were deemed to be not yet conversant with (Western) ideas and institutions of modern self-government. It was feared that if they were granted independence prematurely, some members of their populations would simply impose an authoritarian regime on the remainder, thus obstructing the movement toward authentic political freedom. (The fact that this scenario was frequently played out after decolonization is perhaps an indication of the validity of the argument.) These territories were—as Article 22 of the League Covenant put it—"inhabited by peoples not yet able to stand by themselves under the strenuous conditions of the modern world." Consequently some system of internationalized trusteeship would be necessary until this capacity had been developed. Certain non-Western countries were expected to develop it within a decade or two (Type A mandates, such as Iraq, Syria, and Palestine); in others the process would take considerably longer (Type B mandates, such as Cameroon and Tanganyika); and in still others that were extremely marginal, external supervision and control might be necessary for an indefinite period (Type C mandates, such as Southwest Africa and New Guinea).[15]

This paternalist doctrine was reconfirmed in 1945 by the United Nations Charter (chaps. XI–XIII) even though World War II gave an enormous boost to normative ideas and beliefs of international equality and freedom, which eventually contributed to the repudiation and overthrow of colonialism by undermining and then finally displacing its legitimacy. The charter affirmed "the principle of equal rights and self-determination of peoples" in its first article, but also perpetuated the League doctrine of tutelage in the Trusteeship Council. Echoing the League Covenant, Article 73 declared that U.N. members with foreign territories "whose peoples have not yet attained a full measure of self-government . . . accept as a sacred trust the obligation to promote to the utmost . . . the well-being of the inhabitants of these territories." In the view of the drafters of the U.N. Charter, self-determination was a right that could reasonably be claimed only by peoples who were demonstrably capable of self-government.

The idea of the "self," however, was different: it now focused on colonies—which in most cases were political artifacts formed by Western colonizers—rather than on indigenous ethnolinguistic groups. In most parts of Africa and many other parts of the colonial world there was perhaps little choice in the circumstances: the ethnolinguistic

---

[15] W. Roger Louis, "The Era of the Mandates System and the Non-European World," in Bull and Watson, *Expansion of International Society,* p. 202.

groups were usually too small to be independent or they were too disorganized and disunited, having in many cases been divided and disrupted by colonial rule. If they were given a right of self-determination and self-government, the Third World would become more balkanized than the Balkans. In tropical Africa alone there would be not 40 or 50 independent countries, as there are today, but 400 or 500 or more. African nationalists recognized that this eventuality would leave Africa even more vulnerable to outsiders than it would be if the colonial framework were accepted as the foundation of state jurisdiction. However, since most multiethnic colonies resembled the old empires of Eastern Europe more than anything else, the "self" in self-determination was now a medley, some might say a hodgepodge, of usually very different peoples. This conception is almost the reverse of the idea of self-determination that defined newly independent statehood in Europe in the nineteenth and early twentieth centuries—and again recently in Eastern and Central Europe.

Self-determination now could be claimed only by the indigenous population (in practice by the government) of a former colonial territory—which in many cases was more like an internal empire than a nation-state. Ethnolinguistic groups had no right of self-determination: Karens, Sikhs, Tamils, Biafrans, Bugandans, and many other non-Western equivalents of Poles or Lithuanians or Bulgarians were not about to qualify for political independence. Through no fault of their own, they (like the Kurds of the Middle East or the aboriginal peoples of the Americas) had been consigned to the ranks of the abandoned peoples by the transformation of colonial frontiers—which never recognized them—into international boundaries. They became a striking feature of a newly mobilized world of ethnic politics and multiethnic states.[16] The exclusive definition of foreign or alien rule was rule by Europeans from overseas. It did not include Russian domination of the Islamic countries of the Soviet Union or Chinese domination of Tibet. Nor did it include the subsequent domination of the new states by particular ethnonationalities, such as Sri Lanka by the Sinhalese or the Sudan by Arabic-speaking Moslems from the north. Self-determination in some parts of contemporary Asia and Africa was virtually the same as imperialism in some parts of Eastern and Central Europe before the rise of ethnonationalism.

Independence

After World War II independence was still seen as a question of development: as long as colonies remained in a condition of relative

[16] See Donald L. Horowitz, *Ethnic Groups in Conflict* (Berkeley: University of California Press, 1985).

backwardness socially and economically, they were in no position to take on the burdens of self-government. Independence was subject to social and economic circumstances and was not yet a categorical right of everyone. This was the official ideology and policy of the British Colonial Office during and after the war. In 1943 the colonial secretary declared in the House of Commons that "it is no part of our policy to confer political advances which are unjustified by circumstances, or to grant self-government to those who are not yet trained in its use."[17] In that year a Colonial Office memorandum that discussed the prospects for self-government in West Africa, the most developed part of British colonial Africa, concluded with the observation: "A good many years (perhaps a good many generations though it would be impolitic to say so openly) must elapse" before the transition to African self-government could go beyond the local level.[18]

This conservative thinking carried over into British foreign policy during the planning for the United Nations Organization at the end of the war. A British memorandum prepared for the Dumbarton Oaks conference observed that "the development of self-government within the British Commonwealth" must occur "in forms appropriate to the varying circumstances of Colonial peoples."[19] Not every colony would become entirely self-governing: there were other destinations, marked by varying degrees of independence. In 1946 it was evident to Margery Perham, perhaps the leading British colonial theorist of the day, that "four chief obstacles" still stood in the way of "early and effective self-government" in most colonies: (1) the general populations were still "too unaware" of modern governmental operations to be capable of citizenship; (2) most colonies as yet lacked any basis of national unity; (3) many colonies were so insubstantial that "anything more than a limited internal self-government" was impossible; and finally (4) the level of economic development was still far too low to support a modern state.[20]

This justification for gradual and specific rather than rapid and universal decolonization provoked increasing criticism. The U.N. General Assembly was the focus of much of it. After 1945 colonial trusteeship became unacceptable to a steadily expanding non-Western U.N. membership, which eventually would be the majority. By the 1950s it was

[17] Quoted in A. N. Porter and A. J. Stockwell, *British Imperial Policy and Decolonization: 1938–1964* (London: Macmillan, 1987), p. 156.
[18] See doc. 22 ("Constitutional Development in West Africa") in ibid., p. 177.
[19] Quoted in D. J. Morgan, *Guidance towards Self-government in British Colonies, 1941–1971: The Official History of Colonial Development*, vol. 5 (London: Macmillan, 1980), p. 11.
[20] Margery Perham, *Colonial Sequence: 1930 to 1949* (London: Methuen, 1967), pp. 295, 336–37.

being challenged regularly in resolutions and declarations of the General Assembly. Resolution 421 (1950), for example, called for a study of the ways and means "which would ensure the right of peoples and nations to self-determination"; Resolution 637 (1952) declared that the right to self-determination "is a prerequisite to the full enjoyment of all fundamental human rights"; and Resolution 1188 (1957) held that self-determination was a right deserving due respect from (all) member states.

Final normative victory was heralded by the 1960 General Assembly Declaration on the Granting of Independence to Colonial Countries and Peoples (Resolution 1514), which proclaimed that "all peoples have the right to self-determination" and "inadequacy of political, economic, social and educational preparedness should never serve as a pretext for delaying independence." What not long before had been a widely recognized empirical condition for independence was now merely a "pretext." The declaration was passed in the General Assembly by a vote of 89 to 0, with 9 abstentions. Even the colonial powers were unwilling to go against it. The declaration was considered by Third World states and by many others as a "second charter" of the U.N., promulgated to liberate all remaining colonial peoples.[21] The overwhelming passage of the resolution marked the victory of a far more expansive reading of the charter and constituted in effect a major revision. From about this time arguments to delay independence on empirical grounds (such as levels of development or education) were considered morally inferior to universal claims to self-determination. A new normative idea expressing an absolute and unqualified right to self-government had displaced an old normative idea that made such a right contingent on a demonstrated capacity for self-government.

Opinion on this question changed dramatically not only at the U.N. and in a growing number of world capitals but also in the governing circles of leading Western imperial powers, particularly Britain. By the early 1950s the British government had officially committed itself to a policy that aimed "at helping the Colonial Territories to attain self-government . . . as rapidly as possible."[22] The year of Ghana's independence, 1957, is perhaps the time when British decolonization accelerated and any remaining desire to make independence conditional on development ran out of steam. Nor was Britain alone in dramatically changing its thinking on the question: the French and the Belgians quickly followed suit. Until 1956 the French could scarcely conceive of

---

[21] H. G. Nicholas, *The United Nations as a Political Institution*, 5th ed. (New York: Oxford University Press, 1979), p. 155.
[22] Quoted in Morgan, *Guidance towards Self-government*, p. 21.

colonies in the British manner, as schools for self-government. Yet in 1959 President Charles de Gaulle acknowledged the right of independence of every French colony in subsaharan Africa. All of them gained independence in 1960. In 1955 a leading professor of colonial law, A. A. J. van Bilsen, shocked his fellow Belgians by proposing a plan that envisioned the independence of the Congo (Zaire) within thirty years. Yet independence came a mere five years later.

In his now famous 1960 speech in Capetown, British Prime Minister Harold Macmillan declared categorically: "The wind of change is blowing . . . . Whether we like it or not, this growth of national consciousness is a political fact. We must all accept it as a fact. Our national policies must take account of it."[23] What had to be accepted as a reality was not the emerging military or economic power of the Third World—that had scarcely changed. It was a new normative idea concerning what constituted legitimate and illegitimate sovereignty. European colonial jurisdictions were now illegitimate. To persist in governing them as if nothing had changed was morally unthinkable and politically untenable.

From this time empirical statehood rapidly went into eclipse as a valid ground for determining the right to sovereignty in the Third World. Having previously condemned Portuguese colonialism and South African apartheid as "crimes against humanity," in 1970 the General Assembly in Resolution 2621 declared: "The further continuation of colonialism in all its forms and manifestations is a crime which constitutes a violation of the Charter of the United Nations, the Declaration on the Granting of Independence to Colonial Countries and Peoples, and the principles of international law." A novel idea of equality and self-determination had completely displaced an older idea of inequality and wardship: European overseas rule of non-Western peoples was now condemned as nothing less than a crime against humanity. The colonial and trusteeship system did not and arguably could not survive such a root-and-branch attack on its moral principles and institutional practices.

As indicated, the normative framework of anticolonialism embodied principles of juridical statehood for former colonies which disclose a rights-based model of international relations and law. According to these norms, independence is not a question of political capability or national unity or military power or national wealth or an educated citizenry or any other empirical or utilitarian criterion; it is a question solely of the right of a dependency to have it. If independence is demanded, it cannot be refused. The new state can claim equality with all

---

[23] Quoted in ibid., p. 117.

other states and demand their respect, whatever its internal conditions happen to be. Territorial jurisdiction is defined by formerly colonial boundaries, which acquire an inviolable status. Unsolicited military intervention is categorically prohibited even though the borders of many new states cut across territory occupied by indigenous nations that have a more legitimate claim to it, and even though the governments of many new states are frequently corrupt and not infrequently abusive of human rights. In other words, countries claim independence on the basis of self-determination even though they resemble empires more than anything else. Furthermore, once independence is acquired, not only is the former colonial power obliged to recognize the former colony and to continue to provide it with foreign aid, but all other developed countries are under a similar nonreciprocal obligation, whether or not they have ever been colonial powers.

In this novel scheme—which would have astonished any mid-Victorian imperialist—there is no place for colonies, protectorates, mandates, trust territories, condominia, associate states, or international legal dependencies of any kind. Apart from a few obscure remaining Western dependencies—mostly tiny islands—the only territorial jurisdiction recognized by contemporary international law nowadays is the locally sovereign state. The international system consists exclusively of such states. Formal colonialism is an entirely historical phenomenon. It would be impossible for any elected politician—if he or she did not want to be banished to the political wilderness—to call publicly for the reinstatement of colonialism or even to look back with nostalgia on the colonial era. Today the idea and institution of colonialism is politically dead. From the perspective of yesterday, this is a world turned upside down.

POWER VERSUS LEGITIMACY IN DECOLONIZATION

How should this extraordinary international transformation be explained? Was decolonization at bottom not fundamentally a consequence of altered equations of power and interest—instrumental rationality? Could it not be argued that the Third World really gained independence because of setbacks imposed upon colonial powers by their anticolonial adversaries specifically and the Cold War generally? Were not the anticipated costs from the continued possession of colonies greater than the expected benefits? A skeptic could concede that the change was one of ideas and norms but still contend that the underlying cause of the change was shifts in power and interests which had to be cloaked in ideology.

These are important questions and I have no doubt that this international change had a variety of causes. The "revolt against the West" certainly played a part in it.[24] Instances of indigenous rebels defeating or deterring Western colonial powers by raising the costs of colonialism are important and well known: the Viet Minh in Indochina; the FLN in Algeria; militant nationalist movements in India and Indonesia; guerrilla forces in Malaya (Malaysia), Kenya, Portuguese Guinea (Guinea Bissau), Mozambique, and Angola. Other examples could be cited. These episodes are obviously important and must be taken into account. But they are by no means the whole story of decolonization.

Indeed, if anything, they are the exceptions. According to one historian: "Western Europe's status and capacity . . . was clearly on the wane for most of the twentieth century, and violently so after 1945, but whether that status and capacity fell in relation to Upper Volta or the Gold Coast/Ghana is very doubtful."[25] According to another: "Whatever persuaded the British empire . . . to plan its own demise in tropical Africa, it was not fear of black African freedom fighters."[26] If we consider the debilitated and disorganized condition of so many postcolonial states, particularly although not exclusively those in subsaharan Africa, it is difficult to believe that the Third World nationalists who acquired them from the European powers managed to do so because of superior organization and skill. It seems rather more likely that the adverse conditions of these feeble states reflects (in significant part) the political limitations of those same nationalists and their successors. In other words, the weak states of the Third World arguably tell us more about the right of the Third World to exist in the form of sovereign states than they tell us about its power and capacity to exist in this form.

Utilitarian calculations by the colonial powers were important considerations in their decision to decolonize. But at least in British government discussion papers of the day "there was little sense . . . of Britain being too impoverished for the task of colonial rule."[27] The colonies had not become an economic burden. If anything, interest in hanging on to the colonies and developing them further was renewed in the late 1940s and early 1950s as the West struggled to recover from the war. In a memorable 1947 speech the British minister for economic affairs, Sir Stafford Cripps, declared the colonies could, by reducing

---

[24] See Hedley Bull, "The Revolt against the West," in Bull and Watson, *Expansion of International Society*, pp. 217–29.

[25] R. F. Holland, *European Decolonization, 1918–1981* (London: Macmillan, 1985), p. 300.

[26] R. Robinson, "Andrew Cohen and the Transfer of Power in Tropical Africa," in *Decolonization and After*, ed. W. H. Morris-Jones (London: Frank Cass, 1980), p. 52.

[27] Porter and Stockwell, *British Imperial Policy*, p. 69.

their consumption and increasing their investment in economic growth, make a substantial contribution to the postwar recovery of Britain and the sterling area.[28] One should also remember that at this time the main basis for Britain's and France's claims to be bona fide great powers and self-respecting members of the new U.N. Security Council alongside the two new superpowers was their colonial empires, which added enormously to their territories and populations and not insignificantly to their wealth. Winston Churchill looked at the British Empire in this light during the war, and he and other British leaders continued to do so for some time afterward. Charles de Gaulle and other French leaders took a similar view of their empire at that time.

Something besides declining military power or economic disinterest on the part of the imperial powers was involved in decolonization—certainly British decolonization. The cabinet and colonial papers upon which this judgment is based make reference not to any fundamental alteration in Britain's military posture or economic interests but rather to "the large body of opinion in this country, in Africa and internationally," which by the late 1940s was already demanding "more rapid political, economic and social development" and by 1960 would accept nothing less than complete decolonization—as Prime Minister Harold Macmillan's speech indicates.[29] Foreign policy is undoubtedly affected by calculations of power and interest. But foreign policy in a democracy also is profoundly influenced by the opinion of significant others, not only at home but also abroad.

The Cold War, too, played an important role in decolonization. By 1950 the wartime allies were fundamentally divided into hostile and heavily armed camps, and both the United States and the Soviet Union were (or soon would be) appealing for support from the emergent nationalists of the colonial world. Such appeals, by the United States no less than by the Soviet Union, certainly could not include the justification of colonialism or the rejection of self-determination and self-government. The constraints placed on colonial powers by this sharp division between West and East undoubtedly increased the opportunity for anticolonialists to bid for independence, if necessary by the threat or exercise of force, thereby increasing the hazards and costs of the colonial enterprise. Yet many of the more peripheral parts of the colonial world were, at best, of very marginal interest to the superpowers: their support could not affect the balance of power in the slightest degree. Almost the whole of tropical Africa was in this category. Yet

[28] Doc. 44 in ibid., pp. 278–83.
[29] See, e.g., doc. 40 in ibid., pp. 267–68.

Britain and France retreated completely from this part of the world not long after they departed from southeast Asia, and almost as rapidly.

Underlying all these causes, and others one could come up with, was a fundamental shift of normative ideas and a corresponding change of mind on the part of most sovereign governments and the public opinion influencing them concerning the right to sovereign statehood. When the Soviet Union and the United States appealed for the support of Asian and African nationalists who later became leaders of the non-aligned world, anticolonial ideas framed the only appropriate normative context within which such appeals could be made: they shaped the appeals. In other words, ideas, far from merely serving as the handmaidens of military power and economic interests, were the force that defined what those interests could legitimately be. A new climate of international opinion expressed anticolonial ideas and convictions that could not be ignored or brushed aside even by major powers—at least not if they were concerned about their reputations. By 1960 most states—even most colonial powers—no longer thought a colonial regime was a legitimate form of government. At least they were no longer prepared to defend its legitimacy and lawfulness in public. Most states had by then come to believe that colonial peoples had an unqualified right to be independent, with no further questions asked. It was impossible to argue for the contrary view and expect to be taken seriously. The Portuguese and the Rhodesians and the white South Africans tried it, but to no avail. In fact, they became international pariahs. The universally hostile attitude of the international community toward policies that reflected the practices of the old colonial world is testimony to the purchasing power of the new anticolonial norms.

Britain always insisted on the completion of a constitutional process of decolonization in every colony before it transferred sovereignty to the new government.[30] Apart from the debacles of Indochina and Algeria, much the same could be said of French rule in the majority of its colonies: their African subjects did not violently rebel. On the contrary, they "assimilated the metropole's culture" and participated jointly with the French in a peaceful process of decolonization.[31] The change was explicitly institutional and was understood as such by all parties: it was carried out by referenda and elections and not by the threat or use of force or as a result of sudden change in the economic utilities of the colonies for the imperial power. Consequently, it was not that

[30] See Martin Wight, *British Colonial Constitutions, 1947* (Oxford: Clarendon, 1952), chap. 2.

[31] See Henri Brunschwig, "The Decolonization of French Black Africa," in *The Transfer of Power in Africa: Decolonization, 1940–1960,* ed. P. Gifford and W. Roger Louis (New Haven: Yale University Press, 1982), pp. 223–24.

most Third World nationalists gained independence by defeating the colonial powers or even by making it too difficult or costly for them to persist in their imperial enterprise in the new circumstances of the United States' antipathy to colonialism and the Soviets' willingness and ability to support anticolonial rebellions materially—although such equations and calculations did of course contribute to the outcome. It was rather that nationalists took full advantage of available normative ideas and institutions to press their claim for independence in the confident knowledge that in a democratic age it would be extremely difficult for their democratic adversaries to refuse.

Thus, although power was obviously involved, the anticolonial struggle and victory were fundamentally and finally normative. Decolonization was above all an international change of ideas about legitimate and illegitimate rule and not a change in the balance of power or the economic utilities of imperialism. If it were merely a prudential or utilitarian question and no fundamental change of international opinion on the normative issue of colonies had taken place, it is likely that colonialism would have gone on for quite a bit longer in many places, and in some of them might still be with us. But the colonial enterprise had fallen into moral disrepute by the late 1950s, and in a few more years it would be equated not only with illegitimacy but with inhumanity and criminality. Thus, unless we can point to some dramatic changes at this time in the balance of power or in the balance of material costs and benefits, it seems as though we must resort to normative ideas to explain the change. I do not know of any such dramatic changes. Even though there were now two superpowers whose fundamental conflict divided the world, the military and economic relations between European states and their colonies from 1955 to 1959 were not very different from what they had been from 1935 to 1939. Consequently I am inclined to believe that colonialism ultimately proved defenseless at the level of ideas in a world that was fundamentally different not materially but normatively.

A counterfactual argument can be used to develop this point. If instrumental rationality by itself were a sufficient explanation, decolonization would not have had the general characteristics that in fact distinguish it. If only considerations of power and interests were involved, it would not have occurred as rapidly and widely as it did or been as categorical and unarguable as it was. There would have been far more variation in the timing, pace, and results of independence movements, each depending on the strength of an indigenous political organization, the capacity and resolve of its imperial adversary, the military and economic value of the colony, and so forth. Each anticolonial movement would have advanced or retreated according to a particular equation of power. Each would have developed its own means of resistance with whatever outside support it could muster. Each colonial power would have made its own utilitarian calculations of the advantages and disadvantages, profits or losses, that were likely to result if it persisted in its colonial enterprises. Some powers might have abandoned certain colonies and some might have decolonized entirely, but other powers might have persevered in their colonial enterprises.

Given a rational interest in retaining colonies that were militarily useful or economically valuable and making what I believe in most cases would have been a correct assessment that its nationalist adversaries were paper tigers, each colonial power could have tried to play out the process—perhaps indefinitely in some cases—according to its own interests and timetable. Some colonies would have broken free, some would be struggling still, and some would lack any real prospects of gaining independence. Some anticolonial movements might have run out of steam and failed to achieve their goals. Liberation movements that were of no strategic or tactical use to the Soviet Union in the Cold War logically would have been ignored by them. As we have seen, most of subsaharan Africa was in this category.

Since the morality of colonialism would not have been a fundamental issue in this imagined world of prevailing self-interest, some powers might conceivably have expanded their colonial holdings by acquiring territories of which other powers were prepared to divest themselves— just as business empires buy and sell firms and as the United States purchased Alaska from Russia. This sort of commercial transaction— which was a feature of colonialism and indeed of international relations before the democratic age—would not have been out of the question (as in fact it was, owing to the new norms of equality and self-determination). Furthermore, if utilitarian considerations were the main forces propelling decolonization, the ideology of anticolonialism would not have developed to the extent it did. It would have been largely beside the point. The anticolonial resolutions that took up so much of the time of the U.N. General Assembly, the Commonwealth, and other international bodies would have counted for little—if they had been expressed at all. Indeed, the climate of hostility to colonialism which pervaded both domestic and international politics after World War II and which was rooted in a sense of injustice simply could not have been the noteworthy historical phenomenon that it in fact was.

As it happened in subsaharan Africa, only Portugal, Ian Smith's Rhodesia, and apartheid South Africa acted in a manner consistent with the instrumental argument. For almost fifteen years after 1960 Lisbon refused to acknowledge the general illegitimacy of colonialism and the specific legitimacy of the anticolonial movements in its African territories. In persisting in its unlawful seizure of power for about the same length of time, Ian Smith's regime defied not only the colonial authority—Britain—but also the international community. White South Africa went even further and became the most noteworthy international outcast of the postcolonial era. But these cases are generally regarded as the exceptions and not the rule in African decolonization, which elsewhere was driven far less by the logic of power than by that of legality and legitimacy.

In brief, if power and interests alone had decided the issue, the world today would be less like it is and probably more like it used to be. Decolonization would be strung out over a far lengthier historical period and noteworthy colonies would probably still be in existence. Perhaps there would also be intermediate categories between legal dependency and outright independence, such as associate membership in the U.N. Perhaps other nonsovereign statuses would have been innovated and instituted. Different international organizations might have been formed to deal with them. Much would have depended on local circumstances. As it happened, however, circumstances counted for little: decolonization was a question of right, and no legitimate claimant—no matter the circumstances—could be denied. All of the alternatives were ruled out by the new norms of equality and self-determination. In short, decolonization was fundamentally a revolution not of power but of ideas about what is legitimate and illegitimate in international politics.

Could this observed general pattern not still be accounted for on a utilitarian basis? Suppose we grant that the uniformity and rapidity of decolonization across many cases within a restricted time period is consistent with a normative argument. The skeptic might still argue, however, that the decision facing the colonial powers was no longer whether to retain or abandon authority over a particular piece of overseas real estate but whether to defend or reject the institution of colonialism as a whole. Hence the same decision to decolonize could in principle have been made on a utilitarian, cost-benefit basis at about the same time by all the colonial powers.[32]

This argument assumes that the utility or rather disutility of colonialism would be more or less the same for every colonial power. However, when we consider the actual circumstances and interests of those powers—which varied considerably—this assumption seems unlikely to hold. The relevant socioeconomic differences between states are, as a rule, far greater than those between citizens. Given such differences, it seems far more likely that Britain, France, and Belgium (to take three

[32] I am grateful to Robert Keohane for suggesting this line of argument.

similar cases) would have arrived at different decisions at the same time on the question of decolonization, or at similar decisions at different times—unless something else intervened. The fact that Portugal denied the illegitimacy of colonialism and clung to its African colonies well after 1960—even to the point of fighting for them—suggests that the utilities of colonialism did in fact vary from one colonial power to the next. But the new intervening anticolonial norms were the same for all colonial powers—including Portugal, which could pursue its utilitarian calculations only by defying those norms.

It is important to be clear about the argument to this point. I am not arguing that ideas and norms explain every aspect of decolonization. I am only arguing that power and interests cannot by themselves account for decolonization. But I am explicitly arguing against the view that ideas and norms merely play the role of handmaiden to material costs and benefits. Normative ideas played an important intervening role in changing colonial policy by disrupting the old legal and moral framework of positive sovereignty within which it had been carried on in the past. What for generations had been colonial government as usual became within a decade the death of colonialism.

THE INSTITUTIONALIZATION OF ANTICOLONIALISM

What were the principal normative ideas behind the international change we refer to as decolonization and why did they rapidly infiltrate international relations after 1955? The story is long and complicated, and limitations of space permit only a brief sketch of the main developments.

Colonialism, like any other social or political institution, can be justified and defended or criticized and condemned. The evaluation depends on the standards of conduct prevailing at the time, the presence of sufficient numbers of people who are committed to them and are willing to put them into play, and the opportunity for them to do so. By the 1950s anticolonial ideas were circulating widely within leading Western states and many of their colonies and also within the international community. Substantial numbers of political activists recognized that colonialism was morally vulnerable to criticism on the grounds of equality and self-determination. They were already well represented within political parties or in voluntary groups organized to press their claims. In London and Paris and to a lesser extent Brussels and the Hague—and also by that time increasingly in British and French colonies themselves—ample opportunity existed for opponents of colonialism to criticize not only the policies of the colonial powers but the institution of colonialism itself. International organizations also by then provided important assemblies where the anticolonial view could be registered: annual meetings of the U.N. General Assembly were regular occasions for widely publicized censure of colonialism. Anticolonialism was a refrain not only of Soviet bloc states and China but also of many Western governments—particularly social democratic governments, such as those in Scandinavia.

In short, public opinion hostile to colonialism was by 1955 becoming embedded not only within many countries and colonies but also in the international community at large. This situation was in sharp contrast to that of 1935, when decolonization was still inconceivable—except for a tiny cohort of farsighted and determined non-Western nationalists and their Western acolytes. A 1937 report of the Royal Institute of International Affairs reflected public opinion of the day: "Decolonization proceeds to the goal of independence only in countries which are economically and politically advanced. Over the whole of tropical Africa and the greater part of the Pacific areas this prerequisite has not been attained, and direct advance on Western democratic lines is not feasible."[33] This proposition was so self-evident that the authors felt no need to give any further explanation.

The anticolonial ideology underlying this remarkable shift in public opinion flows from the heart of the Western political tradition, which extols democracy and equality and condemns unrepresentative or discriminatory governance. Although these ideas have been circulating in the West for at least two centuries, they have been institutionalized in most Western countries for a shorter period. The democratic franchise was gradually extended to adult populations over the past century and longer, but women and racial minorities were included only at the final stages in the present century. The democratic franchise initially and for a long time postulated specific qualifications and competence on the part of the voter, ownership of property and education being two common conditions. But these prerequisites were progressively eliminated as workingmen and then women gained the vote—the latter only after World War 1 in most countries. Race was the last restriction on democratic citizenship to be abolished: in the United States racial discrimination became unconstitutional only in the 1950s. The right to vote had become universal and unconditional for all adult citizens of democratic states. A parallel process of democratization focusing on the universal and virtually unconditional right of self-determination occurred in international relations. Just as women and nonwhites could

[33] *The Colonial Problem: A Report by a Study Group of Members of the Royal Institute of International Affairs* (Oxford: Oxford University Press, 1937), p. 255.

ground their demands for the franchise on claims to equal rights and nondiscrimination, non-Western politicians could ground their demands for independence on claims to equality and self-determination.

However, substantial voting restrictions (including property and educational qualifications) were retained in British and French colonies (and also South Africa) long after they had been abandoned in Britain and France. There were two main reasons for this failure to abandon them. The first was a belief on the part of colonial authorities (probably genuinely held by most of them) that the far lower levels of socioeconomic development in the colonies made them necessary. Otherwise self-government simply would not be workable. The second was their belief that race (and in some cases ethnicity) was an accurate predictor of democratic competence—whites being competent and nonwhites being incompetent. (The same belief about women had delayed their acquisition of the franchise in Western democracies.) In most colonies it was easy to equate nonwhites with political incompetence because these populations consisted overwhelmingly of rural folk who had little, if any, exposure to modern conditions.

These firmly held beliefs delayed the institution of democracy in most colonies until well after World War II. Even at that time it was still possible for a British Labour party deputy leader—Herbert Morrison—to declare publicly that transferring colonial governments to Africans before they were ready to take over would be "like giving a child of ten a latch-key, a bank account and a shot-gun."[34] Before the war prevailing public opinion within Western states—including democratic states—did not condemn racial discrimination in domestic social and political life. Nor did it question the ideas and institutions of colonialism. In the minds of most Europeans, equality and democracy could not yet be extended successfully to non-Europeans. In other words, these ideas were not yet considered to be universal human rights divorced from any particular civilization or culture. Indeed, for a century or more race had been widely employed as a concept to explain the scientific and technological achievements of Europeans as compared to non-Europeans and to justify not only racial discrimination within Western states but also Western domination of non-Western peoples.[35] Racial distinctions thus served as a brake on the extension of democratic rights to people of non-European descent within Western countries as well as in Western colonies.

[34] Quoted in Colin Cross, *The Fall of the British Empire, 1918–1968* (London: Macmillan, 1968), p. 262.

[35] See R. J. Vincent, "Racial Equality," in Bull and Watson, *Expansion of International Society*, pp. 239–54.

But as a criterion for determining full citizenship within states and full membership in the community of states race had become discredited by the middle of the present century. The military defeat of fascism and the discoveries of concentration camps and other massive violations of human rights by Nazi Germany did much to discredit laws and policies of racial discrimination in the West.[36] Britain and France could not participate in the Nuremberg tribunal and sign the Universal Declaration of Human Rights (1948) and still continue to draw a fundamental racial distinction between themselves and their colonial subjects in Asia and Africa without appearing to be not only inconsistent but hypocritical. North American domestic laws and policies of racial discrimination were similarly vulnerable. The government of Canada extended the democratic franchise to non-European immigrants (mainly Chinese) about the same time it signed the Universal Declaration of Human Rights.

There is a definite parallel between the extension of domestic citizenship across racial lines in Western countries and the extension of membership in the society of states to non-Western countries or peoples. During the identical period when legalized racial discrimination was being abolished in the United States—between the Supreme Court ruling against racism in *Brown* v. *Board of Education* (1954) and the passing of the Civil Rights Act (1964)—rapid steps toward the abolition of European colonialism were being taken in international relations. This is no mere coincidence. Third World intellectuals and politicians who were campaigning for decolonization were fully aware of these developments, and some of them were in direct contact with Western intellectuals and politicians (white and nonwhite) who were campaigning for racial equality within Western democracies. In Britain, for example, the Fabian Society and the Labour party as well as some of the universities, most notably the London School of Economics and Political Science, were meeting places for such people. There were similar meeting places in Paris, Amsterdam, New York, and other Western cities.

Both the civil rights movement and the decolonization movement are rooted in the same core values of Western political culture—equality in particular—and both disclose a common normative process concerning valid and invalid grounds for drawing social distinctions between individuals and groups. Henceforth race or ethnicity or culture or civilization cannot be used to restrict either citizenship in democracies or membership in the international community. These movements also

---

[36] See Philip Sieghart, *The Lawful Rights of Mankind* (Oxford: Oxford University Press, 1986).

exhibit a similar historical process of consummation or completion. Just as the franchise, once it is partially instituted, can and will be claimed until it is universally provided, self-determination, once it is conceived to be a human right and not something restricted to particular peoples, will be demanded until it is globally installed. There is also an irreversibility about these political norms: once universal suffrage is instituted within a state or self-determination within a state system, there is no going back.

Furthermore, once such ideas as democracy and self-determination are put into political play in a world in which democratic states are prominent players, it is extremely difficult for such states to deny or even ignore them. If the leading colonial powers had been authoritarian states and not democracies, the story might have been very different and colonialism would perhaps still be widespread. As we have noted, the final colonial or quasi-colonial systems to be dismantled were those of authoritarian powers: the Portuguese African empire, Ian Smith's Rhodesia, apartheid South Africa, and, more recently, the Soviet Union. If the Soviet Union had been a democracy, it probably would have had to decolonize the non-European parts of its land empire about the same time that the Western democratic colonial powers decolonized. Almost as soon as Russia declared itself a democracy in 1990–1991 it divested itself of these (and other) territories.

Anticolonialism was also expressed through international organizations established at the end of World War II—the U.N.—or expanded and liberalized afterward—the (British) Commonwealth. Owing to its more restrictive membership and Eurocentric outlook, neither the League of Nations nor the prewar British Dominions Office provided that opportunity. Latin American states took the lead at an early date in making the voice of the Third World heard in the General Assembly. The newer states of the Commonwealth, particularly India, Pakistan, and Sri Lanka, which became independent shortly after the war, added their voices both at the U.N. and at meetings of the Commonwealth. The voice of the Third World was officially expressed by resolutions of the General Assembly, statements of the International Labor Organization and UNESCO, communiqués of Commonwealth conferences, and pronouncements of various other bodies that began to express the non-Western view on world politics. As more and more colonies became independent, their voices were added to the growing anticolonial blocs in such international organizations.

The new states also formed organizations of their own, among them the nonaligned movement, which took initial shape at a conference in Bandung (1955); the U.N. Conference on Trade and Development (1962), which was dominated by the "Group of 77" developing countries; the Organization of African Unity, which was founded in 1963; and many other international bodies one could mention.[37] The society of states centered on the U.N. eventually came to be more elaborate, extensive, organized, and active by far than that associated with the League of Nations or any previous international organization.[38] A significant part of the reason was decolonization: the new states depended on international organization for their survival and welfare far more than most other states.

In short, after World War II institutional bodies, both domestic and international, were available or could be created in which anticolonial ideas and arguments could be injected without much difficulty. Those ideas proved to be contagious. Anyone who tried to justify opposition to them appeared to be denying the core values of Western civilization. Few Western governments, parties, or politicians were prepared to do that. As an indication of the preemptive character of anticolonial ideas, colonial institutions and policies are now not only untenable but even unthinkable. Nowadays it would be about as hard for an independent country to become a colony—even if the people voted to do so—as it would be for citizens of a democracy to sell themselves into slavery. Once fundamental rights are institutionalized, it is extremely difficult to withdraw them or even renounce them. Political and social ideas that take root in a society have a way of foreclosing on the past.

[37] See Robert A. Mortimer, *The Third World Coalition in International Politics* (Boulder, Colo.: Westview, 1984).
[38] See Evan Luard, *International Agencies* (London: Macmillan, 1977).

CHAPTER SIX

The Power of Principled Ideas:
Human Rights Policies in the
United States and Western Europe

KATHRYN SIKKINK

The story of how human rights became an integral and legitimate part of foreign policy and international relations illuminates the power of principled ideas to shape policy. Human rights ideas entered foreign policy debates in the United States and Europe at the same time—in the period immediately after World War II. Nevertheless, the European and American approaches to human rights policy differ considerably in the timing of policy selection, the targets of human rights pressures, and instruments or channels used to implement policy.

In Europe, international human rights policies have been present constantly since World War II, gradually increasing in comprehensiveness throughout the period. In the United States, after a flurry of activity around the drafting of the Universal Declaration and the covenants, human rights policies virtually disappeared for twenty years, only to resurface in the early 1970s. The focuses of human rights activities have also differed: European policies have focused primarily

I acknowledge the very helpful comments of Judith Goldstein and Robert Keohane on earlier versions of this paper, and the suggestions of other participants in the SSRC workshop on Ideas and Politics. An earlier version was also presented to the Program on International Politics, Economics, and Security (PIPES) at the University of Chicago, where the lively discussion it provoked further stimulated the redrafting of sections of the work. The detailed comments of one anonymous reviewer were extremely useful in the final revision.

on the European regional system, U.S. policies on Second and Third World countries. The Europeans are more likely to pursue legal, multilateral human rights policies (either through European institutions or through the United Nations) and to engage in quiet diplomacy, whereas after 1976 the United States was more likely to pursue bilateral political human rights policies and to combine quiet and public diplomacy. There are also important differences among the policies of European countries, ranging from the more activist Dutch foreign policy to the limited human rights initiatives of the British, but the differences between the United States and Europe are the most striking.

How does one explain the emergence of human rights as an international issue area in the years after World War II and the later incorporation of human rights as an important aspect for bilateral foreign policy in both Europe and the United States? And why were human rights policies pursued in such different ways in Europe and in the United States?

One cannot understand the emergence and adoption of human rights policies after the close of World War II without taking into account the unmediated role of ideas. In Europe ideas had a direct impact on policy, leading to the emergence of the European human rights regime in the postwar period, but in the United States, the impact of human rights ideas was delayed by the Cold War. It was not until the convergence of détente, public disillusionment with Vietnam, and the initial successes of the civil rights movement that human rights ideas led to changes in American foreign policy in the mid-1970s. Human rights policies survived the opposition of key figures in the Reagan administration because human rights ideas had become institutionalized in the foreign policy apparatus.

The emergence of human rights policy is not a simple victory of ideas over interests. Rather, it demonstrates the power of ideas to reshape understandings of national interest. The adoption of human rights policies represented not the neglect of national interests but a fundamental shift in the perception of long-term national interests. Human rights policies emerged because policy makers began to question the principled idea that a country's internal human rights practices are not a legitimate topic of foreign policy and the causal assumption that national interests are furthered by support of repressive regimes that violate the human rights of their citizens. Nongovernmental organizations, too, were influential in introducing human rights ideas and reinforcing human rights policies. By the 1980s, these groups had become so well organized and integrated with like-minded organizations in other countries that one can speak meaningfully of a transnational human rights movement. This movement served as a key carrier of human rights ideas and a lobby for human rights policies.

BELIEFS AND HUMAN RIGHTS POLICIES

Human rights ideas involve the interaction of all three types of beliefs that Goldstein and Keohane have summarized in Chapter 1: ideas that define concepts of possibility, stipulate principles, and specify causal relationships. At its most general level, the debate over human rights forms part of a more fundamental debate over the changing nature of sovereignty, since the doctrine of internationally protected human rights offers one of the most powerful critiques of sovereignty as the concept is currently understood, and the practices of human rights law offer concrete examples of shifting understandings of the limits of sovereignty.

The doctrine of state sovereignty implies a double claim of autonomy in foreign affairs and exclusive competence in internal affairs. Under this second claim, the state asserts the exclusive competence to make and enforce laws within its domestic jurisdiction. A citizen's claim against his or her government for violation of internationally recognized human rights clearly offers a direct challenge to the state's prerogatives under the doctrine of internal sovereignty.[1] At their most comprehensive, human rights treaties impose obligations on states in respect to their treatment of their nationals and provide individuals with limited access to international institutions to lodge complaints against their own state or against another state.[2] These treaties and practices are beginning to undermine the standard perceptions of sovereignty, especially in Europe.[3]

Most of the human rights beliefs considered here, however, are principled and causal. Disagreements exist as to whether human rights are a legitimate aim of foreign policy (principled beliefs) and as to what

[1] Nancy Newcomb Haanstad, "Compulsory Jurisdiction over Human Rights and Domestic Jurisdiction," Ph.D. diss., University of Utah, 1984, p. iv.

[2] The main legal instruments providing individuals access to international institutions where they can lodge complaints are the optional protocol to the Covenant on Civil and Political Rights and the American Convention on Human Rights, which automatically grants the right to petition the Inter-American Commission on Human Rights. All of the states in the European system have separately accepted the right of individual petition to the European Human Rights Commission.

[3] In Europe, the real undermining of sovereignty comes from the regional human rights institutions. See Rosalyn Higgins, "The European Convention on Human Rights," in *Human Rights in International Law: Legal and Policy Issues,* ed. Theodor Meron (Oxford: Clarendon, 1984), p. 538.

kinds of foreign policies are most effective in promoting human rights (causal beliefs). Even policy makers and advocates who share principled beliefs about human rights and foreign policy often differ as to causal beliefs about what kinds of policies can most effectively address abuses of human rights.

Human rights ideas also address larger causal arguments about national interest. In the process of foreign policy making, there is considerable uncertainty not only about what constitutes the national interest but also about how it can be promoted. Even if we can agree that it is the interests of the United States to promote stable regimes in the Third World, for example, it is far from clear what leads to stability. During the Cold War, U.S. policy makers believed they were promoting the national interest by supporting anticommunist regimes, regardless of their internal human rights practices. By the mid-1970s, people began to question the causal assumption that support for repressive anticommunist regimes led to stability. An important group of political entrepreneurs argued that the best way to promote stability was to defend human rights and democracy. While some policy makers advocated human rights policy solely from a principled stance, arguing that it was wrong or immoral to support repressive regimes, most mingled principled and causal reasoning in their justification of the human rights policy, arguing that it was both immoral and counterproductive for long-term U.S. interests to support regimes that violated human rights.

A TYPOLOGY OF HUMAN RIGHTS POLICIES

Two related but analytically separate issues form part of a comprehensive human rights policy. The first is willingness to surrender a degree of sovereignty and submit internal human rights practices to some international review. This is the essence of the debate over ratification of a number of human rights treaties, since they involve not only the international codification of norms but also specific mechanisms for the international supervision of domestic practices. Beliefs regarding the nature of sovereignty most actively come into play in this aspect of human rights policy. I call this a multilateral human rights policy because it allows for multilateral supervision of internal practices. To be categorized as having a multilateral human rights policy, countries must have either ratified the optional protocol to the Covenant on Civil and Political Rights or accepted compulsory jurisdiction of the relevant regional human rights court. These criteria are important because they give teeth to a supranational institution to oversee internal practices.

The second part of a comprehensive human rights policy involves the projection of human rights values internationally through an external human rights policy. An external policy exists when explicit human rights legislation or executive policy regulates aspects of foreign policy making so that human rights are incorporated in the foreign policy calculus. This is not to say that human rights issues are taken into account in all bilateral foreign policy decisions. Human rights policy is frequently criticized for being applied selectively or inconsistently. Some critics contend that a human rights policy does not exist unless human rights considerations are given priority in all cases. This is an unreasonably stringent criterion by which to judge any foreign policy. All foreign policy decisions involve the balancing of a variety of considerations. No single consideration, even a geostrategic one, always wins out. For this reason, I use a more limited criterion for defining the emergence of an external human rights policy. A country can be said to have an external human rights policy when it has explicit mechanisms for integrating human rights concerns into foreign policy, and when those mechanisms have modified foreign policy decisions in some cases. Before 1973, for example, human rights were rarely explicitly considered in the United States' foreign policy calculus; after 1976, legislation and executive policy led to the explicit inclusion of human rights criteria in foreign policy decision making.

We can summarize these aspects of human rights policy by arraying the United States and the countries of Western Europe in accordance with the four possible types of human rights policy, as in Figure 1.

Only countries in box I, which have both an external and a multilateral human rights policy, will be considered as having a comprehensive human rights policy. At the other extreme, any country in box IV would have no human rights policy. In boxes II and III are countries with partial human rights policies. The United States is the only country to have an external policy but no multilateral policy. The many European countries in box III have multilateral policies but no explicit external human rights policy.

The historical pattern behind this situation shows a clear progressive trend toward the adoption of human rights policies. With the temporary exception of Greece, all the movement has been away from box IV. Before World War II, no country had a human rights policy; by 1988, the United States and all the countries of Western Europe had some kind of human rights policy.[4] This movement, however, occurred

---

[4] Although the United States has ratified the Covenant on Civil and Political Rights, it is unlikely to move into box I in the near future. Before it could do so it would have to ratify the optional protocol of that covenant or the American Convention on Human Rights and to accept the jurisdiction of the Inter-American Court on Human Rights.

Multilateral human rights policy[a]
(partial surrender of sovereignty)

		Yes	No
		I	II
External human rights policy[b]	Yes	Norway Denmark Netherlands Sweden	U.S.A.
		III	IV
	No	U.K. Ireland Portugal Belgium Spain Austria Italy Switzerland Iceland Greece Luxembourg Finland Germany Malta France Liechtenstein	

Figure 1. Human rights policies of the United States and Western European states

Source: Council of Europe, *Conventions and Agreements: Chart of Signatures and Ratifications of European Treaties: Updating as at 2 March* 1992 (Strasbourg, 1992); United Nations, *Human Rights: Status of International Instruments as at 31 March 1991* (Geneva, July 1991).

[a]To be classified as having a multilateral human rights policy a country must have either ratified the optional protocol to the Covenant on Political and Civil Rights or accepted compulsory jurisdiction of a regional human rights court. All Western European countries have accepted the compulsory jurisdiction of the European Court of Human Rights. The United States, however, has ratified neither the optional protocol nor the American Convention on Human Rights and has not recognized the jurisdiction of the Inter-American Court in accordance with art. 62 of the convention.

[b]To be categorized as having an external human rights policy, a country either must have an explicit bilateral human rights policy through which human rights concerns are incorporated in foreign policy or must have used multilateral channels regularly to file complaints or attempt to change the human rights practices of other states.

gradually. By 1960, a few European countries had migrated from box IV into box III as they accepted the compulsory jurisdiction of the European Court of Human Rights. But it was not until the late 1960s that the first move was made into boxes I and II.

It is particularly interesting that the United States is alone in having an external policy but not a multilateral policy. One could explain the failure to surrender sovereignty as the typical behavior of a hegemon, but why did the United States move toward an externally oriented human rights policy after 1973 when it had none before? And why has it begun to move in the direction of a multilateral policy in the

1990s? The hegemonic explanation does not explain these shifts; to understand them we need to look at the convergence of factors that blocked human rights ideas in the United States from 1953 to 1973, especially the attitudes of cold warriors, segregationists, and advocates of states' rights.

The wide disparities in the timing and sequencing of the adoption of external and multilateral human rights policies suggest that the emergence of these two aspects of human rights policies may have different explanations. While some of these differences are structural, institutional and procedural factors also affect movement within Figure 1. The adoption of an external human rights policy in the United States, for example, requires majority votes in favor of such legislation in both houses of Congress, whereas the adoption of a multilateral policy, because it is achieved by ratification of treaties, requires a two-thirds vote in the Senate. Thus the procedural barrier to the adoption of an internal policy is higher in the United States than in some European parliamentary systems.

THE TIMING OF POLICY SELECTION

Although human rights concerns were not incorporated in the bilateral policies until the 1970s, human rights first emerged as part of the discourse in U.S. and European foreign policy in the aftermath of World War II. The placing of human rights issues on the international agenda is often seen as a direct result of the shocking atrocities of the Nazis during the war.[5] Many Europeans believed that human rights abuses were linked to the causes of the war, and thus thought that protection of human rights could also increase security. The emergence of human rights concerns in many countries at that time reinforces the argument that the experiences of the war served as a powerful impetus for a change in policy. But it does not explain why human rights issues stayed on the agenda in Europe from 1948 until the present but dropped off the U.S. agenda from 1953 to 1973. In Europe, the experience of the Holocaust and the war led to a change in ideas that had a direct impact on policy. In the United States, the initial postwar ideas about the connection between respect for human rights

[5] See, e.g., Jack Donnelly, *Universal Human Rights in Theory and Practice* (Ithaca: Cornell University Press, 1989), pp. 210–11; James Avery Joyce, *The New Politics of Human Rights* (London: Macmillan, 1978), p. 45; Moses Moskowitz, *International Concern with Human Rights* (Dobbs Ferry, N.Y.: Oceana, 1974), p. 8.

and world peace were superseded by the combined ideological forces of anticommunism, isolationism, and segregationist sentiment.

International Precursors to Human Rights Policies before World War II

Human rights were not considered an appropriate topic for international scrutiny and rule formation before World War II. The international precursors to the human rights issue included the movement for respect for human rights during armed conflict, the campaign for the abolition of the slave trade and slavery, the work within the League of Nations for the protection of minority rights, and the early work on the rights of workers in the International Labor Organization. But each of these limited issue areas fell far short of a full-fledged demand for attention to human rights as a legitimate topic for international action.

In two instances nongovernmental organizations played a central role in bringing the issue of human rights to public attention and promoting international action. The Red Cross movement helped bring about the Geneva Convention, which codified humanitarian law, or the rules governing human rights in armed conflict.[6] The effort to protect the rights of people held in slavery, to end the slave trade, and to abolish slavery was led by an amalgam of nongovernmental organizations, the Anti-Slavery League, which helped persuade states to adopt the 1926 convention outlawing slavery.[7]

Period 1: 1941–1953

A qualitative and quantitative change occurred in the treatment of human rights issues in the period after World War II. The concern with human rights as part of the postwar order was articulated by Franklin Roosevelt in his "Four Freedoms" speech in 1941 and was later reaffirmed by Roosevelt and Winston Churchill in the Atlantic Charter.[8] But it was not until the San Francisco conference at which the U.N. Charter was drafted that human rights was first addressed as an area for necessary and legitimate international action.

[6] For a discussion of the role of the Red Cross in international politics, see David P. Forsythe, *Humanitarian Politics: The International Committee of the Red Cross* (Baltimore: Johns Hopkins University Press, 1977), and J. D. Armstrong, "The International Committee of the Red Cross and Political Prisoners," *International Organization* 39 (Autumn 1985).

[7] David P. Forsythe, *Human Rights and World Politics* (Lincoln: University of Nebraska Press, 1983) pp. 7–9.

[8] M. Glen Johnson, "The Contributions of Eleanor and Franklin Roosevelt to the Development of International Protection for Human Rights," *Human Rights Quarterly* 9 (1987): 21–23.

Nongovernmental organizations (NGOs), invited by the U.S. government as consultants to the U.S. delegation in San Francisco, played a pivotal role in securing the inclusion of human rights language in the U.N. Charter, and that language served as the basis for all further U.N. efforts in the human rights area. The initial U.S. drafts of the charter contained no reference to human rights, and the proposals that emerged from the Big Four meeting at Dumbarton Oaks to prepare for the San Francisco conference contained only one such reference.[9] NGOs representing churches, trade unions, ethnic groups, and peace movements, aided by the delegations of some of the smaller countries, "conducted a lobby in favor of human rights for which there is no parallel in the history of international relations," writes John Humphrey, "and which was largely responsible for the human rights provisions of the Charter."[10] The United States' record on human rights at San Francisco was mixed. On the one hand, the United States supported the effort to include human rights language in the charter, but on the other hand, it resisted attempts to include references to economic human rights, and expressed concern over possible U.N. intrusion into domestic jurisdiction. The two other key government actors, the USSR and the United Kingdom, expressed the same concern about domestic jurisdiction.[11] Although the human rights provisions had no teeth at this early stage, states were very wary of the sovereignty implications of the human rights issue.

As a result, the charter's mandate on human rights is less firm than many NGOs desired, calling only for promoting and encouraging respect for human rights, rather than protecting or safeguarding them. Nevertheless, by assigning institutional responsibility for human rights to the General Assembly and the Economic and Social Council and by specifically recommending the creation of a human rights commission, the charter paved the way for all of the later human rights actions within the U.N. system.

Although human rights was placed on the agenda, it still lacked an institutional embodiment. The early period was devoted to drafting rules and building institutions at both the international and domestic levels in the human rights area.[12] The United States was actively in-

---

[9] Jacob Robinson, *Human Rights and Fundamental Freedoms in the Charter of the United Nations* (New York: Institute of Jewish Affairs, 1946), p. 17.

[10] John P. Humphrey, *Human Rights and the United Nations: A Great Adventure* (Dobbs Ferry, N.Y.: Transnational Publishers, 1984), p. 13. Also see Department of State, *The United Nations Conference on International Organization, San Francisco, California, April 25 to June 26, 1945: Selected Documents* (Washington: U.S. Government Printing Office, 1946).

[11] Johnson, "Contributions of Eleanor and Franklin Roosevelt," p. 24.

[12] The Universal Declaration of Human Rights was adopted in 1948. The Covenant on Civil and Political Rights and the Covenant on Economic, Social, and Cultural Rights

volved in the early drafting of the international rules, initially under the leadership of Eleanor Roosevelt. Although during this period, according to Glenn Mower, U.S. policy combined "a commitment to human rights as a worthy end in itself with a judicious use of human rights as a cold war political weapon,"[13] it represented a high point in U.S. participation in multilateral human rights efforts.

During this early period, the paths of U.S. policy and the policies of European states began to diverge in ways that would become even more pronounced after 1953. From 1948 to 1953 the United States continued to engage in negotiations over the content of U.N. human rights documents, but made no effort to draft regional human rights treaties or to submit its internal human rights practices to any form of international or regional scrutiny. The Europeans, in contrast, moved quickly and consciously to build a regional human rights regime.

Human rights issues were present in the earliest discussions of postwar European order. Nongovernmental organizations promoting European unity focused on human rights issues.[14] Their call for a European human rights charter and court was later taken up by the newly created Council of Europe and incorporated into the European Convention on Human Rights. The statute of the Council of Europe does nto merely affirm its commitment to human rights but makes respect for human rights and the rule of law conditions of membership in the council, and any violation of these conditions may result in suspension from the organization.

In the fifteen months between August 1949 and November 1950, the European Convention for the Protection of Human Rights and Fundamental Freedoms was drafted and opened for signature and ratification. The European Convention and its protocols are limited basically to civil and political rights.[15] The regional human rights re-

---

were substantially drafted by 1954 but not approved by the General Assembly and opened for signature until 1966. The two covenants attained the number of adherents required for entry into legal force in 1976. With the entry into force of the Covenant on Civil and Political Rights came the formation of the Human Rights Committee.

[13] A. Glenn Mower, *The United States, the United Nations, and Human Rights* (Westport, Conn.: Greenwood, 1979), p. 36.

[14] Several nongovernmental groups organized to promote European unification after the war united in 1948 to form the International Committee of the Movements for European Unity. The resolutions and the "Message to Europeans" issued by a congress of the International Committee in 1948 "were bursting with the two concepts of democracy and human rights": Ralph Beddard, *Human Rights and Europe* (London: Sweet & Maxwell, 1980), p. 17.

[15] Economic and social issues are discussed in the European Social Charter, which frames these questions differently from the way "rights" are treated in the European Convention and sets up very different machinery for implementation. As a small number of European countries adopted external human rights policies in the 1970s, many economic and social issues such as the right to development were incorporated explicitly

gime, which applies only to the European signatories, granted very strong monitoring powers to the European Human Rights Commission and authoritative decision-making powers to the European Court of Human Rights. By September 1953 the convention entered into force. The defining elements of a "surrender of sovereignty" and of a multilateral human rights policy, however, had to be accepted separately as optional provisions of the European Convention, and that process took longer than ratification of the convention.

Period 2: 1953–1973

Progress on the construction of the European human rights regime continued unabated through 1973. The two crucial elements of the internal human rights policy—the right of individual petition, which allowed individuals to file complaints about violations of the European Convention, and compulsory submission to the jurisdiction of the European Court of Human Rights—were accepted by virtually all the states of Europe during this period. By 1955, the commission gained the competence to hear individual petitions against the six states that had accepted these rights (Sweden, Ireland, Denmark, Iceland, West Germany, and Belgium). By 1958, eight states had agreed to the jurisdiction of the European Court on Human Rights, and the court was established in 1959. Also during this period, a number of European states ratified the U.N. human rights covenants and the optional protocol of the Covenant on Civil and Political Rights, which permits international supervision of domestic human rights practices.

Another path-breaking development came when a few progressive European states moved toward adoption of external human rights policies. A crucial turning point came after the coup d'état in Greece in 1967, when four parties to the European Human Rights Convention— Norway, the Netherlands, Denmark, and Sweden—filed a joint case against the military government of Greece for violation of the convention's human rights provisions. Until then, interstate human rights petitions in Europe had taken the form of a protest by one country against the treatment of its citizens by another country. The Greek case broke new ground because the Scandinavians and the Dutch were using the regional standards established in the European Convention to protest violations of Greek citizens' human rights by the Greek government.

After a thorough on-site investigation, the commission concluded that the Greek military government had indeed violated the conven-

into external policies, but this is a much more recent phenomenon and does not apply to internal human rights policies.

tion's articles; in particular, it held that the Athens Security Police had engaged in torture and ill treatment of persons arrested for political reasons. The European Commission's report led Greece to withdraw from the Council of Europe to avoid expulsion. After democratic government and respect for human rights were restored in 1974, Greece was invited to resume its membership in the Council of Europe.[16] The Greek case demonstrates the European preference for multilateral and legal forms of action even in the implementation of external human rights policies. This gradual but steady progress in the development of the European human rights regime with the partial surrender of sovereignty by European states to the regional and international human rights institutions contrasts dramatically with developments in the United States.

Human rights essentially dropped out of the United States' foreign policy agenda from 1953 to 1973.[17] David Forsythe argues that during the Cold War, the human rights issue was "collapsed into its anticommunist policy."[18] But issues other than anticommunism were also at work to block the adoption of a human rights policy. In 1951 Senator John Bricker of Ohio sponsored a constitutional amendment to protect states' rights against treaties authorizing "any international organization to supervise, control, or adjudicate rights of citizens of the United States."[19] The coalition supporting the Bricker amendment, comprising almost the necessary two-thirds of the senators, included cold warriors, conservatives concerned about states' rights, traditional isolationists, and segregationists who feared that the ratification of U.N. human rights treaties would give the federal government the authority to impose civil rights standards on the states. The Eisenhower administration, worried that the Bricker amendment would tie the hands of the executive branch in the making of foreign policy, successfully blocked the passage of the amendment. But the administration sacrificed the U.N. human rights covenants as the price for defeat of the Bricker amendment; Secretary of State John Foster Dulles formally

[16] A. H. Robertson, *Human Rights in Europe*, 2d ed. (Manchester: Manchester University Press, 1977), pp. 178, 255.

[17] Occasional references to human rights appear in the *Congressional Record* during this period, but the overall tendency was indifference or opposition to U.N. human rights efforts. In 1967 Senator William Proxmire, discouraged by the Senate's refusal to ratify the Genocide Convention, vowed to speak daily about human rights until the convention was ratified, but his comments rarely elicited debate or support.

[18] Forsythe, *Human Rights and World Politics*, p. 104.

[19] Although the amendment was framed in general terms, its supporters were motivated primarily by their opposition to the human rights treaties. See Natalie Hevener Kaufman and David Whiteman, "Opposition to Human Rights Treaties in the United States Senate: The Legacy of the Bricker Amendment," *Human Rights Quarterly* 10 (1988): 309–37.

declared to the Senate in 1953 that the United States would not become a party to the U.N. human rights covenants.

Senator Bricker had emphasized that the purpose of his amendment was "to bury the so-called covenant on human rights so deep that no one holding high public office will ever dare to attempt its resurrection."[20] Bricker used the platform of opposition to the covenants as glue to construct the coalition that supported his amendment. In the face of opposition by the executive, this coalition was unable to master the two-thirds majority needed to pass the amendment, but it managed to block attempts to ratify the human rights covenants for almost forty years.

Period 3: 1973–1984

Human rights reemerged as a significant item in U.S. foreign policy in 1973. The United States adopted an external human rights policy in the 1970s but made virtually no progress toward a multilateral human rights policy until the 1990s.

In the seven years from 1973 to 1980, the United States fundamentally altered its external policy by explicitly incorporating human rights criteria into the foreign policy calculus. Although human rights policy is usually associated with the Carter administration, it actually began in the Congress well before Jimmy Carter was elected. Virtually all of the essential human rights legislation was already in place when he took office.[21] Thus any inquiry into the origins of U.S. human rights policy must examine the 1973–1977 period, when the bulk of human rights legislation was enacted.

Before 1973, no legislation existed to instruct U.S. policy makers to take human rights into account in bilateral relations. Only one officer in the entire Department of State was assigned full-time responsibility for human rights. By 1977, when the Carter administration took office, an assistant secretary of state for human rights and humanitarian affairs presided over a new State Department bureau with a staff of more

---

[20] Duane Tananbaum, *The Bricker Amendment Controversy* (Ithaca: Cornell University Press, 1988), p. 25.

[21] This legislation focused on a much narrower definition of human rights than that contained in the U.N. Universal Declaration of Human Rights. The most basic piece of human rights legislation (sec. 502B of the Foreign Assistance Act of 1961, as amended) identifies violations of human rights as "torture or cruel, inhumane, or degrading treatment or punishment; prolonged detention without charges and trial, causing the disappearance of persons by the abduction and clandestine detention of those persons, and other flagrant denial of the right to life, liberty, or the security of person" (cited in *U.S. Legislation Relating Human Rights to U.S. Foreign Policy*, ed. International Human Rights Law Group, 4th ed. [Buffalo, N.Y.: William S. Hein, 1991], p. 23).

than thirty. The new bureau prepared an annual human rights report for each country that received U.S. assistance. Congress had enacted general human rights legislation governing U.S. military and economic aid and multilateral loans, and country-specific human rights provisions banning military aid to Argentina, Chile, Uruguay, and Guatemala. An important transformation had occurred in U.S. policy: human rights concerns had become embodied in the laws and the institutions responsible for U.S. foreign policy. The Carter administration strongly endorsed the human rights concerns first voiced by Congress and made human rights a central component of its foreign policy. Just as the Greek case demonstrated the possibilities of an external human rights policy in Europe, U.S. policy toward Argentina shows the extent to which human rights were incorporated into U.S. policy in a handful of cases.[22]

Early in the Carter administration, Argentina was chosen as one of three human rights target countries, along with Ethiopia and Uruguay. According to one State Department official, no human rights situation created greater concern in Washington than that of Argentina in the 1970s.[23] In early 1977 the U.S. government reduced the planned level of military aid for Argentina, citing human rights abuses. Later Congress passed a bill eliminating all military assistance to Argentina; it went into effect on September 30, 1978.[24] A number of high-level delegations met with the members of Argentina's ruling junta during this period to discuss human rights, among them a delegation led by Secretary of State Cyrus Vance. In Buenos Aires Vance presented to Argentine authorities a list of approximately 7,000 "disappeared" people in Argentina.[25] The United States voted against approximately twenty-five Argentine loan applications to the multilateral financial institutions, but none of these votes actually led to denial of a loan.

During meetings with President Jorge Videla of Argentina, both

---

[22] This section draws upon the discussion in Lisa Martin and Kathryn Sikkink, "U.S. Policy and Human Rights in Argentina and Guatemala," in *Double-Edged Diplomacy: International Bargaining and Domestic Politics*, ed. Peter Evans et al. (Berkeley: University of California Press, 1993).

[23] Patrick J. Flood, "U.S. Human Rights Initiatives Concerning Argentina," in *The Diplomacy of Human Rights*, ed. David D. Newsom (Lanham, Md.: University Press of America, 1986), p. 129.

[24] Congressional Research Service, Foreign Affairs and National Defense Division, *Human Rights and U.S. Foreign Assistance: Experiences and Issues in Policy Implementation* (1977–1978), report prepared for U.S. Senate Committee on Foreign Relations, November 1979, p. 106.

[25] In addition, in two years the U.S. embassy made more than 1,200 representations to the Argentine government on cases of human rights abuse. See Americas Watch, *With Friends Like These: The Americas Watch Report on Human Rights and U.S. Policy in Latin America* (New York: Pantheon, 1985), pp. 99–100.

President Carter and Vice President Walter Mondale asked Videla to invite the Inter-American Commission on Human Rights (IACHR) to visit Argentina as a means of improving U.S.-Argentine relations.[26] In exchange they offered to release funds to Argentina that had been blocked by the Export-Import Bank because of human rights abuses.[27] In December 1978 the Argentine government invited the IACHR to conduct an on-site investigation. In the months that followed the decision to issue the invitation, the human rights situation in Argentina improved significantly; especially noteworthy was the decline in the practice of involuntary disappearance, for which the Argentine regime had gained international notoriety.[28] The Argentine junta gave in to U.S. pressure to invite the IACHR because it believed the human rights situation had improved and the report would not be damaging. To prepare for the IACHR visit and to refute any condemnations in the final report, however, the Argentine authorities had to improve their human rights practices.[29]

This brief summary highlights the new criteria U.S. policy makers used in making aid decisions as a result of the human rights legislation of the mid-1970s. Similar pressures were used effectively in other Latin American countries—Chile (after 1976), Uruguay, Paraguay, and the Dominican Republic.[30] This simple recounting of bilateral relations, however, leaves out the very substantial behind-the-scenes role played by nongovernmental human rights organizations during this period. U.S. policy makers learned about human rights abuses in Argentina from information supplied by such groups as Amnesty International and the Washington Office on Latin America. Human rights organiza-

[26] Interview with Robert Pastor, Wianno, Mass., June 28, 1990.

[27] Interview with Walter Mondale, Minneapolis, June 20, 1989.

[28] See Asamblea Permanente por los Derechos Humanos, *Las cifras de la guerra sucia* (Buenos Aires, August 1988), pp. 26–31.

[29] Interviews with officials of Argentina's military government, Buenos Aires, July 1990.

[30] Some scholars claim that Carter's human rights policy was not effective. See, e.g., Michael Stohl, David Carleton, and Steven E. Johnson, "Human Rights and U.S. Foreign Assistance from Nixon to Carter," *Journal of Peace Research* 21, no. 2 (1984), and Carlos Escudé, "Argentina: The Costs of Contradiction," in *Exporting Democracy: The United States and Latin America: Case Studies,* ed. Abraham F. Lowenthal (Baltimore: Johns Hopkins University Press, 1991). Most analyses of human rights policies fail to explore the precise linkages between the implementation of policy and the changing human rights practices in specific countries. Such a procedure requires careful comparative research and a longer time frame than most studies employ. For a study that takes this approach and concludes that the policy was effective in the cases in which it was implemented most forcefully, see Kathryn Sikkink, "The Effectiveness of U.S. Human Rights Policy: Argentina, Guatemala, and Uruguay," paper prepared for the International Political Science Association, Buenos Aires, July 21–25, 1991.

tions abroad and in Argentina collaborated with the IACHR to provide crucial information for its report.[31]

In Europe during the same period, important developments continued in both the multilateral and external aspects of human rights policies. The European Human Rights Commission and the court became very active in response to individual petitions in refining the human rights provisions of the convention. Thousands of complaints are submitted to the commission each year. Although only a small percentage of these complaints are found admissible, the actions of the commission and the court have frequently led member states to change their policies and to review existing legislation. Changes in Britain's prison policies, mental health law, and immigration practices, for example, can be traced in part to commission and court responses to a large number of complaints. Virtually all of the court's decisions have gone against the United Kingdom.[32]

A small number of European countries also developed more explicit external human rights policies during this period. The Norwegians and the Dutch have taken the lead by developing specific memoranda and criteria designed to incorporate human rights into foreign policy decision making; they have often acted together with the other Scandinavian countries, whose outlook is similar.[33] The first steps toward institutionalization of external human rights policies in Europe came between 1977 and 1979, several years after similar policies had been adopted by the U.S. Congress. Although the Europeans led the way in developing internal human rights policies, the United States was the first to legislate and institutionalize an external human rights policy.

Period 4: 1980–1992

When Ronald Reagan assumed the presidency in 1981, human rights activists predicted that U.S. human rights policy would disappear. But

---

[31] Emilio Mignone, "Derechos humanos y transición democrática en la sociedad argentina," paper presented at the seminar "Transition to Democracy in Argentina," Yale University, March 4–8, 1990, p. 117.

[32] Henry G. Schermers, "Human Rights in Europe," *Legal Studies* 6 (July 1986): 175–78. Also see Clive Symmons, "The Effect of the European Convention on Human Rights on the Preparation and Amendment of Legislation, Delegated Legislation, and Administrative Rules in the United Kingdom," in *The Effect on English Domestic Law of Membership of the European Communities and of Ratification of the European Convention on Human Rights*, ed. M. P. Furmston et al. (The Hague: Martinus Nijhoff, 1983), pp. 387–428.

[33] See Ministry of Foreign Affairs of the Kingdom of the Netherlands, *Human Rights and Foreign Policy*, memorandum presented to the Lower House of the States General of the Kingdom of the Netherlands on May 3, 1979, by the Minister for Foreign Affairs and the Minister for Development Cooperation; and "Norwegian Development Aid and International Human Rights," in *Human Rights in Developing Countries, 1986: A Yearbook*

despite many successful efforts to undermine and roll back these laws and institutions, U.S. human rights policy survived and continued (albeit in a much more restricted form) during the Reagan and Bush administrations. The public human rights diplomacy characteristic of the Carter administration disappeared, but human rights continued to be an issue in bilateral relations.

When the Senate failed to confirm Reagan's nominee for assistant secretary for human rights, who was on record as expressing disapproval of the human rights policy, it sent a message to the new administration that it would not tolerate the overt dismantling of that policy. The Reagan administration next attempted what amounted to a covert dismantling of the human rights policy. The administration accepted and endorsed the policy in principle while subverting its meaning in practice. This situation led to an interesting demonstration of a phenomenon that Goldstein and Keohane discuss in Chapter 1: the power of ideas to prevail even when the policy makers themselves do not believe them. The Reagan administration's policy makers did not believe in the human rights policy of Congress and the Carter administration, as they made clear by their early endorsement of Jeane Kirkpatrick's critique of Carter's policy. Within a year of taking office, however, the Reagan team changed their human rights policy. A leaked copy of the memo calling for the change indicates that they shifted their stance because they had become aware of broad support for human rights policies among members of Congress, the American public, and the Western allies.[34] Once adopted, the new policy in support of democracy demanded a minimal inner consistency. Reagan administration officials who used the human rights and democracy banner in their crusade against Nicaragua felt obliged occasionally to protect themselves against charges of bias by also criticizing human rights abuses by some right-wing regimes, such as those in Chile and Uruguay.

During this period the United States made its first tentative move in the direction of a multilateral human rights policy. In 1984, for the first time, the Senate ratified a U.N. human rights treaty: the Convention on the Prevention and Punishment of the Crime of Genocide, adopted by the General Assembly in 1948. In the early 1990s the pace of ratification speeded up dramatically. In 1991 the Senate ratified the Convention on the Abolition of Forced Labor and the Covenant against

---

on Countries Receiving Norwegian Aid, ed. Tor Skalnes and Jan Egeland (Oslo: Norwegian University Press, 1986).

[34] Tamar Jacoby, "The Reagan Turnaround on Human Rights," *Foreign Affairs* 64 (Summer 1986): 1071–72.

Torture and Other Cruel, Inhuman, or Degrading Treatment or Punishment, and in 1992 it ratified the Covenant on Civil and Political Rights. The United States is still not moving toward ratifying the optional protocol of the Covenant on Civil and Political Rights or accepting the jurisdiction of the Inter-American Court of Human Rights, so it has not moved into box 1 of Figure 1. But in spite of limiting reservations, these ratifications suggest that the United States is increasingly willing to accept some international human rights obligations.

The Carter administration had signed and submitted the Covenant on Civil and Political Rights to the Senate in 1978. When the Senate held hearings in 1979, witnesses and senators revealed many of the same attitudes that had led to the Bricker Amendment in 1953.[35] Yet by 1992 the legacy of the Bricker coalition appeared to be dying; even Senator Jesse Helms eventually voted in favor of recommending ratification of the Covenant on Civil and Political Rights.[36]

Several important changes had occurred. The most important lobby against the covenants in the 1950s, the American Bar Association, reversed its position on the treaties by the late 1970s.[37] Most important, however, were changes in international conditions. With the transformation of the former Soviet Union and Eastern Europe, U.S. officials expressed increased confidence in multilateral institutions, including the United Nations. Administration testimony on the Covenant on Civil and Political Rights stated that a "radically altered world picture" led them to change their position on ratifying the covenant. "Ratification of the covenant would have been an empty gesture 10 years ago, but now it has new meaning and effect."[38] Specifically, unless the Senate ratified the covenant, the United States could not be a member of the U.N. Human Rights Committee. The administration believed that the Human Rights Committee would become a central forum for shaping future international human rights law, and it did not want the United States to be barred from taking part in that process.

EXPLANATIONS FOR U.S. AND EUROPEAN HUMAN RIGHTS POLICIES

Though the literature on human rights and on U.S. and European human rights policies is copious, few serious attempts have been made

---

[35] Kaufman and Whitehead, "Opposition to Human Rights Treaties," pp. 330–31.

[36] U.S. Senate, Committee on Foreign Relations, *International Covenant on Civil and Political Rights: Report*, 102d Cong., 2d sess., March 24, 1992 (Washington, D.C.: U.S. Government Printing Office, 1992).

[37] Kaufman and Whitehead, "Opposition to Human Rights Treaties," p. 334.

[38] U.S. Senate, Committee on Foreign Relations, *International Covenant on Civil and Political Rights: Hearings* 102d Cong., 1st sess., November 21, 1991 (Washington, D.C.: U.S. Government Printing Office, 1992), pp. 16, 19–20.

to explain the reasons for the emergence of U.S. and European human rights policies or for their similarities and differences.[39] As in the case of the abolition of slavery, with which human rights policy has intriguing similarities, alternative interest-based arguments could be offered.[40]

The Adoption of Human Rights Policies

A realist or neorealist explanation of foreign policy has trouble accounting for the adoption and implementation of human rights policies, except by dismissing them as insignificant. Realists would suggest that human rights policies are adopted to further the economic and security interests of a country. They would expect human rights policies to be used against traditional opponents and not to be used against allies in a way that might undermine the stability of security arrangements. But the essence of a multilateral human rights policy—acceptance of compulsory submission to the court's jurisdiction and of the right of individuals to petition regional and international organizations—involves acceptance of uncertainty about future outcomes, which does not coincide with a standard interpretation of furthering security interests. The realist would predict that the West would use human rights policy most forcefully against communist countries. Yet the most forceful implementations of human rights policies were directed against authoritarian capitalist regimes, such as those of Argentina and Uruguay in the case of the United States and those of Greece and later Turkey in the case of Europe. All of these authoritarian regimes were members of Western military alliances and were adopting economic policies in line with U.S. and European interests: policies of openness to trade and investment. In this sense, implementation of human rights policies was a matter of "getting our own house in order" rather than a simple crusade against the East.

[39] Jan Egeland, *Impotent Superpower, Potent Small State: Potentials and Limitations of Human Rights Objectives in the Foreign Policies of the United States and Norway* (Oslo: Norwegian University Press, 1988), is one of the few works that compare the human rights policies of the United States and a European country. Egeland argues that small countries can have more effective human rights policies than large countries. His definition of effectiveness, however, appears to equate it with the existence of coherent or consistent policies; see pp. 82, 177–79. He demonstrates that Norway's human rights policy is more coherent and consistent than the United States' (a result, it seems to me, more of a parliamentary system than of the size of the country) but does not demonstrate that Norway's policies led to more effective human rights practices in the target countries. The case that Egeland suggests as a failure of the Carter administration's human rights policy—Uruguay—appears as a success in a longer time frame, and the case he lists as a moderate Norwegian success—Sri Lanka—appears problematic.

[40] For a discussion of the relevance of the abolition of slavery to current debates on international relations, see James Lee Ray, "The Abolition of Slavery and the End of International War," *International Organization* 43 (Summer 1989): 405–40.

The Greek case demonstrates the conflict between a human rights policy and a more standard interpretation of security interests. In 1968, when the Council of Europe essentially forced Greece to resign its membership as a result of human rights practices of the military junta, the United States lobbied strenuously against the move, arguing that it would undermine the unity of NATO. Here we see a confrontation between the older definition of national security held by the United States, which did not adopt a human rights policy until the 1970s, and the redefined understanding of national security within the European context. Implicitly, the Europeans were more troubled about the impact of the breakdown of democracy in Greece and the resulting human rights abuses for the long-term security of Europe than they were about the immediate impact that the expulsion of Greece from the Council of Europe might have on the unity of NATO.[41]

When the United States adopted an external human rights policy in the mid-1970s, one key aspect of the policy involved denial of military and economic aid to regimes that violated the human rights of their citizens. This policy was most actively implemented toward such Latin American countries as Argentina, Chile, Uruguay, and Paraguay, and, to a lesser extent, Nicaragua and Guatemala. Realist analysis would not predict the fairly dramatic change in bilateral relations between the United States and these traditional allies. These regimes, which earlier had enjoyed close and cordial relations with the United States, were now subject to aid cutoffs and public discussions of their human rights violations in the State Department's annual country human rights reports. A realist could argue that denial of aid to relatively marginal countries does not constitute a costly policy. In the postwar period, however, the United States had invested large amounts of military and economic aid and elaborate diplomatic and sometimes covert efforts to promote and bolster the kind of anticommunist regimes that they were now attempting to discredit and isolate. The human rights policies were rarely costly in monetary terms, but they implied undermining relationships with Latin American militaries that the United States had been assiduously cultivating for two decades through its military training and aid programs. Latin American militaries increasingly saw the United States as an "unreliable" ally. Such attitudes can be costly in their effects on strategy and reputation.

---

[41] Motivations for the proposed expulsion of Greece from the Council of Europe were mixed and complex. Nevertheless, one can discern a preoccupation with preserving the credibility of the Council of Europe, with the opinion of left-of-center groups within European countries, and with the concern that "what happens in Greece can also happen elsewhere." Besides, most Europeans believed (correctly, it turned out) that Greece would not drop out of NATO if it were excluded from the Council of Europe. See *The Times*

One alternative argument, similar to the materialist explanation of the abolition of slavery, is that although the human rights policies of the United States and European countries did not directly support their economic and security interests, indirectly they helped create an ideological climate in which Western economic and security interests could flourish. These policies, by focusing on a fairly narrow set of gross violations of civil and political rights, helped legitimize and privilege these rights over the economic and social rights that are also part of the Universal Declaration. Just as the movement for the abolition of slavery has been seen as contributing to the legitimation of wage labor, thus reinforcing capitalist values,[42] human rights policy can be seen as a means of promoting the hegemony of capitalist values by emphasizing political freedoms as opposed to economic rights. By focusing on repression, U.S. human rights policy downplayed and deemphasized oppression.

This argument finds support in the fact that the United States focused on political and civil rights rather than on the wider list of rights contained in the U.N. Universal Declaration of Human Rights. The countries with comprehensive human rights policies—Denmark, the Netherlands, Norway, and Sweden—have given more emphasis to economic, social, and cultural rights. But this argument cannot explain why human rights policy emerged when it did or the differences in timing and sequencing of multilateral and external policies. East and West had differed over the priority of the various human rights since the debate over the U.N. Charter. What was it that led the United States to move from rhetorial defense of political rights in U.N. debates to advancing a major new policy of human rights?

Human rights policy was often justified as an essential arm in ideological conflict with the USSR in the Third World and Eastern Europe. Sean MacBride, the Irish minister for external affairs, said on the occasion of the signing of the European Convention on Human Rights: "The present struggle is one which is largely being fought in the minds and consciences of mankind. In this struggle, I have always felt that we lacked a clearly designed charter which set out unambiguously the rights which we democrats guarantee to our people. This convention is a step in that direction."[43] The Carter administration, calling simultaneously for détente and human rights, saw the human rights policy as

---

(London), December 1, 1969, p. 9A; December 5, 1969, p. 5A; December 10, 1969, p. 5C; December 11, 1969, p. 10A; December 13, 1969, p. 9A.

[42] See David Brion Davis, "Reflections on Abolitionism and Ideological Hegemony," *American Historical Review* 92 (October 1987): 800.

[43] Robertson, *Human Rights in Europe*, p. 5.

part of a larger ideological competition with the Soviets.[44] But to say that championship of human rights was perceived as a useful tool in ideological competition between opposing blocs is not at all to say that human rights policy was mainly an epiphenomenon of a broader political and economic struggle.

If human rights policies were the products of competition with the East, one would have expected them to be strongest at the height of the Cold War, and to have declined in importance with the collapse of communism. To the contrary, at the height of the Cold War, human rights dropped out of U.S. policy, to be replaced by an extreme anticommunism that had an entirely different logic; and human rights policies have increased in importance since the end of the Cold War.

A human rights policy emerged in 1973 in tandem with détente. As one might have expected, détente permitted competition between the superpowers to move from the security arena to a more ideological plane, where weapons such as a U.S. human rights policy would become effective. The changes generated by détente created an atmosphere in which values other than anticommunism could come to the fore. But when the revolution in Nicaragua converged with the invasion of Afghanistan and the Iran hostage crisis in 1979, support for détente and for human rights legislation withered.

The changing world structure produced by détente helps us understand the timing of the United States' human rights policy but cannot explain why anticommunism was replaced specifically by a human rights policy or why that policy took the shape that it did. To understand those phenomena we must go back to the 1960s and early 1970s, which proved to tbe a crucial turning point in American elite public opinion.

The Role of Ideas

Policy makers adopted new policies because their ideas had changed. As their views changed, they attempted to articulate a new definition of long-term U.S. national interests that not only accorded with respect for human rights but even used such respect as the fundamental yardstick with which to measure the value of an ally or the potential stability of a regime.

Members of Congress did not adopt a human rights policy in response to pressures from their constituencies. Though polls conducted in the early 1970s indicated public support for vigorous action to pro-

---

[44] Friedbert Pfluger, "Human Rights Unbound: Carter's Human Rights Policy Reassessed," *Presidential Studies Quarterly* 19 (Fall 1989): 708.

mote human rights, human rights were low on the public's list of foreign policy priorities.[45] A study of congressional voting also concludes that the characteristics of representatives' constituencies have little or no effect on the way members of Congress vote on human rights.[46]

Nevertheless, policy makers were aware that concerns for human rights could be framed in ways that strongly appealed to the American public. Tom Harkin of Iowa, a leading advocate of human rights in the House, was heartened to note that a 1975 Harris poll found that 63 percent of the American people felt that the U.S. government had no justification for backing "authoritarian governments that have overthrown democratic governments," and 73 percent opposed U.S. support of a military dictatorship "even if that dictatorship will allow us to set up military bases in that country."[47] Likewise, Jimmy Carter received such positive responses to his discussions of human rights in his campaign speeches that he felt confident of support when he acted on his convictions after his election. Thus one can argue that once the issue of human rights impinged on policy makers' consciousness, they found that they were able to galvanize latent support for human rights in the general public. By 1985, a survey among influential U.S. citizens found that "a more vocal stand for human rights" emerged as the foreign policy issue that enjoyed the greatest support.[48]

What caused policy makers' ideas to change? The set of causal ideas that motivated the United Staes' external human rights policies were not those that drove European multilateral policies. The framers of the Statute of the Council of Europe and the European Convention on Human Rights believed, first, that strong regional action promoting human rights would help prevent a repetition of the grim experience of dictatorship and repression in Europe. Second, the uniting of Europe needed to go hand in hand with an effort to codify and unify moral standards and practices as embodied in the human rights convention. Third, in the emerging conflict between East and West, the human rights convention would serve to set out unambiguously the

[45] Lars Schoultz, *Human Rights and United States Policy toward Latin America* (Princeton: Princeton University Press, 1981), p. 35. Donald Fraser, the member of Congress most responsible for the initial adoption of human rights legislation, said that there was "very little" interest in human rights in his liberal Minnesota district and "no demand" for his human rights work from his constituency: interview, Minneapolis, March 18, 1991.

[46] David P. Forsythe, *Human Rights and U.S. Foreign Policy: Congress Reconsidered* (Gainesville: University of Florida Press, 1988), p. 50.

[47] Tom Harkin, "Human Rights and Foreign Aid: Forging an Unbreakable Link," in *Human Rights and U.S. Foreign Policy*, ed. Peter Brown and Douglas MacLean (Lexington, Mass.: Lexington Books, 1979), p. 26.

[48] Twelfth annual survey, "Who Runs America?" in *U.S. News & World Report*, May 20, 1985, p. 56, quoted in Egeland, *Impotent Superpower, Potent Small State*, p. 172.

rights that Western countries guaranteed their peoples.[49] These beliefs emerged out of the experience of World War II and remained strong throughout the Cold War, thus providing the basis for continuous and gradual progress on development of internal human rights policies. The second set of causal beliefs also served as justifications for the external human rights policies that focused on such states as Greece and Turkey.

In the United States, however, the adoption of both a multilateral and an external human rights policy was blocked by a cluster of more powerful ideas. Here the initial postwar belief in the promotion of human rights as a means of preventing future conflict soon gave way to the dual pressures of anticommunism in the foreign policy realm and conservative states' rights and segregationist sentiment in the domestic realm. Not until both of these more powerful clusters of ideas/interests had subsided could human rights reemerge in U.S. policy. Even then, human rights ideas did not totally displace earlier interpretations of national security, but rather continued to exist with them among members of the Congress, the executive, and the general public. Some policy debates were won by one side, some by the other. During Carter's administration the overall debate was institutionalized in the State Department between the Bureau of Human Rights and the regional affairs bureaus.

A series of issues converged to make political leaders question traditional ideas about American politics and the place of the United States in the world. Mentioning such events as the military coup in Greece, the Vietnam War, the civil rights movement, and the U.S. invasion of the Dominican Republic, one key sponsor of human rights legislation referred to the 1960s as "a decade when events tended to heighten one's sensitivity to human rights issues."[50] Another policy maker said, "The Civil Rights movement, Watergate, Vietnam, a revulsion at the support for repressive regimes, and the intervention of Congress to place human rights conditions as an important aspect of U.S. foreign policy—these were the forces that propelled human rights into the foreign policy debate in the presidential campaign of 1976."[51]

The Vietnam experience led liberals to associate U.S. military and economic assistance with the emergence of repressive policies. The

---

[49] Robertson, *Human Rights in Europe*, p. 3.

[50] Interview with Donald Fraser, Minneapolis, March 18, 1991.

[51] This is the view of a key figure in U.S. human rights policy, first as a member of Senator Edward Kennedy's staff, later as a policy maker in the Human Rights Bureau of the State Department. See Mark L. Schneider, "The New Administration's New Policy: The Rise to Power of Human Rights," in Brown and MacLean, *Human Rights and U.S. Foreign Policy*, p. 8.

links between disillusionment with U.S. policy in Vietnam and the evolution of human rights legislation become strikingly clear in the experience of Tom Harkin, one of the major congressional sponsors of human rights legislation. While Harkin was a congressional staffer he was responsible for the discovery of the notorious "tiger cages" in a South Vietnamese prison that had received U.S. assistance. Vietnam also left another legacy that influenced the adoption of a human rights policy—a desire to restore to the United States the position of moral leadership in world affairs that had been severely eroded by the war. Opposed to the moral ambiguity of realpolitik and the high-handedness of Henry Kissinger, human rights advocates hoped to advance a new type of foreign policy based on traditional U.S. values.[52] In this sense, it was not détente or superpower ideological competition that led to a human rights policy but changing ideas about the need to transform the United States' role in the world.

The civil rights movement also played a role in the change of attitudes toward both external and multilateral human rights policies. By the 1970s, many of the states' rights arguments offered in support of the Bricker Amendment were increasingly irrelevant, because the federal government and the courts had already intervened in the states to promote desegregation. And the civil rights movement contributed more than ideas: a generation of activists trained in its rigors turned their organizational skills to promoting equal rights in the international arena.[53]

Among other ideas that changed was the prevailing understanding of the causes of human rights abuses around the world and the United States' responsibility for them. The traditional view was that human rights abuses were the result of either political culture, despotism, or poverty and underdevelopment. By the mid-1970s, however, the prominence of human rights abuses in such developed countries as Greece, Argentina, and South Korea; in countries with long histories of democracy, such as Uruguay and Chile; and in countries where the United States had had a strong hand in the emergence of authoritarian gov-

---

[52] "The human rights factor is not accorded the high priority it deserves in our country's foreign policy. . . . Proponents of pure power politics too often dismiss it as a factor in diplomacy. . . . But a higher priority is urgently needed if future American leadership in the world is to mean what it has traditionally meant—encouragement to men and women everywhere who cherish individual freedom": U.S. House of Representatives, Committee on Foreign Affairs, Subcommittee on International Organizations, *Human Rights in the World Community: A Call for U.S. Leadership,* 93d Cong., 2d sess. (March 27, 1974) (Washington, D.C.: U.S. Government Printing Office, 1974), p. 9.
[53] E.g., Patricia Derian, Carter's assistant secretary of state for humanitarian affairs and human rights; Andrew Young, U.S. ambassador to the U.N.; and one of Young's top aides, Brady Tyson, had all been very active in the civil rights movement.

ernments, such as Chile, Brazil, and the Philippines, led many Americans to question the traditional views.[54] Reports from human rights organizations indicated that the abuses were being organized and promoted by the highest levels of governments that were receiving U.S. assistance.

As a result of all these changes, the principled belief underlying the new U.S. human rights policy was that a concern with violations of human rights was a necessary and legitimate factor in foreign policy. The causal belief underlying much of U.S. human rights legislation was that the cutoff of military and economic assistance would contribute to improvements in human rights practices in targeted countries.

For some advocates in Congress, however, human rights legislation had a dual purpose: to change the practices of repressive governments and to distance the United States from those practices.[55] The causal logic behind this reasoning was more complex. The cutoff of military and economic aid was believed to send an important symbolic and material message aimed at dissociating the United States from repressive regimes. In the short term, it was hoped that these aid cutoffs would improve human rights, or at least not hurt them; in the long term, such action was aimed at improving the United States' image and restoring its moral legitimacy. Donald Fraser pointed out that the Congress placed especially stringent standards on military aid "because of the symbolic and sometimes practical importance of such assistance in carrying out repressive policy in numerous countries."[56]

Human rights policy emerged both from the changing ideas of congressional incumbents and from the convictions of a new generation of policy makers who entered Congress after the 1974 elections. These "Watergate babies"[57]—the largest freshman class since 1948—not only included a large group of progressive Democrats but in general shared

[54] Schoultz, *Human Rights*, pp. 5–17. These changes in the ideas of policy makers parallel changes in thinking in the academic community about the causes of authoritarian regimes and of the breakdown of democracy. Dependency theory in general and Guillermo O'Donnell's theory of bureaucratic authoritarian regimes were increasingly being discussed and accepted in academic circles in the mid-1970s. Both of these theories called into question traditional assumptions about poverty and abuses of human rights, and placed increasing emphasis on the responsibility of external forces for underdevelopment and repression in the Third World and in the more developed countries of Latin America.

[55] Jo Marie Griesgraber, "Implementation by the Carter Administration of Human Rights Legislation Affecting Latin America," Ph.D. diss., Georgetown University, 1983, pp. 33–39.

[56] Donald M. Fraser, "Congress's Role in the Making of International Human Rights Policy," in *Human Rights and American Foreign Policy*, ed. Donald Kommers and Gilbert Loescher (Notre Dame, Ind.: University of Notre Dame Press, 1979), p. 248.

[57] Cynthia Arnson, *Crossroads: Congress, the Reagan Administration, and Central America* (New York: Pantheon, 1989), p. 11.

a profound distrust of executive power as a result of the Watergate experience. The ideas that led to a human rights policy were already abroad in Congress before their arrival, but the seventy-eight new Democrats in the class of 1974 gave the human rights advocates new leadership and the margin they needed to pass human rights legislation. The Watergate generation also voted for changes in congressional rules that, by increasing the opportunities for junior members' voices to be heard, contributed to the success of the human rights policy. Under the new rules, more actors, some of them without assignments to foreign policy committees, took active roles in raising issues and proposing foreign policy alternatives. Tom Harkin, for example, was the main sponsor of key human rights legislation although he served on none of the committees dealing with foreign affairs.

There was one interesting similarity between the actions taken by the Senate in the early 1950s to prevent an internal human rights policy and the actions taken in Congress in the mid-1970s to initiate an external human rights policy: both responded to a perception of excessive executive power. In sponsoring his amendment Bricker had wanted to limit the power both of the president in the realm of foreign policy and of the federal government over the states. Some of the human rights advocates in Congress in the early 1970s, too, saw the human rights policy they advocated as a means of protesting the increasingly imperial presidency and the realpolitik of Nixon and Kissinger.

IMPLEMENTATION OF HUMAN RIGHTS POLICIES IN EUROPE AND THE UNITED STATES

Human rights ideas were applied to politics in very different ways in the United States and in Europe. Differences can be seen in the focuses or targets of human rights policies and in the types of policy instruments and the channels used to register protests against violations. The Europeans tended to focus on the human rights practices of countries on the margins of Europe, such as Spain, Greece, and Turkey. To the degree that they focused outside the region, they tended to concentrate on Third World countries that had been European colonies, especially in Africa. In the United States, pressures were exerted in two directions: the Jacksonian Democrats and Republicans advocated the use of human rights policy against the Soviet Union and its allies, whereas the liberal Democrats and the Watergate babies identified Third World allies, particularly in Latin America, as the primary targets.

A second difference can be seen in the nature of the human rights policies that were pursued. The Europeans were more likely to use legal instruments and multilateral channels such as those provided by the European Convention, whereas the United States tended to use bilateral channels and more political forms of pressure.

These differences can be traced in part to the degrees of power reflected in the policies of the two regions. A preference for bilateral policies and for public rather than private diplomacy tends to be characteristic of a hegemonic power. It is interesting to note that when Europeans play a crucial role in a less developed country, as the Dutch did in Surinam and the French in the Central African Republic, their policies more closely resemble those of the United States.

Continuity in U.S. and European Human Rights Policies

Europe can claim a record of four decades of expansion and activism in the human rights realm. Except in the case of Greece, the Western Europeans have held fast to the human rights regime. In the United States, although the Reagan and Bush administrations backtracked on human rights, external policies were not completely deserted and some progress was made toward a multilateral policy.

If changing ideas about the causes of human rights abuses go part of the way toward explaining the adoption of a human rights policy, what explains its continuity? The continuation of human rights policies on both sides of the Atlantic, even during administrations hostile to some of the basic concepts, is the result of both a consensus on the importance of a human rights policy and the stickiness of the institutional provisions for implementing it.

The institutionalization of the human rights policy within the laws and policy apparatus of the United Staes made it difficult for administrations that did not support the policy to abandon it completely. In the 1950s and 1960s, human rights concerns were institutionally embedded only in the part of the State Department concerned with the U.N. It was not until the institutional modifications of the 1970s, with the creation of the Bureau for Human Rights and Humanitarian Affairs, and the delegation of human rights issues to specific congressional subcommittees, that a stronger institutional basis emerged for human rights policies. In the 1970s the United States also supported the strengthening of regional human rights institutions within the Inter-American system, especially the Inter-American Commission on Human Rights. These institutions, for the most part the result of the generation and political selection of human rights ideas, contributed to the persistence of those ideas when Reagan came to power.

Human rights ideas embodied in institutions and laws created bureaucratic interests based on the perpetuation of those policies. The most important means by which those ideas were institutionalized were the formation of the Bureau for Human Rights and Humanitarian Affairs of the State Department and the congressional requirement that the State Department issue a human rights report on each country every year. This requirement in turn altered the job requirements of foreign service officers around the globe: for the first time they were instructed to gather systematic information on human rights abuses. Human rights concerns were institutionalized in Congress in the Subcommittee on International Organizations of the House Foreign Affairs Committee.

Human rights ideas were also promoted by nongovernmental organizations already in place and by new interest groups that formed around the issue of human rights. Some, such as Amnesty International, were active before the United States adopted a human rights policy and contributed to the emergence of that policy. Many other organizations, such as Human Rights Watch and the Lawyers' Committee on Human Rights, were organized in the late 1970s, at the same time that human rights policies were being integrated into U.S. foreign policy. Once established, they became a strong lobby in support of continuation of the human rights policy.

The influence of these organizations is unlike that of most groups whose impact is felt in international relations. The groups had no power either numerically or economically; they had no money to contribute to reelection campaigns and rarely were able to mobilize a constituency at the polls. The influence they wielded was a direct result of the reliability of their information and the resonance of their arguments with the moral concerns of policy makers. In view of the fact that citizens' attitudes toward the human rights issue, though generally favorable, were not strongly held, the effectiveness of these small but well-organized groups was extraordinary. Their strength is indicated by their ability to help persuade the Senate to defeat the Reagan administration's initial nominee for the position of assistant secretary of state for human rights and humanitarian affairs.[58]

There was also important interaction between the human rights NGOs and the bureaucratic and institutional interests, links that were mutually

---

[58] An ad hoc group of NGOs that met to coordinate strategy to defeat the nomination of Ernest Lefever provided information to senators who spoke in opposition to Reagan's nominee. Lefever himself referred to "orchestrated" opposition mounted against him. One of the more effective strategies devised by members of the human rights community was a dinner organized by Robert Bernstein, president of Random House and chair

reinforcing though not always congenial. NGOs contributed to human rights legislation by providing information about human rights abuses, by graphically bringing abuses of human rights to the attention of members of Congress and their staffs through personal testimony ("One way they influenced Congress," says Donald Fraser, "was by bringing individuals to visit congressional offices who had personal stories of human rights abuses to tell"),[59] and by encouraging people around the country to write to their representatives in support of human rights. Once adopted, this legislation then provided a focal point for the interest groups' activities. The uses to which the human rights reports were put are illuminating. Because State Department officials did not want to offend the officials of any country or undermine other policy goals, their human rights reports were often weak; but their very weakness became a weapon in the hands of human rights groups, who created an annual event by issuing responses to the State Department reports.[60] The reports and counterreports attracted press coverage, and the critiques held the State Department up to higher standards of reporting.

Human rights policies were also institutionalized in Europe, but there they were more multilateral than in the United States. The early creation of the European Human Rights Commission and the European Court of Human Rights and their increasing activity over the years help explain the longevity and greater continuity of human rights policies in Europe. The court and the commission are generally recognized as the most effective formal institutions for the promotion of human rights.[61] Even when administrations relatively unsympathetic

---

of Helsinki Watch, with Jacobo Timmerman, the prominent journalist who had been imprisoned and tortured by the Argentine government, and key senators on the Foreign Relations Committee, including Claiborne Pell and Paul Tsongas. The senators referred to the dinner several times during the hearings and quoted Timmerman's arguments against Lefever's nomination. Timmerman's appearance in the hearing room was greeted by sustained applause. See U.S. Senate, Committee on Foreign Relations, *Nomination of Ernest W. Lefever: Hearings*, 97th Cong., 1st sess., May 18 and 19, June 4 and 5, 1981 (Washington, D.C.: U.S. Government Printing Office, 1981), pp. 360–61, 205–6, 288.

[59] Interview, March 18, 1991. When asked to identify the most influential groups on human rights outside Congress, Fraser referred to three NGOs, including one coalition that brought together all the human rights groups in Washington. For more on the influence of NGOs on congressional action on Argentina, see the opening statement by Congressman Don Bonker in U.S. House of Representatives, Subcommittees on Human Rights and International Organizations and on Inter-American Affairs of the Committee on Foreign Affairs, *Review of United States Policy on Military Assistance to Argentina: Hearings*, April 1, 1981 (Washington, D.C.: U.S. Government Printing Office, 1981), pp. 3–5.

[60] See, e.g., Human Rights Watch and Lawyers' Committee for Human Rights, *Critique: Review of the Department of State's Country Reports on Human Rights Practices for 1987* (New York, June 1988).

[61] Mark W. Janis and Richard S. Kay, *European Human Rights Law* (Hartford: University of Connecticut Law School Foundation Press, 1990), p. xlii.

to the cause of human rights took power, the range of acceptable actions to show their displeasure or lack of support was limited. Despite the unprecedented number of cases that had gone against the United Kingdom, for example, the Thatcher government renewed the right of individual petition under the convention for five years in 1981 and 1986.

European human rights policies became intertwined with the emerging institutions of the European community. Human rights piggybacked on the momentum of the creation of supranational institutions at other levels. Though the Europeans supported institution building at the international and regional levels, they lagged behind in the creation of national governmental institutions to address abuses of human rights.

CONCLUSIONS

The cases reviewed here appear to indicate that ideas have influenced foreign policy in respect to human rights in two ways. First, the changes in ideas that emerged after World War II led quite directly to the construction of the European human rights regime. In the United States, however, the impact of human rights ideas was delayed by the Cold War. Once adopted, U.S. human rights policies tended to focus on the international scene, whereas European policies focused on Europe.

Two interesting questions arise here: Why did the Cold War delay the adoption of human rights policies in the United States but not in Europe? And why were the policies implemented in different ways? Because the atrocities of World War II were the original shock that led policy makers to craft human rights policies, it is not surprising that European policy focused on Europe. For Europeans, the human rights issue was how to keep such horrors from happening again. The greater immediacy of the issue contributed to the regional focus and the more steady progress. In addition, human rights became part of a larger process, the process of building a unified Europe. Support for human rights policies was intensified by the widespread belief that the unification process depended on a normative agreement, and such an agreement was embodied in the European human rights documents.

For the United States, human rights was an external issue, one easily subsumed by and subordinated to the Cold War, which had emerged at the top of the foreign policy agenda. It was not until détente took the chill from the Cold War and the human rights issue came together with a broader set of ideas that emerged in the later 1960s and early 1970s that human rights began to be applied to U.S. foreign policy in any consistent way. In the early 1970s human rights ideas came to resonate with ideas from the civil rights movement, with the anti-intervention sentiment that grew out of the Vietnam experience, and with the growing distrust of executive power and the desire to reassert the power of the Congress vis-à-vis the president. It was not until the Cold War finally ended with the disintegration of the Soviet Union and the Eastern bloc that the United States began to take its first steps in the direction of a multilateral human rights policy.

The role of the Cold War as a block to human rights policies in the United States is substantiated by the nation's movement toward a multilateral policy in the early 1990s. The Cold War, anticommunism, and the resulting distrust of the United Nations system continuously obstructed external and multilateral human rights policies. Détente in the early 1970s and the end of the Cold War in the early 1990s permitted human rights policies to advance. But these were only necessary conditions, not sufficient conditions for human rights policies in the United States. Those policies owe their being to the ideas that emerged in the wake of the Holocaust and were reinforced by the experiences of Vietnam, Chile, and other repressive regimes. These human rights ideas were championed and carried by nongovernmental organizations. Although eventually human rights ideas became embedded in state institutions, their continued vigor depended upon the active documentation and lobbying of nongovernmental actors.

The effectiveness of human rights organizations can be seen in the early campaigns that were the precursors of the current human rights policies, especially in the Geneva Convention and the campaign for the abolition of slavery; in the inclusion of human rights language in the U.N. Charter; and in the linkage of human rights to the process of the unification of Europe. Such organizations have contributed to the implementation and continuity of human rights policy. NGOs in the United States have often played roles behind the scenes by providing reliable information to policy makers. NGOs play an even more central role in the implementation of European bilateral human rights policies in some of the smaller countries for they are sometimes responsible for producing the reports on human rights practices that influence governments' aid decisions; they may even play an important role in the dispersal of bilateral aid. This survey suggests that in the examination of the role of ideas and politics, at least in a subset of international issues such as human rights and the environment, more attention needs to be paid to the crucial role of nongovernmental actors as the carriers of transformative ideas.

PART III

SOLVING COORDINATION PROBLEMS: IDEAS AS FOCAL POINTS

CHAPTER SEVEN

Ideas, Interests, and Institutions: Constructing the European Community's Internal Market

GEOFFREY GARRETT AND
BARRY R. WEINGAST

As embodied in the signing of the Single European Act 1987 (SEA), the decision of European Community (EC) members to complete their "internal market" by the end of 1992 is one of the most important instances of multilateral cooperation in the postwar period. Its economic objective is the removal of a wide array of neoprotectionist barriers—embodied in national standards, public procurement policies, industrial subsidies, and the like—to facilitate the free movement of goods, services, people, and capital within the EC.[1] The institutional

Earlier drafts of this chapter were presented at the NBER Conference on Political Economics, Cambridge, November 15–16, 1991, and the Stanford/ESCP Conference on the Political Economy of Institutions, Paris, March 26, 1992. We thank Judith Goldstein, Lloyd Gruber, Robert Keohane, David Soskice, and Beth Yarbrough for helpful comments on an earlier draft of this chapter. Special thanks are due to Anne-Marie Burley and Joseph Weiler for sharing with us their insights into European law and the EC's legal system. The editorial assistance of Paulina Favela and the research assistance of Gabriella Montinola are gratefully acknowledged.

[1] It should be noted that the internal market had little chance of being "complete" by the end of 1992, if ever. National governments have steadfastly refused to facilitate the free movement of people within Europe, citing fears of terrorism, drug smuggling, and the like. The elaborate system of agricultural protectionism embodied in the Common Agriculture Policy has not been reformed (despite external pressures from the Uruguay Round of the GATT). Moreover, despite considerable effort on the part of the EC, it is proving very difficult effectively to eliminate trade barriers constituted by many aspects of national regulatory regimes. For an assessment of progress toward the completion of the internal market see Stephen Woolcock et al., *Britain, Germany and 1992.* (London: Pinter, 1991).

structures underpinning the internal market are considerably more elaborate and constraining on member states than has been the norm for international regimes. While the existing EC cannot be described as even a confederal political system, it is clear that the Community comprises at least two fundamental features normally associated with sovereign polities: majoritarian decision making and an authoritative legal system to enforce decisions so made.[2]

The SEA replaced unanimity voting in the Council of Ministers, the fundamental decision-making institution in the EC, with a qualified majority rule (article 100A).[3] In so doing, the members of the Community agreed to overturn the "Luxembourg compromise," which affirmed the right of any member to veto any EC decision of which it disapproved. Moreover, the internal market rules are buttressed by a legal system without precedent in international politics. The EC's legal structure is more akin to a consitutional order than to a normal system of international treaties, in which signatories reserve the right to interpret the extent of their obligations.[4] The European Court of Justice (ECJ) exercises considerable autonomy in the interpretation and application of EC laws. Moreover, these laws have "direct effect" in the courts of member states and override contending national laws. Domestic courts frequently refer cases brought before them to the ECJ for preliminary rulings on the application of relevant EC law (pursuant to article 177 of the Treaty of Rome).

How can these attributes of the internal market be understood? A large literature seeks to explain the conditions under which cooperation may emerge between self-interested states in the anarchic international system. Collective action problems—such as the mutual opening of domestic markets—are endemic to international politics.[5] Couched

---

[2] If the Maastricht Treaty on European Union is ratified, the amount of sovereign authority vested in the EC will increase dramatically (most importantly through the creation of a single European currency and a single European monetary policy).

[3] The exceptions are fiscal matters, the movement of persons, and the rights of workers. Voting weights in the Council are apportioned thus: France, Germany, Italy, and the United Kingdom each have 10 votes; Spain, 8; Belgium, Greece, the Netherlands, Portugal, 5; Denmark and Eire, 3; and Luxembourg, 2. Fifty-four of the 76 votes constitute a "qualified majority."

[4] Eric Stein, "Lawyers, Judges, and the Making of a Transnational Constitution," *American Journal of International Law* 75 (1981): 1–27; and Joseph Weiler, "The Transformation of Europe," *Yale Law Journal* 100 (1991): 2403–83.

[5] Economic theory suggests that unilateral trade liberalization is always in the interest of all countries. However, there are strong domestic political reasons—emanating from the power of producer groups in relation to consumers and the short-term dislocations associated with market adaptation—for national governments to prefer to maintain the ability to protect domestic markets while having unhindered access to foreign markets. See Stephen Magee et al., *Black Hole Tariffs and Endogenous Policy Theory* (New York: Cambridge University Press, 1989).

in terms of the familiar prisoner's dilemma, these problems may be mitigated when interactions are repeated indefinitely, when the rates at which states discount the future are low, and when the value of cooperation is high. Under such conditions, states will be reluctant to free-ride on fellow members for fear of retaliation and loss of reputation.[6]

Without doubt, repeated interaction and the "long arm of the future" play large roles in enabling actors to capture the gains from cooperation. Yet the numerous instances in which cooperation fails to emerge suggest that this understanding is inadequate. Several problems stand out. All arise from fundamental difficulties associated with *ambiguity*. First, there are often multiple paths toward capturing the gains from cooperation and no obvious way for a set of decentralized actors to converge on one of them. Second, the informational requirements for the "evolution of cooperation" are considerable, notably because of the difficulty of identifying and verifying defection (so that transgressors may be punished) and because of problems associated with unanticipated circumstances (in which the meaning of cooperation is unclear). Many scholars argue that political institutions may play significant roles in generating the necessary information for the realization of collective gains.[7]

This scholarship, however, suffers from a further crucial weakness. The literature can tell us why the set of cooperative arrangements that was chosen represented an "efficient" (Pareto-improving) solution to the collective action problem facing participants. But existing studies shed little light on the question why one particular cooperative solution was chosen.[8] In keeping with the basic thrust of transactions costs economics,[9] most studies assume that the institutional arrangements that

[6] The most influential statement of this perspective in international relations is Robert Axelrod, *The Evolution of Cooperation* (New York: Basic Books, 1984). For a more rigorous analysis of the effects of iteration and reputation, see David Kreps et al., "Rational Cooperation in the Finitely Repeated Prisoners' Dilemma," *Journal of Economic Theory* 27 (1982): 245–52; and David Kreps and Robert Wilson, "Reputation and Imperfect Information," *Journal of Economic Theory* 27 (1982): 245–52.

[7] Avner Greif, Paul Milgrom, and Barry R. Weingast, "Coordination, Commitment, and Enforcement: The Case of the Merchant Guild," *Journal of Political Economy* (forthcoming); Robert Keohane, *After Hegemony* (Princeton: Princeton University Press, 1984); Paul Milgrom, Douglass North, and Barry R. Weingast, "The Role of Institutions in the Revival of Trade: The Medieval Law Merchant, Private Judges, and the Champagne Fairs," *Economics and Politics* 2 (1990): 1–23; and Barry R. Weingast, "Institutional Foundations of 'The Sinews of Power': British Financial and Military Success Following the Glorious Revolution" (manuscript, Stanford University, 1993).

[8] Stephen Krasner, "Global Communications and National Power: Life on the Pareto Frontier," *World Politics* 43 (1991): 336–66.

[9] Ronald Coarse, "The Nature of the Firm," *Economica* 4 (1937): 338–405; and Oliver Williamson, *Market and Hierarchies* (New York: Free Press, 1975).

emerge were chosen precisely because they were uniquely efficient solutions to given problems of cooperation. The weakness of such functional reasoning is that in most interesting issues in international relations (and in the social sciences more generally) there are many stable paths to cooperation that cannot readily be differentiated in terms of their consequences for aggregate welfare.[10]

This context provides for the potentially pivotal role of ideas. Shared beliefs may act as "focal points" around which the behavior of actors converges.[11] Moreover, given that most agreements are likely to be incomplete (that is, provisions will not be written to cover every possible conflict between participants), shared beliefs about the spirit of agreements are essential to the maintenance of cooperation.[12] Less prosaically, ideas, social norms, institutions, and shared expectations may influence both the way actors choose to cooperate and the stability of these arrangements over time.

Shared belief systems and focal points, however, do not always emerge without conscious efforts on the part of interested actors. Rather, they must often be constructed. In the context of multiple paths to cooperation, the realization of potential shared gains may be impeded when there is no single "natural" solution but a whole range of possible paths to cooperation. The creation of a set of institutions can fill this void. By embodying, selecting, and publicizing particular paths on which all actors are able to coordinate, institutions may provide a *constructed focal point*. Such institutions can also mitigate potential breakdowns in cooperation associated with ambiguity by providing the critical information about when an actor has defected and by resolving problems raised by unanticipated circumstances. Acting in this capacity, institutions not only provide individuals with critical information about defection but also help construct a shared belief system that defines for the community what actions constitute cooperation and defection.

If this assumption is correct, the widely perceived stark divide between "rationalists" and "reflectivists" is inappropriate.[13] Pure efficien-

---

[10] The most general statement of this problem is the "folk theorem" that for repeated games with nontrivial information structure, an infinite number of strategies can be sustained in equilibrium. For a discussion see Drew Fudenberg and Eric Maskin, "The Folk Theorem with Discounting or with Incomplete Information," *Econometrica* 54 (1986): 533–54.

[11] Thomas Schelling, *The Strategy of Conflict*, rev. ed. (Cambridge: Harvard University Press, 1980).

[12] David Kreps, "Corporate Culture and Economic Theory," in *Perspectives on Positive Political Economy*, ed. James Alt and Kenneth Shepsle (New York: Cambridge University Press, 1990).

[13] Robert Keohane, "International Institutions: Two Approaches," *International Studies Quarterly* 32 (1988): 379–96.

cy- and interest-based approaches cannot generate unique explanations for international cooperation. They can only show ex post facto why the form of cooperation that emerged was Pareto-efficient, and hence that actors could rationally have selected it. In our view, the central concerns of reflectivists—the social and institutional bases of shared beliefs—hold the key to overcoming the deficiencies of functionalist logic.[14]

We suggest that if we are to understand the evolution and operation of the EC's internal market, it is necessary to integrate interests and ideas. Our argument is that a cooperative agreement to complete the single market in Europe based solely on decentralized, self-interested behavior neither could have emerged in the mid-1980s nor would be likely to sustain itself after 1992. Because the participants had—and continue to have—divergent preferences over the potential ways to organize their interactions, the lack of a natural, unique path to cooperation has been a great barrier to the realization of collective gains. Understanding how this barrier can be overcome requires analysis of the role of institutions in the broadest sense: the embodiment and propagation of coordinated expectations about the internal market (that is, the creation of a shared belief system).

The members of the EC clearly had powerful reasons to liberalize their economic relations in the mid-1980s. But the critical issues are why the particular institutional arrangements associated with the internal market were chosen and how they will work. Numerous alternative economic rules could have been used as the basis for EC trade liberalization, from pure laissez-faire to the creation of an encompassing set of EC regulations and standards. It would be difficult to argue that the choice of "mutual recognition" of national practices as the overarching organizing principle of the internal market was not influenced by the European Court of Justice's decision in *Cassis de Dijon* (1979).

Furthermore, the translation of the general principle of mutual recognition into detailed decisions governing the behavior of political and economic actors in the internal market relies heavily on the EC legal system. There undoubtedly are other mechanisms for implementing the internal market, such as enforcement by the EC Commission. But the fact that the principle of direct effect was firmly established pro-

---

[14] It is important to note, however, that ideas as focal points do not represent the only possible solution to the multiple-equilibria problem. Rather, the interests and relative power of different actors may significantly influence outcomes. See Geoffrey Garrett, "International Cooperation and Institutional Choice: The European Community's Internal Market," *International Organization* 45 (1991): 539–64; and Krasner, "Global Communications and National Power." The interaction of ideas, interests, and power are explored at length later.

vided a readily available and effective solution to the problems of incomplete information and incomplete contracting that would otherwise have hindered cooperation in the EC.

At this point, however, the limits of the impact of ideas should be carefully delineated. Mutual recognition was not merely a construction of the European Court. Rather, this principle is consistent with the desire of the major political and economic actors in Europe to liberalize trade. Furthermore, EC members maintain considerable control over the course of rulemaking through the Council of Ministers. More fundamentally, the continued legitimacy of the court and its rulings is contingent upon the support of the governments of EC members. Put simply, the implicit threat of intervention by the member states, either through decisions in the Council of Ministers or through noncompliance with court decisions, ultimately constrains judicial activism in the EC.

More generally, the force of ideas is neither random nor independent. Only certain ideas have properties that may lead to their selection by political actors and to their institutionalization and perpetuation. It is not something intrinsic to ideas that gives them their power, but their utility in helping actors achieve their desired ends under prevailing constraints. Given the complexity and uncertainty of most political economic interactions, appropriate ideas may serve as pivotal mechanisms for coordinating expectations and behavior.

THE POLITICAL ECONOMY OF COOPERATION: A CRITIQUE

It is now conventional to analyze the prospects for realizing mutual gains from cooperation within a group of self-interested actors—be they individuals, interest groups, or states—in terms of the prisoner's dilemma. In this familiar world, all actors would benefit from cooperating to achieve common goals, but each has substantial incentives to defect. So long as interactions are repeated indefinitely, potential gains are large, and the rates at which actors discount the future are low, the threat of retaliation against those who defect and the prospect of loss of reputation in the future provide the means for maintaining cooperation. Despite short-run temptations to defect, individuals will cooperate because they know that future benefits depend on cooperating today—and hence on not inciting retaliation and on attaining reputations as good cooperators.

Recent work has suggested, however, that such arguments break down in the context of ambiguity and incomplete information. Conventional approaches assume that members of society costlessly learn who has defected. Yet in the real world there are many situations in which it is very costly, if not impossible, for all members of a community to discern whether an actor has violated commonly agreed rules. In the medieval trading system of the "law merchant," for example, when an individual trader cheated his partner, the latter was immediately aware that he had done so. All other traders, however, knew only that a dispute had arisen. These outsiders typically had difficulty weighing the veracity of the various claims and counterclaims made by the disputants.[15] Disputes of this type result in uncertainty over defection and may impede the emergence of cooperation or may cause it to break down unnecessarily. If individuals do not always know when a defection has taken place, then defection will not always be punished, and thus the incentives to defect will increase.

Institutions may play an important role in overcoming the adverse effects of incomplete information. Role specialists may be created to whom authority is delegated to administer the rules of the game, to monitor the adherence of members to these rules, and most important, to identify and publicize transgressions by errant members. If institutions can provide these types of information, interactions between self-interested players may then lead to the evolution of cooperation in the manner that is conventionally envisaged (through "tit for tat" and other trigger strategies). Thus institutions need not be granted any sanctioning power to facilitate stable cooperation. Rather they need only provide the information that is required for effective decentralized punishment by members.

But even when the conventional models are augmented with these institutional arguments, they are still liable to a telling criticism. Most studies assume that a given collective action problem has a unique solution—the one that is chosen by the actors. Most interesting interactions in domestic and international politics, however, are likely to have multiple possible solutions that cannot be distinguished in Paretian terms. If there is more than one efficient path to sustainable cooperation, arguments that purport to explain cooperation in terms of efficiency logically must fail.

We can illustrate the dynamics of cooperation problems due to multiple equilibria by nesting a coordination game within the prisoner's dilemma. In the two-player rendering of this game (Figure 1), mutual defection is the dominant strategy of both actors in a given play. Any form of mutual cooperation (C_1, C_1 and C_2, C_2) is preferable to mutual defection, but, as in the simple prisoner's dilemma, each player is tempted to free-ride on the other, so both must be fearful of being

---

[15] Milgrom et al., "Role of Institutions."

suckered. The standard means of supporting cooperation in the prisoner's dilemma does not automatically succeed under these circumstances. Even if iteration were to make the realization of collective gains possible, the players would not necessarily be able to maximize their payoffs. Both have an interest in coordinating around C1 or C2, but these potential equilibria cannot be differentiated in terms of either efficiency or self-interest.[16] Thus this game has no simple "rational" solution.

Player B

		C1	C2	D
Player A	C1	3, 3	0, 0	−1, 4
	C2	0, 0	3, 3	−1, 4
	D	4, −1	4, −1	0, 0

Note: The payoffs to player A appear first.

Figure 1. A pure coordination game nested within the prisoner's dilemma

In this game, showing that both strategy combinations (C1, C1 and C2, C2) are efficient solutions to the dilemmas facing the actors does not explain how or why they would be able to settle on one of them. If more than one set of "rules of the game" would allow the actors to realize mutual gains and if more than one set of institutions can monitor adherence to these rules, models of cooperation need to explain why a particular set is chosen.

But even if it were possible to determine why one set of rules was initially chosen over others, a final important impediment to cooperation would remain. The analysis thus far has assumed that members of a community will be able initially to agree on an exhaustive set of rules to govern all their future interactions. It will always be very costly, however, if not impossible, for actors to construct such agreements. Thus parties will invariably make incomplete contracts that do not specify how participants should behave under all possible circumstances, but rather only sketch general codes of conduct.[17] The stand-

[16] The case in which the actors have different preferences between the two Pareto-efficient equilibria is discussed below.
[17] Kreps, "Corporate Culture"; Paul Milgrom and John Roberts, "Bargaining Costs, Influence Costs, and the Organization of Economic Activity," in Alt and Shepsle, *Perspectives on Positive Political Economy.*

ard prisoner's dilemma formulation of the problem of cooperation thus does not address this issue because it allows no room for ambiguity.

Incomplete contracts present a large challenge for studies based on the notion that institutions merely facilitate adherence to a predetermined set of rules of the game. The reason is that incomplete agreements imply that in certain circumstances, what is required by the rules of the game cannot be determined uniquely. Thus analyses of cooperation must explain how the institutions deal with unanticipated contingencies, and why members acquiesce in the decisions of these institutions as to the application of the rules of the game in specific cases.

Consider the following example of the breakdown of cooperative arrangements in the face of unexpected events.[18] After the United States invaded and defeated Mexico in the mid-1840s, the Hidalgo Treaty established the middle of the Rio Grande as the U.S.-Mexican border. No problems arose for many decades until, early in the twentieth century, the river moved fifty miles south. The United States immediately occupied the land, and a dispute with Mexico arose over whether this action constituted a violation of the treaty. The United States, relying on the letter of the law, argued that it did not. Mexico, interpreting the spirit of the law, argued that the treaty designated the border as the middle of the river at the time of signing, regardless of where it might subsequently move.

How were third parties—critical to the efficacy of all international agreements—to arbitrate this dispute? Without any previous agreement on how to coordinate their evaluations in the face of this unexpected outcome, members of the international community could not agree about whether the United States' action constituted a violation. The critical absence of a set of shared beliefs about whether a violation had occurred proved a primary problem for decentralized coordination: the absence of agreement led to the breakdown of the community punishment mechanism. In fact, it took nearly half a century for this dispute to be settled in the absence of mechanisms for coordinating expectations about determining "fair" borders.

THE MICROFOUNDATIONS OF THE ROLE OF IDEAS: CONSTRUCTED FOCAL POINTS

The above discussion suggests that existing approaches to the politics of cooperation are inadequate in two related ways. First, they fail to

---

[18] We thank Bruce Bueno de Mesquita for bringing this example to our attention.

explain how actors settle on particular rules of the game, including the relevant organizing principles and supporting institutions, from among the many sets that are available. Second, they do not consider the impact of ambiguity and unanticipated contingencies on the role of institutions in the implementation of these rules: how institutions arbitrate disputes that are not directly covered by their mandates, and why members might adhere to their decisions.

Let us return to the question how actors settle on one solution to a cooperation problem when there are multiple sustainable equilibria with no "rational" desiderata (in terms of efficiency or self-interest) for choice. Thomas Schelling's argument about "focal points" suggests a strong role for such factors as culture, history, ideas, and institutional legacies—things that might provide the basis of a shared belief system:

> Most bargaining situations ultimately involve some range of possible outcomes within which each party would rather make a concession than fail to reach agreement at all. . . . Each party's strategy is guided mainly by what he expects the other to accept or insist on; yet each knows that the other is guided by reciprocal thoughts. The final outcome must be a point from which neither expects the other to retreat; yet the main ingredient of this expectation is what one thinks the other expects the first to expect, and so on. . . . These infinitely reflexive expectations must somehow converge on a single point, at which each expects the other not to expect to be expected to retreat.
>
> If we then ask what it is that can bring these expectations into convergence and bring the negotiations to a close, we might propose that it is the intrinsic magnetism of particular outcomes, especially those that enjoy prominence, uniqueness, simplicity, precedent, or some rationale that makes them qualitatively differentiable from the continuum of possible alternatives.[19]

Put simply, some solutions are inherently more likely to emerge because the actors believe that others will choose them too.[20] These beliefs

---

[19] Schelling, *Strategy of Conflict*, p. 70.

[20] Consider the following permutation of the infamous chicken game. Two joggers are moving toward each other on a narrow path in a dense forest. The path is sufficiently wide for both to pass without contact, but the two joggers approach each other down the middle of the path (perhaps the edges are muddy). They share a common interest in separating, but if both move in the same direction they will run into each other. How will the joggers move along the path? If both joggers are American, they might both move to their right (in accordance with American road rules). If both were British, each might instinctively move left. If one were from each country, the probability of collision would probably increase. Furthermore, even if the two joggers were to discuss their rules for engagement before they set out, national origin might still heavily influence how quickly and easily they could settle on a solution to their mutual problem. Kreps makes a similar point with respect to the reactions of foreign students to experimental games with culturally biased expectations: "Corporate Culture," p. 121.

are based not on rational calculations about strategic interests but rather on expectations that are likely to be functions of culture, past practices, existing institutions, organizational routines, and the like.[21] The potential importance of focal points is even greater in the context of incomplete contracting, as David Kreps makes clear:

> . . . in many transactions, particularly ongoing ones, contingencies typically arise that were unforeseen at the time of the transaction itself. Many transactions will potentially be too costly to undertake if the participants cannot rely on efficient and equitable adaptation to those unforeseen contingencies. Note that such reliance will necessarily involve blind faith; if we cannot foresee a contingency, we cannot know in advance that we can efficiently and equitably meet it.
>
> When we speak of adaptation to unforeseen contingencies we cannot specify, *ex ante*, how those contingencies will be met. We can at best give some sort of principle or rule that has wide (preferably universal) applicability and that is simple enough to be interpreted by all concerned. In the language of game theory, unforeseen contingencies are best met by the sort of principle that underlies what Schelling calls a focal point.[22]

If focal points are so important to the resolution of coordination problems, it is important to ask: How do they arise in the first place? As Schelling emphasizes, their value is that they are "conspicuous." Yet many situations may afford no set of actions that is sufficiently conspicuous to serve as the unique focal point; worse, in many situations there may be a multitude of conflicting solutions.

Consider a simple game of cooperation with both multiple equilibria and distributional asymmetries. This game can be illustrated by a simple permutation of the payoff matrix of Figure 1 which transforms the pure coordination game into a "battle of the sexes." In Figure 2, players A and B are no longer indifferent about coordinating on the strategy combinations (C_1, C_1) and (C_2, C_2): A prefers the former, B favors the latter. These problems multiply as the community expands. In situations of this sort, no decentralized consensus is likely to emerge as to which of the many paths to cooperation should be utilized.

It is in such situations that institutions may play an important role in the coordination of behavior. In the absence of a natural or preexisting focal point, an institution can *construct* one by devising the required set of specifications (as to the nature of the agreement, and hence as to what constitutes cooperation and defection) and by making

---

[21] Of course, it could be argued that the weight of "the past" is determined less by the logic of focal points than by such efficiency considerations as "sunk costs."

[22] Kreps, "Corporate Culture," pp. 92–93.

Player B

		C1	C2	D
	C1	3, 2	0, 0	–1, 4
Player A	C2	0, 0	2, 3	–1, 4
	D	4, –1	4, –1	0, 0

Note: The payoffs to player A appear first.

Figure 2. The "battle of the sexes" game nested within the prisoner's dilemma

them known to the community. Without such an institution, actors in the community must first recognize the problem, arrive at a *common* understanding of the problem and its solution, and then recognize and punish defectors. Failure at any one of these steps would lead to the breakdown of cooperation. The existence of an institution might break this chain by transforming each individual's problem to that of observing the pronouncements of the institution. The principal role of the institution would thus be to create a shared belief system about cooperation and defection in the context of differential and conflicting sets of individual beliefs that inhibit the decentralized emergence of cooperation.

In this formulation, institutions and decentralized community enforcement of norms and shared beliefs are thus complementary.[23] The role of the institutions is not to replace the mechanisms of decentralized cooperation but to help them work in precisely those situations in which they alone would fail.[24] Institutions do not take on the role of enforcement but rather help the community to coordinate expectations and interpretations so that decentralized punishment can play that role.

Thus, with respect to the types of problems discussed in the cooperation literature, our analysis of constructed focal points and shared belief systems may generate significant leverage over the questions that cannot be addressed by conventional approaches: the choice of governing principles and their future application in specific cases. This position is clearly consistent with the broad thrust of "reflectivist" criticisms

[23] Greif et al., "Coordination, Commitment, and Enforcement."
[24] Milgrom and Roberts, "Bargaining Costs."

of interest-based approaches.[25] Unlike these critics, however, we do not wish to engage in epistemological debates about the origins of preferences and about structure versus agency. Rather, we simply hope to show that microfoundational and ideational approaches are not mutually irreconcilable and indeed may very fruitfully be integrated.

IDEAS, INTERESTS, AND INSTITUTIONS

The assertion that ideas may play important roles in the generation and perpetuation of cooperation is likely to have raised some skeptical eyebrows among those with realist and rationalist predilections, even if the inability of conventional models to deal with multiple equilibria and incomplete contracting is acknowledged. Two central charges could be made. First, constructed focal points may play important roles in the resolution of multiple equilibria problems when the actors have no preference among the potential outcomes. But when their preferences diverge, the actors' relative capabilities or "power" will have a great bearing on outcomes. Second, if institutions are given autonomy to overcome incomplete contracting problems by interpreting the spirit of the law, there is nothing to stop them from abusing their positions to further their own ends (hence undermining the cooperative agreement). These are serious challenges that must be confronted. But it should be remembered that we wish to integrate ideas and interests rather than segregate them.

Let us begin by assessing the impact of power on choices between contending cooperative equilibria with distributional asymmetries (recall Figure 2). There are good reasons to think that power considerations may play an important part in the choice between such equilibria.[26] Put simply, the powerful are more likely to get what they want. There are many potential sources of power, such as formal first-mover advantages, the ability to make credible commitments,[27] strategic

[25] Fritz Kratochwil and John Ruggie, "International Organization: A State of the Art on the Art of the State," *International Organization* 40 (1986): 753–75; Alexander Wendt, "The Agent-Structure Problem in International Organization," *International Organization* 41 (1987): 335–70, and "Anarchy Is What States Make of It," *International Organization* 46 (1992): 391–425.

[26] Garrett, "International Cooperation and Institutional Choice"; Krasner, "Global Communications and National Power."

[27] Robert Putnam, "Diplomacy and Domestic Politics," *International Organization* 42 (1988): 427–60.

issue linkage,[28] the relative opportunity costs of exit,[29] and differences in the time horizons of actors.[30]

It is perfectly possible, however, that the logic of focal points might operate in this case as well as in the pure coordination game analyzed earlier. Indeed, Schelling explicitly asserts that the outcomes of games with asymmetrical consequences "may not be so much . . . conspicuously in balance with the estimated bargaining powers (of actors) as just plain 'conspicuous.'"[31]

How can we evaluate the impact of constructed focal points and relative power on the resolution of such games? Rather than seek to refute the assertion that "power matters," we suggest that the influence of focal points and shared belief systems is likely to vary significantly with the structure of given strategic interactions. The lesser the distributional asymmetries between contending cooperative equilibria and the smaller the disparities in the power resources of actors, the more important will be ideational factors. Similarly, the effects of focal points will increase with the actors' uncertainty about the consequences of agreements or about their relative capabilities. Thus both power and ideas can be expected significantly to influence the resolution of multiple-equilibria problems, but the relative explanatory power of each is likely to vary significantly with the context.

The second concern of our rationalist skeptic pertains to potential abuses of power by institutions to which authority is delegated. We argued that institutions that embody the shared beliefs of the participants in a cooperative agreement might apply the spirit of the law to contingencies unanticipated at the formation of the agreement, and that this course would be vital to the stability of cooperative arrangements. But once authority is delegated, how can participants be sure that the institution will act in this manner, rather than abuse its authority? This problem is sufficiently important that if the relevant actors could not be sufficiently confident as to the answer to this question, it is improbable that they would delegate authority to such an institution.

To address this issue, it may be helpful to draw parallels with the recent American public law literature that analyzes the constraints on U.S. courts with high levels of formal independence of the executive

[28] Ernst Haas, "Why Collaborate? Issue-Linking and International Regimes," *World Politics* 32 (1980): 357–405.

[29] Albert Hirschman, *National Power and the Structure of Foreign Trade*, rev. ed. (Berkeley: University of California Press, 1980).

[30] Ariel Rubenstein, "Perfect Equilibrium in a Bargaining Model," *Econometrica* 50 (1982): 97–109.

[31] Schelling, *Strategy of Conflict*, p. 69.

and legislative branches of government.[32] These studies stress that the process of lawmaking is ongoing. Unanticipated contingencies will be encountered and they must be dealt with. When courts make individual decisions, however, they must always be aware that their decisions may be overridden by political actors. This process need not entail overt legislative action. Simple noncompliance can also be effective. So long as the members of institutions with delegated powers value their positions, they will act carefully to guard their reputations as fair and just interpreters of the rules of the game. If the members of a cooperative arrangement and the institutions they create to maintain cooperation share similar views about right and wrong, the vexing problem of incomplete contracting may be overcome.

THE SINGLE EUROPEAN ACT: EXPEDIENCY, INTERESTS, AND IDEAS

Having developed theoretical arguments about the role of self-interest and ideas in the evolution of cooperation, let us move to the specific case of the creation and operation of the EC's internal market. It is not controversial to assert that the European economies had powerful incentives to liberalize trade among them in the mid-1980s. In accordance with Ricardian theory, numerous economic assessments suggest that large gains from exchange—gains in productivity, output, and employment—would accrue from the creation of an internal market.[33] Moreover, it is clear that these incentives were stronger in the 1980s than they had been earlier.

Ever-growing dependence on trade combined with more than a decade of poor and declining economic performance ("Eurosclerosis") to increase greatly the benefits of a potential internal market in relation to the costs of participation. The linkages between national economies within Europe grew rapidly in the 1970s.[34] With increasing interdepen-

---

[32] John A. Ferejohn and Charles R. Shipan, "Congressional Influence on Administrative Agencies: A Case Study of Telecommunications Policy," in *Congress Reconsidered,* ed. Larry Dodd and Bruce Oppenheimer, 4th ed. (Washington, D.C.: Congressional Quarterly Press, 1990); Brian Marks, "A Model of Judicial Influence on Congressional Policy Making: *Grove City College* v. *Bell,*" Working Papers in Political Science P-88-7, Hoover Institution, 1988; Pablo Spiller and Raphael Gely, "Congressional Control or Judicial Independence: The Determinants of U.S. Supreme Court Labor Relations Decisions, 1949–1988" (manuscript, University of Illinois, 1991).

[33] Paulo Cecchini, *1992: The Benefits of a Single Market* (Aldershot: Gower, 1988); Michael Emerson, *The Economics of 1992* (New York: Oxford University Press, 1988); and Tomasso Padoa-Schioppa et al., *Efficiency, Stability, and Equity: A Strategy for the Evolution of the Economic System of the European Community* (Oxford: Oxford University Press, 1987).

[34] The openness of the EC economics (exports + imports ÷ GDP) rose from less than 40% in the mid-1960s to over 60% by the early 1980s. Moreover, intra-Community trade

dence, the efficacy of economic strategies based on the manipulation of the domestic market and protection from external forces was significantly reduced, and all governments were forced to concentrate instead on improving the competitiveness of national goods and services in world markets and on adjusting quickly and efficiently to changing market conditions.[35]

Developments in the relationships between European nations and the other major players in the international economy, notably Japan and the United States, also generated incentives for regional integration. The European economies had suffered through more than ten years of industrial unrest and stagflation when the world economy began to recover from the second OPEC shock in the winter of 1982–1983. The American and Japanese recoveries were swift and strong, but the European economies did not rebound nearly so effectively.[36] It came increasingly to be perceived that if European producers were to compete effectively in global markets, something had to be done to redress Europe's trade imbalances with North America and particularly with Japan and the newly industrialized countries of eastern Asia.

In sum, there were strong functional reasons to expect that the members of the EC might seek to complete their internal market after the mid-1980s. The costs of remaining at the status quo were very high. The potential payoffs of an EC internal market were large, irrespective of whether they were viewed in terms of a "fortress Europe" of new and ingenious forms of neoprotectionism or as accruing from the logic of comparative advantage and economies of scale.

Efficiency-based reasoning also suggests that the creation of an internal market would have entailed significant delegations of authority to supranational institutions. There were, however, numerous potential paths toward cooperation. Without an explicit agreement on the path of cooperation, the nature of defection would have been ambiguous. Moreover, it would have been very difficult to monitor the behavior of all actors in the large and complex European economy even if defection

---

as a portion of the total trade of EC members also grew in the same period from under one-half to over two-thirds. For a more detailed analysis see Per Manus Wijkam, "Patterns and Production of Trade," in *The Dynamics of European Integration*, ed. William Wallace (New York: Free Press, 1990).

[35] Geoffrey Garrett and Peter Lange, "Political Responses to Interdependence: What's Left for the Left," *International Organization* 46 (1991): 539–64.

[36] U.S. growth in 1984 was 6.7%, compared with −2.5% in 1982, whereas growth rates for the EC had changed from significant negative figures in the early 1980s only to 2.4% by 1984. More important from a political standpoint, the disparity in unemployment performance was even larger. The U.S. rate declined from its zenith of 9.5% in 1982 to 7.1% in 1985, while EC unemployment continued to over 10% by 1985.

were theoretically clear-cut. Finally, unforeseen contingencies were likely to be endemic.

Arguments showing that some form of institutionalized internal market was likely to emerge in Europe after the mid-1980s, however, cannot shed much light on the question of the specific form the market would assume. Numerous economic principles and supporting institutional infrastructures could, hypothetically, sustain an internal market, with scant grounds for distinguishing between them in terms of efficiency. Economically, an internal market could have been based on pervasive deregulation at the national level, with no concomitant re-regulation at the EC level. Alternatively, an array of EC regulations could have been layered on top of existing national regimes. With respect to political institutions, the EC members could have supported the internal market by granting more executive power to the commission, by ceding more authority to the European Parliament, by reforming the Council of Ministers, by creating a more federal Europe (with an authoritative government and judiciary, for example), or some combination of these measures.

The point of these hypothetical scenarios is simply to show that no natural route toward cooperation existed. Thus one had to be constructed. The basic economic principle that emerged for ordering the internal market was mutual recognition: goods and services that may legally be sold in one country should have unrestricted access to other markets.[37] The decision by the member governments to choose this principle in the mid-1980s postdated the assertion of the European Court of Justice in *Cassis de Dijon* (1979) that mutual recognition was already EC law.

This evolution accords with our argument about the need to construct focal points when they do not naturally exist. A large range of methods could have been used to underpin the move toward integration. The court's decision did not *force* the members of the EC to adopt mutual recognition. The fact that they did so—in signing the SEA and in endorsing the commission's White Paper on Completing the Internal Market—suggests that the court's decision acted as a focal point around which EC members could coordinate their bargaining.[38]

It would be interesting to speculate as to what might have happened in the absence of the *Cassis* decision. Without such a focal point, the process of negotiation might have been more drawn out but still would

---

[37] Health and safety and environmental considerations override this principle.

[38] Renaud de Housse and Joseph Weiler, "The Legal Dimension," and Robert Keohane and Stanley Hoffmann, "Conclusions: Community Politics and Institutional Change," both in Wallace, *Dynamics of European Integration*.

ultimately have arrived at the same outcome. But a stronger "ideas matter" argument can be made. What would have happened if members of the EC had in fact not approved mutual recognition and wished instead for a more highly regulated internal market, contra *Cassis de Dijon?* To have created such a market would have entailed repudiating both the authority of the court and, more significant, the document on which the EC was founded, the Treaty of Rome (1958), since the court asserted that the treaty's declared objective of the "removal of all barriers to movement" necessarily implied mutual·recognition. It is always extremely difficult to obtain the necessary unanimity for treaty revisions. It would have been even harder to do so if the revisions entailed rejection of the spirit of the Treaty of Rome and the letter of EC law. It was far more likely that any revisions would have been coordinated around the focal point of mutual recognition. The force of ECJ decisions is thus not necessarily limited to their legal standing. As Schelling observed more generally: "Precedent seems to exercise an influence that greatly exceeds its logical importance or legal force. . . . Sometimes, to be sure, there is a reason for a measure of uniformity . . . but more often it seems that there is simply no heart left in the bargaining when it takes place in the shadow of some dramatic and conspicuous precedent."[39]

Lest we present a one-sided interpretation of the internal market, it is important to note at this point that mutual recognition was the preferred economic principle of the most powerful political and economic actors in Europe. The stances of the "big three" countries in the EC—Britain, France, and Germany—toward trade liberalization converged markedly in the early 1980s.[40] Thatcher obviously supported mutual recognition in virtue of its laissez-faire connotations. The German center-right coalition also favored it because its highly competitive firms could only gain by greater freedom of access to foreign markets.[41] The failure of François Mitterrand's "Keynesianism in one country" experiment led him to assume a much more liberal internationalist stance from 1983 on. Furthermore, all large European companies became ever more frustrated by the barriers to their carrying on of business beyond national borders. In addition to pressuring their governments, big business lobbied the Brussels establishment directly

---

[39] Schelling, *Strategy of Conflict*, pp. 67–68.

[40] Andrew Moravcsik, "Negotiating the Single European Act: National Interests and Conventional Statecraft in the European Community," *International Organization* 45 (1991): 19–56.

[41] It should be noted here that the German government was the loser in *Cassis*. Opposition to specific court decisions, however, by no means negates the more general assertion that the German government was a strong proponent of mutual recognition.

as to the virtues of laissez-faire, and the commission was very receptive to these suggestions.[42]

The concerns of the big three governments may also explain the primary political reform of the Single European Act—the introduction of qualified majority voting in the Council of Ministers with respect to most matters pertaining to the internal market.[43] Historically, it had proved very difficult for the supporters of market liberalization to push measures through the council under the prevailing unanimity rule. When the big countries came to agree on the merits of liberalization, numerous initiatives were blocked by the social democratic governments of southern Europe, especially Greece. Indeed, even though Thatcher vehemently opposed circumscribing national sovereignty (as exemplified by her Bruges speech in 1988), she was prepared to support the introduction of qualified majority voting on internal market matters (so long as areas such as the social dimension were excluded). The qualified majority system significantly reduced the ability of the smaller EC members to block liberalization measures, so that Britain, France, and Germany (and their allies in the Low Countries) would often be able to push through measures.

In sum, then, (1) to say that the internal market was warranted on efficiency grounds is to take only the first step toward understanding European cooperation. To stop there is to neglect the central political questions about the precise form of European integration and the distributions of the costs and benefits. (2) Ideas—manifest in the ECJ's mutual recognition decision—and the interests of the powerful European actors were consistent with the process that culminated in the ratification in 1987 of the Single European Act. It is thus difficult to disentangle the independent effects of these two factors.

A more clearly articulated distinction between the roles of ideas and interests can be drawn with respect to the institutional mechanisms for translating the intent of the SEA into the day-to-day operation of the internal market—the EC's legal system.

THE COURT OF JUSTICE, EUROPEAN LAW, AND IMPLEMENTING THE INTERNAL MARKET

The basic political mechanism for moving from the general objectives of the SEA to a detailed internal market can be stated briefly. The

---

[42] Wayne Sandholtz and John Zysman, "1992: Recasting the European Bargain," *World Politics* 42 (1989): 95–128.

[43] Moravcsik, "Negotiating the Single European Act."

commission's white paper proposed more than 270 measures deemed necessary to complete the internal market.[44] The Council of Ministers may vote by qualified majority on whether to implement these proposals.[45] Most decisions duly passed by the council have the status of "directives."[46] Directives formulate guidelines for action, to be translated into domestic legislation by national governments. Once a directive becomes part of national law, it may be enforced conventionally (and hence be supported by all the sanctions available to domestic courts). If this procedure is followed—as it has been in many instances[47]—there is no puzzle to adherence to internal market rules: they simply become part of national law.

Internal market rules, however, can be implemented in many other ways. In each the European Court of Justice plays a powerful role.[48] Figure 3 depicts this more complex array of implementation mechanisms. To explore the intricacies of these implementation paths, it is helpful to investigate the options available to a private party that believes it has suffered from the transgression of an internal market rule (by an individual, a firm, or a national government).[49] As we mentioned earlier, the SEA envisaged that the council would pass a directive relevant to the grievance, that this directive would be legislated into national law, and hence that the aggrieved party could bring suit in a

[44] In keeping with the spirit of *Cassis*, the white paper comprised what was considered to be the minimum set of issues that needed to be harmonized to achieve a functioning single market without internal barriers. Thus the bulk of the white paper's proposals concern technical standards and health and safety provisions.

[45] The passage of internal market directives requires the participation of both the commission (which alone has the right to make proposals) and the European Parliament (which has limited veto rights). The council, however, remains the preeminent decision-making institution in the EC. For detailed analyses of the interactions of the commission, council, and parliament since the passage of the SEA see Garrett, "International Cooperation and Institutional Choice," and George Tsebelis, "The Power of the European Parliament as a Conditional Agenda Setter," papers presented at the Annual Meeting of the American Political Science Association, 1992.

[46] By the middle of 1992, over three-quarters of these directives had been approved by the Council of Ministers.

[47] The United Kingdom and Denmark have the best records for legislation implementing internal market directives. The southern European states have tended to be laggards. This pattern is a result of the fact that most directives that thus far have been passed by the Council of Ministers have dealt with the elimination of barriers to the free movement of goods and services rather than the creation of a more interventionist internal market.

[48] The discussion of the EC legal system draws heavily on Anne-Marie Burley and Walter Mattli, "The Law and Politics of the European Court of Justice: Law as a Mask," *International Organization* (forthcoming); Koen Lenaerts, "The Role of the Court of Justice in the European Community," *University of Chicago Legal Forum* (forthcoming); Stein, "Lawyers, Judges"; and Weiler, "Transformation of Europe."

[49] Individuals cannot petition the ECJ directly. The Treaty of Rome reserves this right for member states (art. 70) and the commission (art. 169). Thus, to delineate the full scope of the EC legal structure, it is better to begin with cases in national courts.

domestic court. But this sequence (the upper left corner of Figure 3) represents only a small part of the implementation game tree. All decisions are subject, through one mechanism or another, to review by the European Court.

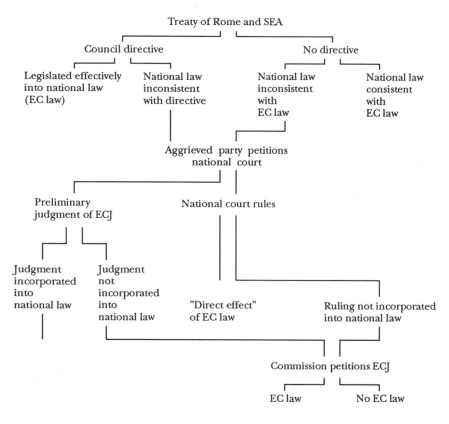

Figure 3. The implementation of internal market directives

What can the aggrieved party do if it believes that national law is inconsistent with a directive that has been passed by the council (because the national government either has not legislated the directive into national law or has done so inappropriately) or if no directive exists and the party believes prevailing national law is inconsistent with the Treaty of Rome or the SEA? In either case, the aggrieved party may petition a domestic court and ask for a judgment that the rights accruing to it under the Treaty of Rome and subsequent pronouncements of the EC have been violated. A national court hearing such a case has two basic options. It may simply apply what it believes to be EC law (the doctrine of "direct effect") or it may ask the European Court of Justice for a preliminary ruling as to the status of EC law with respect to the case at hand (pursuant to section 177 of the Treaty of Rome). If by either of these procedures the national court rules in favor of the plaintiff, EC law will effectively have dominated both the will of the national government and existing national law. This is the so-called supremacy of EC law. The aggrieved party that does not receive a favorable ruling in the national court may request that the EC Commission petition the ECJ directly. At this point, the court will make an explicit determination about the nature of EC law.

This system has been quite effective. Indeed, in numerous instances European law has constrained the behavior of members even in areas that impinge directly on the traditional authority of national governments. Two types of cases should be highlighted: those in which the legal system has upheld directives passed by the council against the opposition of national governments; and those in which domestic courts (and ultimately the ECJ) have gone even further to enforce as EC law measures that have not been approved by the council (as envisaged by the SEA).

First, in numerous cases domestic judges and the European Court have upheld directives against the wishes of national governments. The case of public procurement provides an interesting example. Preferential procurement decisions have long been important instruments of protection in the EC, allowing governments to favor domestic contractors in the granting of public contracts. In 1989–1990 the EC passed a series of directives severely limiting the scope for such preferential treatment.[50] In light of these directives, some governments have chosen to open up public tenders to foreign firms. In 1990, for instance, a German company won the contract to build the Marseilles metro and an Italian corporation was awarded the tender to construct a road bypass around Lyon.

Furthermore, in one important instance a direct threat to bring an action before the Court of Justice led a government to alter its behavior significantly with respect to the awarding of a large public contract. After receiving numerous bids from firms in many countries, the Danish government decided in 1989 to give the contract for the building of the Great Belt Eastern Bridge, between Denmark and Sweden, to a domestic contractor. A British-French consortium believed that its tender was more competitive, and took its complaint to the EC Commis-

[50] The primary areas exempted from the directives are energy contracts and public transport.

sion. The commission threatened to prosecute the Danish government in the ECJ. Fearing an adverse judgment by the court, the Danish government ultimately agreed to pay costs and damages to the foreign consortium rather than to proceed with the case (which it probably would have lost).[51]

Second, pro-EC judicial activism has recently been taken even further. The British government has long wished to protect its national fishing industry against open competition. Among other things, it has refused to register foreign fishing boats as legitimate farmers of British waters. Moreover, the Conservative government was a leading partner in a coalition in the Council of Ministers which blocked the passage of a commission proposal to liberalize the European fishing industry. As a result of this intransigence, Spanish fishermen brought a case in a British court seeking a declaration that the government's behavior violated EC law (even though no fishing directive had been issued).

This case eventually was heard by the ECJ in 1991 (*Commission v. United Kingdom*). The court ruled against the British government. It argued that the commission's proposed directive to the council was in accordance with the EC treaties and so should have been passed by the council. The court reasoned that the commission proposal thus became EC law, even though enough members in the council (including Britain) voted against it to defeat its passage as a directive.

From the perspective of traditional international law—in which the rights and obligations generated by treaties are determined solely by the contracting parties themselves—the legal structure of the EC and the case law outlined above are quite extraordinary. The system of laws is one that is far more akin to that of an entrenched written constitution that empowers the judiciary to act as its guardian.[52] But the EC is not a federal political organization; at best it might be considered a very loose confederation. Neither the Treaty of Rome nor the SEA created new supranational "sovereign" institutions above national governments. Moreover, there is no formal institutional linkage between the European Court and national judiciaries: the ECJ's decisions formally do not affect national legal systems. Finally, the court's sanctioning powers are very limited. It has no formal jurisdiction over private parties. Its decisions are supposed to be binding on national governments, but it

[51] In 1990, after an Italian subsidiary of Du Pont had appealed to the commission, the ECJ ruled that an Italian law requiring 30% of contracts to be awarded to firms based in southern Italy violated the public procurement directive. The response of the Italian government to the ruling is not yet clear. If the government modifies the law, however, this case would represent an even greater encroachment of EC law on national politics.
[52] Stein, "Lawyers, Judges."

cannot enforce such decisions directly. The commission may fine firms that breach EC law, but not governments.

Thus the keys to the effectiveness of the EC's legal system are the doctrine of direct effect and the willingness of national courts to refer cases to the ECJ for preliminary judgment. The vast majority of cases determined by EC law are decided either in national courts (applying existing EC law) or through preliminary judgments of the ECJ. In either case, the great force of European Court decisions is incommensurate with its formal attributes.

The decisions of the ECJ have had an enormous impact on the evolution of this "constitutional" system. The mandate for the ECJ emanating from the Treaty of Rome is to enforce the provisions of the treaty, all decisions made in accordance with it (by the council and commission), and any subsequent revisions of the treaty (such as the SEA). The Treaty of Rome did not make clear, however, the status of EC law vis-à-vis national laws. So long as the domain of EC law was limited to cases brought before the Court of Justice, it was likely that national governments would view court decisions as conventional treaty obligations to be determined as they saw fit.

This situation was transformed in the path-breaking *Van Gend* case (1963). The Court of Justice ruled that to protect the rights of individuals and other private actors with respect to the Treaty of Rome, the treaty must have "direct effect" in national courts (recall that individuals do not have recourse to the ECJ). Then in *Costa v. ENEL* (1964) the court extended the principle of direct effect to the "supremacy" of EC law over national laws (irrespective of when the national law was written). Finally, in *Van Duyn* (1974) the court ruled that even directives that had not been legislated into national law became EC law as soon as they were passed by the Council of Ministers. Of course, in virtue of the two earlier cases, the court is not limited to making decisions on the basis of directives, but rather may rule that the Treaty of Rome or the SEA mandates or proscribes certain behavior even if the council has not yet passed an appropriate directive. This is precisely the thrust of the court's ruling in *Cassis de Dijon*.

But this situation creates a puzzle: The mere assertion by the Court of Justice of the direct effect and supremacy of its rulings on EC law cannot explain the effectiveness of the European legal system. The critical question is why the sovereign nations of the EC—and particularly national governments and judiciaries—have acquiesced in the ECJ's extraordinary restructuring of the legal system. Eric Stein contends that the ECJ was able to increase its power simply because of a lack of interest on the part of national governments.[53] Lack of interest may have been part of the explanation before the signing of the SEA, but it seems far less plausible in the context of the completion of the internal market. The whole purpose of the introduction of qualified majority voting in the council was to expand the scope of the internal market. Expansion of the internal market would necessarily entail a concomitant expansion in the scope of the ECJ's power.

Why, then, did the members of the EC not circumscribe the role of the court in the SEA? The logic of constructed focal points provides a simple and powerful answer. Reform of the Treaty of Rome is always very difficult because of the requirement of unanimity. Given the pre-existence of a stable legal system, it could be considered unlikely that all the member states would have been able to agree on some alternative arrangement (especially when there was no obvious option).

It should also be pointed out, however, that the EC legal system was actually—and seemingly paradoxically, given its consequences for national sovereignty—consistent with the interests of member governments in liberalizing trade in the EC. In order to make this argument, one must view the delegation of authority to the ECJ in terms of the monitoring and incomplete contracting problems confronting EC members.

MONITORING, INCOMPLETE CONTRACTING, AND THE ROLE OF THE EUROPEAN COURT

Recall that a central objective of actors wishing to engage in stable cooperation in complex environments is the construction of institutions that monitor the behavior of participants, identify transgressions, and apply the general rules of the game to myriad unanticipated contingencies. Now consider the hypothetical case of the EC's internal market without an effective legal branch: members agreed to the general principle of the market (mutual recognition), to qualified majority decision making in the council, and to the implementation of these rules by the commission.

We expect that compliance with such rules would not be high because it would be relatively easy for disaffected parties to ignore internal market principles when there are ambiguities with respect to compliance—either in what constituted defection or in the monitoring of

---

[53] Ibid.

behavior.[54] Even though the commission's staff has grown rapidly since the mid-1980s, it is still far too small to scrutinize all economic transactions within the EC effectively. The creation of a legal system in which it is in the interests of a party that believes it has not been treated in accordance with an internal market directive to seek recourse to the courts is an effective means for dealing with this problem.

In the EC legal system, monitoring is not only decentralized but also highly efficient. To see its efficiency, let us explore how this institution inhibits potential defection by an individual government. At the apex of the system, the ECJ has no formal sanctions over national governments that ignore its decisions. Nonetheless, the existence of the EC legal system has dramatically changed the nature and consequences of violations of the mutual recognition principle. Without this legal system, it would be difficult for governments to observe defections and to evaluate their significance. Moreover, even if all governments could independently come to their own judgments on these matters, nothing ensures that they would arrive at the same decisions. Given these expectations, the incentives for any government to flout internal market rules would be substantial.

The EC legal system dramatically transforms the problem. First, it implies that if a government defects, it must do so in a very public way, much like the basketball player who must raise a hand after committing a foul. Other governments no longer need to uncover potential violations, or investigate their importance, or determine whether a particular action constitutes a transgression. Instead, they need only observe the pronouncements of the courts. The ability of aggrieved individuals to bring such behavior to the attention of the courts—and of the courts to paint scarlet letters on offenders—greatly reduces the incentives for such behavior. The loss of incentive in turn facilitates the logic of retaliation and reputation in iterated games. So long as EC members value effective participation in the internal market more highly than they do the benefits of defecting from rules that affect them adversely, it is unlikely that governments will jeopardize their positions through flagrant violations of commonly agreed rules.[55] It should be noted,

[54] Roger G. Noll, "The Economics and Politics of Deregulation," Jean Monet Chair Papers, the European Policy Unit at the European University Institute, Badia Fiesolana, Italy, 1992.

[55] Of course, some matters are of such vital concern to member governments that the sanctions of retaliation and lost reputations will be insufficient to dissuade them from violating internal market rules. Many of these matters were anticipated in the SEA (the areas not subject to qualified majority voting). Furthermore, it is well understood that some governments on occasion simply will not be able to abide by internal market rules, and in such cases others are unlikely to punish such behavior. In these senses, the system

however, that this system is far from perfect. As is well known, there still are instances in which member governments can evade court rulings—by appealing, for instance, to environmental or health and safety concerns to justify protectionist practices.[56] Indeed, Martin Shapiro has argued that the existence of such loopholes most likely represents a lack of consensus between members on how far the free market principle should be pushed.[57]

At this point it should also be emphasized that the combination of the Treaty of Rome, the SEA, and even the directives pertaining to the internal market do not constitute a complete contract by the EC members. The treaties only propose general guidelines for the form the completed internal market should assume. Directives are not detailed provisions that are intended to be applied directly and literally. Indeed, it is inconceivable that the members of the EC could have sought to write an exhaustive set of rules to govern the internal market. Rather, they knew that if they were to forge a cooperative agreement with any chance of longevity, they would have to do so on the basis of an incomplete contract, delegating to another institution the application of its general intent to specific cases. This is precisely the role played by the ECJ in the internal market: to uphold and interpret the doctrine of mutual recognition in all disputes that arise.

The ECJ and Political Accountability

The last point about incomplete contracts and the delegation of authority to the ECJ brings to center stage an issue that we have thus far addressed only in passing. If this significant delegation of authority is to be in the interests of the EC's members, the court must faithfully implement the spirit of the internal market rules to which they agreed. Given that members have not objected to the extension of the power of the EC legal system, they must be confident that the court does fairly apply the principle of mutual recognition. Many observers have asserted that there is no basis for this confidence. According to this view, the court not only acts without close surveillance but does so in

---

for implementing the internal market is made even stronger by its recognition of cases in which adherence is simply out of the question.

[56] Noll, "Economics and Politics of Deregulation."

[57] Martin Shapiro, "European Court of Justice" (manuscript, University of California at Berkeley, 1991).

a manner that furthers its own preferences rather than those of the member states.[58] We believe that this conclusion is unwarranted.

Our logic is based on the new approach to studying the courts and especially the interaction of the courts and political officials. This approach, known as positive political theory (PPT), has been applied with considerable effect to critical issues in American public law.[59] The arguments can readily be extended to the EC legal system.

We begin with the observation that courts in general wish to maintain their authority, legitimacy, and independence. To do so, they must strive to act in ways that elected officials do not frequently reject.[60] Courts whose rulings are consistently overturned typically find themselves and their role in the political system weakened. As a consequence, the actions of courts are fundamentally "political" in that they must anticipate the possible reactions of other political actors in order to avoid their intervention.

The main implication of the observation is this: Embedding a legal system in a broader political structure places direct constraints on the discretion of a court, even one with as much constitutional independence as the United States Supreme Court. This conclusion holds even if the constitution makes no explicit provision for altering a court's role. The reason is that political actors have a range of avenues through which they may alter or limit the role of the courts. Sometimes such changes require amendment of the constitution, but usually the appropriate alterations may be accomplished more directly through statute, as by alteration of the court's jurisdiction in a way that makes it clear that continued undesired behavior will result in more radical changes.

---

[58] Burley and Mattli, "Law and Politics"; and Stein, "Lawyers, Judges."

[59] PPT has had a significant impact on public law, as witnessed by the striking set of special issues and symposia of law journals devoted to this topic over the past few years. Recent instances include "Positive Political Theory and Public Law," *Georgetown Law Journal* 80 (1992): 457–807; "Constitutional Law and Economics," *International Review of Law and Economics* 12 (1992): 123–296; and "Symposium on Positive Political Theory and Administrative Procedures," *Law and Contemporary Problems* (forthcoming). The conclusions that follow draw heavily on John A. Ferejohn and Barry R. Weingast, "A Positive Theory of Statutory Interpretation," *International Review of Law and Economics* 12 (1992): 263–79; Marks, "Model of Judicial Influence"; and Matthew McCubbins, Roger Noll, and Barry R. Weingast, "Positive and Normative Models of Due Process: An Integrative Approach to Administrative Procedures," *Journal of Law, Economics, and Organization* 6 (1990): 307–32.

[60] It should be remembered that courts are made up of individual justices whose tenures are shorter than those of their institutions. The reasons why individual judges are interested in maintaining the reputation of their institutions can be derived from intergenerational models in which the tenures of judges overlap. Equilibria may evolve between them in such a way that the authority of older judges is supported by the younger ones in exchange for the elder judges' forbearance to make decisions that will undermine the authority of the court as a whole.

This is not to say that courts are without some latitude. Indeed, one of the main objectives of PPT is to show the conditions under which the scope for autonomous behavior by judges is large and when it is small. Judges virtually always have some latitude. But a set of decisions that would provoke an explicit reaction against the court is equally possible. The principal conclusion of PPT is that *the possibility of such a reaction drives a court that wishes to preserve its independence and legitimacy to remain in the area of acceptable latitude.* While this proposition implies that the courts retain a degree of discretion, it also implies that their decisions are in no sense unconstrained.

The autonomy of the ECJ is clearly less entrenched than that of the Supreme Court of the United States. Its position is not explicitly supported by a constitution. One of the thirteen justices of the European Court is selected by each of the twelve member states, and their terms are renewable every six years. Many are likely to seek government employment in their home countries after they leave the ECJ.[61] Moreover, there is no guarantee that the trend to ever greater European integration—legal or otherwise—will continue. At any moment, the opposition of a few states would be enough to derail the whole process.

This observation suggests that the European Court should be at least as sensitive as the Supreme Court to the preferences of other important political actors, and would choose not to act in ways that they would disapprove. The justices of the European Court have an interest in furthering their powers to interpret and to extend the rules of the internal market (and European law more generally). This constraint is at least as powerful for domestic judges as it is for those sitting on the ECJ bench. By following the doctrine of direct effect and by referring cases to the ECJ for preliminary rulings, judges in domestic courts can significantly increase their authority vis-à-vis their national governments. But they cannot push this activism too far, lest they provoke a backlash by their governments.

The court knows that decisions against individual states are liable not to be followed by disaffected governments if they deem the court's rulings to violate fundamental national interests. The opprobrium of individual states, however, would be ineffective if the vast majority of members favored the court's decision (given the logic of the preceding section). A more serious threat to the ECJ's authority would arise if it were to incite a qualified majority in the Council of Ministers to write detailed directives that would more tightly circumscribe the court's

---

[61] It should be noted, however, that ECJ decisions are reported as the consensus of all justices. As no dissenting opinions are published, it is difficult for any national government to ascertain precisely how "its" judge is behaving on the court.

autonomy, despite the efficiency costs in doing so. The ultimate threat against the EC legal system is a revision of its treaty base. If the justices were to act far enough outside the range of outcomes acceptable to all members, the member states could act fundamentally to circumscribe their powers through further amendments to the Treaty of Rome—limiting, for instance, the extent of direct effect, or the areas in which EC law has supremacy over domestic law.

In sum, the broader institutional structure of the EC creates strong constraints against the court's willingness to act in ways that most members would deem unfair. Although the European Court of Justice can, in theory, rule a directive to be "unconstitutional," as a practical matter it will do so only when that ruling has widespread community support. To ignore this constraint would be to invite an explicit reaction that would overturn a court decision (by a directive, for instance) or worse, directly alter the scope of the court's autonomy, authority, or jurisdiction. Given these implied institutional constraints, the ability of the European Court to interpret broad directives facilitates the application of the internal market to situations not envisaged by the council members when they made their decisions.

Our argument about the EC legal system can be distilled to three points. First, the system works because the courts and the member states share a common framework about how the "internal market" should be applied in specific cases. With the principle of mutual recognition acting as a focal point, the European Court attempts faithfully to apply this basic principle to the wide array of cases it confronts. Second, the force of its rulings depends on acceptance by the member states of the changes in the European market that the legal system effects.

Our final point concerns the observation commonly made by legal scholars that the ECJ has the last word in the operation of the internal market. But as we have suggested, this assertion ignores a fundamental and ongoing interaction between the court and relevant political actors. Because a judicial decision may provoke a political reaction, the court does not have the final say.[62] The fact that a court's decisions are neither overturned nor the subject of considerable controversy does not demonstrate that it exercises real discretion. The opposite conclusion is also consistent with the same observation.[63] A court that can take decisions that will provoke an adverse political reaction may prevent those reac-

[62] Ferejohn and Weingast, "Positive Theory of Statutory Interpretation."
[63] Barry R. Weingast and Mark J. Moran, "Bureaucratic Discretion or Congressional Control? Regulatory Policy Making by the FTC," *Journal of Political Economy* 91 (1983): 765–800.

tions by avoiding such decisions. An absence of political reaction thus may reflect the court's willingness to steer away from the set of controversial decisions, not its discretion. Put another way, the absence of controversy or reaction may be the result of a highly constrained but politically sophisticated court rather than an unfettered and activist one.

The latter view may, in fact, characterize the ECJ, notwithstanding the very different arguments of legal scholars.

Toward a Theory of the Role of Ideas

The arguments we have presented have implications for a theory of the role of ideas in politics. Much of the literature on ideas is subject to two basic criticisms. First, ideas are a dime a dozen. For every idea that appears to play a major role in politics, tens of thousands play no role at all. Rarely do scholars explain why the idea they study had an impact when so many others did not. Second, too often an argument about the role of ideas amounts to an assertion that an idea mattered without a persuasive explanation for why or how it had influence. Such assertions often are entirely plausible. The problem is that invariably the events in question can be explained in numerous other ways that assign the ideas an ancillary role; that is, the ideas are epiphenomenal and some other variables—such as material interests—ultimately bear the causal weight.

Arguments about material interests should constitute the null hypothesis in research into the role of ideas. Yet few scholars who argue for the role of ideas provide persuasive evidence against the null hypothesis, thus simply leaving us with plausible but unsubstantiated assertions that the null hypothesis can be rejected.

A theory of the role of ideas must therefore go beyond the mere assertion that ideas matter. It must explain why one particular idea mattered, why it made a difference (that is, merits the status of independent causal variable). This is precisely what we have sought to achieve here. We argue that the impact of ideas with respect to cooperation between players—in this case the members of the EC, but they could equally well be any group engaged in a collective endeavor—is a function of three interrelated phenomena: (1) the gains to be expected from cooperation among a relevant set of players; (2) an idea that expresses these gains from cooperation; and (3) a mechanism devised to translate the idea into a shared belief system so as to affect expectations, and hence behavior. The mechanism may be thought of as an "institution" comprising elements both formal (organizational) and informal (shared understanding about and expectations of "fair" behavior).

Each of the three components must be taken into account if the role of ideas is to be understood. The first consists of the parties' motivations to cooperate.[64] The second associates the reasons for collective action with an idea. The third factor—the mechanism for translating the idea of collective action into reality—is clearly the most important. It helps explain why the idea—as implemented via a social mechanism—was necessary to capture the gains from cooperation.

The key to the success of an idea is that it be capable of being transmitted through a mechanism in a way that affects behavior in a desirable way from the standpoint of the members of a community. Our argument shows why, without the idea and its embodiment in a mechanism that changes or establishes a set of shared expectations about behavior, outcomes would be different from those we observe.

Ideas are important because they communicate the potential gains that may accrue from exchange, especially in situations in which some change in behavior must occur before these gains can be captured. Yet ideas are *not* self-implementing, because there are myriad ways to generate the associated gains. We have argued that decentralized attempts to cooperate by a community of agents are unlikely to succeed in these contexts. There is typically no unique path to cooperation; and for this reason and because of unanticipated events, what constitutes defection from a cooperative arrangement is unavoidably ambiguous.

In our approach, cooperation is facilitated by institutions that mitigate the problem of ambiguity in a variety of ways: by constructing a focal solution; by making declarations or judgments about what occurred in the past (on the occasion of an alleged defection, for example); and by determining what should occur from now on in the face of an unanticipated event. When such declarations are transparent, they potentially resolve problems of ambiguity.

But such mechanisms constitute only a necessary part of the solution, for the newly created role specialists must also be given the incentives to use their authority to benefit the community. Ideas here play a key role. In order to succeed, institutions must embody and perpetuate a *normative system* that translates the general idea for capturing the gains from cooperation into specific expectations and behaviors that make it

[64] The notion that the role of ideas embodies a notion of common interest or cooperation is familiar to rational choice theorists. But it also plays an important role in other arguments. For example, one of the major advocates of the role of ideas, Ernst Haas, argues that "all international organizations are deliberately designed by their founders to 'solve problems' that require collaborative action for a solution." See Ernst Haas, *When Knowledge Is Power* (Berkeley: University of California Press, 1990), p. 2.

possible to capture them. It is a normative system because it requires the institution to define what constitutes cooperation and defection, and hence good and bad behavior.

The necessity to create a successful normative system, in turn, places strong and direct bounds on the decisions and constructions issued by the institution. In the context of a set of actors voluntarily participating in an attempt to cooperate, the system must not only capture the potential gains from cooperation but distribute them in a manner that makes all better off. Otherwise, participation would fall off and the attempt would fail.

In the context of European integration, scholars have long trumpeted the importance of ideas. Most generally, the idea of a "united Europe" has for several decades animated a host of actors and focused attention on the possibility of a radical political and social organization for Europe. Our focus is not on the general process of this larger role of ideas but on the next step: how a specific idea or set of ideas translates into action. In the case of the EC, we must move beyond the notion of a united Europe to a set of institutions that have a hope of implementing the idea. In the absence of such institutions, the general inspiration underlying the idea must fail.

This problem is especially important for Europe because none of the EC institutions possesses clear sovereign authority. Participating nations remain free, in principle, to reject the system. If a sufficient portion of the participants disapproved of the set of policies and decisions, they would either reject or reconstitute the EC. This possibility in turn provides the principal incentive for the organs of the EC to create a normative system that serves the interests of the participants. Failure to do so risks the success of the entire enterprise.

In our model, ideas are important because they play a role in coordinating the expectations that are necessary to sustain cooperation among a set of players with divergent preferences. The idea must therefore squarely match its environment so that it facilitates the interaction of players to allow them to realize collective goals. Hence it is likely that the "right" idea will emerge only rarely, but that when it does, it will prove to be the catalyst that transforms politics. In this context idea and interests are intimately related; we must understand both if we are to understand how a set of individuals can overcome the impediments to cooperation.

In sum, our methodology has been to show that the null hypothesis—that the emergence and maintenance of cooperation can be explained purely in terms of self-interested behavior and the role of formal organizations—is inadequate in the case of the European internal market. We have done so by taking such arguments very seriously. Hence we have established scientific credibility for the assertion that "something else" must be added to the explanation. In turn, we have developed a model for the role of ideas that delineates precisely how shared beliefs facilitate the effective operation of the internal market. In so doing, we hope we have addressed the two challenges that habitually are made against ideational arguments.

CHAPTER EIGHT

Structure and Ideology: Change in Parliament in Early Stuart England

JOHN FEREJOHN

Institutions are limited in the kinds of things they can do. Parliaments, as "representative" institutions having relatively little control over their memberships, generally find it difficult to organize themselves to participate actively in government. The relative equality of members makes difficult the development of internal mechanisms of coordination and control that would permit a collective body to take rapid and effective action. Not surprisingly, such institutions find it easier to specialize in legislative or deliberative activities than in administrative or governing ones. This specialization, however natural, is a matter of degree, and legislatures have played a greater governmental role in some circumstances than in others.

Historians have sometimes argued, indeed, that there is an inexorable trend in this direction: that we should see in parliamentary history a series of generally successful attempts to grasp "the initiative" from nonelective institutions.[1] This view—that the democratic impulse is immanent in human history—is no longer so popular among historians as it once was, both because of the implausibility of linear theories of history in light of modern events and because of some critical failures

---

[1] These ideas were ubiquitous among English historians of earlier generations, including Wallace Notestein, *The Winning of the Initiative by the House of Commons* (1924), and S. R. Gardiner, *History of England from the Accession of James I to the Outbreak of the Civil War*, 10 vols. (1883–1884).

of evidence to support it.[2] As social scientists, however, without embracing linear theories, we might nevertheless expect that there might be specifiable conditions under which legislatures would be more powerful participants in government. This is the issue we begin exploring here.

Parliamentary institutions, as collectivities, can become effective participants in governing only to the extent that they can create and sustain internal hierarchical or vertical relations of power among independently chosen members that permit them to react promptly and effectively to external events.[3] Each such creation rests on a set of shared supporting beliefs and expectations that serves both to explain and to justify the inequality of powers to relatively equal members.[4] This structure of beliefs and expectations must have the property that all the agents find it rational to act in such a way that the institutional structure is sustained. That institutions and ideas are locked in a relation of mutual dependence is, in fact, one of the central notions underlying the game-theoretic analysis of institutions. From a static point of view, it is both unimportant and impossible to untangle the causal relation between these elements. From the standpoint of historical analysis, however, the causal connection between ideas and institutions is a central explanatory issue.

Structural accounts in international relations say that international structural relations play a decisive role in determining internal governmental organization and practice. Nations surrounded by hostile neighbors, or whose economies are strongly involved with others, are pressed to adopt different institutions, practices, and public cultures than those shielded from political or economic competitors by distance or geographic impediment.[5] Ideas and ideologies, if they play any causal role at all in this story, serve only intermediate purposes, mediating between international structures and domestic institutions. Other-

---

[2] For a powerfully argued version of this view as it applies to the period under study here, see Conrad Russell, *Parliaments and English Parliaments, 1621–1629* (Oxford: Oxford University Press, 1979). Russell's views are not unanimously accepted, however, and a number of younger historians seem to think the questions of evidence more arguable than he seems to. See Richard Cust and Ann Hughes, *Conflict in Early Stuart England* (London: Longman, 1989).

[3] Historically, various systems of organizations have evolved in legislatures: committees, parties, the speakership, etc.

[4] A common example is the practice of selecting internal leaders by election or by seniority, or according to some other convention, together with a set of shared beliefs regarding such a practice as legitimate and predictive.

[5] For a strong statement of such a view see Charles Tilly, *Coercion, Capital, and European States* (Cambridge, Mass.: Blackwell, 1992). See also Ronald Rogowski, *Commerce and Coalitions* (Princeton: Princeton University Press, 1989).

wise, they are mere rationalizations for changes that would have occurred anyway.

While structural theories have the attractions of simplicity and power, they seem better at accounting for institutional change after the fact than at predicting it. We can see this by examining the two comparative perspectives that animate this essay. In seventeenth-century Europe, within apparently similar structural circumstances, we observe both the rise of absolutism in France and other continental powers (with the decay and disappearance of representative institutions) and the simultaneous development of parliamentary institutions and practices in England.[6] There are good reasons to think that structural circumstances catalyzed both of these internal institutional changes, but it is not at all clear that the natures of the changes were predictable from structural circumstances by themselves. A committed realist might respond that this apparent failure is traceable to an inadequately developed description of structural circumstance. Such an account might, for example, point to England's geographic separation from the continent.

To take a second axis of comparison, over the course of the previous four centuries England had frequently been involved in long and expensive wars with France and Spain. In some respects, these earlier conflicts seemed to place England in structural circumstances similar to those it faced at the beginning of the Thirty Years' War. Yet, in the face of those earlier pressures, English governmental institutions and practices changed only incrementally and certainly seemed in little danger of disappearance.[7] Structuralism requires an account of how English international circumstances early in the seventeenth century differed from those forty years or two hundred years earlier. Here geographic isolation does not seem available as an explanatory hypothesis. The incompleteness of structural explanations points to the need to supplement them with other causal mechanisms. For this reason, I develop a hypothesis that emphasizes the role of ideas in generating and supporting institutional arrangements.

---

[6] As well as less thematic evolutions in Germany and Italy.

[7] Two particular episodes of institutional evolution seem especially noteworthy. At the end of the fourteenth century, extensive involvement in France forced English kings to summon parliaments very frequently—between 1370 and 1420 some fifty parliaments were called—and this period witnessed the establishment of a regular role for the Commons in the making of statutes, the origin of the Commons' right to assent to revenue bills, and the creation of the Speaker. Similarly, Elizabeth's wars with Spain produced frequent parliaments, multitudinous proposals for legislation, and, relatedly, an increased use of committees to consider and expedite these proposals. While both periods produced significant institutional developments, there was very little change in the institutional role of Parliament or in the way that role was understood. Indeed, during the fifteenth century, the Speaker rapidly became effectively an officer of the crown, and

Like most other European states in the seventeenth century, England could be characterized as a mixed monarchy in which the authority of the king was limited by an expectation of consultation with various "representative" institutions. This combination of monarchical and representative expectations can be traced both to the relative political weakness of kings in extracting wealth from their people and to medieval (and ancient) ideas about authority. The requirement of consultation was particularly strong in areas of government finance. Most European monarchs were required to (or found it expedient to) obtain the consent of their estates in order to raise revenues beyond those due to them as feudal lords. Everywhere in Europe, these expectations produced and sustained conflict between monarchs and their estates as to what kinds of taxes required consent and what kinds were due the king either by right or by virtue of prerogative powers.

By the beginning of the seventeenth century, however, these widely shared expectations as to the division and nature of authority came under pressure from new circumstances. These new circumstances amounted to this: Religious conflicts between and within European states produced situations in which the pragmatic requirements of statecraft increasingly separated monarchs, who had to conduct "realistic" foreign policies across confessional lines, from their more fervent countrymen.[8] These conflicts frequently led to (expensive) military action and therefore to a demand for revenues that called for parliamentary action. Increasing consciousness of the separation between the monarch and his subjects—often expressed in the common belief that kings were influenced by bad counselors or were not taking counsel at all—produced a chronic distrust of monarchical courts throughout Europe. The consequence of this endemic distrust was, on the one hand, to strengthen absolutist and divine-right ideologies, and on the other, to support various strands of mixed constitution theory and theories based on some form of consent. These bifurcated ideological developments in turn gave direction to the institutional changes that were already under way.

These ideological divisions affected seventeenth-century England particularly strongly. The incompleteness of the Reformation there produced profound religious division and distrust within the governing elite. England's chronic vulnerability to French, Spanish, and Dutch threats made foreign policies that would prevent these forces from coalescing very attractive. Such policies tended either to involve concili-

---

after the end of the Elizabethan Spanish wars, parliaments and committees became much less frequent.

[8] The "countrymen" were generally elites, of course.

ation of one or the other major Catholic power or extensive and expensive military action, which would force the king to try to obtain additional resources from his subjects. Not surprisingly, kings usually preferred conciliation to warfare. Conciliatory policies, however, provoked chronic, religiously motivated distrust of the king and his counselors. This chronic distrust delimited the set of acceptable and stable institutional arrangements that could evolve.

War, Religion, and Parliament

From the very beginning of his reign, James I faced an international situation in which the outbreak of religious warfare was always a possibility. England's major continental rivals—France, Spain, and Austria—were powerful Catholic states in the grip of Counterreformation sentiment. A policy aimed at forestalling confessional confrontation seemed especially attractive in this circumstance. Yet any such foreign policy was bound to be distasteful to the more reformed English Protestants, who preferred to make common cause with the Dutch Calvinists and with the Protestant German princes engaged in struggles against the Habsburgs. The keystone of James's policy was his plan to marry his children into the leading Protestant and Catholic ruling families, thereby diminishing the likelihood of war with the major Catholic powers and permitting England to play a mediating role in confessional struggles. Even if this policy had been completely successful, the concessions needed to secure either a Spanish or a French marriage for his son grated on Protestant sensibilities and produced a sense of separation between the more reformed England Protestants and James's court.

The marriage policy was, however, not successful in preventing the outbreak of religious war. The acceptance of the Bohemian crown by James's son-in-law Frederick, the Calvinist elector of the Palatinate, produced a sharp Austrian military reaction that expelled Frederick from Bohemia and eventually from the Palatinate as well, producing powerful pressure for an English military response. To this end, James summoned a parliament to request money to resist the Habsburg forces. Partly for religious reasons, many members of the 1621 parliament displayed enthusiasm for a war against the Habsburgs in Germany. This enthusiasm produced a rapid parliamentary agreement to two subsidies.

James remained determined to confine the struggle narrowly to the Palatinate, however, and not to engage in any broader European war. He restricted the use of the parliamentary subsidies to mercenary forces and pursued a diplomatic course with Spain. While mercenaries fought Habsburg forces in the Palatinate, James increased the diplomatic pressure to marry Prince Charles to the Spanish infanta in the hope that the Spanish Habsburgs would help restore the Palatinate to Frederick without the need for a military confrontation. As negotiations proceeded, however, the price of a marriage became clearer: in addition to requiring a permanent Catholic presence in the queen's court, the Spanish demanded increased toleration of English Catholics and pressed James to allow Catholic peers to raise English troops to fight in the Habsburg armies.

Reformed Englishmen and members of Parliament were exceedingly anxious about these events, particularly as they seemed likely to lead to the possibility of a Catholic heir to the English throne. Indeed, parliamentary criticism of the "Spanish match" in 1621 led James angrily to dissolve Parliament and to imprison several of its leaders. The dissolution, however, left James without sufficient funds to conduct an active military policy and placed the marriage policy at the center of the English defense of the Palatinate. It also made English policy completely hostage to the Spanish, who were in no hurry to conclude negotiations as long as their forces were prevailing in Germany. Moreover, it left the MPs to go home to report that they had voted new taxes without any consideration of grievances.

With the failure of the marriage policy and the growing financial demands of the mercenaries in Germany, Prince Charles and Buckingham, the royal favorite, persuaded James to summon another parliament to prepare for military action against Spain. The king refused to break with Spain without a parliamentary commitment—in the form of subsidies—to help pay off the mercenaries and to support a Spanish war. He feared that "I should be bound and they leap free and leave me naked and without help." In view of their experiences in 1621, however, members of Parliament were very reluctant to provide subsidies before grievances had been attended to. Sir Henry Anderson worried aloud: "Dangerous to return into the Country, and tell them of Subsidies; dangerous again not to give."[9] In the end, Parliament voted to provide subsidies but retained some control over them by delegating authority for disbursements to a parliamentary committee, in return for a promise of royal attention to grievances at future sessions.[10] Un-

[9] Thomas Cogswell, *The Blessed Revolution* (Cambridge: Cambridge University Press, 1989), pp. 200, 201.
[10] After the 1624 parliament, a number of parliamentary leaders were severely pressed to explain their votes. For example, Sir Robert Phelips, who had worked hard to pass the subsidies, was accused "by a member of the rival county faction of . . . seeking favour

fortunately both for him and for the MPs, James died before any future sessions could be convened, and members had once again to return home having imposed new taxes.

James's death had more far-reaching implications. Unlike his father, Charles was disposed to pursue active and assertive policies in domestic as well as foreign affairs. Moreover, whereas James's religious beliefs fitted well with the various strains of Calvinism popular in England and Scotland at the time, Charles was more attracted to Arminian views, which not only rejected central Calvinist doctrines but supported a hierarchical organization of the church. Not very surprisingly, such views were regarded as "popish" by many contemporaries. While Elizabeth and James, as monarchs, were attracted to relatively hierarchical forms of church organization that allowed religion to serve state interests, they appointed bishops with diverse views on these matters. As a result, religious conflict within the established church was largely avoided during most of their reigns. Charles and his advisers were more inclined to be consistent in their ecclesiastical policies, and such consistency was likely to sharpen religious conflicts between the king and others.

Charles's first parliament met in circumstances of a costly war with Spain, and members, having twice returned home to justify new taxes to their countrymen, were in no mood to be generous. Many of the same parliamentary leaders who had supported Charles's war policies in 1624 now opposed his urgent requests for immediate supply in 1625, and Parliament refused to grant the traditional lifetime customs revenues to the king, limiting the right to take tonnage and poundage to one year. Believing that Parliament had committed itself to a Spanish war in 1624, Charles felt betrayed, and when an attempt was made to impeach Buckingham, he dissolved the Parliament. Christopher Thompson concluded that "the King was resolved thereafter . . . not to recall the assembly if it could be avoided" and instead to find new nonparliamentary sources of revenue.[11] To this end he not only sold off royal lands but also reneged on royal debts and engaged in various forms of coercive borrowing.

Though these extraparliamentary financial measures were partially successful, they did not return nearly enough revenue to support an active war, and after the defeat of an underequipped naval expedition

---

so hard that he neglected other business, and of suppressing petitions the county wanted to have presented in Parliament" (Russell, *Parliaments*, p. 19).

[11] Christopher Thompson, "Court, Politics, and Parliamentary Conflict in 1625," in Cust and Hughes, *Conflict*, p. 187.

at Cadiz, Charles agreed to another parliament. The king summoned the 1626 parliament for the purpose of financing the war, but the members themselves had accumulated a substantial agenda of grievances, including both religious and administrative issues arising from royal policies. Parliament agreed in principle to provide four subsidies, but its archaic methods made progress on legislation slow. And when the issue of Buckingham's impeachment arose again, the king dissolved parliament to save his counselor, though it had not yet produced either subsidies or legislation.

The failure of parliamentary supply and the widening of the war to France led Charles to resort again to extraparliamentary methods, continuing to take tonnage and poundage and ultimately imposing a forced loan. Unlike earlier forced loans, which fell largely on selected wealthy individuals, this one was administered by the subsidymen in the same manner as parliamentary subsidies were imposed. Whether by design or not, the loan came to appear to be a tax imposed without parliamentary consent, and as such it produced widespread constitutional objections. Faced with open refusals to pay by local elites—many of them charged with collecting the loan—the Privy Council employed coercive measures to obtain compliance throughout 1626 and 1627, and while the amount raised was equivalent to five subsidies, the political costs of this course of action were substantial.[12]

After the failure of the English expedition to relieve the Huguenots at La Rochelle, Charles reluctantly agreed to summon another parliament. This decision, according to Richard Cust, "was obviously taken because of the Crown's financial needs" as well as "because tradition and the weight of opinion within the Council favoured such a course of action."[13] The closeness of the decision is reflected in Charles's attempt to require that the country show its loyalty by subscribing to his request for ship money. When the Parliament finally met, his insistence once again on immediate supply was as much a demand for subordination as a demand for the needed funds.

When the Parliament met in the spring of 1628, the political costs of the coercive policies that the king had followed between 1626 and 1628 became apparent. The collection of the forced loan had, in the Five Knights case, led the crown to insist on its power to arrest people

---

[12] See Richard Cust, *The Forced Loan and English Politics, 1626–1628* (Oxford: Clarendon, 1987). For a theoretical treatment of this phenomenon see Bruce Bueno de Mesquita and David Lalman, *War and Reason* (New Haven: Yale University Press, 1992), chap. 5.
[13] Ibid., pp. 325, 88.

without showing cause.[14] The existence of large military forces—raised
on the prerogative in the absence of statutory authorization for a mili-
tia—and the concomitant necessity of billeting them sometimes required the government to employ martial law to commandeer local
services. Ordinary citizens found that their rights were liable to be
tested in military rather than ordinary courts. Common law seemed
unable to limit these royal impositions on liberty and property, and the
king appeared able and willing to govern without any source of authority other than proclamation.

In light of these events, Conrad Russell writes, the 1628 parliament
"came to Westminster with the conscious and deliberate aim of vindi-
cating English liberties." There was a "remarkable unanimity" on four
complaints, each arising out of the administration of the war, and each
of which found a place in the petition of right: the forced loan, arbitrary imprisonment, billeting, and martial law.[15] Though nearly everyone (including the council) conceded that these acts were illegal and
should be ended as soon as possible, there was substantial disagreement
as to how they could be prevented. The main issues of the session were
finding a legislative vehicle and language that were acceptable to both
Lords and Commons and getting the king to give an acceptable answer.
All this was a precondition to finishing work on a subsidy bill. The king,
with badly needed funds held hostage to the effort to circumscribe his
prerogative powers, found it expedient to confirm the petition. The
king's acceptance was so grudging and vague that some MPs pushed
for additional legislative action, and this pressure led to a prorogation.

The second session of the Parliament met early in 1629 and was as
completely occupied with issues of religion as the first session had been
with parliamentary liberties. Charles had appointed some notorious
Arminians to prominent bishoprics, and had begun an attempt to impose ecclesiastical discipline on the church in ways that were frighten-
ing to Calvinist MPs. With the five subsidies voted in 1628 not yet
collected, all Charles could have hoped for from the 1629 session was
legislation legalizing the tonnage and poundage. As he was taking these
revenues anyway out of "necessity," it is hard to see how a parliament
determined to get him to renounce Arminianism could have succeeded.
Faced with its humiliating demands, Charles felt forced to dissolve the
Parliament before any legislation had been produced.

The dissolution made the idea of summoning future parliaments

---

[14] Five knights were arrested for refusal to pay the loan. Rather than permit the case
to test the legality of the loan, the king insisted on his (prerogative) right to imprison
without showing cause. Though the court did not rule for the crown, the knights remained in jail and so the king's claim was effectively vindicated.

[15] Russell, *Parliaments*, pp. 343–44.

unappealing to the king, but he knew that the only way to avoid parliaments was to stay out of war. After the collapse of the parliament called in 1629, therefore, Charles proceeded to extricate England from its costly wars with France and Spain and to undertake extensive reforms that both improved his revenues and limited the costs of his government.[16] These actions permitted Charles to conduct English government without parliaments for more than a decade.

PARLIAMENTARY PRACTICES AND INSTITUTIONS

In the early seventeenth century, parliaments were largely occasional assemblies infrequently called "for a specific purpose laid before it by the crown."[17] Parliaments were usually called when extraordinary revenues were needed, primarily in times of war, to provide the king with resources beyond those he could raise on his own. While Parliament met on the king's business, its members usually wished to secure advantages for their localities, usually by petitioning either the king or Parliament for relief from administrative practices that weighed heavily on their constituents.

A parliament was, in this sense, a circumstance of exchange between the king and his subjects: "the King wanted extraordinary supply," Russell notes, "and his subjects wanted to reform, usually by legislation, things which they thought were in need of change."[18] But the nature

[16] For a discussion of Charles's extensive efforts to achieve financial and administrative reforms, see Kevin Sharpe, *The Personal Rule of Charles I* (New Haven: Yale University Press, 1992).

[17] Mark Kishlansky, *The Rise of the New Model Army* (Cambridge: Cambridge University Press, 1979), p. 11. Historians disagree as to the nature of the early Stuart parliaments. Whig historians saw Parliament as an institution with an awareness of its powers, filled with men who consciously pursued large principles and were eager to vindicate the constitutional authority of representative institutions in English government. These historians saw in the politics of the time a struggle for legislative "initiative" between nascent political parties—the "country," centered in the Commons, against the "court"—a struggle that came, inevitably, to a head in the Civil War.

More recently revisionist historians have seen in Parliament an occasional assembly of locally oriented provincials, largely unconcerned with larger political issues, trying as best they could to preserve the autonomy of their local society and their places in it against incursions from an increasingly nationally oriented royal administration. Parliamentarians, according to this view, cared about national issues only when and insofar as they touched on local ones: fundamentally, they wished to avoid imposing taxes on their countrymen. Political cleavages are not between Parliament and the court but rather predominantly between courtiers. Parliament, these historians claim, is better seen as a field of action than as a unified actor. Parliament's resistance to crown policies is best understood as the fragmented resistance of separate, insulated localities against attempts by the national government to impose taxes or regulations.

[18] Russell, *Parliaments*, 35.

of this exchange was always ambiguous: the king regarded it as a matter of a free exchange of gifts, whereas members of the Commons often saw it as more of an ordinary transaction. Whatever its basis, MPs regarded a linkage between subsidies and grievances as desirable, as they dreaded the prospect of returning to their constituencies having imposed new taxes without addressing popular complaints about government. Sounding a note familiar to a student of modern legislatures, Sir Francis Seymour worried that "if wee should graunt the King Subsedyes before our Greivances are debated and redressed our Judgements may very weell be questioned and it may give the Country (whom wee serve) cause to blame the men whom they have chosen as consenting to their sufferance."[19] Recognizing these fears, the crown did not usually try to make parliamentary subsidies the first order of business in a new parliament, but usually proposed them only after the grievances had been treated. But this practice of addressing grievances before supply was probably more a sign of a well-functioning polity than a royal recognition of parliamentary rights.[20]

Parliamentary institutions were well suited to ensure that only those statutes that were largely consensual were enacted. "The guiding principles of the parliamentary method," writes Mark Kishlansky, "were unencumbered debate and the quest for unanimous resolution. Free debate . . . was persuasive discussion, reasoned argument among men uncommitted to predetermined positions."[21] The formal rules of debate in the chambers were cumbersome: three (actual) readings were required of each bill before it could be enrolled, and members were permitted to speak to an issue no more than once. These procedures made formal consideration of complicated legislation difficult, and for this reason both chambers made use of committees (including committees of the whole house to circumvent the archaic rules of debate). But legislative committees were typically composed of like-minded men, because members opposed to a legislative proposal—specifically, those

[19] Quoted in Derek Hirst, *Representative of the People?* (Cambridge: Cambridge University Press, 1975), p. 173.

[20] The idea of a connection between revenues and grievances was already quite old by the seventeenth century. See A. L. Brown, "Parliament, c. 1377–1422," in *The English Parliament in the Middle Ages*, ed. R. G. Davies and J. H. Denton, pp. 109–40 (Philadelphia: University of Pennsylvania Press, 1981).

[21] Kishlansky, *Rise of the New Model Army*, p. 11. More recently Sheila Lambert has asked whether some of the evidence Kishlansky presents was unambiguous testimony to the centrality of consensus in that period. The ritual by which a defeated minority in the House were to go out and bring the bill into the chamber, which Kishlansky regarded as a signal of their acceptance of the outcome, was probably in disuse by the late sixteenth century, and in any case might as well have been a method of "rubbing one's opponent's nose in his defeat": "Procedure in the House of Commons in the Early Stuart Period," *English Historical Review* 95 (1980): 736n.

who spoke against it on the floor—would not be put on a committee to consider it.[22] Thus committees were hospitable places to work out agreements among supporters of a proposal, but they were less effective at conciliating those opposed to it. In any case, committee actions still had to be considered in the chambers, where, because of cumbersome rules of debate, proposed statutes would often be referred back to committee repeatedly without being decided.

Divisions were rare, except on unimportant matters that were not felt to warrant the time to discuss in the committee of the whole. If a conflict could not be resolved, the matter was either referred to an ad hoc committee (of supporters) to craft an acceptable version or simply left "to sleep." These rigidities were amplified by the bicameral structure and the cumbersome methods available to resolve disputes between the chambers and, of course, by the fact of an absolute royal veto.

Not surprisingly, in view of the combination of rigid procedures and consensual expectations, little legislation got through Parliament. Locally oriented legislation failed to attract widespread interest, and more nationally oriented proposals—those aimed at restricting general administrative and regulatory practices, for example—could not gain consensual support. As Russell said, "there were too many bills before the Commons, and too little agreement on which were important, to permit very much progress."[23] Subjects with grievances tended to seek aid elsewhere, in the Privy Council, with prominent lords and courtiers, or by petitioning the king himself.

These considerations were reflected in the careers of members of Parliament. The most able and prominent of them—such men as Robert Phelips, Edward Coke, Francis Seymour, and Thomas Wentworth—aspired constantly to careers beyond Parliament. These prominent and important "Parliament men" regularly, and often vainly, sought the support of patrons and positions as courtiers. They were smart and ambitious men who gravitated to places where real power was excercised—primarily to the court. Perhaps it was because their court-centered aspirations were so often frustrated, and because Parliament was so often in session during the 1620s, that such men turned more and more of their attention and effort to Parliament at that time.

But even for the ordinary member—the one who rarely spoke and, if he did, never on large issues—local influence depended crucially on

---

[22] Historians disagree as to whether this practice was general or confined to private bills, and as to its age. According to Lambert ("Procedure in the House of Commons," p. 759n), it appears that outright opponents of legislation may generally have been kept off of committees but that in some cases everyone who had spoken to a question would be put on.

[23] Russell, *Parliaments*, p. 41.

his relationships with the court. The king appointed both the justices of the peace and the deputy lieutenants—the principal (unpaid) administrative officers of the state—and could, if he wished, name local rivals to these posts. Moreover, because local grievances were often more efficiently dealt with at court, the MP was well advised to devote attention in that direction if he wished adequately to represent the interests of his constituents.

Events in the sixteenth century began to alter traditional expectations about Parliament's role in English government. For a variety of reasons, royal fiscal instruments became less able to finance the government.[24] By the turn of the seventeenth century, even after a period of fiscal innovation and with church holdings largely sold off, royal revenues were able to support only a modest court, even in peacetime.[25] James, like Elizabeth before him, needed (and claimed) both additional revenue sources (sales of monopolies and offices, impositions on trade, etc.) and various forms of credit to support his administration. Moreover, James ran an expensive court, and it was doubtful how long his revenues, even expansively defined, could support it, even in peacetime.[26] Other sources of revenue traditionally required Parliament's consent.[27]

James's need for additional funds caused him both to call parliaments to press revenues and continually to explore new and controversial revenue sources that transgressed parliamentary expectations. When England was not at war, these royal innovations exposed chronic "constitutional" tensions over revenues that had existed in England for hundreds of years. Royal demands for revenues strained parliamentary institutions and expectations while at the same time they increased the king's dependence on parliamentary leaders. Predictably, early Stuart parliaments often ended in deadlock and disarray, sometimes without

[24] An excellent survey of the decline in royal revenues is found in Conrad Russell, "The Poverty of the Crown and the Weakness of the King," in *The Causes of the English Civil War* (London: Oxford University Press, 1990), chap. 7.

[25] Wallace MacCaffery, "Parliament and Foreign Policy," in *The Parliaments of Elizabethan England*, ed. D. M. Dean and N. L. Jones, pp. 65–90 (Oxford: Basil Blackwell, 1990); and J. D. Alsop, "Parliament and Taxation," in ibid., pp. 91–116.

[26] ". . . under James I, . . . royal extravagance caused the level of ordinary expenditure to rise disproportionately to any increase in the ordinary revenue which was achieved through such measures as the growth in impositions, the more extensive adoption of customs farming and the screwing up of the farmers' rents": Robert Ashton, *The Crown and the Money Market, 1603–1640* (Oxford: Oxford University Press, 1960), p. 38.

[27] See ibid.; Douglass North and Barry R. Weingast, "Constitutions and Commitment: Evolution of the Institutions Governing Public Choice in 17th Century England," *Journal of Economic History* 49 (1989): 803–32; Barry R. Weingast, "Institutional Foundations of the 'Sinews of Power': British Financial and Military Success Following the Glorious Revolution," in *Fiscal Crises and the Growth of Representative Institutions*, ed. Philip Hoffman and Kathryn Norberg (Stanford: Stanford University Press, forthcoming).

providing revenues, sometimes with parliamentary leaders imprisoned or exiled, and almost always with the king asserting the right to raise revenues on his own. In wartime, as the need for revenues became more urgent, the pressure on parliamentary institutions became correspondingly more intense.

These effects of international circumstances on parliamentary organization and practices are scarcely surprising. With each new parliament its members, facing the prospect of explaining new taxes to their countrymen, articulated new demands for legislation treating administrative abuses, many of which arose from previous royal efforts to raise revenues.[28] The conduct of war, which inevitably called for collection of taxes and conscription of troops, was increasingly another source of grievances. As a result, interest grew in bills concerning patents and monopolies,[29] informers,[30] concealments,[31] as well as in a revived mechanism of impeachment.[32]

By increasing the need for revenues, wars traditionally produced new parliaments and therefore new elections. Elections called forth contestants for seats in the Commons and produced pressures for a broadened franchise at least in the county seats.[33] The increased frequency of parliaments also led to more continuity of both membership and leadership and to more frequent interaction among the members. At the same time, many issues tended to be carried over from one parliament to the next and occasioned the use of similar internal practices.[34] Parliament made somewhat more use both of (more or less) standing committees with specific jurisdictions[35] and of the committee

[28] Sharpe, *Personal Rule of Charles I*, pp. 75–100.

[29] The crown sold rights to regulate trade and commerce in various areas as methods both to control markets and to raise revenues from a nonparliamentary source.

[30] Informers were used by the crown to increase the regularity with which various statutes were enforced and especially to control underassessment of taxes by local officials.

[31] The crown sold the right to conduct "title searches" for lands that properly belonged to the crown, and, not surprisingly, this right frequently led to extortion from men who occupied such lands.

[32] Some historians believe that impeachments are best understood as evidence of intra-court politics—one court faction attacking a prominent member of another faction with the permission of the king—rather than of increased parliamentary powers. The point is that Parliament had become the forum for these attacks.

[33] Such pressures were due partly to the effect of inflation on the franchise requirement and partly to the effects of parliamentary actions in widening the borough franchises. See Hirst, *Representative of the People?*

[34] Bills that were left to "sleep" were routinely put on the new parliament's agenda.

[35] Lambert, "Procedure in the House of Commons," identifies the traditional grand committees, which were traceable well back into the sixteenth century, as grievances, religion, courts of justice, and trade. In addition, committees on supply were commonly appointed. The committee on elections, never technically a grand committee, was to become more important in the Stuart period.

of the whole—both to process the larger work load and to modify or circumvent cumbersome internal restrictions on debate.[36] These increases in institutional continuity had the effect of making Parliament somewhat more important as a venue of political action, both for the king and for ordinary members.

Less tangible changes were perhaps even more significant. There was increased attention to parliamentary "boundaries," and therefore to Parliament as a distinct institution within English government whose rights and privileges had to be protected. By taking over the settlement of disputed elections from the Privy Council,[37] by protesting royal interference with parliamentary speech and action, and by insisting on its constitutional responsibility for levying taxes, the Commons attempted to assert some control over its institutional boundaries. Perhaps an even more striking instance of attention to boundaries is the decline in the powers of the Speaker, who was essentially an officer of the king in the House, to control the flow of legislation: the Speaker's agenda powers, his power to adjourn, and his power of recognition were more frequently challenged and overridden in the 1620s.[38] If this awareness of boundaries did not lead to the development of a sharp division between the court and Parliament, it did help to articulate a consciousness within which parliamentary rights and privileges were endowed with concrete significance.

From a historical perspective, these changes can be seen as an instance of what Nelson Polsby has called legislative "institutionalization."[39] Political leaders both inside and outside Parliament began to see it as something more than an "occasional assembly," as having established rights and privileges, as having internal structures and norms,

[36] The practice of using large committees—made up of nearly the whole house—increased in the late sixteenth century, often at the urging of the government, with the apparent purpose of allowing government representatives more effectively to influence parliamentary outcomes. The use of large committees forced changes in other parliamentary practices, such as the times for meetings and for considering private bills. The transition from these large committees to the formal device of the committee of the whole occurred in the Lords in 1606 and more gradually in the Commons. In any case, in the 1620s much of the Commons' business was transacted in such committees.

[37] Hirst, *Representative of the People?*

[38] Lambert, "Procedure in the House of Commons," concludes that the decline of the "speaker's powers between 1601 and 1629 was real." She argues that "the speaker's dual role, as mouthpiece of the Commons to the king, and as the channel of crown control of the House, could be played out satisfactorily only so long as reasonable harmony prevailed" (p. 775).

[39] Polsby's criteria for an institutionalized system were these: differentiation from its environment (boundaries), an internal division of labor, and the use of universalistic norms and rules in the conduct of business. See Nelson W. Polsby, "The Institutionalization of the U.S. House of Representatives," *American Political Science Review* 62 (1968): 144–68.

and as having a regular role in the conduct of government, especially in the realm of public finance.[40] I emphasize that we should not see these changes as a "winning of the initiative" by an assertive parliament. Indeed, some of them, such as the increased use of the committee of the whole, were urged by the crown on a reluctant house. Others are best seen as essentially defensive reactions to constituent expectations or to royal pressures and, indirectly, to pressures from the international system.[41] However they were seen by contemporaries, these changes had the effects of increasing both the institutional integrity of Parliament as a social system and the extent to which its members saw it as having rights and privileges that needed to be guarded against royal incursions.

CHANGING GOVERNING EXPECTATIONS

The changed circumstances of the 1620 parliaments can be understood within a broader set of expectations in respect to government, held not only by Englishmen but by Europeans generally. Like most governments on the continent, England's was a mixture of monarchy and "representative" elements. The prevalence of mixed monarchies in Europe might be traced to a characteristic ambivalence in medieval views of authority[42] between what Walter Ullmann has termed a "de-

[40] We can see an earlier period of institutionalization during the crisis-ridden years of the late fourteenth century, which saw nearly annual parliaments, during which the Commons came to be an accepted part of Parliament and to have a regular "right" to agree to revenue requests. During the same period the role of Speaker originated and the incumbent was given some degree of control over the Commons' agenda.

[41] In the short run these attempts were failures: after the acrimonious dissolution in 1629, Charles stopped calling parliaments altogether and English governmental practices under his personal rule came to resemble those on the continent. But, viewed over a longer perspective, institutions do not cease to exercise power simply because they lose their material existence. The set of expectations, memories, and beliefs surrounding parliament continued, albeit in disembodied form, throughout the 1630s, to converge with the drastic need for revenues a decade later.

[42] It is obviously impossible to do justice to the rich variety of medieval views on government in the span of this chapter or to trace these views to scholastic or legist sources. For present purposes the materials I need are those relating to the idea of mixed constitution or mixed monarchy. The idea that monarchical and representative institutions naturally coexisted in a well-functioning polity (whether secular or ecclesiastical) was widely held by the late thirteenth century, and such ideas had particularly broad appeal in the realm of taxation and finance. These practical ideas could be and were grounded in a variety of theoretical conceptions of the state, most but not all of which would fit within a broadly Aristotelian scheme. See Brian Tierney, *Religion, Law and the Growth of Constitutional Thought* (Cambridge: Cambridge University Press, 1982); and James M. Blythe, *Government and the Mixed Constitution in the Middle Ages* (Princeton: Princeton University Press, 1992).

scending" view that saw the prince as God's lieutenant on earth and an "ascending" view that located authorization in the consent of those affected by a public action.[43] Mixed monarchy accommodated both modes of authorization, but at the price of permitting a potential for conflict among these institutions.

The potential for conflict among medieval institutions was manageable institutionally and doctrinally as long as people generally accepted the existence of a natural law, and believed that this law could and would be discovered by institutionally competent actors. As these ontological and epistemological beliefs began to collapse under the weight of the religious conflicts of the sixteenth and seventeenth centuries, the contradictory views of authorization began to pull apart, setting up sharply opposed paths of institutional "reform."

This conflict came to be particularly sharp in the realm of taxation and government finance, domains closely connected to waging wars. Throughout Europe, representative institutions played a role in levying taxes in the sixteenth and early seventeenth centuries. When kings needed to raise money, they felt they had to (and ought to) consult their estates—the Estates General in France, the Imperial Diet, the German Estates, the English Parliament—to help them do so. Public finance within medieval kingships rested on the principle that both the king and his subjects were self-sufficient and were normally able to support themselves "of their own" domains.[44] The king, while elevated above his subjects in status and responsibilities, was expected to have enough revenues to support his court and the limited activities of his government. Except in extraordinary circumstances—typically wars, plagues, or famines—he would not have to impose on his subjects for either revenues or service. If such circumstances arose, he would summon a parliament, as the representatives of landed and commercial wealth in the country, and present his case that circumstances really were extraordinary, and Parliament, in turn, was obliged to consent to supply the king's needs if its members were convinced by his argu-

---

[43] The descending aspect is well expressed by the ancient legal maxim "quod omnes tangit ab omnibus tractari et approbari debet": "What touches all should be approved by all." Walter Ullmann argued that authority throughout the Middle Ages always had both a "descending" (from God) and an "ascending" (from the people) aspect, in *Principles of Government in the Middle Ages* (London: Methuen, 1961). A survey of medieval and Roman sources of these doctrines can be found in Arthur Monahan, *Consent, Coercion, and Limit* (Leiden: E. J. Brill, 1987). Monahan shows that this principle is traceable to Roman sources before the time of Justinian and also that its application was very widespread within both secular and religious governing institutions throughout the Middle Ages.

[44] This portrait is drawn largely from G. L. Harriss, "Medieval Doctrines in the Debates on Supply, 1610–1629," in *Faction and Parliament*, ed. Kevin Sharpe, pp. 71–103 (London: Methuen, 1985).

ments. Parliament's obligation to supply the king's needs was matched by the king's obligation to take measures to protect the country.

Within this system of ideas, authorization flowed not from the fact of consent but rather from the extraordinary circumstances. Subjects were obliged to consent in such circumstances, and if they withheld consent (as they sometimes did), the king could rightfully impose taxes without it. Authorization was seen, therefore, as a factual matter. If the kingdom's welfare was at risk, the king was obliged to act and the parliament was obliged to supply the means for him to do so. Parliamentary consent was the *recognition* of this situation, not the creation of authorization for taxation. Consent did not create authority but was evidence of an authority that already existed.

For our present purposes, it is important to recognize the centrality of *trust* in reconciling the elements of divine authorization and popular consent in the medieval kingship. Subjects and king had to believe not only that both king and Parliament could recognize an extraordinary circumstance but also that no one had a systematic interest in misperceiving or misrepresenting one. Failures to arrive at correct judgments were thought to be grounded not in any deep conflict of interest but in human frailty, and these frailties were not concentrated in one or the other constitutional element. The natural state of affairs, therefore, was one in which both rulers and ruled trusted each other to act as they should to recognize and pursue common purposes within the limits of their particular competences.

Once the mutual trust between the king and Parliament started to erode, the conflict between the ascending and descending conceptions of authorization began to surface. Two alternative theories of justification were embedded in mixed monarchy, each of which articulated a distinct role for Parliament in English government. Each of these theories was continuous with medieval conceptions in important respects: each differed from them with regard to only a single empirical premise, but each suggested a different answer as to the foundation of justified authority in contemporary England. Medieval kingship theory rested on two assumptions: that the king and his subjects had a common purpose and that both could be expected to determine what it required. Both new theories retained the belief in a common purpose but they disagreed as to the body that was better able to find or to pursue it.

Royalist Theories

We can identify two main variants of royalist theory. One version sought to ground the authority of the crown in a delegation of authority directly from God. Because the king's actions were authorized by

God, they did not require any additional justification either from a visible church or from representative institutions such as Parliament. A good king would, of course, be religious and would make use of representative institutions to obtain counsel from those with special wisdom, but his failure in either respect would in no way undermine the authority of his acts or the obligation of his subjects to obey.

The other royalist theory grounded the authority of the king in necessity. This variant, which contemporaries often traced to Machiavelli's concept of raison d'état and to Bodin's notion of sovereignty, saw the king as responsible for the common good of the realm and regarded the prerogative powers as necessarily unbounded by any other law, whether customary or parliamentary. These princely powers were rooted, instead, in the common purpose of the community itself.

Royalist theories understood parliamentary "privileges"—the prerogative of the Commons to originate revenue legislation, the obligation of the king to hear and respond to grievances set forth by the Commons, and so forth—not as fundamental rights but as concessions freely given by wise and generous kings for the convenience of the realm and revocable at will. Royalist views of the Parliament's role in taxation were clearly expressed by Charles in 1628: "If you (which God forbid) whould not give that supply, which this kingdom and state requires at your hands in this time of common danger, I must, according to my conscience, take those other courses, which God has put into mine hands."[45] Charles here asserted both a medieval claim—the reference to "common danger"—and royalist ones—his allusions to God's authorization to "take other courses" and to the notion of necessity of state.

The king's will is, on these views, securely placed above other sources of law (including common and canon law) and cannot be restrained by them. The king can address grievances through statute (in Parliament) if he chooses, but statutes so produced are not seen as superior to royal proclamations. Parliament may be a useful place for the king to get advice and counsel as to what the best course of action may be, but it has no independent source of authority.[46]

Consent Theories

What I shall call consent theory was a loose and contradictory set of ideas that emerged gradually over the course of the previous century.

---

[45] Johann Sommerville, "Ideology, Property, and the Constitution," in Cust and Hughes, *Conflict*, p. 52.

[46] It should be emphasized that while the prerogative was not confined by either statute or common law, it was regulated, as were the king's actions, by a deeper law, traceable to

It is important to emphasize that the consent theories articulated in the 1620s were backward looking, aimed at protecting ancient liberties against what were seen as royal incursions. The most conservative strand of consent theory was articulated by Sir Edward Coke, among others, and has been called by J. G. A. Pocock the Ancient Constitution Myth or the Common Law Mind.[47] On this view, the king's prerogative authority as well as that of parliamentary statutes was defined and constrained by an ancient customary law that was occasionally confirmed (but not made) by Parliament—notably in Magna Charta.[48] This idea, that ancient usage and custom gives law (including statutes) its authority, fits comfortably with medieval understandings (especially the upward view cited earlier); its chief difference from earlier understandings is its perception that the king seems to be getting things wrong.

Another strand, apparently more modern, was expressed by John Selden in the context of the debate on the petition of right in 1628. Selden argued that the ancient foundation of common law was not itself sufficient to constrain the royal prerogative and protect ancient liberties. "The same power that established the common law must establish martial law, and were it established by Act of Parliament, it would be most lawful."[49] Selden asserted that the authority of common law and prerogative both had to be located in statute—that is, in parliamentary act. Parliament's authority was, however, derived from its ancient pedigree, so in this sense Selden's consent theory was conservative of the ancient constitution. Selden's insistence on the authority of statute and his view that common laws originated in ancient statutes were not typical of his contemporaries—in principle, he disagreed with Coke, the preeminent articulator of common law ideology, as much as with the king.

The key idea of all strands of consent theory as it applied to finance was this: If the king could not persuade Parliament to provide him with revenues, he was not justified in imposing taxes himself. Doing so would be illegal and wrong and subjects would be justified in refusing to pay. Unlike royalist theory, consent theory rested on the assumption that, as regards the taking of property, representative institutions were

---

God or nature. Royalist theory was not, therefore, absolutist in the Hobbesian sense of identifying legitimate state acts with the commands of the sovereign.

[47] J. G. A. Pocock, *The Ancient Constitution and the Feudal Law* (Cambridge: Cambridge University Press, 1987).

[48] It is important to note that when I speak of Parliament in this period, I always include the king as a member. The standard formulation of "the king in Parliament" was expressed institutionally in the royal veto.

[49] Quoted in Russell, *Parliaments*, p. 352.

more competent than the king to make correct judgments about necessity.[50] As it evolved out of common law ideology, consent theory was espoused by Coke and others as a deeply conservative understanding of English legal practices.[51]

The "Parliament men"—Edward Coke, Francis Seymour, Robert Phelips, and others—insisted that the chambers of Parliament, and especially the House of Commons, were ancient institutions that had been a part of English government since its inception in the dim and unremembered past, and did not owe their authority to this king or to any past king. Parliamentary privileges originated in customary practice or common law; they were not granted by any king and were genuine rights that could not be abridged by royal action. Moreover, the excercise of these rights intrinsically required the retention of private rights of judgment and therefore of consent through Parliament. On this view, the king's executive authority or prerogative is severely limited by common law (for Coke) and by statute (for Selden) and, though it may be necessary for timely and effective government, it cannot form the basis of justified authority. Rather, governmental authority flows from the practice of consent through formal acts of Parliament, and this requirement has been embedded in the English constitution from time out of memory.

Conflicting Implications of Royalist and Consent Theory

These two political conceptions—each a close relative of medieval conceptions of mixed monarchy—provided distinct ways to give moral force to political action (or to withhold it) and thereby provided distinct ways to understand the authority of the commands of the state. Most important for our purposes, each theory provides an account of how Parliament should relate to other English institutions, how it should be structured, what business it should do, and how it should do it. Each theory contained within it appraisals of parliamentary practices and therefore of ideas as to how they might be reformed.

From the royalist viewpoint, legislative stalemate and delay, while sometimes surprising or irritating, was not fundamentally corrosive

---

[50] This version of consent theory is essentially cognitive in the sense that Parliament's acts are acts of recognition of what the common good requires. As such it is closer to the medieval notion of consent than the modern one, in which acts of consent constitute authority rather than recognize it.

[51] Selden was as concerned as Coke to provide a foundation for the protection of ancient liberties, but the foundation he provides seems less conservative than Coke's in that it is the ancientness of the constitution, and particularly of Parliament, rather than that of the laws that authorizes state action.

of governmental practice. Such delays might be seen as a sign that deliberations were not yet ripe for decision and should be continued. Institutions that produced deadlock in the absence of consensus might, in this sense, have seemed better than more decisive ones. If Parliament could not agree on a course of action, the king could address problems on his own, and more swiftly and efficiently at that. Since consent played no constitutive role in authorizing governmental acts—it was merely a sign of the health of the commonwealth—its absence did not undermine the authority of royal commands.

From the perspective of consent theory, things were completely different. Cumbersome internal institutions prevented Parliament from addressing serious and persistent problems at both the national and local levels. Satisfactory solutions to these problems inevitably involved the imposition of burdens on some for the benefit of others. Such public acts needed to be explained and justified, especially to those called upon to make sacrifices. Parliament was the institution constitutionally best able to provide justifications of this sort, and its inability to do so shifted power but not authorization toward the court. The situation called for reform—both within the Parliament, to make it more efficient in producing legislation, and in its relations with the king, the authority of whose acts rested on a foundation of consent.

EXPLANATION OF INSTITUTIONAL CHANGE: CAUSES AND REASONS

The study of the role of ideas in social action intrinsically involves difficult issues in social science. We want social science theories to provide causal explanations of events in the same sense that scientific explanations of physical or biological phenomena seem to do. At the same time, we want social science theories to give an account of the reasons for or meanings of social action. We want to know not only what caused the agent to perform some act but also the agent's reasons for taking the action. Good reason-giving explanations are supposed to show how it is that the action "makes sense" or is intelligible; such accounts may be thought of as rationalization for or interpretations of action.

Social science theories generally attempt to reconcile these two demands by seeking the causes of action in intentions. The causal accounts of actions we seek take beliefs, preferences, values, intentions, ideas as causal agents. From this point of view, the problem of understanding the role of ideas in social action is, then, that ideas are supposed both to play a causal role in the genesis of actions and at the same time to rationalize or make actions intelligible.[52] These two explanatory requirements inevitably conflict. Within rational choice theory, for example, an actor's desires are supposed to be causally efficacious—someone's thirst causes her to drink—and also to give reasons for or justifications of the action. Material circumstances by themselves—the absence of liquids in the body's tissues—without the intentional state (thirst) might also be causally efficacious if there happened to be some (reflexive) causal mechanism directly connecting drinking with the absence of water. But such circumstances by themselves could not make the *act* of drinking intelligible from the standpoint of the agent; such a mechanism might explain the behavior of taking in liquids while not accounting for drinking as an act at all.

In principle, then, the positive and interpretive requirements of theories of action are independent. That social theories are both positive and interpretive requires that they be both causal and intentionalist in their structure, seeing actions as caused by intentional or purposive states. That actions are so produced opens the possibility that intentional states are independent of material ones and that complete theories of action must not only account for action in intentional terms but also explain the evolution of the intentional elements themselves.

Ideas play an important role in this story in two distinct ways. At one level, potentially verifiable beliefs about the world can be both causally significant and determined by what I call an "interpretive requirement." The king's belief that a parliament would not provide adequate revenues to conduct necessary military operations made him reluctant to summon one. The failure of the king to call parliaments or to deal reasonably with them when he did call them induced parliamentarians to doubt his respect for ancient representative institutions and therefore to grant him less revenue than he asked, in order to increase his dependence on them for revenues. Expectations or beliefs of this sort guide strategic choices and are themselves shaped by those choices.

Less obviously, nonverifiable beliefs—specifically normative beliefs about the relationship of God's will, popular consent, and political authorization—can be causally significant as well. Virtually everyone thought both that the king's authority was derived from God and that some kind of popular consent was necessary for his authorization; these two beliefs lie at the core of late-medieval political thought. That such beliefs can be causally efficacious is evident; it is less clear that they may evolve endogenously. Though neither of these beliefs is veri-

---

[52] This problem was elegantly stated and discussed several years ago by Donald Davidson in "Reasons and Causes," in *Essays on Actions and Events* (Oxford: Oxford University Press, 1980).

fiable, the tension between them made them jointly susceptible to certain empirical occurrences. Thus, if—as happened periodically in medieval England—a king comes sharply into conflict with his subjects, questions about his authority will arise (as they did in Magna Carta). Moreover, if the conflict becomes sufficiently chronic to undermine the authority of princely action, the nature of political authorization itself will come into question. In this sense, the (normative) theory of authorization can be "forced" to change under pressure of empirical events.

Given traditional English understandings of English institutions, the fiscal requirements of war "required" the king to summon parliaments and thereby recreate a characteristic bargaining relationship with his subjects and their delegates in Parliament. That war put this pressure on English institutions was not, however, new to the seventeenth century. What was new to this century was the breakdown of the traditional relationship of trust between the king and his subjects. Throughout the debates on the petition of right in 1628 the king's supporters insisted more and more shrilly that the subjects trust the king's judgment. Attorney General Heath argued in the Lords that "God has trusted the King with governing the whole. . . . As the King is trusted with the coins and monies of the kingdome, of his absolute power . . . he may turn our gold and silver money into brass or base money, and in one instant undo his people thereby. The answer is, he will not do it: he is trusted."[53] Heath's argument failed to stop the Lords from agreeing to the petition of right, and more fundamentally it failed to stop the quest for a coherent basis of governmental authority. This failure cannot, I think, be laid at the feet of the Stuart kings; it is rooted in a deeper ideological shift, traceable to the Reformation, which undermined the possibility that authority could still be based fundamentally on trust between king and subject.

In a sense, the transition in this period was between two strategic equilibria: one based on extensive trust between crown and subject and the other based on more explicitly formulated rules and procedures for resolving conflict. As long as the king and his subjects trusted each other to behave as they should, the medieval kingship theory gave an adequate account of authority, and rigid parliamentary institutions were well suited for the limited job they had to do. When that trust failed, the role of parliamentary action had to be either vastly reduced or dramatically increased. Either parliaments would meet seldom and then only to provide extraordinary revenues, or they would have to become much better able to produce the legislation needed to account for the activities of English government.

[53] Quoted in Russell, *Parliaments*, p. 367.

The notion that there were (at least) two equilibria, each supported by appropriate expectations, is to be expected in any circumstance of strategic complexity. Less obvious is the dynamic process leading to the collapse of the equilibrium based on trust and its replacement by another. Here the story runs as follows. When James asked the parliaments of 1621 and 1624 to support his efforts to restore the Palatinate, they readily complied, acting under the traditional governing expectations. It was James's duty to defend England's claims and Parliament's duty to assist him. It was the fact that the royal policies failed—that the Spanish negotiations collapsed, that James's mercenaries were unable to defend the Palatinate, and that the French marriage led to repeated religious concessions to Catholics—that led to a dramatic decline in trust in the king and a destabilizing of the original equilibrium.

Succeeding parliaments became much more stingy in providing revenues, effectively requiring Charles to impose nonparliamentary taxes and to employ coercive methods to collect them in order to continue the war. Whether these new taxes were illegal or not was ambiguous under medieval kingship theory; it depended on whether parliamentary judgment was sufficiently occluded to justify the king's resort to other means. Royalist theories, as they relied on the king's judgment, regarded the new taxes as legal and supported an equilibrium in which Parliament would play little role in English government. Consent theories, as they relied on parliamentary judgment of necessity, judged the taxes illegal and supported an equilibrium in which parliaments were more central to ordinary government. It is the fact that both of these theories were slight variants of traditional theory that limited the number of equilibria that could be reached to two.

Both theoretically and practically, Parliament's role in English politics underwent a profound transformation during the 1620s. This transformation was rooted in the dissolution of traditional ways of understanding the political and social world. Men could no longer assume that they were engaged in a common project or that their ruler's interest and their own were fundamentally the same. Moreover, even when a ruler and subjects could be believed to have a common purpose, it became less possible for each to believe the other capable of good judgment. This sense of separate purposes and separate judgments limited the range of acceptable institutions by placing increasing emphasis on those arrangements that required leaders to obtain public agreement before taking costly action.

PART IV

THE INSTITUTIONALIZATION
OF IDEAS

CHAPTER NINE

Westphalia and All That

STEPHEN D. KRASNER

The conventional view that the Peace of Westphalia of 1648 marks a turning point in history is wrong. The Peace of Westphalia was not a clear break with the past: political entities with exclusive control over a well-defined territory existed well before the Peace, and feudal and universal institutions, which were eventually extinguished, continued well after it.

The view that the Westphalian system implies that sovereignty has a taken-for-granted quality is wrong. The actual content of sovereignty, the scope of the authority that states can exercise, has always been contested. The basic organizing principle of sovereignty—exclusive control over a given territory—has been persistently challenged by the creation of new institutional forms that better meet specific material needs.

Both the slow extruding out of universal and feudal institutions and the contested nature of sovereignty can be explained primarily by material, not ideational, factors. The rich variety of political ideas available in Europe in the fifteenth, sixteenth, and seventeenth centuries made it easy for political leaders to legitimate institutional innovations that were motivated by economic and military opportunities.

Westphalia is an icon for international relations scholars. The Peace of Westphalia of 1648 is routinely understood to have ushered in or codified a new international order, one based on independent sover-

I thank David Abernethy, Bruce Bueno de Mesquita, Jack Donnelly, Frank Dobbin, Neil Fligstein, Judith Goldstein, David Gress Wright, Robert Keohane, John Meyer, Susan Okin, and John G. Ruggie for their comments on earlier drafts of this chapter.

eign states rather than on some earlier medieval concept of Christendom, or feudalism, or empires. History, however, is not so neatly compartmentalized. The provisions of the Peace itself reflect medieval conceptualizations more than modern ones. The treaties of Münster and Osnabrück, which made up the Peace of Westphalia, dealt primarily with feudal issues such as hereditary succession in specific German principalities, the system by which the Holy Roman emperor was elected, representation in the diet and imperial courts of the empire, and fiefdoms in northern Germany for the victorious king of Sweden. The passage of the treaties most often cited, the one giving German principalities the right to sign treaties, is only one element in a document of more than forty pages.

The Peace did not mark the end of the Holy Roman Empire, one of the two great universal institutions of the medieval world. The empire was not formally abolished until 1806. The papacy, the other great universal institution, is still with us, although in very much diminished form. Even before the Peace, England was a well-defined territorial entity with a hierarchical structure of control, and the city-states of northern Italy had effectively freed themselves from the external control of the papacy and of the Holy Roman and Byzantine empires by the thirteenth century.

While the term "the Westphalian system" does accurately capture the fact that the efficacy of universal institutions has been virtually eliminated, it is misleading in suggesting that there has been agreement on the scope of authority that could be exercised by sovereign states. The positive content of sovereignty, the areas over which the state can legitimately command, has always been contested. The claim to exclusive control over a given territory has been challenged both in theory and in practice by transborder flows and interference in the internal affairs of states.

The nature and level of control exercised over flows across territorial boundaries—the movement of people, goods, finance, ideas, and information—has varied across states and over time. Some states have very effectively regulated some kinds of activities, such as the movement of goods, but not others, such as the movement of people. Even the most powerful states have found it extremely difficult to block the penetration of their national boundaries by radio waves. Ideas, from the Reformation to rock and roll, have been transmitted across borders despite the efforts of sovereign political authorities to control them. Billions of dollars' worth of illegal drugs enter the United States and other countries every year. In the contemporary world individual states could isolate themselves from international capital markets, but only at great economic cost.

Even the exercise of authority over activities exclusively within a given territory, generally regarded as a core attribute of sovereign states, has been problematic in practice and contested in theory.[1] The most dramatic challenge has involved efforts by external actors to control the way a state treats its own citizens or subjects. In the sixteenth and seventeenth centuries, states concluded international agreements containing provisions in respect to the treatment of religious dissenters. The final act of the Congress of Vienna provided for the prohibition of the slave trade, though not of slavery itself.[2] After World War I the newly created states of Central Europe accepted restrictions on their treatment of minorities, including, for instance, guarantees of primary education in minority languages.[3] The United Nations Declaration of Human Rights and the Helsinki accords both have provisions outlining the appropriate array of rights, referred to as human rights, that should be accorded to individuals regardless of the policies of their governments. In the contemporary world, political systems based on ethnic exclusion are condemned, and states that have engaged in such practices, such as South Africa, have been subject to external pressure, including economic sanctions.

While universal institutions have been eliminated, other institutional forms that do not conform with the basic organizing principle of sovereignty, exclusive control over all activities within a given area, have been created. In the nineteenth century European powers established protectorates, assuming control over the foreign but not the domestic policies of some weaker areas; outright colonization, in contrast, was fully consistent with sovereignty. The Exclusive Economic Zone, formulated during the United Nations Law of the Seas Conference and now accepted by states even though the final treaty was never ratified, gives littoral states control over the exploitation of resources within the 200-meter isobath or the end of the continental shelf, but not the right to regulate shipping in the same area. The Antarctic is governed by the Antarctic Treaty regime, most of whose members have rejected claims of sovereignty over the continent. The European Community may evolve into an institutional structure in which the territorial exercise of authority varies with the issue area—monetary policy might be set for all of Europe by a single central bank, while social behavior might

---

[1] Robert Jackson, *Quasi-States: Sovereignty, International Relations, and the Third World* (Cambridge: Cambridge University Press, 1990), p. 6, refers to the "basic prohibition against foreign intervention" as the *Grundnorm* of sovereign statehood.

[2] Ibid., pp. 72–73.

[3] The two best treatments of the minorities question are C. A. Macartney, *National States and National Minorities* (London: Oxford University Press, 1934); and Inis L. Claude, Jr., *National Minorities: An International Problem* (Cambridge: Harvard University Press, 1955).

be regulated in different ways by different regions. Sovereignty has always been contested both with respect to the scope of authority exercised by states and by institutional arrangements that do not conform with exclusive territorial control.

In the effort to construct sovereignty, ideas have been used to codify existing practices rather than to initiate new forms of order. Ideas have not made possible alternatives that did not previously exist; they legitimated political practices that were already facts on the ground. Ideas have been one among several instruments that actors have invoked to promote their own, usually mundane, interests. The Europeans of the fifteenth, sixteenth, and seventeenth centuries had an unusually rich mix of conceptualizations to draw on, which included not only the extensive political argumentation that had been generated by divisions within Christianity but also the thought of the classical world which had been recovered during the Renaissance. A wide variety of ideas and cognitive structures were available to European leaders, an advantage they enjoyed over the more isolated civilizations of the Americas, Africa, and even Asia.

The impact of ideas about the sovereign state system has been felt over time because they have been embodied in institutions. In this embodied form ideas reinforced the positions of some actors and undermined those of others. Having established nascent bureaucracies and courts, the kings of Europe could invoke concepts of sovereignty to strengthen these institutions against the claims of rival transnational authorities, especially the papacy. Over time the position of the administrative units of sovereign states strengthened and that of the church bureaucracy weakened. The idea of sovereignty was used to legitimate the right of the sovereign to collect taxes, and thereby strengthen the position of the state, and to deny such right to the church, and thereby weaken the position of the papacy. Only as national states became increasingly effective and powerful actors, capable of limiting the authority claims of other actors, did the Peace of Westphalia come to be understood as a decisive break with the past.

THE CONVENTIONAL VIEW

This perspective, which emphasizes the contingent and pliant character of sovereignty, especially with regard to the actual exercise of authority, the scope of state control, can be contrasted with a widely held view among international relations theorists and international lawyers which sees Westphalia as a major, perhaps a decisive, break marking the transition from the medieval to the modern world. In one variant this conventional view simply refers to behavioral regularities. In another, a more reflective perspective, it points to changes in the deep or generative structure of the system.

Gianfranco Poggi, in his *Development of the Modern State*, says that an international system composed of independent states, each with its own territory, was "consecrated by the Peace of Westphalia [1648], the cornerstone of the modern system of international relations."[4] Kalevi Holsti, in a survey of peace and conflict since the seventeenth century, writes that "the Peace of Westphalia organized Europe on the principle of particularism. It represented a new diplomatic arrangement—an order created by states, for states—and replaced most of the legal vestiges of hierarchy, at the pinnacle of which were the Pope and the Holy Roman Emperor."[5]

Leo Gross, one of the leading postwar students of international law, asserted that Westphalia detached international law from any particular religion. Westphalia placed Protestant and Catholic states on the same footing.[6] Public international lawyers have generally traced the beginnings of the modern international system to the Peace of Westphalia.[7]

Among contemporary students of international relations John Ruggie has been the most probing, imaginative, and illuminating of those that have argued that the period around Westphalia, if not Westphalia itself, represents a break with the past, a change in the deep generative structure in the nature of the international system. Ruggie suggests that changes in dynamic density can lead to changes in structure. He argues that population pressure, widening markets, the expansion of systems of justice, and the elimination by rulers of domestic challengers led to a change in the deep or generative structure of the system; a change from the heteronomous structure of the medieval world to the modern structure of sovereignty.[8] Ruggie points to three important

---

[4] Gianfranco Poggi, *The Development of the Modern State: A Sociological Introduction* (Stanford: Stanford University Press, 1978), p. 89, cites Leo Gross, "The Peace of Westphalia, 1648–1948," *American Journal of International Law* 42 (1948): 20–41.

[5] Kalevi J. Holsti, *Peace and War: Armed Conflicts and International Order, 1648–1989* (Cambridge: Cambridge University Press, 1991), p. 25.

[6] Gross "Peace of Westphalia," p. 22.

[7] David Kennedy, "A New Stream of International Law Scholarship," Institute of International Public Law and International Relations, Thessaloniki, Greece (August 1988), p. 29 (mimeo). One public international law text from the interwar period states, for instance: "But since the peace of Westphalia of 1648, the principle of complete independence has been accepted by statesmen, and embodied in the international code of the civilized world": T. J. Lawrence, *The Principles of International Law*, 7th ed. (Boston: D. C. Heath, 1923), p. 116.

[8] John Gerard Ruggie, "International Regimes, Transactions, and Change: Embedded Liberalism in the Postwar Economic Order," in *International Regimes*, ed. Stephen D.

principles or ideas associated with the beginning of the state system. The first was that the ruler had the right to choose between Protestantism and Catholicism. The second was that within their own domains territorial rulers had the same standing as the emperor. The third was the rediscovery of the Roman concept of exclusive property rights, which could be used as a model for sovereignty.[9]

In sum, the conventional perspective is that Westphalia reflects a break with the past, a passage from the medieval to the modern world.

THE PEACE OF WESTPHALIA

The texts of the Peace of Westphalia, which was composed of the Treaty of Osnabrück and the Treaty of Münster, do not provide much evidence for the assertion that the Peace itself was any kind of decisive transition point. The Peace brought to an end the Thirty Years' War, which had devastated the center of Europe, especially the Germanic lands. It was a complicated document with provisions regarding the satisfaction of various dynastic claims, division of territory, the practice of religion, the constitution of the Holy Roman Empire, and other matters. The Treaty of Osnabrück was concluded between the Habsburg monarch who was the Holy Roman emperor and the Protestant ruler of Sweden; the Treaty of Münster was concluded between the emperor and the Catholic king of France. The princes of the empire were included in the negotiations at the insistence of the victorious powers, France and Sweden, a move that weakened the position of their most important opponent, the Habsburg emperor.[10]

The basic issue at Westphalia was how the empire, which had lost the war, would satisfy France and Sweden, which had won.[11] The more general problem was to find some way of dealing with the religious disorders that had torn Europe apart for a century. The Thirty Years' War, the bloodiest confrontation in which religious disputes were con-

---

Krasner, pp. 195–231 (Ithaca: Cornell University Press, 1983), and "International Structure and International Transformation: Space, Time, and Method," in *Global Changes and Theoretical Challenges*, ed. E. O. Czempiel and J. N. Rosenau, pp. 21–35 (Lexington, Mass.: Lexington Books, 1989).

[9] John Gerard Ruggie, "Finding Our Feet," *International Organization* 46 (Autumn 1992).

[10] E. A. Beller, "The Thirty Years' War," in *The New Cambridge Modern History*, vol. 4, *The Decline of Spain and the Thirty Years' War, 1609–48/59* (Cambridge: Cambridge University Press, 1970), p. 352.

[11] A. W. Ward, "The Peace of Westphalia," in *The Cambridge Modern History*, vol. 4, *The Thirty Years' War*, pp. 400–405 (Cambridge: Cambridge University Press, 1907).

sequential, resulted in more than two million battle deaths—greater carnage than in any conflict before World War I.[12]

The Peace imposed a territorial settlement that was advantageous to the victors, France and Sweden. France was granted control over the bishoprics of Metz, Toul, and Verdun, which had been under de facto French control for a century. Alsace was granted to France by Austria, even though Austria's claim to Alsace was questionable. Austria had an undisputed claim to some parts of Alsace but dubious claims over other areas that were under the control of the local nobility. One provision of the Treaty of Münster states that the ancient privileges that these local nobles had enjoyed with regard to the empire should be retained with respect to France, but another provision grants France "all manner of Jurisdiction and Sovereignty."[13]

Sweden's fundamental territorial objective, to secure a position on the southern shore of the Baltic, was accepted at Westphalia. Sweden received Eastern Pomerania, the islands of Rügen, Usedom, and Willin, the bishoprics of Bremen and Verden, and the port of Wismar—not in full sovereignty but as fiefs of the Holy Roman Empire.[14] The ruler of Sweden occupied seats in the imperial diet as the duke of Bremen, Verden, and Pomerania, the prince of Rügen, and the lord of Wismar. Sweden was also given places in the circles of Upper Saxony, Lowery Saxony, and Westphalia.[15] The prerogatives of the ruler of Sweden were specified with regard to appeal to either of the imperial courts—the Aulic Court or the Imperial Chamber. Sweden was given the right to erect a university and to collect certain tolls. The Hanseatic towns in the areas ruled by Sweden were, however, to maintain their traditional liberty and freedom of navigation.[16]

Thus, while the transfer of territory by the emperor and the empire to France was consistent with a world conceived of as being composed of sovereign states, the settlement with Sweden, structured in terms of fiefdoms controlled by the ruler of Sweden within the Holy Roman Empire, was based upon an older set of understandings. Even in the

---

[12] Charles Tilly, *Coercion, Capital, and European States, A.D. 990–1990* (Cambridge: Basil Blackwell, 1990), pp. 165–66.

[13] Treaty of Münster, reprinted in *Major Peace Treaties of Modern History, 1648–1967*, ed. Fred Israel (New York: McGraw-Hill, 1967), arts. LXXVI, p. 31 (quote); LXXI, p. 30; LXXIV, p. 31; Ward, "Peace of Westphalia," pp. 404–6; Beller, "Thirty Years' War," p. 353.

[14] Treaty of Osnabrück, reprinted in *The Consolidated Treaty Series*, vol. 1, *1648–1649*, ed. Clive Parry (Dobbs Ferry, N.Y.: Oceana, 1969), art. x, pp. 244ff.; Ward, "Peace of Westphalia," pp. 403–4; Beller, "Thirty Years' War," p. 354.

[15] The circles were administrative structures within the Holy Roman Empire that were charged with a variety of administrative and military functions for a specific set of territories.

[16] Treaty of Osnabrück, art. x.4.

redistribution of territory, perhaps the most straightforward aspect of the Peace of Westphalia, there is no unambiguous commitment to a modern conception of a world made up of sovereign territorial states. The statesmen at Osnabrück and Münster had available to them a variety of institutional forms, and they saw no problem in cobbling together arrangements that now appear anomalous.

Several provisions of the Peace dealt with the practice of religion. Religious differences had precipitated a series of devastatingly costly wars in Europe, both international and civil. The major intellectual proponents of the theory of sovereignty, such as Jean Bodin and Thomas Hobbes (who wrote the *Leviathan* after the Peace of Westphalia but *De Cive* before it), were attempting to find some way to end these bloody sectarian struggles. The Peace of Westphalia, like the Peace of Augsburg of 1555, tried to establish a set of commonly accepted principles regarding the practice of religion that would govern relations between sovereigns and their subjects. While legitimating the existence of Protestantism within the empire, Augsburg had placed the choice of religion in the hands of the ruler.[17] This was not a formula for stability; Christians concerned about the disposition of their eternal souls were disinclined to allow their secular sovereigns to choose their religious persuasions.

Westphalia attempted to insulate religion from politics. The Peace did not explicitly reject the principle that the ruler had the right to determine the religion of his subjects (a principle completely consistent with conventional notions of internal sovereignty), but several of its provisions constrained the authority of the sovereign. The most important provided that a sovereign who changed his religion could not compel his subjects to change theirs. Religious practices were to be restored to the situation that existed on January 1, 1624. Religious practices on which ruler and subject were in agreement as of that date were to continue unless they were changed by mutual consent. Catholic orders were to stay Catholic; Lutheran orders were to stay Lutheran. Those Catholics who lived in Lutheran states or Lutherans who lived in Catholic states were given the right to practice their religion in the privacy of their homes, to educate their children at home, or to send them to foreign schools. Subjects were not to be excluded from the "Community of Merchants, Artizans or Companies, nor depriv'd of

[17] There were two exceptions. In eight imperial cities inhabited by both Protestants and Catholics, both faiths were given the right to exist. The Habsburg ruler Ferdinand I also promised, in a secret agreement not formally part of the Peace, that Lutheran nobles and townspeople living in ecclesiastical territories could continue to practice their faith. See John Gagliardo, *Germany under the Old Regime* (London: Longman, 1991), pp. 16–17.

Successions, Legacies, Hospitals, Lazar-Houses, or Alms-Houses, and other Privileges or Rights" because of their religion. Subjects were not to be denied the right of burial, nor was any amount they were charged for burial to differ from that levied on those who adhered to the religion of the state. Dissenters (Catholic or Lutheran) who did not have any rights of religious practice in 1624 and who wanted to move or were ordered to move were to have the freedom to do so and were given five years to sell their goods.[18]

Cities with mixed Lutheran and Catholic populations (Augsburg, Dunckelspiel, Biberach, Ravensburg, Kaufbeuren) were to permit the free practice of religion by Catholics and Lutherans. In the first four of these municipal cities, offices were to be divided equally between Catholics and Lutherans.[19]

The emperor granted members of the Silesian nobility who were Lutherans the right to continue to practice their religion provided that they did "not disturb the publick Peace and Tranquillity." They were also given the right to build three churches. Magistrates of both religions were admonished to forbid any person to criticize or impugn the religious settlement contained in the agreement and in the earlier Treaty of Passau.[20]

The Treaty of Osnabrück provided that Catholics and Lutherans should be equally represented in the assemblies of the empire. Religious issues were to be decided by a consensus of both Catholics and Protestants. Representatives at the imperial courts were also to include members of both religions. If the judges hearing a case divided along religious lines, then the case could be appealed to the diet. If there were cross-cutting cleavages with respect to religion, then a case could not be appealed.[21]

Rights given to Lutherans and Catholics were also extended to Calvinists. In the event that a territory that adhered to one Protestant church (the Lutheran) came to be ruled by an adherent of another (the Calvinist) the new ruler was to have the right to practice his own religion, but he was prohibited from attempting to change the religion of his subjects or of churches, hospitals, schools, and revenues. The new ruler was enjoined from giving "any trouble or molestation to the Religion of others directly or indirectly." The community was given the right to name ministers, and the prince was to confirm them "without

---

[18] Treaty of Osnabrück, art. v, secs. 11–23, pp. 219–25; secs. 28–30, p. 229.
[19] Ibid., sec. 25, p. 226; sec. 7, p. 217.
[20] Ibid., sec. 31, pp. 230–31; sec. 41, p. 234.
[21] Ibid., sec. 42, p. 234; sec. 45, p. 238.

denial." Religious toleration was, however, limited to Lutherans, Calvinists, and Catholics.[22]

The Peace of Westphalia did not address the vexing problem of religion according to the precept of sovereignty developed by Bodin or Hobbes.[23] The treaties did not sanction the right of rulers to do whatever they pleased with regard to the practice of religion within their own territories. The Peace dictated a set of internal practices for much of the Holy Roman Empire, the area of Europe most riven by doctrinal divisions; it did not simply endorse the Peace of Augsburg, which gave the sovereign absolute power to establish sectarian practices. In the area of religion, the central political question of the seventeenth century, Westphalia was less consistent with modern notions of sovereignty than Augsburg, which had been concluded almost a century earlier. Westphalia recognized some rights for both Protestants and Catholics, rejected the right of rulers to change religious practices within their territories arbitrarily, and required consensus on religious matters in the diet and in the imperial courts.

The inherent tension between sovereign prerogatives and international pressures reflected in the treaties of Westphalia is manifest in many later controversies about human rights. The practices of individual states with regard to slavery, the rights of national minorities, and the exclusion of ethnic minorities have been subject to international scrutiny, criticism, and pressure. Here, as elsewhere, sovereignty is a contingent concept whose actual content depends on the balance of resources—cognitive, economic, and military—among political actors.

The treaties also dealt with other constitutional issues related to the empire. The number of electors was raised to eight to restore an electorship to the Count Palatine.[24] The rights of succession for the ruling house of Bavaria were spelled out, including a provision that the elec-

---

[22] Ibid., art. VII, pp. 239–41. For treatments in secondary sources, see Beller, "Thirty Years' War," p. 355; Ward, "Peace of Westphalia," pp. 411–14.

[23] Bodin was less prepared than Hobbes to cede absolute power to the sovereign. Bodin argued, for instance, that the sovereign was constrained by natural and divine law and was obligated to follow the Salic Law, which prohibited a female ruler. Bodin favored religious toleration on the grounds that it was impossible to be certain about questions of religion and that efforts to repress Protestantism could tear France apart, but this was not an area where he recognized any formal or theoretical constraint on the sovereign's right to legislate. See Quentin Skinner, *The Foundations of Modern Political Thought*, 2 vols. (Cambridge: Cambridge University Press, 1978), 2:244–54.

[24] The electors were those rulers of the empire who had the power to elect the emperor. Since the Golden Bull of the fourteenth century there had been seven electors. The seventh electorate, however, had been transferred from the count Palatine to the ruler of Bavaria.

toral seat held by Bavaria would disappear were there to be no male heir.[25]

For the conventional interpretation of the Peace of Westphalia, which underscores 1648 as a break with the past, the most important provisions of the treaties were the ones that gave the princes of the Holy Roman Empire the right to conduct their own foreign policies, to conclude treaties with other states within and without the empire. The section of the Treaty of Münster which recognizes the right to make treaties provides that all of the electors, princes, and states of the Holy Roman Empire should

> enjoy without contradiction, the Right of Suffrage in all Deliberations touching the Affairs of the Empire; but above all, when the Business in hand shall be the making or interpreting of Laws, the declaring of Wars, imposing Taxes, levying or quartering of Soldiers, erecting new Fortifications in the Territorys of the States, or reinforcing the old Garisons; as also when a Peace of Alliance is to be concluded, and treated about, or the like, none of these, or the like things shall be acted for the future, without the Suffrage and Consent of the Free Assembly of all the States of the Empire; Above all, it shall be free perpetually to each of the States of the Empire, to make Alliances with Strangers for their Preservation and Safety; provided, nevertheless, such Alliances be not against the Emperor, and the Empire, nor against the Publick Peace, and this Treaty, and without prejudice to the Oath by which every one is bound to the Emperor and the Empire.[26]

The Treaty of Münster is forty-two pages long. It contains 128 provisions. The right to make treaties is given in one sentence of a section that spells out the rights of states within the Holy Roman Empire to participate in the deliberations of the empire and concludes with an admonition that no treaty should be directed against the emperor and the empire. Only after the fact can this provision be read as an endorsement of the principles of sovereignty, which deny any restraint on the way states may conduct their foreign policies.

The presence of the princes of the empire at Münster and Osnabrück undermined the hierarchical claims of the emperor. The princes were in attendance, however, not because of an ideological commitment to sovereignty but because Austria, whose ruler was also the emperor, had been defeated in the Thirty Years' War.[27] France and Sweden

---

[25] Treaty of Osnabrück, art. IV, secs. 1–44, pp. 202–11; Treaty of Münster, art. XIV, p. 13.

[26] Treaty of Münster, art. LXV, pp. 27–28; a similar provision is found in the Treaty of Osnabrück, art. VIII, sec. 1, p. 241.

[27] With only one exception, all Holy Roman emperors from the 14th century until the abolition of the empire in 1806 were Habsburgs, even though the emperorship was an

wanted to undermine the power of the Habsburgs, who also ruled Spain. The major princes wanted to enhance their autonomy. The provision that the princes of the empire could conduct their own foreign policies, albeit with some constraints, was a manifestation not of a principle or idea but rather of the immediate political interests of France, Sweden, and the larger German principalities.

Moreover, the treaty-making power recognized at Westphalia had already been put into practice. The more powerful German states that were part of the empire had conducted independent foreign policies before the conclusion of the Peace. Both the Palatinate and Brandenburg, for instance, concluded alliances with the Dutch Republic around 1605. Both the Protestant and Catholic rulers within the empire had formed alliances among themselves before the outbreak of the Thirty Years' War.[28]

Westphalia was but one step in the long-term erosion of the position of the emperor. Every important change in the Holy Roman Empire from the Golden Bull of 1356 to the Final Recess of the Imperial Deputation of 1803 involved either a reduction in the emperor's power or an increase in the power of the princes, or both. Westphalia was only the most notable of these developments.[29]

In sum, the Peace of Westphalia was not a decisive break with the past. It codified existing practices more than it created new ones. It reflected the short-term interests of the victorious powers, France and Sweden, rather than some overarching conceptualization of how the international system should be ordered. Only in retrospect did Westphalia become an icon that could be used to justify further consolidations of the sovereign state against rival forms of political organization.

European Heterogeneity

No part of Europe suddenly changed from a medieval to a modern institutional structure. The driving force behind the elimination of feudal institutions was material, not ideal: changes in the nature of military technology and the growth of trade, which systematically favored states that could take advantage of siege guns and elaborate

---

elective office. The Habsburgs, as the hereditary kings of Bohemia, held one of the electoral seats. As hereditary rulers of Austria they controlled the most powerful state in Germany.

[28] Geoffrey Parker, *The Thirty Years' War* (London: Routledge & Kegan Paul, 1984), p. 2; Gagliardo, *Germany under the Old Regime*, pp. 23–24.

[29] Joseph Gagliardo, *Reich and Nation: The Holy Roman Empire as Idea and Reality, 1763–1806* (Bloomington: University of Indiana Press, 1980), p. viii.

defenses, and organize and protect long-distance commerce. The diversity of Europe's intellectual capital, with ideas from the classical world recovered during the Renaissance mingling with Islamic and various Christian perspectives, provided actors who had material resources, military or economic, with a rich repertoire of legitimating conceptualizations from which to choose. Over a long period of time territorial states were able to reduce dramatically the importance of the two universal institutions of the medieval world, the Catholic Church and the Holy Roman Empire. The elimination of rivals to the sovereign state does not, however, imply that the positive content of sovereignty, the internal and external scope of state control, has been ubiquitously accepted.

Heterogeneity and irregular change, rather than the working out of some deep generative grammar, have characterized institutional developments in Europe. Some medieval kingdoms, such as England, closely resembled modern sovereign states. In the contemporary world not only is the specific content of state authority subject to challenge, but sovereignty itself as the constitutive principle of political life continues to be tested, most notably by the European Community.

The Holy Roman Empire

Westphalia is seen as a critical turning point because it has been understood to mark the end of the Holy Roman Empire, which, along with the papacy, was one of the two major universal institutions of the medieval world. The empire had been understood as the spiritual and secular heir of the Roman Empire. Some spokesmen for the empire claimed that it held authority in all of Christendom, even in those areas that had never been part of it, such as England.

The Holy Roman Empire did not, however, disappear either in law or in practice in 1648. It was not formally abolished until Napoleon's conquests in 1806. While its most important institutions, especially the diet, atrophied during the eighteenth century, others remained robust.

There were four kinds of entities in the empire: ecclesiastical states, imperial cities, estates of imperial counts and knights, and secular states. The first three supported the empire, as did the smaller secular states. The larger secular states, such as Brandenburg, were antagonistic to the empire.

Ecclesiastical states were ruled over by prince prelates of the Catholic Church, who were usually elected by chapters, most of whose members were lay princes. The ecclesiastical states were eager to maintain the empire. Almost all of them were quite small. Shorn of the legitimacy they derived from the empire, they would be even more vulnerable to the predatory attacks of their larger neighbors. The ecclesiastical states were not abolished until the Final Recess of 1803, the last constitutional change in the empire before it was terminated in 1806. Some 3.25 million people lived in the ecclesiastical states at the time they were dissolved and secularized or absorbed by neighboring territories.

The fifty-one imperial cities accounted for less than 2 percent of the population of the empire. In general the cities had stagnated because of changes in trade routes and war, but some, including Hamburg, Frankfurt, and Lübeck, did prosper. These cities were generally run by self-perpetuating patrician oligarchies. The imperial cities were strong supporters of the empire, which provided them with special prerogatives denied to other cities. The status of the imperial cities was ended at Napoleon's insistence in 1803, with six exceptions: Lübeck, Frankfurt, Bremen, Hamburg, Nürnberg, and Augsburg. These cities were charged with the obligation of remaining neutral even if the rest of the empire was at war.

The small estates of the imperial counts and knights lay principally in the south and west of Germany. The imperial counts and knights were strong defenders of the imperial constitution and of the emperor. Only within an imperial structure could they maintain independence.[30] The imperial knights continued to exist until the empire was dissolved in 1806. They had judicial powers within their territories and paid taxes directly to the emperor.

The first sustained attack on the knights' prerogatives came in 1791, when the Hohenzollerns began to assert full sovereignty over the territory of Ansbach-Beyreuth. The Hohenzollerns required payments directly to the Prussian government and prohibited payments to the emperor, the Habsburg ruler of Austria, who was their main rival. Other princes followed the Hohenzollerns in eliminating the prerogatives of the knights, sometimes by actual fighting and attacks on castles. When the status of the knights was abolished in 1806, their lands were absorbed by the contiguous territorial states.[31]

The secular states varied enormously in the nature of their internal constitutions and in size. The largest were Electoral Saxony, Brandenburg, Bavaria, the Palatinate, Hesse, Trier, and Württemberg. They were all ruled by hereditary right. In general, the rulers of the secular states opposed the prerogatives of the emperor and sought to strengthen the role of the imperial diet. In the last 150 years of the empire, however, the smaller states gave more support to it. The largest

---

[30] Ibid., p. 5.
[31] Ibid., pp. 228–32.

secular states, and ultimately the largest of them all, Brandenburg/ Prussia, emerged triumphant in the nineteenth century.

During the several-hundred-year history of the Holy Roman Empire this conglomerate of disparate entities was knitted together through five major institutions.

The Emperor

The emperor was elected by seven or eight leading hereditary nobles and archbishops. During most of the empire's history, from the Golden Bull of 1356, when the system for selecting the emperor was established, to its demise in 1806, the electors were the archbishops of Trier, Cologne, and Mainz, the margrave of Brandenburg, the king of Bohemia, the duke of Saxony, and the count Palatine of the Rhine. In every election save one between 1438 and 1806 the ruler of the house of Habsburg was chosen. Habsburg Austria was the largest political entity in the empire, and by the seventeenth century the income the emperor derived from his imperial position was negligible—another reason why the rich and powerful Habsburgs were usually the only serious contenders for the office.

The power of the emperor steadily eroded, especially after 1519, when the candidate was forced to make capitulations to the electors for the first time. These capitulations or promises accumulated over time. The most important was the expansion of *Landeshoheit,* which gave the imperial estates the right to exercise control within their own territories. The emperor could act only to resolve disputes between states or in matters that affected the whole empire collectively.

The emperor did retain some feudal rights. All land in the empire was theoretically held as a fief granted by the emperor. The emperor could depose a territorial ruler for a breach of feudal obligations or violation of criminal law. Such sanctions were imposed almost to the end of the empire, though only when the target was both weak and odious. The emperor could establish new nobles, but only with the consent of the immediate terriorial lord. He could organize universities, confer postal monopolies, and appoint members to the two highest imperial courts.

The Imperial Diet (Reichstag)

The diet consisted of three councils—the Council of Electors, the Council of Princes, and the Council of Cities. The Council of Electors was of course composed of the electors. The Council of Princes was composed of two groups, secular and ecclesiastical princes. This council had a total of 100 votes, but some larger states had more than one vote.

The Council of Cities was the least important. Its right to meet with the diet was recognized only in 1648.

Each of the three councils voted separately. A majority was needed to commit each council to a proposal. Two of three councils were needed to send a proposal to the emperor. In practice, however, the Council of Cities was never allowed to cast a deciding vote. If the emperor approved, the proposal became law. If the emperor disapproved, the proposal died.

The Peace of Westphalia provided that religious measures required the approval of both Protestant and Catholic representatives. The Protestant group, dominated by secular princes, was much less supportive of the emperor than the Catholic group, which was dominated by ecclesiastical representatives and smaller states.

By the middle of the eighteenth century the diet was defunct. It met continuously after the late seventeenth century but accomplished virtually nothing. The power of the major secular princes continued to increase and the requirement of the Peace of Westphalia that religious issues be dealt with on the basis of consensus made it difficult for the diet to act.

The Imperial Courts

There were two imperial courts—the Imperial Cameral Tribunal and the Aulic Council. Both were essentially defunct after Westphalia. The Imperial Tribunal was chronically underfunded, and by the middle of the eighteenth century the backlog of cases may have reached 60,000. The emperor could grant rulers the right to exclude the possibility of appeal to either of the supreme courts. By the eighteenth century all of the major states had secured from the emperor the right to prevent appeals to the imperial tribunals, thus acquiring total control of their own judicial systems. The courts did not have any direct power to implement their judgments. They had to rely on the compliance of local rulers, with the result that judgments against powerful rulers were never carried out.

The Imperial Circles

The imperial circles were first established in the sixteenth century. There were ten circles. The princes of each circle met in their own assemblies and were given the power to keep peace, regulate imperial coinage, and mobilize contingents for the imperial army. After Westphalia some of the circles were extinguished by powerful princes. The circles of Burgundy and Austria, composed exclusively of Habsburg lands, were never significant. In areas dominated by smaller princes, however, such as Franconia and Swabia, the circles did function effectively after Westphalia.

The Imperial Army

The emperor usually contributed at least 50 percent of the forces that made up the imperial army. Circles and individual princes contributed the remaining forces. The larger princes resisted the creation of a more powerful imperial army, which could threaten their own autonomy.[32]

In sum, the Treaty of Westphalia did not mark a decisive end of the Holy Roman Empire and the creation of a new international order based on sovereign states. The empire continued to exist after Westphalia, and not merely as an empty shell. One historian has argued that "the peace [of Westphalia] was not the tombstone of the empire but a charter which gave it another century-and-a-half of life."[33]

If a generative grammar was at work, it was buried very deep. Actors used the rich repertoire of institutional forms that had been bequeathed to them. The institutions of the empire persisted because some actors found them useful. The existence and identity of the imperial knights and the ecclesiastical states were dependent on the viability of the empire. Some of the smaller states could use the institutions of the empire, especially the imperial circles, to balance against their larger neighbors. The autonomy of some of the most important cities was enhanced by their imperial status. The position of the emperor gave the Habsburg monarch some leverage throughout Germany.

The Final Recess of 1803, which eliminated the ecclesiastical states and most of the imperial cities, was imposed after Napoleon's conquest of the left bank of the Rhine. Napoleon abolished the empire completely in 1806 because he wanted to create a number of fairly large and coherent German states on the right bank—states that would be large enough to resist Austria but would be beholden to and therefore not a threat to France.[34] The Holy Roman Empire came to an end at the beginning of the nineteenth century because its termination served the interests of the most powerful actor in the European system, Napoleonic France. The institutions of the empire had weakened over hun-

---

[32] The discussion of the institutions of the Holy Roman Empire is based on ibid., chap. 2; David Maland, *Europe at War, 1600–1650* (Totowa, N.J.: Rowman & Littlefield, 1980), p. 14; Georges Pages, *The Thirty Years' War* (New York: Harper & Row, 1970), p. 34; Parker, *Thirty Years' War*, pp. 16–18; and Roger Wines, "The Imperial Circles, Princely Diplomacy, and Imperial Reform, 1681–1714," *Journal of Modern History*, 1967, pp. 3–6, 18–19.

[33] Wines, "Imperial Circles," p. 2.

[34] Gagliardo, *Reich and Nation*, pp. 194–95.

dreds of years because the national state was better able to command material resources. The empire suffered slow erosion, not a dramatic collapse. The concept of sovereignty was well developed long before the existence of the Holy Roman Empire was formally terminated; it was Napoleon's *levée en masse*, not Bodin, Hobbes, or Vattel, that led to the empire's demise.

The Medieval World

The medieval system in its ideal typical form was characterized by what John Ruggie has referred to as a heteronomous form of organization. Different actors did different things. Their obligations overlapped and sometimes conflicted because vassalage was not strictly hierarchical. One's sovereign was one's superior; but the king's sovereignty did not place him outside of the political order. The highest power was the power to judge, not the power to legislate; God's law, custom, and natural law were the sources of legal precepts. Society was understood as a great chain of duties. Individuals held multiple hereditary titles. The distinction between domestic and international politics was not simply blurred, it had little or no conceptual meaning. Ambassadors regarded themselves as representatives of Christendom, not simply as servants of the particular ruler who had appointed them.[35]

This schematic depiction of the medieval world should not, however, mask the fact that institutions and behavior varied considerably. In theory the feudal order was characterized by heteronomous institutions with different functional tasks that supposedly would promote peace and harmony among all elements in the society. In practice violence was endemic among the nobility and between the nobles, the monarchs, and the church. Actual political practices hardly conformed with Christian ideals. Vassalage, which rewarded loyal servants with land, provided subordinates with resources that they could and did use to challenge their nominal superiors.[36]

Institutional structures as well as practices were in a state of flux. By

[35] Ruggie, "Continuity and Transformation in the World Polity," *World Politics* 35 (1983); Joseph R. Strayer, *On the Medieval Origins of the Modern State* (Princeton: Princeton University Press, 1970), p. 13; Michael Mann, *The Sources of Social Power* (New York: Cambridge University Press, 1986), p. 376; Poggi, *Development of the Modern State*, chap. 2; Bertrand de Jouvenel, *Sovereignty: An Inquiry into the Political Good* (Cambridge: Cambridge University Press, 1957), pp. 171–76; Garrett Mattingly, *Renaissance Diplomacy* (Boston: Houghton Mifflin, 1955); C. S. Lewis, *English Literature in the Sixteenth Century Excluding Drama* (Oxford: Clarendon, 1954), pp. 48–49.

[36] Markus Fischer, "Feudal Europe, 800–1300: Communal Discourse and Conflictual Practices," *International Organization* 46 (Spring 1992).

1300 the actual practice of sovereignty existed in parts of Europe even if it did not have a clear intellectual rationale or even a name.[37]

Entities most clearly resembling sovereign states first appeared in northern Italy. In 1000 the pope, the Holy Roman emperor, and the Byzantine emperor claimed to rule the Italian peninsula, but in fact the more than two hundred cities on the peninsula enjoyed effective de facto control of their own affairs.[38] Virtually all of the land was divided among the cities. Nobles acknowledged the authority of the cities, which were organized in accordance with a republican form of government.

The city-states were able to establish themselves in part because their enemies, the papacy and the Holy Roman Empire, were unable to act effectively. The papal schism greatly weakened the power of the church in northern Italy. When the pope attempted to reestablish control after his return to Rome, Florence successfully resisted. Ironically, it was a papal revolt against the emperor, leading to the Avignon exile, which contributed to the creation of the "first omnicompetent, amoral, sovereign states."[39]

The conflict between the empire and the papacy also weakened the position of the empire. The empire could not repress the cities of northern Italy in part because it was opposed by the papacy. Frederick Barbarossa invaded twice, but on the second occasion he was defeated by the combined forces of the Lombard League, and in the Treaty of Constance of 1183 he gave up his right to interfere with the internal affairs of the cities. In the middle of the thirteenth century a series of wars were fought between the cities and the emperor Frederick II, from which the cities emerged victorious. By the beginning of the fourteenth century, the emperors realized that they could not conquer the northern Italian cities.[40] The struggle between the papacy and the empire created a political and geographic space within which a new political form, one based on exclusive territorial rule, could develop.

The position of the northern Italian city-states was undermined by changes in military technology and trade routes. By the sixteenth century they were doomed by the development of large armies and heavy artillery. The commercial links of the northern Italian cities were also weakened by the large navies and large merchantmen of Spain, England, and Holland, all of which began to send oceangoing vessels into the Mediterranean in the sixteenth century.[41]

[37] Strayer, *Medieval Origins*, pp. 9, 13, 57.
[38] Tilly, *Coercion*, p. 40.
[39] Mattingly, *Renaissance Diplomacy*, pp. 47–49.
[40] Skinner, *Foundations*, 1:3–8.
[41] Tilly, *Coercion*, pp. 65, 77–78.

The first large geographic area to move toward what would be recognized as modern sovereignty was England. England had achieved political unity as early as the tenth century. During the thirteenth century, loyalty began to move from local authorities to the king. A sense of national identity had begun to emerge by the fifteenth century. By 1300 the nobles could not impose new taxes without the king's approval. The king could make laws. A hierarchical judicial system was established, with the king's courts as the final arbiters. The king asserted the right to tax the clergy without asking the permission of the pope. When the barons protested, or even when they rebelled, they did not try to destroy centralized institutions, although the War of the Roses shattered English unity during the fifteenth century.[42]

In France the Hundred Years' War wreaked havoc on all political institutions, but the monarchy was harmed the least. France proceeded more slowly toward a unified government. As in England, law and finance were the central institutions of the king. The king asserted that the royal court had final say in all judicial disputes. The king's right to impose taxes was gradually accepted. Jeanne d'Arc could emerge as a national heroine even though she had grown up on the eastern reaches of the French kingdom.

In 1200, however, the writ of the king was fully secure only on the Île-de-France. The king extended his rule through conquest, beginning with the defeat of the king of England, who had held much of northwest France. Provinces were added through marriage and inheritance. The French king did not insist on uniform laws and practices in all provinces. Unification was secured piecemeal through the appointment of royal officials in the provinces rather than by pressure to compel the provinces to conform with identical laws and practices. At the same time, some effort was made to achieve financial uniformity. Hence France developed a multilayered administration that was less efficient and centralized than England's.[43]

Medieval Ideas

The confusing character of political life in the late Middle Ages—something resembling sovereign city-states in northern Italy, the clear beginnings of sovereign control in England, more nascent development in France, the complicated Holy Roman Empire in Germany—was re-

---

[42] Kenneth H. F. Dyson, *The State Tradition in Western Europe: A Study of an Idea and Institution* (New York: Oxford University Press, 1980), p. 38; Strayer, *Medieval Origins*, pp. 43–48.
[43] Strayer, *Medieval Origins*, pp. 48–56.

flected in a similar level of heterogeneity in the realm of ideas. All European thinkers accepted the concept of Christendom, a unified society that was governed by divine law. But exactly what divine law entailed and who interpreted it on earth were matters of continuous dispute. All claimants invoked the deity and none more vigorously than the pope. The pope claimed to be the supreme ruler and promulgated canon law in secular as well as religious areas. The advocates of papal supremacy argued that secular rulers derived their power from the pope; that the empire was a beneficium granted by the papacy. This claim, however, was never universally accepted in the west. The representatives of the emperor maintained either that he was the sole final authority in Christendom, deriving his power directly from God, or that the emperor and the pope shared an equal claim from God.[44]

There were even more serious challenges to the papacy's affirmations of secular as well as religious authority. From the late thirteenth century on an antipapalist school of thought denied that the church was a political community at all and asserted instead that it was a community of the faithful. Marsiglio of Padua, for instance, argued that the papacy had no claim to secular authority and that the ultimate authority of the church rested not with the pope but with a council composed of all Christians. He maintained that the church could not wield any coercive power, and that if such power were invoked, it had to be exercised by a secular legislator, the ruler of a republic.[45]

Kings and their intellectual supporters developed claims against the assertions of both the pope and the emperor. From the Merovingians on, European kings described themselves as king "by the grace of God." The notion of the king's two bodies symbolized the theory that the king was at the same time both a mortal ruler and a representative of an immortal God. Kings claimed that they held the powers of the emperor within their own kingdoms, and that the authority of the emperor was limited to questions that affected all of Christendom. The doctrine that the king was emperor in his own domain implied a distinction between internal and external affairs.

The Thomistic perspective, which dominated thought in the later Middle Ages, had a place for the pope, the emperor, kings, and estates, all of which were understood to be part of Christendom. Each component was normally bound by law. In exceptional circumstances, however, any one of the actors might assert authority on the basis of divine law if some other actor violated that law. The pope could not disturb

---

[44] F. H. Hinsley, *Sovereignty*, 2d ed. (Cambridge: Cambridge University Press, 1986), p. 77.
[45] Skinner, *Foundations*, 1:18–22.

the peace of a kingdom. The magnates could resist unjust assertions of authority by the king. The kings could normally rule within their own kingdoms, but if they violated divine law they might be rejected from without by the pope and emperor and from within by the magnates. Thus, while none of the writers of the late Middle Ages developed a modern notion of sovereignty because they still conceived of Europe as a single community of Christians, of which France, for instance, was merely a component part, they did vigorously debate the specific prerogatives of the parts.[46]

Even more indicative of the fluid relationship between power and ideas is the ability of the northern Italian city-states, the progenitors of modern sovereign states, to develop an intellectual rationale that legitimated their independence from both pope and emperor—an independence that ultimately rested on their economic resources and military prowess. Writers defended the liberty of their cities, by which they meant both noninterference in their internal affairs and their right to be governed by republican institutions. They rejected the prevailing view that there was only one ultimate political authority, the emperor, and that the individual kingdoms of Europe were provinces of the empire. By the beginning of the fourteenth century, jurists in northern Italy asserted that the hierarchical claims based on Roman law were invalid in theory because they did not hold in practice. The northern Italian cities, and other parts of Christendom as well, did not, in fact, obey the emperor. These writers maintained that inasmuch as the cities of northern Italy had been exercising their liberty, the emperor had to recognize that they were sovereign and independent.[47]

In sum, the medieval world did share a community of discourse, but within this community a very wide variety of specific authority claims could be justified. Though there was universal agreement on the centrality of divine law, agreement was never universal on what divine law meant or who could interpret it. There was always a variety of political forms in Europe. The emperor might claim to be the inheritor of Rome, but in practice his authority never extended across all of Europe. England developed a centralized political structure before France. The power of the pope waxed and waned. Kings, popes, and emperors all had intellectual rationales that legitimated their claims to make authoritative decisions.

Most strikingly, a new political entity, the city-states of northern Italy, which were characterized by republican forms of government and territorially demarcated authority, generated new political ideas to legiti-

[46] Hinsley, *Sovereignty*, pp. 85–90, 95–99.
[47] Skinner, *Foundations*, 1:7.

mate powers and prerogatives that they had created through economic and military prowess. The ideas themselves were drawn not only from the new tradition of civic humanism but also, in Florence and elsewhere in northern Italy, from the more medieval tradition of scholasticism; existing intellectual orientations could be reinterpreted in strikingly new ways once political circumstances changed.[48]

Only after the ideas became embedded in institutional structures were they consequential for political behavior. Initially the ideas were just hooks to justify actions that were motivated by considerations of wealth and power, not by visions of justice and truth. European leaders were fortunate in having many hooks because of the richness and diversity of European intellectual tradition. The medieval world had certain central tendencies but also internal contradictions, not a deep generative grammar. Chance and power, *fortuna* and *virtù*, launched local historical trajectories, especially in England and northern Italy, that led in practice to political entities that could assert practical control over a given territory. Supporters of these entities then developed intellectual rationales for facts on the ground.

THE MODERN WORLD

Lest the institutional and intellectual ambiguity of the medieval world appear quaint, it is worth reflecting that the modern world, the post-Westphalian world, also cannot be so neatly classified as the conventional view suggests.

European rulers continued to hold multiple titles after Westphalia. After 1714 the electors of Hanover were also the kings of England. Some of George I's English subjects complained that he put the interests of the Holy Roman Empire above those of England. The electors of Brandenburg were also the kings of Prussia, but Prussia was not part of the Holy Roman Empire. The electors of Saxony were the kings of Poland from 1697 until 1763.[49]

Europe's interactions with other areas of the world created unique challenges and generated new institutional solutions. Colonial activities in the seventeenth century were spearheaded by trading companies that were formally private although they were chartered by the state. These companies carried out their own foreign policies and they had their own military establishments.[50] During the nineteenth century the

---

[48] Ibid., pp. 114–52.
[49] Gagliardo, *Reich and Nation*, p. 10.
[50] Holsti, *Peace and War*, pp. 59–60.

enormous disparity between the more advanced states of Europe and weaker areas of the world led to a variety of inventive institutional arrangements. Direct colonization was consistent with the principle of sovereignty—all of the activities and people within a defined geographic area were governed by the same authority structures, although those structures might be located several thousand miles away. The British Empire, for instance, was treated as a single state in international law.[51]

The Europeans did not, however, always resort to outright colonization. In Kuwait and other areas, the British, for instance, established protectorates, which were characterized by a differentiation of authority structures across issue areas. In 1899 the ruler of Kuwait ceded control over much of Kuwait's foreign policy to Britain. In subsequent agreements Kuwait agreed not to trade in arms or slaves and to give Britain veto power over foreign access to Kuwaiti pearl and oil resources. Britain was given the exclusive right to establish a post office in Kuwait and to rent port facilities in Shuwaikh. In 1925 a British order in council gave the British government jurisdiction over British nationals in Kuwait and over several other classes of people, some of whom were Kuwaiti.[52]

In international finance nineteenth-century European lenders engaged in a variety of practices that violated the *Grundnorm* of sovereignty, noninterference in internal affairs.[53] When states defaulted, lenders set up collection agencies that directly transferred state revenues to foreign creditors. Such agencies were established for Bulgaria, Greece, Serbia, Persia, the Ottoman Empire, and Argentina. In Egypt, for instance, Ismail Pasha agreed in 1876 to the creation of the Caisse de la Dette, whose officials were appointed on the recommendation of the British, French, Italian, and Austrian governments, to control customs duties in Cairo and Alexandria, the salt and tobacco taxes, and other sources of revenue. In return for a consolidation loan in 1895, Serbia created a monopolies commission controlled by foreign

[51] Jackson, *Quasi-States*, p. 17.

[52] Mary Ann Tetreault, "Autonomy, Necessity, and the Small State: Ruling Kuwait in the Twentieth Century," *International Organization* 45 (Autumn 1991).

[53] The doctrine of nonintervention was explicitly articulated by Christian von Wolff and Emerich de Vattel in the latter half of the eighteenth century. It was further developed in the nineteenth century, especially by Latin American jurists. See Emerich de Vattel, *The Law of Nations; or, Principles of the Law of Nature Applied to the Conduct and Affairs of Nations and Sovereigns* (Philadelphia: T. and J. W. Johnson, 1852), p. 12; Ann Van Wynen Thomas and Aaron J. Thomas, *Non-intervention: The Law and Its Import in the Americas* (Dallas: Southern Methodist University Press, 1956), pp. 5–6, 55–62; R. Vincent, *Nonintervention and International Order* (Princeton: Princeton University Press, 1974), pp. 26–27; Hedley Bull, "Introduction," in *Intervention in World Politics*, ed. Bull (Oxford: Clarendon, 1984), p. 4, and Stanley Hoffmann, "The Problem of Intervention," in the same volume, p. 11.

lenders to administer the revenue from the state tobacco, salt, and petroleum monopolies, liquor taxes, some stamp taxes, and some railway and customs revenues. Revenues were committed to the payment of foreign loans. The receipts were never deposited in the Serbian treasury.[54]

During the nineteenth century and at the conclusion of World War 1 the major western European powers and at times the United States systematically intervened in the internal affairs of central and eastern European countries in efforts to protect the rights of first religious and then ethnic minorities. In 1830 Britain, France, and Russia signed a protocol guaranteeing Greek independence which stated that all religious groups should be treated equally. At the congress convened to deal with the consequences of the Balkan wars of the mid-1870s, the representatives of the great powers agreed that religious toleration would be one of the conditions of recognition of new members of the international community; such stipulations were included in the treaties regarding Romania, Serbia, Montenegro, and Bulgaria. At the conclusion of World War 1 Austria, Hungary, Bulgaria, Turkey, Poland, Yugoslavia, Romania, Czechoslovakia, Greece, Albania, Latvia, Lithuania, and Estonia were pressured into making elaborate commitments to protect the rights of minorities as a condition of their statehood, recognition by the international community, or admission to the League of Nations. These treaties covered such matters as guarantees of primary education in the languages of minority groups and, in the case of Poland, a commitment not to hold elections on Saturday because to do so would violate the Jewish Sabbath.[55]

The contemporary world also includes a variety of institutions and practices that violate the central characteristic of the sovereignty regime—exclusive control over a given territory. As we saw earlier, the Exclusive Economic Zone (EEZ), which was delineated in the United Nations Conference on the Law of the Seas, provides for control over exploitive activities up to the 200-meter isobath or the end of the continental shelf, but not over shipping. In the Exclusive Economic Zone states have control over some activities but not others. Freedom of the seas applies to shipping, but the state exercises control over fishing and mineral exploitation. Although some major countries, including the United States, have not accepted the Law of the Seas Treaty, a large number of states have accepted the EEZ.

---

[54] Herbert Feis, *Europe, the World's Banker, 1870–1914: An Account of European Foreign Investment and the Connection of World Finance with Diplomacy before World 1* (New York: Norton, 1965), pp. 384–97, 266–68.

[55] Discussions of the minorities treaties can be found in Claude, *National Minorities*, p. 55, and Macartney, *National States*, p. 34.

The international regime for the Antarctic also violates conventional notions of sovereignty. Some twenty-five states are members of the Antarctic Consultative Group. Seven of these states have claimed sovereignty over parts—sometimes overlapping parts—of the continent. The others have not. The Antarctic is not itself a sovereign entity or part of some other sovereign entity. Control is shared among several states. At the same time, however, the Antarctic regime makes no effort to establish an authority structure that supersedes states. The signatories of the treaty are national states.

The most ambitious present-day challenge to conventional sovereignty is the European Community. Undoubtedly at some point it will become obvious whether the EC has generated a real alternative to the national state—not simply a larger European state but a political entity in which authority structures in various issue areas are not coterminous with territory. Decision makers in what are now sovereign states may have control over some kinds of activities while Community structures have control over others.

At the present moment, however, the basic nature of the Community is not clear. The work of some analysts implies that the EC is best understood as a conventional international organization in which policies and behavior are functions of the preferences and power of member states.[56] Other studies suggest that the Community has already transcended sovereign statehood. If, for instance, the Maastricht Treaty is fully implemented, a European monetary authority will be independent of state control. At the same time, however, states will retain the ultimate authority to withdraw from the system; but the costs of withdrawal will be so high for some states that they will never exercise this right. Would a situation in which monetary policy was set by a European monetary authority but decisions on other issues were taken by national or regional governments be consistent with sovereignty even if states still retained the formal juridical right to dismantle the Community? The fact that European leaders—and academic analysts, for that matter—do not have a clear answer to this question has not prevented new institutional arrangements from being designed.

Hence before and after Westphalia the notion of sovereignty has been, in one way or another, up for grabs. The Peace was not a clear beginning of a new era of sovereign states or a clear end of the medieval period. Entities acting like territorially based sovereign states existed

---

[56] Andrew Moravcsik, "Negotiating the Single European Act: National Interests and Conventional Statecraft in the European Community," *International Organization*, Winter 1991; Geoffrey Garrett, "The European Internal Market: The Political Economy of Regional Integration," *International Organization* 46 (Spring 1992).

well before 1648, and medieval practices, including the continuation of the Holy Roman Empire, continued well after. The clearest story line of the last thousand years is the extruding out of universal alternatives to the sovereign state. The Holy Roman Empire has completely disappeared and the papacy is only an enfeebled version of the spiritual authority and material power that it wielded before the Reformation, although the pope can still bring out a big crowd for a guy who doesn't sing or use much in the way of sound equipment. As the European Community and the Antarctic Treaty system indicate, the dominance of the sovereign state as an organizational form has not prevented experiments with alternatives. Brussels may be the new Rome.

The actual content of sovereign authority—the scope of state control, both internally and externally—has never been generally agreed upon. The Peace of Westphalia included provisions that constrained the right of government to change religious practices. In the nineteenth century Britain attacked Portuguese ships and Brazilian ports to end the slave trade. After World War I extensive guarantees of minority rights were included in international treaties. After the defeat of Iraq in the Gulf War of 1991, the victorious powers set up a zone of protection for Kurds in northern Iraq. New problems have generated new institutional solutions. Actors with more material power have imposed their views on those with less.

Ideas and Institutional Change

No deep structure is evident in the heterogeneous and fluid character of political order from the Middle Ages to the present. The driving forces behind the gradual elimination of universal institutions and the predominance of the sovereign state were material, not ideational. Territorial states benefited from the development of long-distance trade that they could protect and organize and from new military technologies that advantaged larger units. New political practices created a need for legitimating rationales.

In Europe these rationales were relatively easily found because of the heterogeneity of intellectual traditions from which Europeans could draw.[57] The conceptualizations of the classical world and of various lines of thought within Christendom and to a lesser extent Islam

---

[57] Quentin Skinner's two-volume *Foundations of Modern Political Thought* offers a superlative picture of the complexity of European intellectual debate from the fourteenth through the sixteenth centuries.

were available to rulers seeking an intellectual justification for their policies. A variety of lines of argument could flourish in Europe because the multiplicity of political entities offered physical protection and material support. An imperial system such as China's provided little space for new ideas because there was no place to hide from the imperial writ. In societies without written languages, the manipulation and recombination of concepts was more difficult. Europe, sitting on the edge of the Eurasian landmass with its many political units, was ideally situated to generate a rich variety of political ideas.

Independent territorially based states developed in northern Italy by the eleventh or twelfth century because of trading opportunities and divisions within the Holy Roman Empire and the papacy. These city-states quickly found intellectual support for their autonomy. In the fourteenth century Bartolus, Marsiglio of Padua, and others, drawing on newly rediscovered classical sources and the arguments of the conciliar movement, insisted that the cities of northern Italy had the right to freedom from external interference and to their republican form of government.[58]

In the early sixteenth century Lutheranism provided a powerful intellectual rationale for the absolute power of secular states. Luther argued that there was no separate church; the church was the community of all Christians. Each individual had to seek his or her own salvation, which could not be secured by a distinct priesthood. He rejected all papal claims to authority. Luther maintained that because God is omniscient, secular rulers must be divinely ordained. Initially he also argued that there was no right of active rebellion against civil authorities.

Luther was motivated by religious, not temporal, concerns, but secular rulers were quick to seize upon his doctrines. By the 1530s, scarcely a decade after he had posted his ninety-five theses, rulers in England, Denmark, Sweden, and parts of Germany had endorsed Lutheranism and rejected any claim of authority by the Catholic Church. The king became the head of a national church and Lutheranism provided a ready rationale to justify the confiscation of church lands and revenues.[59] Rulers chose the ideas that best suited their political and material needs. Lutheranism offered a powerful intellectual rationale for those monarchs who wished to break completely with Rome.

If Lutheranism provided one justification for secular rulers, the writings of Jean Bodin, a Catholic, provided another. Bodin's *Six Books of the Commonwealth* was a rebuttal of Protestant theories of revolt that had been developed after the excesses of the Counterreformation had

[58] Ibid., 1:7, 18–22; 2:349–58.
[59] Ibid., 2:1–108.

led even Luther to abandon his prohibition against rebellion. For Bodin, writing at the height of the Huguenot uprising, the fundamental objective of any government was to ensure order. Bodin argued that taking up arms against the king, even if the king had become a tyrant, was never justified. He explicitly condemned Huguenot writings that justified revolt against tyranny, even though he recognized that the sovereign ought to be bound by divine and natural law. Bodin's absolute prohibition against insurrection led him to the conclusion that no earthly power could stand above the sovereign. If the sovereign was not supreme, then some actor could claim dominion and justify revolt. The sovereign commands; he cannot be commanded. The commands of the sovereign cannot be challenged even when they are unjust. The sovereign must answer only to God.[60]

Hobbes, writing almost a century later, took an even more extreme position. Hobbes recognized hardly any limitation at all on the power of the sovereign save the fact that psychological panic may drive individuals to disobey the sovereign's commands in time of war. Hobbes wanted to legitimate an absolutist political system that could end civil disorder in England. Both Bodin and Hobbes wrote long after territorial states or city-states had formed in Europe. They were driven to a more extreme defense of sovereign control by the disorders that were engendered by the religious wars of the sixteenth and seventeenth centuries.

Bartolus, Marsiglio, Bodin, Hobbes, and many other writers provided European rulers with a variegated menu of intellectual ideas from which they could draw to justify their policies. These ideas tapped deep traditional, especially Christian, roots. The large repertoire of principles available to European thinkers, and to European rulers, allowed them to make dramatic institutional innovations without utterly shocking the sensibilities of their constituencies. Legitimacy rests on shared understanding, and in Europe such shared understandings could be constructed on a wide range of beliefs.

If the range of available ideas is more limited, the ability of a polity to respond effectively to new conditions can be constrained. The Balinese nobles self-destructed in the face of encroachments by the Dutch in the nineteenth century because they could not incorporate European rulers into their cosmology.[61] The Mesoamericans, who had been isolated from other civilizations, were unable to comprehend the Spanish because their beliefs allowed for only two kinds of mortals: sedentary

---

[60] Ibid., pp. 284–87.

[61] Clifford Geertz, *Negara: The Theatre State in Nineteenth-Century Bali* (Princeton: Princeton University Press, 1980).

civilized and barbarians. The Spanish were neither one nor the other; therefore the Aztecs placed them in the only other available category, the sacred. They thought the Spaniards were gods—a mistake that, along with European diseases and the Spaniards' ability to secure local allies, proved fatal to Aztec civilization.[62] Where the number of ideas is limited, sudden external shocks can be devastating. In Europe the rich mix of available ideas facilitated the construction of new legitimating rationales for political entities, sovereign territorial states, whose material situation had been advantaged by economic and military changes.

Changing material conditions, however, and the continued variety of political ideas have also made it difficult to secure any general agreement on the scope of sovereign authority. While universal institutions have dramatically weakened, the prerogatives of sovereign states have been constantly contested. International human rights clash with the principle of nonintervention in the internal affairs of other states. More powerful states assert extraterritorial economic prerogatives. Economic sanctions are levied against politics that discriminate according to race. Moreover, the extruding out of old universal authority structures, the papacy and the Holy Roman Empire, has not precluded efforts to create new institutional structures that transcend sovereign national states. Some of these structures, such as the British Commonwealth, have failed; others, such as the European Community, may succeed.

In 1948 Leo Gross wrote in the *American Journal of International Law* that the "Peace of Westphalia, for better or worse, marks the end of an epoch and the opening of another. It represents the majestic portal which leads from the old into the new world."[63] Gross's interpretation has been referred to many times, perhaps because it is one of the few articles in English on the Peace of Westphalia. But it is wrong. Westphalia was not a beginning or an end. Sovereign practices had existed hundreds of years before 1648 and medieval practices continued for hundreds of years after. The actual content of sovereignty and the principle of exclusive control have been, and continue to be, challenged.

[62] Octavio Paz, "The Food of the Gods," *New York Review of Books*, February 26, 1987, p. 7.
[63] Gross, "Peace of Westphalia," p. 28.

CHAPTER TEN

Coping with Terrorism: Norms and Internal Security in Germany and Japan

PETER J. KATZENSTEIN

Germany and Japan have been deeply affected by the traumatic defeat they suffered in World War II. Their "Hollandization"[1] as a consequence of that war is reflected in the transformation of both countries from the leading challengers in the international states system in the first half of the twentieth century to the leading trading states in the international economy at the onset of the twenty-first century.[2] Profoundly suspicious of military issues and deeply afraid of being drawn into military engagements, both states have been unable to sidestep security policy altogether. For they have been compelled to defend the state's security inside their borders. In comparison with their practices in the recent past, the physical coercion that these two trading states apply in securing their internal security is very small. Nonetheless, the power of the police in both states has measurably increased during the

Some of the material in this chapter is drawn from Peter J. Katzenstein, *West Germany's Internal Security Policy: State and Violence in the 1970s and 1980s*, Cornell University, Center for International Studies, Western Societies Program, Occasional Paper no. 28 (1990), and Peter J. Katzenstein and Yutaka Tsujinaka, *Defending the Japanese State: Structures, Norms, and the Political Respones to Terrorism and Violent Social Protest in the 1970s and 1980s*, Cornell University, East Asia Program, 1991. I thank Judith Goldstein, Robert Keohane, David Laitin, T. J. Pempel, and Robert Smith for their criticisms and suggestions on a previous version of this chapter.

[1] John Mueller, *Retreat from Doomsday: The Obsolescence of Major War* (New York: Basic Books, 1989), pp. 95–96.
[2] Richard Rosecrance, *The Rise of the Trading State: Commerce and Conquest in the Modern World* (New York: Basic Books, 1986).

past two decades. And in both cases that growing police power has moved away from a preoccupation with reacting to the threat of civil war or massive social unrest to focus on generating the social intelligence necessary to prevent the threats that terrorism and violent social protest pose for the state.

Informed by different norms, Germany and Japan have accomplished this task in different ways. The strengthening of state power through changes in legal norms in Germany betrayed a profound fear that terrorism was challenging the core fiber of the state and thus of the social order. Eradicating terrorism and minimizing the effects of violent social protest were tantamount to overcoming the specter of a Hobbesian state of nature. In Japan, the close interaction of social and legal norms revealed a state living symbiotically within its society and not easily shaken in its very foundation. Eliminating terrorism or containing violent social protest was the task of a Grotian community. Conversely, Germany's active involvement in the evolution of international legal norms conveyed a conception of belonging to and participating in an international Grotian community. Japan's lack of concern for the consequences of pushing Japanese terrorists abroad and its generally passive stance were based on a Hobbesian view of the international system.

Germany and Japan have operated under similar international constraints and opportunities provided by the United States' hegemony and its gradual decline. And both have organized their domestic politics for the pursuit of economic prosperity and competitiveness in international markets rather than national grandeur and power in the international state system. But why do these structural similarities fail to account for the differences in the ways Germany and Japan have accomplished such important tasks as defending state security against internal threats?

The answer to this question lies in the fact that most variants of structural analysis take as a given the normative context in which actors define their interests. But structures often embody different norms and thus give different cues as to what actors should do. And in times of change when structures crumble, these norms acquire particular importance in informing actors about the interests they hold. Should the German army send East German equipment to the Middle East while permitting its air force to fly missions from Turkish airfields, or should Germany be adamant about not participating in the out-of-area engagement of NATO troops? Should Japan send unarmed soldiers to the Mideast, pay a lot of money, or do nothing? The situation was analogous when the social environment of the German and Japanese states changed in the late 1960s in reaction to the Vietnam War, among other things. German and Japanese officials confronted difficult choices. Should large-scale social protest be tolerated? Should it be crushed with a massive display of police or paramilitary force? Or should it be contained through a reorganization and reequipment of national police forces? And was the upsurge of terrorism in Germany and Japan best combated with new or traditional security policies? The answers to these questions were not obvious to either the Germans or the Japanese.

In such situations of uncertainty actors fall back on the world view they have acquired over time—that is, a mixture of causal and principled beliefs about how the world works, and how one should behave in it. On questions of security policy German and Japanese views have been molded decisively by the memories of the enormous costs of the Nazi regime and Japan's military dictatorship as well as the disastrous loss of World War II. Thus normative context that informs the interests of actors matters a great deal.

Norms that are institutionalized matter in particular because they more easily find expression in law and culture. Institutionalized norms express a world view that influences behavior not only directly, by setting standards of appropriateness for behavior, but also indirectly, through selective prefabricated links between values that individuals or collectivities habitually rely upon to address specific problems. Institutionalized norms thus are not only a set of preferences or values motivating behavior. And they do not influence behavior merely by prescribing the ends of action. Institutionalized norms affect behavior also indirectly by offering a way of organizing action rather than specifying only the ends of action.[3]

Some may call this style of analysis "loosely rationalistic"; others may prefer to call it "loosely culturalist." But this perspective permits us to sidestep the weakness that impairs much of the analysis that focuses only on interests. Both interest-driven and norm-driven styles of analysis often assume the ends of action: "rational," individualistic, arbitrary preferences or "irrational," consensual, cultural values. These two perspectives fail to appreciate the normative context of the process by which interests are defined. And they frequently overlook the fact that social or individual action is typically part of an institutionalized repertoire of action. Indeed, the styles or strategies of action are more persistent than the ends that individuals or societies seek to attain. The prefabricated links that institutionalized norms establish are part of a

---

[3] Ann Swidler, "Culture in Action: Symbols and Strategies," *American Sociological Review* 51 (April 1986): 273–86.

collective consciousness that creates habits of interpretation and repertoires of action.[4]

Norms do not float freely in social and political space. They are shaped by history and institutions. To most observers the dramatic decline in Germany's and Japan's militarist norms since 1945 is self-evident. The epochal events of the 1930s and 1940s, embodied in institutional structures such as the demilitarization of the police, had significant effects on subsequent policies of internal security. The analysis falls squarely into the historical rather than anthropological mode of political culture studies.[5] Norms work their effects through historically created institutions and experiences; they are not determined solely by such deep social structures as religion and language. And while the norms that help historically evolving national cultures can be studied among larger collectivities rather than small groups, they are not all made out of one piece of cloth. The degree of divergence between legal and social norms, for example, is a matter of some importance.

Domestic and international norms cannot be analyzed only through the study of behavior.[6] Norms reflect unspoken premises. Their importance lies not in being true or false but in being shared. For these premises themselves often create the evidence that confirm their validity. Norms can be violated by behavior; but they cannot be invalidated. They specify rules rather than regularities. Friedrich Kratochwil and John Ruggie insist that shared meanings are the center of any study of norms. We must grasp, by whatever method appears appropriate, how actors interpret themselves and the world. For the norms that inform action emerge in and through the shared interpretations and shared expectations that constitute standards for judging action. Norms offer a context that affects the interest and behavior of actors in complex ways. They cause, guide, and inspire action. What matters is not only the compliance of actors with forces that determine their behavior and thus make it amenable to explanation and prediction. What matters also is the competence of actors to interpret themselves and the world and to share these interpretations with others.

---

[4] Emanuel Adler, *The Power of Ideology: The Quest for Technological Autonomy in Argentina and Brazil* (Berkeley: University of California Press, 1987), pp. 11, 15; James N. Rosenau, "Before Cooperation: Hegemons, Regimes, and Habit-Driven Actors in World Politics," *International Organization* 40 (Autumn 1986): 849–94.

[5] Thomas Berger, "The Reluctant Allies: The Genesis of the Political Military Cultures of Japan and West Germany" (manuscript, MIT, Department of Political Science, 1991), pp. 13–14.

[6] Friedrich Kratochwil and John Gerard Ruggie, "International Organization: A State of the Art on an Art of the State," *International Organization* 40 (Autumn 1986): 753–75; Emanuel Adler, "Cognitive Evolution: A Dynamic Approach for the Study of International Relations and Their Progress" (manuscript, Harvard University, 1988); John Gerard Ruggie, "International Structure and International Transformation: Space, Time, and Method" (manuscript, La Jolla, Calif., 1988); Nina Tannenwald, "How Norms Matter

What is true of domestic norms holds also for international norms. Agreement on norms in the international community is achieved either through parallel or converging national legislation or through international treaties. Treaties may directly specify norms that become binding after they have been translated into national legislation. Or, alternatively, they may articulate general principles that inform the process of norm setting through national legislation without specifying the norm itself. The difference between international and domestic societies lies in the number of people and the density of institutions involved in defining and interpreting norms. In international society that task is reserved to a few scores of scholars of international law whose writings constitute many of the data that provide the basis for the advice they give to their national governments about the evolution of international norms.

We can fruitfully explore the role of norms by looking at the domestic and international politics of Germany's and Japan's policies of internal security. The definition of terrorism is strongly contested politically. There are two basic types of terrorism: individual terrorism and state terrorism. Furthermore, terrorism can be waged by right-wing or left-wing political radicals. Because groups on the radical left were at the center of the concern of the German and Japanese governments on questions of internal security during the last two decades, I shall deal only with acts of terrorism perpetrated by those groups. Among the political elites of Western democracies a shared if imprecise definition of terrorism has emerged during the last two decades. Terrorist acts are crimes designed to affect at least one putative social norm, to attract maximum publicity, and to instill fear. Many terrorist acts violate the rules of war. All of them depend on violence or the threat of violence directed against private or public targets. Terrorists are politically motivated and often work in small groups. Unlike other criminals, they often take credit for their actions while also seeking to conceal their individual identities.[7]

TERRORISM AND GOVERNMENT RESPONSE

Terrorism and Violent Social Protest

Although Germany has not been immune to international terrorism, most incidents of terrorist activity have been committed by domestic

---

in International Relations: Berlin 1948 and the Cuban Missile Crisis" (manuscript, Cornell University, 1988).

[7] Brian M. Jenkins, "The Study of Terrorism: Definitional Problems" (manuscript, Rand Corporation, 1980), pp. 2–3; Noemi Gal-Or, *International Cooperation to Suppress*

groups. The Red Army Faction and the Revolutionary Cells on the left and some neo-Nazi groups on the right have targeted prominent politicians and businessmen as well as United States military installations and personnel. Between 1970 and 1979, 649 attacks by left-wing groups killed 31 people and injured 97; 163 other people were seized as hostages. Terrorist groups committed at least thirty bank robberies, which netted millions of deutschmarks. Between 1980 and 1985 the total number of terrorist acts rose to 1,601.[8]

Since there are no reliable data on the number of German terrorists, the media always repeat government estimates of about 20 activists, 200 sympathizers who may help with money, cars, or apartments, and a supportive social milieu of about 2,000 to 20,000 people among whom sympathizers and activists are recruited. Compared to the official data on the membership of radical organizations of the left (63,000), of the right (22,000), and among foreigners (117,000), these are small figures.[9] Furthermore, terrorist acts pale numerically in comparison with the total annual numbers of estimated criminal acts (10 million), recorded criminal acts (4 million), and suspects investigated by the police (1.5 million). Less than half of the suspects are prosecuted and less than a third of those prosecuted are convicted; only a tiny portion of those convicted are sent to jail.[10] These aggregate figures reveal how seriously the police and the government take terrorism in Germany. Terrorist acts and violent demonstrations account for about 15,000 crimes against state security, that is, about one-third of 1 percent of all recorded criminal acts. Yet between 5 and 10 percent of all police personnel in Germany are assigned to the state security divisions of the various police forces, excluding a force of about 25,000 that protects Germany's border and acts as a reserve in the case of large-scale public demonstrations.[11]

Terrorism (New York: St. Martin's Press, 1985); Kay Hailbronner, "International Terrorism and the Laws of War," *German Yearbook of International Law* 25 (1982): 169–98; Nicholas G. Kittrie, "Reconciling the Irreconcilable: The Quest for International Agreement over Political Crime and Terrorism," *Yearbook of World Affairs* 32 (1978): 208–36; Jack P. Gibbs, "Conceptualization of Terrorism," *American Sociological Review* 54 (June 1989): 329–40.

[8] Hans Josef Horchem, "Terrorism and Government Response: The German Experience," *Jerusalem Journal of International Relations* 4, no. 3 (1980): 51; Eva Kolinsky, "Terrorism in West Germany," in *The Threat of Terrorism*, ed. Juliet Lodge (Brighton: Wheatsheaf, 1988), pp. 61, 73.

[9] Hermann Borgs-Maciejewski, *Was jeder vom Verfassungschutz wissen sollte: Aufgaben, Methode, Organisation* (Heidelberg: Decker & Müller, 1988), pp. 44–45.

[10] Bernd Wehner, "Wir wissen nicht, was wir wissen . . . obwohl wir es könnten," *Kriminalistik*, no. 12 (December), 1980, p. 538; Heiner Busch, Albrecht Funk, Udo Kauß, Wolf-Dieter Narr, and Falco Werkentin, *Die Polizei in der Bundesrepublik* (Frankfurt: Campus, 1985), pp. 260–69.

[11] Enno Brand, *Staatsgewalt: Politische Unterdrückung und innere Sicherheit in der Bundesrepublik* (Göttingen: Werkstatt, 1989), p. 142; Rolf Gössner, "Auf der Suche nach den verlorenen Maßstäben," *Demokratie und Recht*, no. 2, 1987, pp. 145–50.

Like Germany, Japan has experienced a spate of terrorism and violent social protest during the last three decades that has originated from within its own society. But in contrast to the German Red Army Faction, Japan's Red Army, after a brief period of operation at home in the late 1960s and early 1970s, moved abroad. North Korea and the Mideast became staging areas for a series of spectacular and brutal international operations during the next two decades.[12] At home massive demonstrations against the U.S.-Japan Security Treaty in 1960 and the antiwar movement in the late 1960s as well as the renewal of the treaty in 1970 spawned a number of social movements. Some of them, such as the movement opposing the construction of an airport at Narita, on the outskirts of Tokyo, relied on violence as a symbolic tool as much as a method of self-defense.[13] But other groups, such as Chukaku, mobilized a small cadre of professional militants involved in bombing attacks or the launching of homemade, primitive missiles from apartment houses or cars. The targets of these attacks typically were members of Japan's political and economic establishment, including in recent years the Emperor system. These attacks have occurred in waves over the last two decades. Between 1969 and 1988 the Japanese police reported 236 bombing attacks and 531 guerrilla actions.[14] The international scope of its actions may have earned the Japanese Red Army greater international notoriety than its German namesake. But Japan, with twice the population of Germany, has probably had only half as many incidents of terrorism.

This is not to argue that terrorism and social violence are less important politically in Japan than in Germany. Japan's low overall crime rate, after all, is unique among the advanced industrial countries. Though Germany is a relatively orderly and crime-free society by American standards, Japan's crime rates are lower by a factor of 3 for murder, 4 for burglary, 6 for rape, and 31 for robbery. Estimates of the number of militant cadres operating inside such organizations as Chukaku vary greatly. Four of Japan's five radical groups and ten of about thirty affiliated sects are prone to violent or terrorist actions. Estimates provided by various branches of the Japanese police indicate that the radical left, which in Japan, too, accounts for the bulk of violence and terrorism, appears to have about 14,000 activists and another 20,000 sympathizers. The number of professional militant cadres in

---

[12] Patricia G. Steinhoff, "Hijackers, Bombers, and Bank Robbers: Japanese Managerial Style in the Radical Left," *Journal of Asian Studies* 48 (November 1989): 724–40.

[13] David E. Apter and Nagayo Sawa, *Against the State: Politics and Social Protest in Japan* (Cambridge: Harvard University Press, 1984).

[14] Peter J. Katzenstein and Yutaka Tsujinaka, *Defending the Japanese State: Structures, Norms, and Political Responses to Terrorism and Violent Social Protest in the 1970s and 1980s* (Ithaca: East Asia Program, Cornell University, 1991), Appendix.

large organizations such as Chukaku lies in the hundreds. Other militant organizations have many fewer. The Red Army, for example, has about two dozen cadres abroad and a few hundred sympathizers inside Japan. As in Germany, the police mobilize a disproportionate number of their forces to deal with these few radicals. The police's penchant for secrecy is so great that only rough estimates are possible. While the official number of security police is probably only about 5,000—that is, about 50 percent fewer than the analogous forces in Germany—the flexible deployment of personnel in Japanese bureaucracies makes it possible to allocate, on a temporary basis, perhaps up to one-quarter of Japan's total police force of 240,000 to the issue of internal security.[15]

Government Policy

In Germany the incidence of terrorism and large-scale social protest reinforced a modernization and quantitative expansion of the police that was a key part of the Social Democratic reform program of the 1970s. More important than the considerable quantitative expansion in personnel and financial resources were the qualitative improvements and the change in the basic mission of the police. The guiding image was no longer a state of emergency caused by civil war and insurrection incited by East German infiltrators. Instead the line separating normality and emergency became blurred. In trying to anticipate possible threats to state security, the police changed from reacting to social developments to trying to prevent them from arising in the first place. Improved methods of collecting, storing, and using information were seen as the most promising approach to dealing with the terrorist threat even at the cost of what liberal democrats charged was a serious loss of civil liberties.

New forms of police investigation have come to supplement traditional police work. "Computer matching" *(Rasterfahndung)* was developed in the 1970s to combat terrorism. In the hope of making police work more efficient and effective, large numbers of data were scanned to identify overlapping clusters of what were considered to be suspicious traits of target populations. In the 1970s the police got access to the files of utility companies, for example, and thus could identify those customers who paid their bills in cash or through third parties. This group of potential suspects was narrowed further through checks with data on residence registration (which is compulsory in Germany), auto-

[15] Ibid., pp. 8, 25–29, 47–84; Peter J. Katzenstein, *West Germany's Internal Security Policy: State and Violence in the 1970s and 1980s* (Ithaca: Western Societies Program, Center for International Studies, Cornell Studies in International Affairs, Occasional Paper no. 28, 1990), pp. 12–13.

mobile registration, receipt of social security or child-care payments, and the like. The names that remained on the list were potential terrorist suspects: they were young and single, were not registered, had no automobiles, and paid their bills in cash. Traditional police searches then focused on this target group. If, in addition, these suspects lived in large apartment buildings with underground garages and exits that were unrestricted even during rush hour, they were put under police surveillance, especially if they had changed their locks as soon as they moved in, received little or no mail, insisted on having a telephone installed right away, paid their rent in cash in advance, and kept their curtains closed even during the day.[16] "Preventive" and "intelligent" police work in the name of internal security was thus informed by abstract social categories that the police had defined, rather than concrete evidence that a suspect had been involved in specific terrorist acts.

The home-grown high-tech approach to problems of internal security was complemented by an activist stance that favored international policy coordination to contain the threat of terrorism in Germany. A policy statement from the mid-1980s articulates the position of the German government very clearly: a liberal sharing of information to facilitate a preventive search of international terrorists by national police forces; far-reaching agreements on police cooperation across national borders; simplification of intergovernmental judicial assistance in general and of extradition in particular; and harmonization of national legislation in areas pertaining to antiterrorist policy. The German government has displayed its activist stance wherever it could in multilateral arenas, among others in the United Nations; at the economic summit meetings; in Interpol; in the Schengen Agreement, recently concluded among some members of the European Community; and in the Working Group for Combating Terrorism, convened within the framework of European political cooperation.

Perhaps most far-reaching during the last fifteen years has been the international coordination of antiterrorist policies under the auspices of the key intergovernmental system of cooperation, TREVI (Terrorism, Radicalism, Extremism, Violence, International). A standing conference of the ministers of interior and justice of the member states of the European Community (EC), TREVI is not a part of the European Community, probably because it wants to avoid parliamentary oversight. But the ministers meet, often on the same day, both under the auspices of TREVI and in their capacity as members of the Council of

---

[16] Brand, *Staatsgewalt*, p. 69; *Bürgerrechte und Polizei*, "Rasterfahndung" (CILIP 6), August/September/October 1980, pp. 16–21; David H. Flaherty, *Protecting Privacy in Surveillance Societies: The Federal Republic of Germany, Sweden, France, Canada, and the United States* (Chapel Hill: University of North Carolina Press, 1989), p. 73.

Ministers of Interior of the EC. TREVI was the result of what was largely a German initiative in 1975, at the height of one of the terrorist waves in Germany. TREVI and its various working groups provide not only for regular high-level contacts but also for regular, institutionalized cooperation in the area of practical police work affecting antiterrorist policy.[17]

TREVI and the other multilateral arrangements provide arenas that facilitate the intense bilateral contacts that tie the German police to their partner organizations in other European states. These contacts often involve the sharing of intelligence information and the furthering of professional contacts with the police forces of other states, including an exchange program of police officers with France. More important, they facilitate cooperation of the police at the local level, in particular in border areas, which has become quite extensive after a 1987 administrative agreement concluded between Germany and France.

In sharp contrast to the high-tech image that Japanese industry has projected during the last two decades, the Japanese police have relied primarily on their traditionally close relations with the public in their efforts to defend Japan's internal security. The access to society that the German police apparently sought in the computer in the 1970s has always been available to the Japanese police through numerous organizations that link them to civil society. The local police station *(koban)* has always served as an instrument of surveillance. Annual house calls by policemen are still standard and are designed to elicit regular and detailed information on individual citizens. Such innovations as massive searches of apartment complexes and the creation or extension of myriads of other police support organizations with a combined total of millions of individual contact points have provided the Japanese police with rich sources of information that the German police, lacking such an osmotic relation with society, have sought to gain through high technology. The Japanese police strategy appears less like the proclaimed German shift from reactive to preventive policing than as an adaptation and extension of a social surveillance system that was already in place.

The Japanese approach was very successful in the early 1970s. Whereas successive generations of the Red Army Faction have operated inside Germany, the Japanese police succeeded in pushing the Japanese Red Army offshore within a couple of years. In the 1970s it was said that Japan was good at exporting TV sets and terrorists. Yet, these methods have not had much effect in containing the attacks staged by the militant cadres of such organizations as Chukaku. When radicals hold down steady white-collar jobs, do not participate in any political

---

[17] Katzenstein, *West Germany's Internal Security Policy*, pp. 23–27, 52–53.

activities, and lead apparently normal lives, as these militant cadres do, it is almost impossible to track them down.

Japan has taken a much less activist stance than Germany in the international dimensions of its policy of internal security. The apparent shift from an accommodating policy toward terrorist demands in the 1970s to an unyielding one in the 1980s has not yet been tested seriously; to date the Japanese government has been spared the agonizing choices that the Red Army posed to it in the 1970s. But during the last decade the rhetoric of internationalism has increased on questions of internal security, as on most other important issues the government has faced. But translating this general political commitment to international policy coordination into concrete initiatives has been an excruciatingly difficult process for the Japanese. The convening of the Conference on Security Matters for the Asia-Pacific Region in June 1988, under the auspices of the National Police Agency (NPA), is a case in point. It was the first such high-level meeting that the NPA had convened since 1945 and thus it represented a watershed in the postwar history of Japan's policy of internal security. But at the conclusion of the meeting several governments were simply unwilling to sign the final communiqué.

Furthermore, in contrast to Europe, Asia has no indigenous legal framework that might offer the kind of multilateral forum that Japan is interested in creating. With its residue of Chinese, French, German, and American legal traditions, Japan is living side by side in Asia with India and the Philippines, for example, which are shaped by the legacy of the English and the American judicial and police systems. Weak as it is for reasons of geographic isolation, the operative police cooperation that ties Japan to other countries thus is restricted to bilateral relations in particular crisis situations. Confronted with explicit threats from the Red Army and other extremist groups, Korea and Japan, for example, cooperated, for the first time since 1973–1974, in making the security preparations for the Seoul Olympic Games of 1988. And with the exception of its relations with the United States, in contrast to Germany and most other continental European states, Japan deals with the issue of extradition not on the basis of treaties but on the basis of reciprocity.

DOMESTIC NORMS AND INTERNAL SECURITY POLICY

Germany

The norms characterizing Germany's domestic policy of internal security are centered on the idea of the lawful state *(Rechtsstaat)*. It is the central concept that informs the self-understanding of the police, the elite civil servants, and the politicians as they deal with questions of terrorism. The lawful state is an abstraction that is not based on any substantive rule of law. It is the state, not social norms or moral values, that is the foundation for Germany's legal norms.[18] The concept of the state is "imbued with connotations of 'right' and 'law' which logically as well as normatively precede any particular type of regime such as democracy or authoritarianism."[19] The police do not simply enforce the law. In the words of the Police Administrative Law of 1931, the police are the business of the state. "In effect, the police emanate from the state, not from the people, in philosophy as well as in practice."[20] The state thus transcends the role of mere enforcer of a set of rules. The power of the state is legally controlled, but in the interest of defending state security it also can be legally imposed. West Germany's Basic Law balances its commitment to the primacy of individual rights with the provision that they can be limited, by, among other things, the principle of loyalty to the constitution. Organizations hostile to the constitutional order are explicitly prohibited (art. 9, sec. 2).[21] On questions of state security, and perhaps more broadly, the state legitimates itself.

It is important to note that in Germany changing social norms are typically codified in legal language. Constitutional amendments in this legalistic culture are thus passed with great regularity. Between 1949 and 1983 forty-nine articles of the Basic Law were altered, thirty-three were added, and seven were deleted. By contrast, Japan's constitution has not been altered since the end of World War II, and the constitution of the United States has been changed only about two dozen times during the last two hundred years.[22] In Germany the lawful state plays

[18] Regina H. E. Cowen, *Defense Procurement in the Federal Republic of Germany: Politics and Organization* (Boulder, Colo.: Westview, 1986), pp. 32–33; John E. Finn, "Constitutional Reconstruction, Militant Democracy, and Antiterrorism Legislation in the Federal Republic of Germany" (manuscript, Wesleyan University), p. 346.

[19] Peter J. Katzenstein, *Policy and Politics in West Germany: The Growth of a Semisovereign State* (Philadelphia: Temple University Press, 1987), p. 383.

[20] Erika S. Fairchild, *German Police: Ideals and Reality in the Post-War Years* (Springfield, Ill.: Charles C Thomas, 1988), p. 121.

[21] Peter Weiss, "Joe McCarthy Is Alive and Well and Living in West Germany: Terror and Counter-Terror in the Federal Republic," *New York University Journal of International Law and Politics* 9 (Spring 1976): 63–64; Erhard Denninger, ed., *Freiheitliche demokratische Grundordnung: Materialien zum Staatsverständnis und zur Verfassungswirklichkeit in der Bundesrepublik*, 2 vols. (Frankfurt: Suhrkamp, 1977); Peter Hammans, *Das politische Denken der neueren Staatslehre in der Bundesrepublik: Eine Studie zum politischen Konservatismus juristischer Gesellschaftstheorie* (Opladen: Westdeutscher Verlag, 1987).

[22] Jürgen Seifert, *Das Grundgesetz und seine Veränderung*, 4th ed. (Neuwied: Luchterhand, 1983), p. 4, and *Grundgesetz und Restauration*, 3d ed. (Neuwied: Luchterhand, 1977).

a central role in guaranteeing that government activity rests on a solid foundation of constitutional legality.

This normative context explains why the German political elite responded to the rash of terrorist attacks in the 1970s and 1980s with twenty amendments of the penal code passed between 1970 and 1989.[23] Before the 1970s the provisions of the penal code tended to make it difficult to open criminal proceedings against suspects without specific evidence. The definition of an offense against the state was narrowly drawn. Public prosecutors had to identify and charge principal suspects. Citizens were under no general obligation to report terrorist activities to the police. But the changes in the law that have been made during the last two decades amounted to ensuring the state's right to security against attacks from radicals, even at the cost of infringing on traditional civil liberties.

Article 129a illustrates with particular clarity this shift in legal norms to facilitate the protection of state security. Revised in 1976 and again in 1986, it has granted state officials broad discretionary powers. It forbids the "support" or "advertisement" of terrorist organizations and, under certain conditions, permits the police to arrest individuals even in the absence of any suspicion of criminal activity. In fact, it subjects to criminal proceedings issues concerning criminal intent rather than criminal behavior. The extension of the government's coercive power beyond criminal behavior is virtually unknown in other European countries, as well as Japan. But it has been an essential element of German political practice. Furthermore, Article 129a centralized the power to prosecute all cases involving terrorist activities in the hands of the Office of the Federal Prosecutor, sidestepping the possibility of a long appeals process. And it linked the judicial treatment of terrorist suspects to some of the most controversial procedural reforms of the penal code in the 1970s. According to Article 129a, merely being suspected of supporting a criminal organization constitutes a criminal act and thus provides legal justification for the issuance of a search or arrest warrant. The conviction rate of suspects charged under Article 129a has been extremely low. Between 1980 and 1987 only 30 of the 2,700 preliminary investigations initiated by the federal prosecutor under the provisions of Article 129a, or a little more than 1 percent, have led to convictions.[24] Another study cites a figure of 6 percent for all court cases brought under the authority of Article 129a.[25] The legal

---

[23] Katzenstein, *West Germany's Internal Security Policy,* pp. 32–33.

[24] "Gewalt Weihnachten," *Der Spiegel,* November 14, 1988, p. 66; Falco Werkentin, "Stellungnahme zur Frage der ersatzlosen Auflösung der P-Abteilungen in der Staatsanwaltschaft Berlin" (manuscript, Humanistische Union, Landesverband Berlin, 1989), p. 6.

[25] Brand, *Staatsgewalt,* p. 174; Gössner, "Auf der Suche," p. 156.

restrictions under which the police and prosecutor operate thus have been weakened, and so have individual rights; the power of the police and the protection of state rights have been strengthened.[26] In sum, the legal norms that are invoked against terrorist activity and suspects reveal a state intent on strengthening its own security as the sole source of law. A working group of NATO concurred with this conclusion in the late 1980s when it noted that "antiterrorist legislation in West Germany is extremely severe."[27]

Japan

Japanese legal norms, unlike those of Germany, are deeply embedded in social norms rather than constitutive of them. This difference is reflected in the sizes of the legal professions of the two countries. With only half the population of Japan, Germany in the 1980s had, in proportional terms, six times as many judges, five times as many lawyers, three times as many private attorneys, and a third more procurators.[28] But the difference is also a matter of quality. In contrast to Germany, Japan has declared none of its radical organizations illegal since 1945. The normative context in which Japan's internal security policy is conducted is distinguished by a porous border between formal and informal authority. In Japan, argues David Bayley, government "is not the result of an explicit act of fabrication by an existing community, the product of making a constitution. Government is not added on to community; it is intrinsic to community, as parentage is to family."[29] In contrast to Germany, Japan has avoided passing a spate of legislation on questions of internal security. In the 1970s and 1980s the Diet passed only a handful of laws or amendments dealing with internal security.[30] The reason for this legal passivity lies in a political stalemate

[26] Detlev Krauss, "The Reform of Criminal Procedure Law in the Federal Republic of Germany," *Juridicial Review* n.s. 24 (December 1979): 209–10; Sebastian Cobler, "Plädoyer für die Streihung der Artikel 129, 129a StGB," *Kritische Justiz* 17, no. 4 (1984): 407.

[27] North Atlantic Assembly, Working Group on Terrorism, *Final Report* (Brussels, 1987), p. 37.

[28] John O. Haley, "Sheathing the Sword of Justice in Japan: An Essay on Law without Sanctions," *Journal of Japanese Studies* 8 (Summer 1982): 274; Dan Fenno Henderson, *Conciliation and Japanese Law: Tokugawa and Modern*, vol. 2 (Seattle: University of Washington Press, 1965), pp. 195–96; Robert J. Smith, *Japanese Society: Tradition, Self, and the Social Order* (Cambridge: Cambridge University Press, 1985), p. 43; Citizens Crime Commission of Philadelphia, *Tokyo: One City Where Crime Doesn't Pay* (Philadelphia, 1975), p. 33; Masao Oki, "Japanese Rights' Consciousness: The Nature of Japan's Judicial System," *Look Japan*, January 10, 1984, p. 5.

[29] David H. Bayley, "Learning about Crime—The Japanese Experience," *Public Interest* 44 (Summer 1976): 65–66.

[30] Katzenstein and Tsujinaka, *Defending the Japanese State*, Table 5.

over an attempt to strengthen the legal and political position of the police that has continued since the late 1950s, despite recurrent efforts by conservatives in the Liberal Democratic Party (LDP) to review this issue. Confronted with this political reality, the police have adapted Japan's tradition of bureaucratic informalism to deal with problems of internal security.

The police practice of informalism *(unyo)* does not amount simply to arbitrary police discretion. But in permitting a very flexible application of police powers, it gives a very broad definition to the legal restraints under which the police operate. The practice of informalism is, generally speaking, the most important norm guiding police action on questions of internal security. It describes the basic intentions of police officials rather than the surface appearance of their public statements. It does so in two distinct ways. It systematically applies a variety of minor laws and ordinances to cover the legal void left by political stalemate in the Diet. And it systematically, and on the whole successfully, has broadened the interpretation of the small number of security and police laws that do exist, in particular Article 2 of the Police Law as well as the Police Duties Execution Law. Leading police officials in the 1980s were very explicit about the fact that in providing "comprehensive security" the police self-consciously made intelligent use of their powers to conduct investigations under all existing laws and ordinances.

Many police practices that appear highly questionable in light of minimal existing legislation thus are not deemed illegal by the courts, which have normally taken a conservative and passive attitude toward the practice of bureaucratic informalism. The police have remained untouched by the provision for the compulsory prosecution of the abuse of authority. Of the 1,785 charges brought against the police between 1948 and 1977, only 7 cases were prosecuted; and of these only 4 ended in convictions. "Not only is the small number of cases being prosecuted conspicuous, but so is the low conviction rate, especially in view of the fact that the average conviction rate of all Penal Code violations has been more than 95 percent in Japan."[31]

But legal norms are by no means the only normative context for Japan's policy of internal security. Public opinion, as revealed by surveys and by published commentary, weighs heavily on the behavior of the police and the decisions of the public prosecutors and judges. Karel van Wolferen, for one, concludes that "the social sanctioning role played by the Japanese press must be seen in the perspective of the practical

---

[31] Masayuki Murayama, "A Comparative Study of Police Accountability: A Preliminary Work" (manuscript, University of California, Berkeley, 1980), p. 69.

shortcomings of the Japanese legal system."[32] Informal processes of social control have been very important in conditioning police policy since 1945, and the police have made self-conscious efforts to cultivate public opinion and not to act against public sentiment. In the face of widespread student unrest in the late 1960s, the security and riot police delayed a crackdown on student radicals for almost two years, until 1969, when public sentiment had swung away from the students and behind the government and the police.

This attention to public opinion has had stunning results. An institution that was totally delegitimized between 1945 and 1960 has now become fully accepted by the public. "Even people who tend to have a skeptical attitude toward the police . . . admit that abuses of power by the police are minimal."[33] Complaints lodged against the police with the civilian review boards of the Ministry of Justice have declined steadily since 1948 and numbered about 100 a year in the 1980s, in a population of more than 100 million.[34] We do not know whether the number is so low because the public has a favorable perception of the police or because the public is aware that complaints against the abuse of police authority are very rarely prosecuted. But three national surveys conducted in 1983 revealed that among eight major public institutions, the police were rated most favorably, ahead of the press, business, and government. It is thus no accident that the public views the police as the main defenders of human rights in Japan.[35] Much of that goodwill derives from the daily activity of the police in community life and their deliberate efforts to convince the public that public and police are on the same side in the effort to maintain a civil society. But whatever its source, the public's support allows security and riot police great flexibility in their daily concern with internal security.

INTERNATIONAL NORMS AND INTERNAL SECURITY

Germany

The abstract universalism that typifies Germany's domestic norms has made it easy for German officials to view the German state as part

---

[32] Karel van Wolferen, *The Enigma of Japanese Power: People and Politics in a Stateless Nation* (New York: Knopf, 1989), p. 225. See also Lawrence Ward Beer, *Freedom of Expression in Japan: A Study in Comparative Law, Politics, and Society* (Tokyo: Kodansha, 1984); Edward P. Whittemore, *The Press in Japan Today . . . A Case Study* (Columbia: University of South Carolina Press, 1961).

[33] David H. Bayley, "Police, Crime, and the Community in Japan," in *Institutions for Change in Japanese Society*, ed. George DeVos (Berkeley: Institute of East Asian Studies, University of California, 1984), p. 192.

[34] Smith, *Japanese Society*, p. 125.

[35] Katzenstein and Tsujinaka, *Defending the Japanese State*, pp. 133–35.

of an international community of states seeking to protect itself against subversive attacks. Embodied in the Holy Roman Empire of the German people, the ancient concept of universal sovereignty stood for an international community that encompassed various parts of Germany.[36] Germany's interest in the strengthening of international community since 1945 thus has an important historical precedent. Specifically, Germany has participated with great energy in the process of furthering the evolution of international norms prohibiting terrorist activities, and in several key episodes has in fact played a leading international role. Its active role in furthering the evolution of international legal norms since 1949 was partly a concerted attempt to regain a measure of the legitimacy that the Nazis and their international legal specialists of the New Order had squandered.[37] More important, in the last two decades this active role has been shaped by the characteristic weight that German political leaders have accorded legal norms in domestic politics.

Although, in part for reasons of bureaucratic politics, Germany's involvement in the process of norm definition has been more circumscribed in the U.N. than in various European fora, Germany did take the leading part in the formulation of the 1977 U.N. Convention on Terrorism. The subject of terrorism was included on the agenda of the General Assembly at the request of the Federal Republic, and a German chaired the group that drafted the convention.[38] The German government did not press ahead with this initiative in the hope of overcoming the political disagreements over the definition of terrorism that had divided the General Assembly during the preceding decade. Rather it evidently wanted to put its domestic antiterrorist policy on the broadest conceivable footing. Clarifying and universalizing the principles that informed that policy were integral parts of this political effort.

The same impulse is noticeable in other international arenas, such as the economic summits convened by the advanced industrial states since 1977. The subject of terrorism was raised for the first time at the Bonn summit in 1978, apparently without prior staff work, at a time when Chancellor Helmut Schmidt was very much preoccupied by the issue. In their final communiqué the seven heads of state condemned

---

[36] Louis Dumont, "Are Cultures Living Beings? German Identity in Interaction," *Man* n.s. 21 (1986): 591.

[37] Detlev F. Vagts, "International Law in the Third Reich," *American Journal of International Law* 84 (July 1989): 661–704.

[38] Rainer Lagoni, "Die Vereinten Nationen und der internationale Terrorismus," *Europa-Archiv* 32, no. 6 (1977): 171–80; Robert Rosenstock, "U.S. Supports Establishment of U.N. Ad Hoc Committee on Drafting of Convention against Taking of Hostages," *U.S. Department of State Bulletin* no. 76 (240177) (January 24, 1977), pp. 72–75.

terrorism and threatened to discontinue air service to any country that offered sanctuary to terrorists or hijackers.[39] Since the Group of Seven is politically more homogeneous than the United Nations and accounts for 70 percent of the total air traffic in the Western world, the summit was a promising international arena for the German government. But it was also clear that the political consensus that emerged at the Bonn summit did not really set any norm and had no legally binding force according to customary international law.

From the perspective of the German government, Europe offered the advantage of furthering the evolution of international norms in a setting of relative political homogeneity. In the hope of informing or guiding national legislation, for example, the Council of Ministers of the Council of Europe summarizes existing international practices and interpretations in regard to various issues, including those that involve international criminal activity. Working under the auspices of the council, the European Committee on Crime Problems has facilitated the signing of a number of international conventions.[40] And the decisions of the European Court of Human Rights in Strasbourg are binding on national courts and governments. In the area of human rights, which includes the norms affecting state reaction to terrorism, Western Europe has developed a regime as strong as any to be found in other regions of the world.[41] Because they touch on key aspects of state sovereignty, norms concerning the evolution of the practices of state coercion, embodied in international penal law, are hampered by obstacles that are greater than any in the areas of international civil or commercial law. But despite these impediments, international norms have in fact spread also in the area of public law and have partially converged in national legal practice.

Germany's confident participation in the process of furthering the evolution of international law was very apparent in the central role it played in developing the European Convention on the Suppression of Terrorism, passed in 1977—arguably the most important international convention to establish international norms and procedures for combating terrorism. The convention derives from the 1957 European Convention on Extradition, amended in 1975 and 1978, and the 1959 European Convention on Mutual Assistance in Criminal Matters,

[39] Robert D. Putnam and Nicholas Bayne, *Hanging Together: Cooperation and Conflict in the Seven-Power Summits* (Cambridge: Harvard University Press, 1987), pp. 86–87.

[40] Erik Harremoes, "Activités du Conseil de l'Europe dans le domaine des problèmes criminels (1975–1980)," *Revue de Science Criminelle et de Droit Pénal Comparé*, no. 1 (January–March), 1981, pp. 57–70.

[41] Jack Donnelley, "International Human Rights: A Regime Analysis," *International Organization* 40 (Summer 1986): 620–24.

which was amended in 1978. Based on a political initiative by the German minister of justice, the convention was drafted by the Council of Europe.[42] The Federal Republic was strongly committed to the passage of the convention and ratified it without reservation as early as 1978, in the hope of setting an example for the other members of the Council of Europe.[43] Eventually all members except Malta and Ireland followed suit. With some justification one critic of the convention has argued that it is an "international manifestation of the theory of the 'strong state'—that states hold in reserve strong and wide-ranging powers with which to suppress possible dissent. Germany particularly . . . is generally associated with this view."[44]

Broadly speaking, the convention shifts attention away from the individual right to political asylum, a concern characteristic of the 1930s, 1940s, and 1950s, toward the threat of terrorism, a preoccupation of the 1960s and 1970s. In a sharp break with earlier agreements articulating international norms of conduct, Articles 1 and 2 of the convention stipulate that certain kinds of crime shall never be considered political, notwithstanding their political motivation or content.[45] The convention lists the offenses covered by the term "terrorist crime" and requires signatories to cooperate as widely as possible on all criminal activities covered by its text and, when necessary, to rely on binding arbitration.

Germany's active involvement in the spread of international norms of antiterrorism, especially in Europe, has also found a receptive forum in the Conference on Security and Cooperation in Europe (CSCE). This is arguably the most important institution for moving Western and Eastern Europe in the direction of a pan-European peace order, an idea that has inspired Germany's Eastern policy during the last two decades. The final document of the CSCE, signed in Vienna in January 1989 by all European states except Albania, as well as by the Soviet Union, the United States, and Canada, echoes the European Convention of 1977. "The participating states unreservedly condemn as criminal all acts, methods and practices of terrorism, wherever and by whomever committed . . . and agree that terrorism cannot be justified

---

[42] Robert A. Friedlander, "Terrorism and International Law: Recent Developments," *Rutgers Law Journal* 13 (Spring 1982): 493–511; David Freestone, "Legal Responses to Terrorism: Toward European Cooperation?" in *Terrorism: A Challenge to the State*, ed. Juliet Lodge, pp. 195–226 (New York: St. Martin's Press, 1981); Gal-Or, *International Cooperation*.

[43] Gal-Or, *International Cooperation*, p. 256.

[44] Freestone, "Legal Responses," p. 215.

[45] Michael Schubert, "'Terrorismusbekämpfung' als Vorwand für die Kriminalisierung politischer Konflikte," *Vorgänge* 25, no. 2 (1986): 87–114.

under any circumstances."[46] The signatories of the final document agreed also to stand firm in the face of terrorism, to strengthen bilateral and multilateral cooperation to combat and prevent terrorism, and to ensure the extradition or prosecution of all persons implicated in acts of terrorism. In short, the international norm against terrorism has evidently spread during the last two decades and Germany has been very much in the forefront of attempts to strengthen that development.

Japan

With only a few exceptions, Japan is in full agreement with the evolving international human rights foundation that informs the antiterrorist policy of the major Western democracies. But the social embeddedness of Japanese law and its situational logic have made it more difficult for Japan than for Germany to involve itself actively in furthering the evolution of international legal norms prohibiting terrorism. Furthermore, Japan's social consensus has favored the notion of Japan's uniqueness in the contemporary international system. The extension of the abstract universalism of German law into a larger European space has no Japanese analogue. The process appears to have worked rather in reverse. When the Japanese government confronted a dangerous threat from the Red Army, operating abroad in the 1970s, it enacted six domestic laws so that it could ratify five international treaties that it had signed previously. In other words, the existence of international norms shaped the evolution of Japan's domestic legal norms on questions of internal security. But the effect of these security laws remained largely symbolic and had little bearing on the practical work of the police and the legal profession dealing with questions of internal security.

Furthermore, Japan has not yet been forced to act on the strength of the international antiterrorist conventions it has signed and ratified and thus to demonstrate that in fact it regards them as binding. And in none of the international organizations has Japan taken a leading role in seeking to further international norms of antiterrorist policy. In 1973, for example, it voted together with France in the legal committee of the International Civil Aviation Organization against a proposal, supported by the United States, Britain, and Canada, among others, backing collective action against states that refused to interrupt air

---

[46] "Excerpts from East-West Agreement on the Protection of Human Rights," *New York Times*, January 17, 1989, p. A12.

service with states that were granting safe haven to terrorists.[47] And in the 1980s Japan failed to ratify two international conventions dealing with the security of airports and of oil-drilling platforms, even though it had sponsored one of them. Finally, Asia simply has not evolved any kind of regional framework of organizations that would give Japan an opportunity to play a more active role. On the question of human rights, as on many other issues of international law, "in Asia there are neither regional norms nor decision-making procedures."[48]

In contrast to Germany and other European states, Japan views international legal norms not as a process but as a product, not part of the evolution of its domestic law but as a given attribute of international society to which it must adjust. International law is a tool of diplomacy to further the interests of states. It is not a process by which the creator of norms is in turn bound. The Japanese approach to international legal norms is more narrow and tactical than the German. It lacks an "internationalism in the sense of identification with the international community, with human kind as a whole, that is, rather than in the sense of 'good neighbour' punctiliousness about international obligations—which the Japanese have in good measure."[49]

This is not to argue that the Japanese lack any conception of international norms. Like the people of other states, they seek to generalize to the international realm the institutions and practices that shape domestic norms. But their avenue for doing so is through the process of international technology, as any student of the American or European automobile industry will readily testify, rather than through international law. In contrast to Germany, Japan lacks in international society what it has in domestic society, an ideology of law and a moral vision of the good society. Without the dense set of social relations that characterize domestic society, what remains in international society is a world of "connections," of interests and reciprocity that look merely opportunistic when stripped of their thick domestic social context. For the Japanese, to act in accordance with one's international responsibility means to do what is expected of a country whose influence in the world is rapidly rising. It means conceiving of Japanese interests in the longer term. It does not mean conceiving of the "self" in broader terms, on the basis of a vision that might resemble the abstract universalism of German legalism or the self-confident assertiveness of Anglo-Saxon

[47] Mark E. Fingerman, "Skyjacking and the Bonn Declaration of 1978: Sanctions Applicable to Recalcitrant Nations," *California Western International Law Journal* 10 (Winter 1980): 141.

[48] Donnelly, "International Human Rights," p. 628.

[49] Ronald Dore, *Flexible Rigidities: Industrial Policy and Structural Adjustment in the Japanese Economy, 1970–80* (Stanford: Stanford University Press, 1986), p. 245.

liberalism. For Japan to transcend its interest-driven approach to questions of international norms would require nothing less than a fundamental domestication of international society by Japan—the extension, that is, of its deep social fabric abroad. While this process is certainly under way in several economic and social policy domains, any substantial and sustained change along these lines would constitute a very important break in the domination of the international system by the West.

NORMS AS ANALYTICAL CONSTRUCTS FOR EMPIRICAL ANALYSIS

The normative context of policy is important if we wish to understand better the constitution of policy interests. Since norms and interests are normally converging, it is very difficult to establish empirically the primacy of one over the other. We should therefore make problematic what is often taken to be axiomatic, the interests of actors. To stipulate actors' interests on the basis of abstract notions of structure is often to bypass a significant question we must grapple with if we wish to understand why political actors behave the way they do. To focus on the norms that inform the interests that drive policy, however, is not to assume that norms provide the only plausible explanations, to the exclusion of all other factors. Norms do not determine outcomes for two simple reasons. They are contested, and they are contingent.

Norms Are Contested

Terrorism is a violent contestation of prevailing norms. A focus on the normative context in which Germany and Japan debated and implemented their antiterrorist policies thus must consider the elementary fact that norms are normally contested. These focal "points of concern"[50] reveal an agreement within society or between societies about what it is that is worth arguing about, a source of significant data for an understanding of the normative context of policy. In both Germany and Japan that point of concern in the domestic debate involved the dominant legal and political establishment on the one hand and a civil libertarian countergroup and occasional court judgments on the other. In the evolution of international norms there was some opposition among German and European specialists in international law (a small elite group that at the same time both constitutes and

[50] David Laitin, "Political Culture and Political Preferences," *American Political Science Review* 82 (June 1988): 590.

interprets to their respective governments the evolution of international norms) as well as among politicians to the spread of Germany's strong state norm. Japan's apparent passivity on questions involving the evolution of international norms, on the other hand, voided any substantive public debate because of a broad social consensus on the uniqueness of Japanese culture in the modern world.

In Germany the Basic Law itself reveals a tension between the rule of law that constitutes the state as the sum of laws duly passed by Parliament and individual rights securely anchored in a natural rights tradition, on the one hand, and legal strictures imposed on state—that is, executive—power without constituting the state in a truly liberal, parliamentary fashion, on the other.[51] This ambiguity has been at the center of debate between the German mainstream and its more radical democratic critics who champion a more vigorous defense of civil liberties. Occasional partisan disagreements in Germany, as elsewhere in Europe, have centered on the trade-off between the need for effective protection against terrorism and executive discretion on the one hand and a concern for freedom of expression, the protection of individual rights, and parliamentary supervision on the other. Finally, some of the German responses, such as the redrafting of article 129a of the Penal Code, which now includes issues of motivation and intent as well as overtly criminal behavior, are in such substantial disagreement with the legal doctrine and practice of other European states that they are typically not covered in any of the bilateral and multilateral treaties that Germany has signed. In a couple of cases this has been the cause of considerable friction between Germany and some of its neighbors.

Conflicts over the evolution of domestic norms that affect international security policy have been rare and more muted in Japan than in Germany. Occasionally, as in the late 1960s and early 1970s, a conservative legal establishment that has favored a passive stance in the face of the informal practices of the police has been confronted by a small group of reform-minded lawyers and judges intent on protecting the civil rights of political demonstrators. But generally speaking, the Supreme Court in particular has gone out of its way to avoid ruling on politically sensitive cases, has tried to muffle reformist lawyers, and thus has had a substantial effect on lower court rulings. Japan's relative lack of political conflict over and passive attitude toward the evolution of international norms demonstrate that this issue has simply not been

---

[51] Busch et al., *Polizei in der Bundesrepublik*, pp. 53–58; Albrecht Funk, Udo Kauß, and Thomas von Zabern, "Die Ansätze zu einer neuen Polizei: Vergleich der Polizeientwicklung in England/Wales, Frankreich und der Bundesrepublik Deutschland," in *Politik der inneren Sicherheit*, ed. Erhard Blankenburg, pp. 71–76 (Frankfurt: Suhrkamp, 1980).

a focal point of concern.[52] A widely shared assumption holds that Japan is unique in the international system and that the specific requirements of Japanese society as well as the situational logic of Japan's legal norms do not connect easily with the evolution of more abstract Western norms as codified in international public law. The comparison between Japan and Germany demonstrates that different focal points for political conflict will yield different equilibria. Different political systems exhibit different forms of rationality.

Norms Are Contingent

Norms themselves are not the sole determinants of the interests that shape actors' political choices and political outcomes. At a minimum, any comprehensive analysis must also include the structural conditions that shape interests, choices, and outcomes. These structures differ in Germany and Japan along three dimensions: the organizational structure of the state, the relations between state and society, and the links between the state and transnational structures.

On questions of internal security Germany's federal system and the system of alternating coalition governments has been modified by procedural and institutional responses that have sought to integrate the police and intelligence services into one centralized structure. In comparison with other policy domains in Germany, the issue of internal security is characterized by a remarkably centralized state structure. But the proliferation of coordinating interagency bodies, standing committees of the various state governments, and the political and bureaucratic conflicts between ministries headed by politicians belonging to different parties leave the image of a decentralized structure in comparison with the flexible centralized organization of the Japanese security policy in the National Police Agency and the Metropolitan Police Department. The difference in structure is equally clear in the relations between state and society on questions involving internal security. The distance that the stark German differentiation between state and society (Obrigkeitsstaat) imposes is incomparably greater than our finds in the osmotic relation between formal and informal centers of authority in Japan's familial state. Finally, for reasons of geography and history alone, the German state is much more closely linked to other state structures, especially in Europe, than is Japan, which still suffers from a deep sense of isolation from the world community.

While the organization of the state is not unconnected to the role of norms that help shape policy formulation, its primary effect is on the

[52] Laitin, "Political Culture."

implementation of policy. The structure of state-society relations in these two cases corresponds clearly to the directive role of legal norms in Germany as contrasted with the social embeddedness of Japan's legal norms. And the links between the state and transnational structures which are so much stronger in Germany than in Japan correlate with the activist stance Germany has chosen in furthering the evolution of international norms in contrast to Japan's passivity. In short, the effects of at least two of the three dimensions of structure parallel the domestic and international norms of the two countries.

Both norms and structures predispose Germany to abstract universal norms that facilitate the government's choice of a high-tech approach to the gathering of social "intelligence" and of active involvement in the international process of strengthening universal norms of antiterrorism. Conversely, Japan's norms and structures favor socially embedded and thus nationally specific norms that make plausible the government's effort to elicit social "intelligence" through the adaptation of existing institutions and practices and to remain passive in the furthering of international norms of antiterrorism.

CONCLUSION

Important differences in Germany's and Japan's policies of defending state security against threats posed by terrorism and violent social protest cannot be explained solely in terms of their domestic structures or the international structures that condition policy in the international system. An explanation of Germany's and Japan's policies of internal security must also pay attention to the normative context that frames political choices. Does this argument hold for other instances of internal security policy, such as Germany's and Japan's antidrug policies? And could it be extended to the issue of external security?

Antidrug policies are accorded very high priority in Germany's and Japan's internal security policies. In domestic affairs as in antiterrorism policy, a great gulf yawns between a German policy that expresses primarily the legal norms of a relatively autonomous state and a Japanese policy that relies heavily on the social embeddedness of the Japanese state. And in international affairs Germany has chosen a more activist and cooperative approach to the containment of the flow of illegal drugs than Japan has taken.

Modeled on the American approach, Germany's antidrug policy is informed by the concept of "extended defense." The government's 1988 antidrug report defines the concept clearly. "Of decisive importance for inhibiting the import of stimulants is the effort to build a line of defense in producer and transit countries. This requires close international cooperation."[53] In the 1980s Germany stationed thirty-seven police officers in twenty-one countries, primarily in the Third World. "The European government with the greatest number of law enforcement agents stationed abroad is West Germany," writes Ethan Nadelmann. "[Police] agents also demonstrated their willingness to conduct operations on foreign soil, even to the extent of riling foreign governments. In these respects as well as in its adoption of . . . proactive investigative techniques [of the sort employed by the Drug Enforcement Agency (DEA) in the United States], the German federal police agency has consciously emulated the DEA." Furthermore, the networks of European police that operate in the area of antiterrorism policy—such as TREVI and the Schengen Accord—also support Germany's active international stance. In domestic politics Germany's antidrug police units have become "the most innovative and aggressive in Europe. . . . In Germany, more than in any other country, both the Länder [state] and the federal police have adopted the DEA models of investigation with few inhibitions." Backed by legislative changes among all of the European police forces, the German police use undercover operations most extensively.[54]

Japan's antidrug policy rests on one main strategy, "to isolate not only drug dealers, but also the users from the rest of the population."[55] In this as in all other areas of crime, Japan's police have been very effective. Only when Japan's social structure was deeply disrupted, as it was in the first postwar decade, did the drug problem take on epidemic proportions. But the restabilization of Japan and the tough penalties that were imposed quickly ended that epidemic and left Japan, despite some sharp increases in drug-related offenses in the 1970s and 1980s, with a drug problem that by American standards is minuscule.[56] The close involvement of the Japanese police with local communities is a

[53] Berndt Georg Thamm, *Drogenfreigabe: Kapitulation oder Ausweg? Pro und contra zur Liberalisierung von Rauschgiften als Maßnahme zur Kriminalitätsprophylaxe* (Hilden: Verlage Deutsche Polizeiliteratur, 1989), p. 182.

[54] Ethan Avram Nadelmann, "Cops across Borders: Transnational Crime and International Law Enforcement" (Ph.D. diss., Harvard University, Department of Government, 1987), pp. 86, 295, 269, 285, 288.

[55] National Police Agency, *Anti-Drug Activities in Japan* (Tokyo: Japan International Cooperation Agency and National Police Agency of Japan, 1990), p. 3.

[56] Richard H. Friman, "The United States, Japan, and the International Drug Trade: Troubled Partnership," *Asian Survey* 31 (September 1991); Minoru Yokoyama, "Development of Japanese Drug Control Laws toward Criminalization," paper presented at the International Conference on Crime, Drugs, and Social Control, Hong Kong, December 14–16, 1988; Masayuki Tamura, "Yakuza and Stimulants: Drug Problems in Japan" (manuscript, National Research Institute of Police Science, Tokyo, n.d.).

key to policy success. Since drugs are widely seen as a risk not only to the individual but to society at large, drug users are regularly reported to the police even by family members. And the police remain confident that the social barriers to drugs will hold up. With arrests for drug-related offenses decreasing sharply in 1989, the Japanese police exuded optimism. "What we are thinking of is how to create an anti-drug society."[57]

Japan has frequently professed its readiness to cooperate internationally despite a domestic drug problem that is not of grave concern; but it never ratified the 1971 U.N. Convention on Narcotics and Psychotropic Substances. Despite the criminalization of drug-related offenses, enforcement measures in Japan have remained relatively lax by American standards. The Ministry of Justice was successful in blocking long-standing demands by the National Police Agency that the police be granted legal powers that are considered quite normal in the United States and to some extent in Germany, including undercover operations, surveillance, wiretaps, and access to bank records. The limitations under which the police are operating in Japan have occasioned constant complaints by DEA representatives stationed in Japan. For lack of national legislation, even the monitoring of money-laundering operations, regarded as essential if the police are to close in on the drug-related activities of organized crime, has been stalled for years despite intense international pressure. Japan's participation in a "global partnership" in the American war against drugs, signed by Prime Minister Kaifu and President Bush in September 1989, thus was not motivated by serious concern about drugs. It was instead seen as a way of cementing relations with Japan's most important trade partner and security guarantor at a time of mounting political friction between the two countries. Because the deployment of military forces abroad is prohibited by its constitution, Japan has refused to participate in the eradication or interdiction of drugs abroad, a major part of America's war on drugs. Instead Prime Minister Kaifu agreed in September 1989 to provide economic and technical assistance and cooperation to encourage drug-exporting countries to diversify their economic bases. It did so apparently with little interest in the substance of policy. A special Japanese assistance program to Colombia which was part of the war on drugs, for example, provided funds for a new sewer system for Bogotá and the purchase of audiovisual equipment for the government's music archive.[58]

Germany's and Japan's external security, like their internal security,

---

[57] National Police Agency, *Anti-Drug Activities*, p. 5.
[58] Friman, "United States," pp. 885–86, 888.

cannot be explained fully by structural factors alone. Nearly fifty years after their unconditional surrender to the Allied forces, Germany and Japan appear to have won the cold war that the United States and the Soviet Union waged. Under the protective umbrella of the United States, these two trading states are no longer subject to the temptations of military glory and territorial conquest, which had led to their cataclysmic defeat in World War II. Instead Germany and Japan have focused their political attention on enhancing their competitiveness in international markets while at the same time maintaining viable political relations with the United States as well as with their European and Asian neighbors. The widespread aversion to the use of military force "has become institutionalized in Japanese and West German societies and has become a central feature of their new political culture."[59] Their reaction to the Gulf War in 1991 demonstrated that Germany and Japan are facing political possibilities for growing international influence that they are unwilling to exploit. Hundreds of thousands of antiwar demonstrators in the streets of Bonn and unseemly wrangling in the Japanese Diet reinforce the impression that the trauma of the defeat of 1945 continues to have deep effects on Germany's and Japan's national security policies.

These effects can be gauged only through a consideration of the normative contexts in which policies are formulated and implemented. And the normative contexts of Germany and Japan differ. In domestic politics, German policy has been informed by norms expressed in the concepts of "moral leadership" and the "citizen in arms." These concepts were coined deliberately to forestall the reappearance of German militarism. And they were deliberately institutionalized to foster the growth of an army that was actively supportive of democratic values. As the two concepts indicate, the reform effort aimed at the exercise of authority within the armed forces as well as the pattern of relationship between the military and society. Although the issue of Germany's rearmament was hotly contested in the 1950s, there was virtual unanimity in all political quarters that an unconstrained military would be an invitation to total disaster. The concept of moral leadership was designed to instill political consciousness and responsibility in West German soldiers without endangering military preparedness. Some of the ideas that informed the concepts of moral leadership and the citizen in arms were patterned along the lines of the concept of social partnership that has informed labor-management relations in West Germany since 1945. The modern soldier has become a professional with a distinctive competence, including courage, leadership qualities, and com-

[59] Berger, "Reluctant Allies," pp. 1–3.

mitment, but he no longer has any claim to uniqueness. The principles that were to guarantee the full integration of the military into a civilian society and its subordination to a democratic system of government, though at times sharply contested in politics, were in the end legally codified between 1954 and 1957 and "signified a dramatic break with the Prussian-German military tradition."[60] These moral norms were also institutionalized in a School of the Armed Forces for Moral Leadership, created in the 1950s, and in two military academies set up in the early 1970s.

In the international realm German policy since 1945 has been informed by the concept of security partnership. Konrad Adenauer's Western policy embraced West Germany's membership in NATO and the European Community because they promised both to help defend the Federal Republic against the threat from the Soviet Union and to regain West German sovereignty. But with political conditions changing in the 1960s, the Federal Republic became a leading proponent of NATO's adoption of the Harmel Report in 1967. The report stated that NATO should transcend its traditional role as a defense alliance and involve itself actively in furthering the process of détente. The Harmel Report provided the international basis for West Germany's Eastern policy in the 1970s and 1980s, which helped normalize relations between West Germany, the Soviet Union, and the Eastern European states, including the German Democratic Republic. The process of normalization with the East, like that of Western integration, was informed by the concept of security partnership in an international community of nations. Before 1945 the concept of community was coupled almost by definition with the adjective "national." After 1945, however, Germans thought and talked about domestic affairs primarily in terms of civil society. Germany did belong, however, to the Atlantic Community, the European Community, and now an emerging pan-European peace order. The idea of the international state system as a security partnership is evidently patterned in part on the West German system of social partnership which has regulated conflict between business, unions, and some of the other major interest groups. Though the precise meaning of the concept of security partnership has been politically contested, the wish to see Germany fully integrated in a variety of international partnerships in the broader community of nations is broadly shared.

This view of the world is alien to Japan. Economic and social considerations have been central to Japan's definition of "comprehensive secu-

---

[60] Donald Abenheim, *Reforging the Iron Cross: The Search for Tradition in the West German Armed Forces* (Princeton: Princeton University Press, 1988), p. 167.

rity." Japan's economic reconstruction created stunning successes in export markets in the United States and throughout the world. The story of economic success marred by protectionist backlash abroad has become repetitive as Japan has conquered world markets first in mature industries and subsequently in modern ones. Japan's response to the political consequences of its economic success has been very consistent. Until the mid-1980s Japan engaged in tough bargaining and eventual pragmatic compromise on some kind of "voluntary" export restrictions. Only in the last few years has an uncomfortable awareness spread in Tokyo that Japan may be called upon to develop more comprehensive political solutions to the international political disruptions that its economic prowess is creating.

Japan's normative vision centers on the notion of an economic partnership in an international society of states. In this world view what holds the world together, both at home and abroad, is interests, not common norms that tie actors together in common projects. Cooperation is made possible by flexibility in the redefinition of short-term interests as long-term interests. The extraordinary ability to redefine one's interest is based on the deliberate attempt to foster ongoing, interest-based relationships, in domestic politics as well as in international affairs. The Japanese "self" is extended to incorporate at least some relevant portions of the "other" so that the expectation of an ongoing interest-based relationship is met.[61] This approach differs greatly from the purely market-based approach of the United States, with its assumption of self-contained and autonomous actors. But it differs also from the German and European experience, which increasingly is putting into question the very notion of a national self. Japan's approach to international life is more accepting than Germany's of vulnerability in economic and security affairs. But Japan lacks the German experience of becoming enmeshed with the political structures of numerous neighbors in international institutions and policy projects.

Our analysis of international and domestic politics will remain incomplete if it neglects the normative context that helps define the interests of actors. Incompleteness is of course essential to the enterprise of developing compelling explanations in the social sciences. But the assumption that actors know their interests, though convenient for analytical purposes, sidesteps some of the most important political and intriguing analytical questions in contemporary politics. With established political structures crumbling in various parts of the world, conventional structural analysis needs to be modified and extended. The

[61] Esyun Hamaguchi, "A Contextual Model of the Japanese: Toward a Methodological Innovation in Japanese Studies," *Journal of Japanese Studies* 11, no. 2 (1985): 289–321.

idea of letting go of the assumption that interests are fixed will disturb those who look for a fixed Archimedean point to plant their feet and gain the analytical leverage that they assume will help them to explain the world. I hope I have shown that in a fluid world some advantage may derive from being more nimble-footed. It is possible to do theoretically informed and empirically oriented research on the normative context that informs the interests political actors hold.

Index

Cornell Studies in Political Economy

A Series Edited by

PETER J. KATZENSTEIN